VICTORIAN EXPLORER

THE AFRICAN DIARIES OF CAPTAIN WILLIAM G. STAIRS 1887 - 1892

EDITED BY JANINA M. KONCZACKI

NIMBUS PUBLISHING

Nimbus Publishing Limited
PO Box 9301, Station A
Halifax, NS B3K 5N5
(902) 455-4286

Design: Arthur B. Carter, Halifax

Printed and bound in Canada by Best Book Manufacturers

Canadian Cataloguing in Publication Data
Stairs, William G.
Victorian explorer
ISBN 1-55109-103-8

1. Stairs, William G.–Diaries. 2. Explorers–Zaire–Diaries. 3. Explorers–Canada–Diaries.
4. Emin Pasha Relief Expedition, 1887-1889–Personal narratives, Canadian. 5. Katanga
Expedition, 1891-1892–Personal narratives, Canadian. I. Konczacki, J. M. II. Title.

DT363.2.S73A3 1994   967.51'022'092   C94-950200-6

CONTENTS

FOREWORD

Charles Ritchie, the accomplished Canadian diplomat, once wrote with the charmingly perceptive candour of youth, "I prefer diaries to memoirs. They are less made up afterwards." The observation reflects the happy security of the reader, not the habitual anxiety of the writer. Later, on the publication of diaries of his own, he felt compelled to add a rueful second thought: "They are also less flattering to the ego of the author."[1]

Ritchie, who lived as a boy only a short walk from the residence in which William Grant Stairs had been raised some forty years earlier, had no cause to worry. The diaries that he felt obliged to describe as "mountains of evidence against me" have deservedly met with universal acclaim.[2]

Stairs by contrast was not a litterateur, but he shared Ritchie's desire "not ... to hurt the feelings of the living or cause distress to the friends and relatives of the dead." To this problem, Ritchie thought, the "only real answer ... would be for the diarist to die before publication or for those mentioned in the diary to die before him."[3] Stairs thought differently, as we shall see, but in the end he had no choice in the matter, and time has given him recourse to both of the remedies that Ritchie decided to reject.

Stairs's diaries were composed "in the rough" and more than a century ago, during the course of two expeditions into the interior of Africa. The first, the Emin Pasha Relief Expedition (1887-89), was led by Henry M. Stanley. The second, the Katanga Expedition (1891-92), was under the command of Stairs himself. It was completed just a few days before his death from a recurrent attack of malaria, when he was but three weeks short of twenty-nine.

Until Dr. Janina Konczacki's recent discoveries, only the Emin Pasha diaries had been known to the family, whose early attempts to publish them began shortly after the turn of the century. According to W. G. Stairs's last will, the diaries were to be placed in his mother's safe keeping, with instructions not to publish them during Stanley's lifetime. But my grandfather, Henry Bertram (or "Harry") Stairs, who was William's younger brother, took the view that some editing might be in order. Writing to his sister, Hilda, in 1908, he suggested that "when that event [Stanley's death] should happen the diaries should be published" and "the original should be followed with the greatest care and exactitude, nothing being altered except the spelling and grammar, if necessary."[4] At the same time, however, he felt that negative references to Stanley ought to be removed: "There are in the diary passages reflecting somewhat upon Stanley and my idea in these matters would be to leave out such portions, indicating the omission by a few asterisks. There are also some personal references in the diaries which could be treated in the same way."[5]

It appears from this passage that Harry may not have known that Stanley had died four years earlier, in 1904. In any case, Hilda was less solicitous than Harry of Stanley's reputation. "If there are passages not complimentary to Stanley," she wrote in reply, "it will not do him any harm and may do good to the memory of Major Barttelot and others. After the first rush of praise Stanley fell suddenly in the estimation of the British public—as a man he was a strong bully."[6]

Harry Stairs had arranged as early as 1902 to have the Emin Pasha diaries transcribed to type by one of his office stenographers in her spare time,[7] but in the end the efforts of the family to publish them came to naught. Harry himself died in 1940, and in 1950 another sister, Anna P. Stairs (1868-1953), donated them to the Public Archives of Nova Scotia, making them available to the general public.[8] Various historians who were aware of their importance expressed from time to time an interest in having them published, but were deterred by the dimensions of the task. Scholarly expertise would be required, along with prodigious effort, infinite patience, and a great deal of time.

Notwithstanding these formidable obstacles, however, Dr. Janina Konczacki ultimately decided to initiate the project. She did so, not as a service to the family, but as a contribution to scholarship, and the enterprise consumed much of her research activity over a period of eight years. During the course of it she was able to unearth not only the Emin Pasha diaries, but the Katanga diaries as well. In what follows she presents them in fully annotated form, and in the company of a profile of Stairs himself that brings his tale, and his character, fully to life.

Much of the record that appears in these volumes will seem quaint and archaic to contemporary readers, and some of it reprehensible. Stairs was neither an original nor a rebellious thinker, and his values and aspirations are those of his time and place. His story is one that Rudyard Kipling could have written, and one of which Lord Baden-Powell would have approved. Today, with the benefit of hindsight and the experience of a more complicated understanding of our world, we take a different view.

But Stairs's world was not so long ago. My father was raised on Kipling as a boy, and even in maturity he loved to read his work. As a child in a Nova Scotian elementary school in the late 1940s, I shared with my classmates a comforting reassurance that came from viewing above the blackboard a map of the world in which the territories of the British Empire and Commonwealth, carefully outlined in red, seemed everywhere to dominate the topography. And in my high school in English Montreal, Kipling's *Captains Courageous* (1897) was still prominent in the syllabus.

The diaries that Stairs left behind clearly tell us a great deal about the British (and Belgian) Empires and their servants, and even more about the history of their rough and sometimes oblivious intrusions into the societies of Africa. They may also, however, teach us something about ourselves—about the communities that have succeeded those with which Stairs was so closely familiar and of which he was so obviously a part. To the extent that this is so, our debt to Dr. Konczacki—and to the diligence, skill, and determination that she has brought to her task—is especially great, as anyone who reads with care the pages that follow will quickly discover.

Denis Stairs,
Halifax, Nova Scotia
January 1994

PREFACE

In the late 1870s only a small part of the African continent was under European rule. In the north and in the west of Africa the French control was very tenuous. Britain had small enclaves in Gambia, Sierra Leone, and Lagos, which were still largely dominated by African rulers. The Portuguese rule in Angola and Moçambique was confined to a few coastal trade centres. French presence in East Africa was similarly limited to a few coastal bases. South Africa, where deep penetration dated to an earlier period, was the only exception.

Towards the end of the nineteenth century, most of the African continent was carved up by European powers. This intensification of partitioning activity dated back to the Berlin Conference of 1884-85, prior to which Germany had annexed South-West Africa (Namibia), Togoland, the Cameroons, and extensive areas of East Africa (formerly Tanganyika). Another country which contributed significantly to the "scramble" for African territory was Belgium. In 1876 Leopold II, the king of the Belgians, created the African International Association, which became active both commercially and in the field of scientific exploration in Central Africa.

Leopold's real intention was to create a private colonial empire in Africa which was to be based on a commercial monopoly. He availed himself of the services of the already well-known explorer H. M. Stanley who, between 1879 and 1884, was active in the Congo and managed to establish a land and water transport system between the Congo River estuary and Stanley Falls (Kisingani). Having created the Congo Free State, Leopold II took steps to prevent the colony from falling into the hands of the other European powers. He founded the *Association Internationale du Congo* (AIC) in 1882 and sought its recognition by other countries. The timely recognition of the AIC by Germany strengthened Leopold's position at the Berlin Conference, which was to serve as a platform for resolving the vexing problems of contemporary colonial competition. Britain decided to side with Germany in favour of King Leopold II, who emerged from the conference as the head of the newly created Congo Free State of approximately 900,000 square miles (2,400,000 square kilometres).[1]

Meanwhile, until the German intrusion into East Africa, the partitioning activities in that part of the continent appeared less intense than in other parts of Africa. This was due mainly to the traditional British policy of keeping out of East Africa by relying on the loyalty of the sultan of Zanzibar, whose dominion extended over the coastal areas of the mainland. The latter was viewed by London as the protector of the private British interests. Over a period of time problems were created by the Arabs, who were active in the interior and who, after 1884, became increasingly hostile towards the Europeans in general and the British in particular. In their drive for political dominance, they antagonized the Baganda Christians who rebelled against them. Conflicts began to multiply. The British East Africa Company, founded in 1888, could not intervene effectively. Although in theory it had the powers of a government, in practice it did not possess the resources to enforce its rule. Seeing the lives of the European missionaries threatened, Britain was forced to occupy Uganda (1894) and Kenya (1886). This move was prompted by the fear that with the collapse of the rule of law in these territories, Germans could be tempted to invade them.[2]

With the exception of King Leopold II, who promoted predatory exploitation of the natural resources, other partitioning powers did not expect immediate financial returns. In the words of Lord Rosebery, the British Secretary for Foreign Affairs in 1893, the British in Africa were "pegging out claims for the future." He also claimed that partition "has been forced upon us."[3]

The two expeditions that are the subjects of Stairs's diaries took place shortly after the Berlin Conference (1884-85). The conference not only created colonial rivalries but also generated great interest in the exploration of the African interior. Consequently it was not difficult to find sponsors for such undertakings as the Emin Pasha Relief Expedition, which aimed at rescuing Emin Pasha, a European serving in the Egyptian administration as a governor of Equatoria. The outbreak of an insurrection in 1881 led by Mohammed Ahmed El Mahdi and the rapid spread of his *jihad* (Muslim holy war) to the Equatorial Province forced Emin Pasha to retreat to the south, where he established his new headquarters in the neighbourhood of Lake Albert. A prolonged breakdown of communication with Emin Pasha created intense concern about his fate, both in Egypt and in England. The fall of Khartoum, the capital of the present-day Sudan, and General Gordon's death aroused the sensibility of the European public, and events in the Equatorial Province received a considerable measure of publicity. An expedition was organized by private initiative in Britain, with the assistance of the Egyptian government, for the relief of Emin Pasha. It was headed by Henry M. Stanley.

One of the men whose life was caught up in the web of political activities following the Berlin Conference, was a young Canadian from Halifax—Capt. William G. Stairs. In 1887 Stairs joined the Emin Pasha Relief Expedition as a member and in 1891 became the leader of the Katanga Expedition. He left behind diaries describing the exploits of the two expeditions which permit us, in the post-colonial period, to acquaint ourselves with the innermost thoughts and observations of this Victorian explorer.[4]

The sponsorship of the Emin Pasha Relief Expedition stemmed partly from King Leopold's interest in extending his sphere of influence over parts of Equatoria. For this reason, he was ready to give conditional support to Emin Pasha, whose hold on that province was becoming increasingly tenuous.

The connection between Stairs's expedition to Katanga and Leopold's partitioning activities was even more direct. Msiri's kingdom, though nominally incorporated into the Congo Free State, was not yet "effectively occupied" as stipulated by the Berlin Conference. Under these circumstances, the door was left open to any colonial power determined to proclaim the territory its own. It was no secret to the Belgians that Cecil Rhodes had an interest in the supposed mineral riches of the Katanga region and of his designs to extend the British South Africa Company's sphere of operations into that area. Hence, the purpose of Stairs's expedition was to establish effective control over Msiri's kingdom, thereby thwarting any possible designs Rhodes may have had.

Apart from the *Emin Pasha Relief Expedition Diaries,* Captain Stairs's papers include a scrapbook with an interesting collection of personal memorabilia including some press-cuttings from contemporary newspapers, and a few letters and photographs. The diaries consist of five booklets bearing many signs of wear and extensive damage. They range in size from 11 in. x 8 in. to 7 in. x 4½ in. (28 cm x 20 cm to 18 cm x 11.5 cm) and have flimsy carton covers with the exception of journal 4. The latter is bound in stiff untanned leather (possibly impala skin) on which tufts of brown hair are still visible. The five journals cover the following periods: journal 1–20 January-23 September 1887; journal 2–24 September 1887-24 January 1888; journal 3–25 January-20 December 1888; journal 4–21 December 1888-31 May 1889; and journal 5–1 June-26 October 1889.

There are many sketches of maps, scenery, and African artifacts that are of considerable interest. The writing is difficult to decipher, and for this reason, circa 1902, Henry Stairs had the diaries transcribed by a typist. However, the typed version is incomplete and contains many inexactitudes. According to H. Gerald Stairs, the son of Henry Stairs, a number of "Uncle Will's trophies, such as native shields, spearheads, knives, arrowheads, etc. are in the McCord Museum at McGill University in Montreal."[5] This information appears to be inaccurate as none of these objects were found by the editor during her visit to the museum in the summer of 1979.

During the Emin Pasha Relief Expedition, William G. Stairs often complained of the shortages of writing materials and damage to his diaries. For instance, in the introduction to his journal 3 (entry of 25 January 1888), he wrote with resignation: "this [book] being the last one that I have got and still we are good for two years in Africa. This book has passed two or three nights under water and a great many months crushed up in a bag, so that its form is sadly altered." This passage from the diary reveals both the living conditions on the Emin Pasha Relief Expedition and the fact that the writing in the diaries would be badly smudged. Indeed, the condition of the diaries presented a considerable obstacle to transcription. Hence, the reader of this volume will encounter the occasional "[word illegible]."

On 31 March 1888, Stairs complained of a lack of pens or pencils. All his pens had rusted and he was forced to borrow one from William Hoffmann, Stanley's white servant. Journal 1 and part of journal 2 were still written in black ink, but entries between 29 November 1887 and 24 January 1888 are written in pencil, indicating that all of his ink supply had come to an end. When his ink was running out, he diluted its remnants with water until, according to his description, it resembled "American public picnic lemonade."[6] Then he tried out an old Arab method of making *fari* ink by burning the stalks and husks of rice and boiling the residue. To his deep disappointment the ink thus procured "seemed to be rather watery-looking stuff."[7]

Once the black ink had come to an end, all subsequent entries in the diary are in pencil and then in a light brownish ink, faded with the passage of time, making his writing very difficult to read. It is not clear from which source his supply of pages and ink came be-

Arrow-heads – full size – Upper Aruimi Villages

Taken from village of Msiduru

...18 inches long.

Length of arrow 18"

Length of arrow 18"

Needle.

The length of these arrows is about 18", the heads are very beautifully made & as sharp as razors; the bow used is about three feet long.

Arrow heads (Upper Aruwimi) sketched by W. G. Stairs

tween 24 January 1888 and the beginning of June 1889, when he was presented with a notebook by Emin Pasha in which are recorded the entries of his fifth and final journal.[8]

The complete *Emin Pasha Relief Expedition Diaries* run to approximately 145,000 words. Almost two-thirds of the original diaries are printed here together with editorial narrative and comments whenever omissions were made. The latter are indicated by ellipses. Although the reduction in size was dictated by economic necessity, care was taken to minimize the loss of interesting particulars by excluding entries, or parts of them, which were of an uneventful nature.

The subject matter was divided into chapters which do not correspond to the original divisions in the journals; the latter are of very unequal length and do not reflect well the distinct phases of the expedition. The entry dates indicate the current month, a procedure which is absent in the diaries, but which is a source of considerable inconvenience to the reader of the original manuscript.

Great care was taken to reproduce an exact version of the diaries. In order to avoid confusion, corrections were made in the spelling of names of people, various localities, geographical terms, and African words. It is important to note here that it was customary for villages to be named after the founding chief, for example "Kavalli" or "Kavalli's" refer to the same thing—the village or settlement. Whenever possible, geographical terms were made consistent with those used by Stanley in his book *In Darkest Africa* (first edition 1890), which can be considered the best contemporary source of information in these matters. This procedure has also been dictated by an effort to use place-names most appropriate to the historical context, thus avoiding anachronisms. Some of these names have been changed since independence, for example the Belgian Congo is now Zaire, and Katanga is known as Shaba. As for the misspelled names of people and the Swahili words, the former are corrected in the notes and the latter explained in the Appendix B, "Glossary of Swahili Words."

The publication of Stairs's diaries corrects the claim made in 1968 by the editor of *The Diary of A. J. Mountenay Jephson* that with the appearance of the latter "the documentation of the Emin Pasha Relief Expedition is as complete as it is ever likely to be."[9] It is only now that such a claim can be fully justified. The significance of Stairs's diaries goes far beyond the fact that it provides one more version of events related in the diaries and memoirs of the other members of the Emin Pasha Relief Expedition.[10] With the exception of Jephson's diary, which was discovered in 1955, other narratives were written specifically for publication and for this reason alone their authors were restrained in expressing their opinions and in reporting some of the more controversial or unpleasant events. They do not share the spontaneity, openness, directness, and tartness of Stairs's writing, although his style is often deficient of the customary literary standards.

Clearly, it is not the elegance of expression that matters. Above all, Stairs is a keen and penetrating observer writing about Stanley, the leader, the other members of the expedition, Emin Pasha, and his subordinates in a frank and unrestrained manner. He felt free to express his biting criticism and to condemn actions he finds reprehensible. It is a pity that the many biographies of Stanley, published in the past, failed to take full advantage of these rich and at times shocking comments so vividly expressed in Stairs's diaries. His observations concerning the behaviour of some of the African members of the expedition and the local population are often far from flattering. The unrestrained language in which

June '88   Fort Bodo

Monday 18th 7 men at work on Nelson's house - others under Uledi
at work making a garden. Have made Isassi a Nimishara.
Have tied up the sheep and goats in the North field; another goat died
from exhaustion yesterday caused by hard travelling. Nobody seems
to know much about gardening here, one has just to depend on luck
& what little one picked up when a kid. Nelson's hand is still
bad & his whole system seems out of order; it was hard on him the
other day after volunteering to lead the men to Kilonga Longa to fall
sick again and not be able to go. It would astonish a good many
people at home to see the state some of our men are in; ulcers 2½" + 3"
in diameter right into the bone; why even with the best of treatment
these would take months to heal; our only method is to make the men wash
their sores very often + twice a day parade + again of cold water
well syringed into the ulcer & then bind the sore tightly, up no. Great
quantities of rain fell last night. Wound Chronometer.

Tues 19th At work on garden & Nelson's house - men on latter getting
leaves for roof. In garden we made 4 or 5 large bed - I planted
some more onion seeds, some peas, & some Bringalls, & also a
small knoll to the East of the trees we planted with pumpkin
seed - all these seeds Parke brought with him. I am rather afraid they
will not do well as now it is past the planting season & things
do not thrive. My tobacco which grew so well at first is now at a
standstill. Fkirmi very ill with heart disease, we are afraid
he will not last long. Abedi who had measles is now all right.
Wound Chronometer:

Bushmens' Spear Heads
FORT   BODO.

Arrow.

Tower - Ft Bodo - 1888.

Page from Stair's diary written at Fort Bodo

he expresses such views might offend the feelings of many of today's readers, more sensitive to the human dignity of people of all races than were Victorian explorers.

A considerable part of the diaries is devoted to the description of geographical observations, climatic characteristics, folklore, agriculture, and problems of health in the tropics. Historians interested in the Congo Free State will find valuable comments on the state of local affairs, the relationships with the Arabs, and the work of the European missionaries, including the latter's activities in East Africa.

The record of Captain Stairs as an explorer would not be complete without a narrative of his expedition to Katanga of which he was the commander. The only source of information available in English until now was Dr. Joseph A. Moloney's book *With Captain Stairs to Katanga,* published in London in 1893, which is now a rare bibliophilic item, known only to a few experts specializing in that part of Central Africa. Through sheer accident, the editor came across a reference to what seemed to be an article written by Stairs on Katanga, which appeared in 1893 in a long-discontinued Belgian journal *Le Congo Illustré.*

To the surprise of the editor, the presumed article turned out to be the long missing Katanga diary published in French in nine installments of approximately 58,000 words. The editor had the French diary translated into English and a somewhat abridged version constitutes Part 3 of this volume. All attempts to locate the original manuscript failed. The contents of the *Katanga Expedition Diary* have been divided here into eight chapters to bring it into conformity with the divisions adopted in Part 2: *The Emin Pasha Relief Expedition Diaries.*

According to the contract signed between Stairs and the Company of Katanga, Stairs was obligated to submit periodically detailed reports on the progress of the expedition. These reports, in the form of a diary, aroused great interest among the company directors, and it was decided to publish them in a journal. Its more concise version appeared in *Le Mouvement Géographique* in 1892. As the diary was intended for the eyes of the company's directors, its literary style is far superior to that of the Emin Pasha Relief Expedition. It contains invaluable firsthand information on the prevailing conditions in Central Africa, and there are many controversial comments concerning the African population. Yet, the narrative is always vivid and interesting, reaching a dramatic finale in Stairs's confrontation with Msiri, the deaths of the latter and Bodson, the tragedy of the return journey, and the decimation of the caravan through starvation and illness.

Part 1, a profile of Captain William G. Stairs, is sketched by the editor. It cannot claim to be a comprehensive biography as much information on his early life, prior to his African expeditions, is missing, and according to a family spokesman it is doubtful whether it will ever be uncovered. What is known of his life has been included in the first chapter. As the primary purpose of the editor's work was to make the two diaries available to a wider audience, Stairs the diarist is allowed to speak to the reader in his own words. This form of autobiography provides a fuller portrait, reflecting the lights and the shadows of this unusual personality. There is no doubt that William Stairs was a remarkable young man and a true Canadian, embodying all the ideals of the late Victorian era. It was the editor's laborious, but rewarding task, to rediscover what can rightly be considered as part of our Canadian heritage and to sweep away the thick dust of oblivion. The second and third parts contain the diaries as noted above.

The Appendices should assist the reader in several ways. Appendix A, "The Chronological Table of Events," introduces an element of order into the multiplicity of events that took place, particularly during the Emin Pasha Relief Expedition. Appendix B, the "Glossary of Swahili Words," is simply a necessity for anyone who is not familiar with this African language and who may wish to know the meaning of the numerous Swahili words used without explanation by Stairs.

The editor felt that the colourful and controversial personalities of Tippu Tib, a famous trader and the governor of the Stanley Falls Region, and of Msiri, the king of Garengaze, deserved more than mere explanatory notes (see Appendices C and E). In Appendix D, Stairs's views on colonial policies of his time are confronted with the realities of African life and the actual practice of the territorial acquisitions.

The problem of tropical disease, particularly in the light of contemporary knowledge, was of paramount importance in the exploration and extension of colonialism. Intensified caravan movements contributed to the spread of various diseases to geographical areas where they were previously unknown. Relevant facts and comments can be found in Appendix F.

I would like to thank all persons and institutions without whose help the completion of my editorial work would not have been possible. First and foremost I express my gratitude to Dr. Denis Stairs, the grand-nephew of Capt. William G. Stairs and to the late Dr. Phyllis Blakeley, the former Provincial Archivist for Nova Scotia for their kind assistance and permission to publish the Stairs diaries. I also wish to express my appreciation to the following members of the staff of the Public Archives of Nova Scotia for their unstinting assistance and interest shown in my work: Dr. Brian Cuthbertson, the Public Records Archivist; Mr. Allan Dunlop, Assistant Archivist; Ms. Darlene M. Brine, Research Assistant; Ms. Mary Ellen Wright, Research Assistant; and the staffs of the following libraries for their invaluable help: the Library of Congress; the University of Rochester Library, Rhodes House, Oxford; the Province of Nova Scotia Legislative Library; Metropolitan Toronto Central Library; McGill University Library; McCord Museum at McGill University; Dalhousie University Killam Memorial Library; the Halifax City Regional Library; and Mrs. Hildred Senger for making Jones's private family archives available to me. My special thanks go to Dr. Wayne B. Ingalls, Director of Research and Special Projects at Mount Saint Vincent University for his tremendous support when it was most needed.

Thanks are also due to Dr. John Norris, Professor and Director, Division of the History of Medicine, University of British Columbia; Dr. John Owen, Professor of Social and Preventive Medicine, University of Saskatchewan, and Professor John Flint of the History Department, Dalhousie University, for their valuable comments. I am of course, fully responsible for any errors of fact or interpretation that remain.

I especially want to thank the following persons at Nimbus Publishing whose interest in and work on the text of the manuscript was a gratifying experience: Dorothy Blythe, managing editor, P. Joanne Elliott, production editor, Arthur B. Carter, the designer, who deserves full credit for his artistic design, and Paula Sarson, copy editor, with whom I spent many hours giving the manuscript its final form. As well, my thanks and appreciation to Mr. Gary Shutlak, Map and Architectural Archivist and Photo and Documentary Art Archivist at the Nova Scotia Archives, for his dedication in tracing some of the photographs that are included here. Working with all these people in the production of this work was, for me, an enjoyable and memorable experience.

My research was materially facilitated by a Mount Saint Vincent University grant during the summer of 1980 and in 1982 and 1983, for which I am deeply grateful.

This work has been published with the help of a grant from the Social Sciences and Humanities Research Council of Canada.

I also thank the Public Archives of Nova Scotia for permission to reproduce photographs from their photograph collection.

I also wish to thank Professor Arthur Keppel-Jones for his invaluable advice, Professor Kenneth Dewar for his assistance, Professor Elizabeth Jones for translating the Katanga diary and for reading and commenting on parts of the manuscript. Above all, special thanks are due to my husband whose unfailing encouragement made the completion of this work possible.

Janina M. Konczacki
Halifax, Nova Scotia
January 1994

Captain William G. Stairs

PART ONE

CAPTAIN WILLIAM G. STAIRS:
A PROFILE

The Stairs's family home in Halifax, Nova Scotia,
prior to its demolition in the 1930s

(Public Archives of Nova Scotia)

THE FORMATIVE YEARS AND AFRICAN ADVENTURES

FAMILY ROOTS

Capt. William G. Stairs lived to be only twenty-eight, but he stands out as one of the most active Canadians engaged in Africa towards the end of the nineteenth century. It was on that continent that he spent the most eventful periods of his short life. He took part in the famous Emin Pasha Relief Expedition, headed by H. M. Stanley, that set off in the early months of 1887 and returned in December 1889. Seventeen months later, Stairs himself led a Belgian expedition to Katanga and died in Africa on 9 June 1892. The best documented period of his life, not unnaturally, is that of his exploits in Africa, though we have a few particulars, too, about his earlier years. He kept diaries—an excellent source of information—and these are supplemented by the memoirs of his companions on the two expeditions. Not enough material is available to warrant the writing of a full biography, but it is possible to outline the activities and attitudes of this late Victorian explorer.

William Grant Stairs was born on 1 July 1863, the sixth child and the second son of John Stairs and Mary Morrow of Halifax, Nova Scotia. At the time of his birth his family had been prominent in the city for nearly a century. William's ancestor, Denis Stairs, came to North America from Belfast around the middle of the eighteenth century. He first settled in Port Royal on the island of Grenada and then moved to Philadelphia, where he died in the early 1760s, leaving a substantial estate to his son and his widow. Though Stairs are found in Ireland and Scotland, the family is of English origin, the name being quite common in both Kent and Bedfordshire. During the seventeenth century, some members of the family moved to Scotland and from there Ireland, which explains Denis's connection with Belfast. It is also known that Denis Stairs belonged to the Church of England—an indication that he was of English rather than Irish or Scottish descent.[1]

Denis's son John arrived in Halifax from New England during the 1760s when the recently founded city began to attract new settlers lured by the prospect of excellent trading opportunities in fish, lumber, and other natural products, as well as by the lucrative business of furnishing the local garrison with military supplies. In 1775 John married Joanna Stayner who was originally from Boston. They moved to Philadelphia where Joanna died. Upon re-marriage, John left his children under the care of Joanna's brother in Halifax.

One of the sons, William (1789-1865), founder of the Stairs Line of wooden ships, which sailed all over the world, became a prosperous merchant, a distinguished citizen and politician. He became a member of the Legislative Assembly, the eighth mayor of Halifax, and a member of the Legislative Council. He was a friend and strong supporter of Joseph Howe, Nova Scotia's prominent entrepreneur and statesman. William's marriage to Margaret Wiseman was blessed with ten children—seven daughters and three sons. Of the three sons, William James and John deserve particular attention.

William James (1819-1906), the uncle of our explorer, created a precedent in the Stairs family by showing a strong interest in the local militia. In 1862, he became lieutenant colonel of the 4th Halifax Regiment of Militia (eventually 63rd Battalion, Halifax Rifles).[2] This did not prevent him from achieving considerable success in business. He also took an active part in politics, and strongly opposed Confederation.[3] In 1868, following his father's footsteps, he became a member of the Legislative Council of Nova Scotia. In private life he enjoyed a reputation as a ladies' man, but was also accused of being too harsh with his children, particularly with the boys to whom he applied a martinet's notion of discipline.

His brother John (1823-1888), also a stern disciplinarian and our William Grant's father, was somewhat stiffly and conventionally described thus in an obituary that appeared in the *Acadian Recorder*: "Mr. Stairs never sought or accepted public position and was strictly business in his methods and habits, and of unvarying integrity; while those who knew him, knew him best and were strong admirers of his many estimable qualities."[4]

A few surviving records show that there was more to his character than this. At the age of twenty-one, John joined the family firm as a partner. Eight years later he married Laura Silver, who shortly afterwards developed tuberculosis. Two years after Laura's death, John married Mary Morrow whose sister Susan was William James's wife. The family ties between the Stairs and Morrows became even closer, when in the same year, Helen Stairs, William's and John's younger sister, married Robert Morrow, the brother of Susan and Mary.[5]

Unlike his father and his brother William James, John took no active part in politics or public affairs, though he was one of the staunchest opponents of Confederation and was said to have flown the Pilot Jack at half-mast on Dominion Day.[6] In all likelihood this was his expression of the dissatisfaction with the British government's pressure on Nova Scotia to join the Canadian Confederacy.[7] John feared that Nova Scotia's prosperity would come to an end with the advent of Confederation—an opinion which, in subsequent years, proved to be only too true.

All his energies were devoted to business activities. His main interest lay in ship chandlery though he was always ready to take up any kind of business that appeared promising . He had extensive trade relations with the Magdalen Islands' fishermen, whom he supplied with fishing gear, food, and other goods, which were paid for in salt fish. This in turn he shipped to the west Indies where it was traded for sugar, molasses, and rum, for which there was a ready market in Halifax.

John was notoriously tight-fisted with his employees. One of his office boys, Charlie Wainwright, received a wage of two dollars a week, while John's income was reputed to be about forty thousand dollars per annum.[8] The master's irascibility earned him the nickname of "Hellfire John." Another of the office boys, Scott Chisholm, remembered that he "was always terrified of the old man because he was so stern." John's grandson, H. Gerald Stairs, presents a somewhat modified picture of this Victorian paterfamilias: "Apparently the whole family went in awe of John, though none of them could understand why, as his voice was never raised in anger at home and he never touched them. In fact, according to my father he hardly spoke at all. Maybe he didn't have the chance. After all he had a wife, four talkative daughters and five sons. In any case, though he made little effort, John seems to have had the ability to make people respect him."[9]

In 1861 John built a residence—"Fairfield"—on the northern shore of the North West Arm, which was then a considerable distance from the centre of Halifax. His immediate neighbours were his brothers-in-law Alfred Jones and Robert Morrow. One can picture something approaching a Dickensian idyll of domestic bliss: the numerous offspring of three families growing up together in lively rural surroundings. Constant child-bearing, however, took its toll on John's second wife. William Grant lost his mother when he was barely eight years old. Mary Morrow died in 1871 after the birth of her eleventh child. The following year John married again, taking the governess of his children as his third wife.[10]

Late in 1887 John fell ill with cancer.[11] Shortly afterwards he left for Cannes, in the south of France, where he spent his last days. He tersely told one of his sons the reason for his departure was: "I'll be damned if I'll give my business enemies the satisfaction of seeing me die by inches."[12] Nothing reflects better the nature of his personality than this statement. John died on 22 March 1888.[13]

THE FORMATIVE YEARS

Little is known about William Grant's childhood and adolescence. His early years were spent playing with his Jones and Morrow cousins who lived close by. As a young man he was to write delightedly of the pleasures of living in an English country house—colonial-style pleasures that he must have known as a child. A small capital like Halifax, which numbered thirty-one thousand inhabitants at the time of Confederation, had to generate its own entertainment and amusements. Social activities consisted mostly of house parties, picnics, fishing, sleigh rides, skating parties, and amateur theatricals.[14]

After attending primary school at Fort Massey Academy in Halifax, where he was enrolled until the autumn of 1875, he went with his younger brother John (Jack) to Scotland. At the Merchiston Castle School in Edinburgh he continued his education for the next three years.[15] He has been described as being "shy and reserved in the presence of the masters, but active and playful among the students."[16] One is inclined to suspect that this attitude towards his superiors was the result of his upbringing at home, where everyone lived in fear of the head of the household. Later when he became a soldier, William Grant must have found it easy to obey orders and natural to expect the same from his subordinates.

At the age of fifteen he returned to Canada and attended the Royal Military College at Kingston, Ontario, where he completed his training in 1882. It seems that a military career appealed to him, and although he earned first class honours and the rank of sergeant, his marks did not qualify him for either of the two army commissions offered that year. In September 1882 Stairs left for New Zealand where he obtained a position as a civil engineer on a railway construction project in a district near Hawke's Bay. Living in very primitive conditions, he gained invaluable experience in surveyorship and mapping.

While in New Zealand he accepted an invitation from the British War Office to apply for entry into the army, which was offering commissions to the graduates of the Royal Military College whose graduating marks were satisfactory. Upon receiving the telegram, Stairs left for England. He entered Chatham and was gazetted a lieutenant in the Royal Engineers in June 1885. There he went through a course of professional instruction.[17] It is interesting to read Stairs's own comments on the sudden change in his life: "What a strange existence mine has been when I compare it with that of my army friends! I left my country when I was only a youngster of twelve to go to school in a foreign country. Next I spent four years in Kingston. Then I found myself in the virgin forest of New Zealand where, for two years [and] nine months, I led an open-air life in the wilds working hard all through the rainy days of a New Zealand winter and eating coarse, tough food. And then suddenly I found myself transported to Chatham and London, leading a diametrically opposed life, eating my fill, sleeping as long as I liked, with no special precautions to take for my safety, and not having to work and think very hard."[18]

For a time, at any rate, it seems that he enjoyed this new style of living. The only drawback was the routine of army garrison life, to which he found it difficult to adjust.

At that time Stairs was twenty-two years of age, fast approaching physical maturity. Surviving photographs show us a handsome man, though of a somewhat stern demeanour. Other records indicate how he appeared to his colleagues. Dr. Moloney, a member of Stairs's expedition to Katanga, described thus his impressions when meeting him for the first time:

"I must confess, that the tall, fair, and delicate-looking young man, whom I found seated in the coffee-room, appeared, at first sight, very unlike the typical African traveller; but his interrogatory showed, at any rate, that he did not waste time in beating about the bush. 'Can you shoot?' he asked; and when the question had been answered in the affirmative, there came a second and apparently subsidiary query, 'Have you brought your testimonials?' After a rapid glance at those documents, Captain Stairs informed me that my capacities for the undertaking seemed superior to those of his other correspondents."[19]

Directness and conciseness characterize a good soldier. They were amongst Stairs's most marked qualities as Henry M. Stanley was quick to discover. In a letter to General Wolseley at the War Office he wrote:[20]

"Lieut. [sic] W. G. Stairs R. E., with whom I was previously unacquainted sent me a letter of application for a position on the Emin Pasha Relief Expedition. As I was then receiving applications by the hundred from all ranks his letter would doubtless have escaped attention had it not been for the clear, direct, concise form of the application. It read very different [sic] and was so sensible compared to the others that it arrested the attention, and consequently I became anxious to secure him. I have never had cause to regret it."[21]

To be selected was considered a privilege and many candidates used every subterfuge possible to achieve this coveted distinction. It was no secret that two of the applicants tipped the scale in their favour by subscribing £1,000 each to the relief fund.

James S. Jameson did so out of his own pocket and A. J. Mounteney Jephson was assisted financially by his cousin, the Countess de Noailles. Although the selecting committee was not quite convinced of their suitability, it could not resist the argument of a generous donation.[22]

The Origins of the Emin Pasha Relief Expedition

Much has been written about the Emin Pasha Relief Expedition by Stanley himself, by most of the white participants, and by many historians.[23] What follows then is merely some concise background information and a brief outline of the role played by W. G. Stairs in the expedition.

Emin Pasha, whose original name was Edward Schnitzer, was born in 1840. He spent his early years in what was then Prussia, showing from the first an intense interest in natural history. For a time he studied medicine, but having experienced some bitter disappointments at university, and unable to find employment in his profession, he decided to go abroad. Schnitzer visited a number of European countries, and finally, in 1865 landed in Turkey, where he settled. His functions ranged from that of a quarantine- and sanitary-officer to various political missions. By 1872 he was naturalized. In 1875 he went to Egypt and within three years rose to the high position of governor of the Equatorial Province.[24]

In 1820 the Ottoman Empire, then a declining power, embarked on its last conquest by invading the Sudan, a territory which was fragmented into a number of independent kingdoms and chiefdoms. The establishment of Turko-Egyptian rule was a gradual process and the new rulers made extensive use of European administrators and explorers.[25] First Baker and then Gordon was appointed governor of Equatoria,[26] the southernmost province of the Sudan. Between 1870 and 1876 they subdued the territory south of Gondokoro and by doing so, extended the area over which Emin was eventually to rule.[27] Between 1877 and 1879 Gordon expanded his control over the whole of the Sudan.

Equatoria lay along both sides of the Bahr el Jebel River (the Nile). It was roughly triangular in shape. The base of the triangle, some 450 miles (700 kilometres) long, touched the shores of Lake Albert and was parallel to the equator, while its tip was barely 50 miles (80 kilometres) to the south of the confluence of the Bahr el Jebel and Bahr el Ghazal Rivers. The western side of the triangle was strongly concave towards its centre.

In 1876 Edward Schnitzer assumed the name and title of Effendi Hakim–"Effendi" meaning a man of high social position and authority. In 1878 he was appointed governor of the Equatorial Province and given the title of Bey–a title given to higher officials.[28] An insurrection led by Mohammed Ahmed El Mahdi broke out in 1881, and gradually ousted the Turko-Egyptian administration from the Sudan. When Khartoum fell in January of 1885, the territories to the south were isolated. Threatened by the Mahdists, Emin Pasha removed his seat of government to the south. In July Emin reached Wadelai, the last of his headquarters in Equatoria, situated on the Bahr el Jebel (the Nile) some 35 miles (50 kilometres) north of Lake Albert. As the prospect of a re-conquest of the Sudan from the north was remote, Emin decided to open a line of communication with the east coast,

Emin Pasha

from where news and supplies could reach him.[29] He also considered the possibility of retreating further to the south, but in order to make this option possible, he had to secure the goodwill of Kabarega, the ruler of Unyoro.

Accordingly, in January 1886 he sent to that king's court Dr. Wilhelm Junker, a German explorer who had joined him some time earlier.[30] The timing of these negotiations proved highly inopportune. At the beginning of March war broke out between Unyoro and Uganda, and Kabarega ordered Junker out of the country. The latter managed to reach the Ugandan capital, Kampala, where he discovered that King Mutesa had been succeeded by his son Mwanga, who was known for his hostility towards Europeans. Seeing the futility of his mission and prompted by his private interests, Junker left for Zanzibar.[31]

Towards the end of February 1886, Emin received several letters. One, from Nubar Pasha, the Egyptian prime minister, instructed him to abandon Equatoria and to proceed to Egypt via Zanzibar as the government had decided to give up the Sudan. He also received instructions from Sir John Kirk, the British consul in Zanzibar, advising him how best to effect this retreat to the coast. Furthermore, the Reverend Mackay, the agent of the British mission in Uganda,[32] provided him with details of General Gordon's death, an event with which Emin was apparently already acquainted. The bearer of this correspondence was Mohammed Biri, an Arab from Tripoli, who was reputed to have rendered good services to the International African Association.[33] Junker, who met Mohammed Biri in Unyoro, managed to secure his assistance in establishing contacts between Equatoria and Uganda.[34]

Apart from Junker there was another European in Emin's entourage who was affected by Mahdi's *jihad,* namely Gaetano Casati.[35] In May 1886 Emin entrusted Casati with the task of resuming negotiations with Kabarega.[36] However, because of a conflict between the land-holding chiefs on the one hand and a faction of mercenaries and resident Arab traders on the other, Casati's mission at Unyoro failed, and his position became increasingly precarious. In January 1888 he was imprisoned but managed to escape and return to Wadelai.[37]

From November 1884 there was no information forthcoming about the fate of Emin Pasha. During the long period of silence, Junker's brother, a St. Petersburg banker, hired a German, Dr. Fischer, to head an expedition from the east coast to Equatoria. On arriving at the northeast corner of Lake Victoria, Fischer was forced to turn back because of the Kabaka's (the local ruler's) hostility.

A similar attempt was made by an Austrian, Oscar Lenz, who chose a western route via the Congo River. Lenz, too, was unsuccessful in his efforts. On reaching the Upper Congo, he was unable to find porters willing to cross the unknown and dangerous country.[38]

A third expedition was organized by private initiative in Britain and assisted by the Egyptian government. The British government, however, remained lukewarm if not indifferent to the whole enterprise. It was wary of any financial responsibility—direct or indirect. Aware, too, that an expedition of this sort might cause conflict, it feared any possible political or military involvement—the Khartoum disaster was all too recent. So acting independently of the government, Sir William MacKinnon set up the Emin Pasha Relief Committee,[39] which met for the first time late in 1886 under his chairmanship.[40] The amount of money needed to cover the costs of the expedition was estimated at

£20,000. One-half of it was to be subscribed by the Egyptian government and the rest was to be obtained from donations made by the Royal Geographical Society and private individuals, the most generous donor being Sir William MacKinnon himself. In fact, the relief fund was oversubscribed. The Egyptian government donated £14,000 and with funds obtained from other sources the total reached was £33,368. Expenses came to £27,709.[41]

The leader chosen for the expedition was Henry M. Stanley, an already well-known explorer and an old friend of MacKinnon's. Later we shall examine the hypothesis that there was community of interest between these two men who played an active role in the partition of Africa. Officially Stanley was still in the employ of Leopold II of Belgium, so he required the latter's permission to accept the leadership of the expedition. The Belgian king, however, was quick to see what advantages he might draw from this situation.[42]

Apart from Stanley, there were nine European officers who participated in the expedition in various capacities. Lt. William Grant Stairs was enlisted on condition that he obtain leave of absence from the army. This Lord Wolseley readily granted him. William Bonny, a sergeant in the Army Medical Department (AMD), was engaged as a medical assistant. The remaining two military men, enlisted in London, were Maj. Edmund Musgrave Barttelot of the 7th Fusiliers and Capt. Robert H. Nelson of Methuen's Horse. The latter had been active in the Zulu campaigns.

Other members of the expedition were civilians. John Rose Troup, who had previously been employed in the Congo, spoke Swahili. A. J. Mounteney Jephson was very eager to join, but in Stanley's opinion lacked experience.[43] Subsequent events show him to be a valuable member of the expedition; as a skilled navigator, he was able to take charge of the expedition's steel boat.[44] James S. Jameson was interested in natural history and had experience hunting wild game in South Africa.[45] Jephson and Jameson strengthened their case by subscribing £1,000 each to the relief fund.

Two additional officers were recruited en route. In Alexandria, Dr. Thomas H. Parke, also of the AMD, applied to Stanley for the position of surgeon and was accepted.[46] Besides proving to be an excellent doctor, he also left a vivid account of the expedition. Marching in the interior of Africa, Stanley encountered Herbert Ward, a young man with whom he was much taken. Ward had travelled in New Zealand and Borneo, had been in the service of the Congo State and now volunteered to join the expedition.[47] He became something of a favourite with Stanley and this was to cause much ill-feeling among the other officers.

In the articles of enlistment, which members of the expedition had to sign, Stanley inserted a restrictive clause to be observed by all the participants. This stated that no account of the expedition was to be published before six months had elapsed after the publication of the official account prepared by Stanley himself. The reason for this rather strange precaution was that Stanley was still smarting from criticism of the accounts he had written of his two earlier expeditions.[48]

Essential to an expedition of this sort were, of course, the bearers. At that time Zanzibar was the main centre of recruitment, so it was from there that the expedition would have to set out. One of Stanley's main organizational problems was solved when the sultan consented to his hiring six hundred Zanzibari porters. Human porterage was to be assisted by forty pack donkeys. Ten others for riding were also ordered. All together an

Henry M. Stanley

Lieutenant William G. Stairs, R.E.

Surgeon Thomas H. Parke

Captain Robert H. Nelson

Arthur J. Mounteney Jephson

amount of £7,354 was spent on stores and equipment, excluding the Remington rifles and ammunition, the gunpowder, and the percussion caps, which were sent by the Egyptian government. The British War Office also provided some more ammunition at no cost.[49]

Equipment included a steel boat 28 feet (8½ m) long consisting of twelve 75-pound (34-kg) sections, each of which had to be carried by two porters. The amount of ammunition taken was quite formidable: 2 tons of gunpowder, 350,000 percussion caps, 100,000 rounds of Remington ammunition, and 35,000 special Remington cartridges, 50,000 Winchester cartridges, and 30,000 Gatling cartridges.[50] For reasons we shall see, it was deemed necessary to despatch this extraordinary amount of ammunition to Emin Pasha.[51] So it was to this that the advance column of the expedition gave priority at the expense of the cloth, which was left behind at Yambuya, thus depriving the caravan of the ability to procure foodstuffs. It is not difficult to guess the consequences of this decision.

As the expedition had to be assembled at Zanzibar, it seems logical that the route chosen would start from the east coast. Four possible routes were indeed considered but for various reasons were rejected. The first began at Mombasa, crossed Masailand and continued north of Lake Victoria towards Wadelai. The second began at Bagamoyo and passed through Lake Victoria and the hostile Uganda territory. The third also started at Bagamoyo, continued via Msalala, south of Lake Victoria, then through Karagwe and turned north towards Lake Albert. The fourth passed through Tabora and Ruanda, a country unknown to European travellers. On all these routes there was a high risk of massive desertion by the Zanzibari porters.[52]

It was decided to approach Equatoria from the west. The expedition was to round southern Africa by ship and disembark at Banana Point on the mouth of the Congo. It would travel to the interior via the Congo and Aruwimi Rivers, then march on to the southern tip of Equatoria near Lake Albert, where they hoped to find Emin Pasha.

Later we shall have occasion to note that this choice of route was influenced by the ambitions of Leopold II. Stanley could, however, point to three ostensible advantages: first, a flotilla of steamers could transport the expedition up the Congo River; second, they did not expect any shortage of water and food; third, the predominantly Zanzibari porters would be less inclined to desert.[53]

The subsequent course of the expedition along the Congo route reveals the weakness in Stanley's arguments. The river route proved difficult: there were disastrous shortages of food, many of the porters died, and others deserted when the caravan passed through Arab areas of influence.[54] In effect, Stanley's ignorance of the real conditions of the terrain and its inhabitants, his over-sanguine expectations, and his errors in judgement were to cost the expedition very dear. He estimated that the whole expedition would take eighteen months, whereas it took him thirty-three months to accomplish his mission, almost double the time.[55]

To this day, there is considerable debate as to whether any ulterior motives lurked behind the relief expedition's offer of help to the refugees from Equatoria. Official arguments in favour of the expedition insisted on its humanitarian intent. Was this merely a smoke screen to hide its real purpose? There is, in fact, some evidence to show that both British merchants and the Belgian king had something to gain from the expedition.

In October 1886, J. F. Hutton, a member of the so-called "MacKinnon clan," proposed to MacKinnon the establishment of a commercial syndicate that would open up a direct route to Lake Victoria and the Sudan in order to develop trade. A chartered company was to be set up to control the East African territories involved in these activities. Hutton could then regard the relief expedition as the first step towards the realization of his plan.

The aim of the expedition changed from that of "relief" to that of support for the man who might now become a useful tool to MacKinnon and his associates.[56] Stanley was well-aware of the new circumstances:

"Early in October 1886, Sir William MacKinnon and Mr. J. F. Hutton, ex-president of the Manchester Chamber of Commerce, had spoken with me respecting the possibilities of conveying relief to Emin, with a view to enable him to hold his own. To them it seemed that he only required ammunition, and I shared their opinion."[57] In a speech made later, in January 1890, at a banquet in Cairo, Stanley stated quite plainly that his English friends thought that Emin should not abandon his province.[58]

The "unofficial mind of British imperialism" might plot and plan,[59] but according to many commentators official British policy towards East Africa showed a distinct reluctance to act and viewed most private initiatives in the area with extreme caution.[60] With Lord Salisbury's ministry (1885-1892) some changes came about and its colonial policy became more active.[61] In spite of some initial misgivings, the government gave its approval to the Emin Pasha Relief Expedition. The creation of the Imperial British East Africa Company in 1887-88 formally embodied this new policy.[62]

Meanwhile Leopold II of the Belgians had his own uses for the expedition and was in a position to impose certain conditions given that Stanley was still formally in his employ. One of the conditions was indeed the adoption of the Congo route which, on first consideration, seems so curious. A letter of 7 January 1887, written by Count de Borchgrave on behalf of Leopold II to Stanley, makes this quite plain: "The king has suggested this road merely so as to lend your services to the expedition, which it would be impossible for him to do were the expedition to proceed by the Eastern coast."[63] There is no doubt that the king had imperialist designs on Equatoria, so one of the undisclosed aims of the expedition was to establish a line of communication between the Congo and that province. Leopold was prepared to retain Emin as the governor of the territory which would pass under the control of the Congo Free State and to grant him financial assistance of between £10,000 and £12,000 a year.[64]

To further his aims Leopold authorized Stanley to enter into negotiations with Tippu Tib, a powerful ivory- and slave-trader, whose sphere of influence extended over the territory of the eastern Congo through which the expedition was to pass.[65] Tippu Tib was to be bribed with the governorship of the Stanley Falls district, which was de facto under his control. In exchange for this arrangement Tippu Tib was to grant free passage to the expedition. By accepting the governorship, he became Leopold's employee. Paradoxically, the champion of the anti-slavery movement availed himself of the services of a suspected slave-trader in order to achieve his imperialistic aims.

In view of the open and secret negotiations that preceded the expedition, one is tempted to ask whether Leopold II and MacKinnon were aware of each other's designs with regard to Equatoria. Furthermore, what was Stanley's own position vis-à-vis his two employers?

Unable to count on the support of his own government, King Leopold II approached Prime Minister Gladstone, but the idea of Anglo-Belgian cooperation in the Sudan did not appeal to the British prime minister.[66] There is no evidence that the king ever discussed his plans with MacKinnon, or that either of them was aware of each other's aims. Were their schemes mutually exclusive? In the opinion of Roger Anstey this was not necessarily so, as prior to the formation of the British East Africa Company, MacKinnon was not in a position to take responsibility for Emin Pasha, whereas Leopold had the resources to do so. Had Leopold succeeded, Equatoria would then remain in friendly hands and MacKinnon would be allowed to develop trade within the free trade zone as defined by the Berlin Act.[67] Leopold's earlier approaches to the British government add some plausibility to the view that some form of cooperation was possible. Furthermore, should the Free State be unable to survive, as many believed could be the case, the British would then be in an excellent position to occupy at least part of Equatoria.

As for Stanley, he viewed Leopold's and MacKinnon's proposals as mutually exclusive alternatives, but he seems to have shown considerable indifference to the charge of duplicity. Is it possible that he depended on his own diplomatic skills and cunning to weather any such accusations, or did he believe that a stroke of luck would deliver him from difficulties that could arise in the future? Stanley—a confirmed egocentric—is known to have paid little attention to the interests of the others, and as Barbara Emerson aptly observed, his prime consideration was his "ego-boosting and the material for another bestseller."[68]

THE COURSE OF THE EMIN PASHA
RELIEF EXPEDITION

A brief outline of the course of events that took place on the Emin Pasha Relief Expedition is essential to the understanding of this late Victorian intrusion into Africa. With the exception of a few explanatory remarks the material presented in this section is based primarily on Stairs's diary.[69]

Early in February 1887 Stairs, accompanied by Jephson and Nelson, arrived in Egypt. There he was joined by Stanley, Dr. Parke, Barttelot, Jameson, Stanley's servants, William Hoffmann, and Baruti, as well as by some sixty-one Sudanese askaris fitted out by the Egyptian government. They reached Zanzibar on 22 February. After the embarkation of six hundred Zanzibaris, a number of other Africans, as well as Tippu Tib and his party (which included several wives), the expedition proceeded by way of the Cape of Good Hope to Banana Point on the estuary of the Congo River. They arrived on 18 March and two days later disembarked at Matadi, close to the cataracts. From there they had to march for some 235 miles (370 kilometres) to Stanley Pool. It was on this march that Stanley met Herbert Ward who volunteered as a member of the expedition and was accepted. At Stanley Pool, further transport was provided by a flotilla of steamers. These took them up the Congo as far as Yambuya, beyond which point navigation was impossible. Because of unforeseen circumstances, too few boats were supplied, so some men and their loads were left behind at Stanley Pool. They were to be brought up to Yambuya later.

After the arrival at Yambuya on 15 June, Stanley decided to divide the expedition into two parts which he called respectively the "rear" and the "advance" columns. The advance column, led by himself and consisting of Stairs, Nelson, Jephson, Parke, Hoffmann,

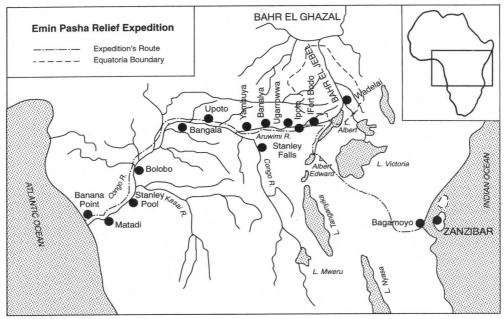

Emin Pasha Relief Expedition

—·—·—·— Expedition's Route
— — — — Equatoria Boundary

BAHR EL GHAZAL

BAHR EL JEBEL

Wadelai

Upoto

Bangala

Yambuya

Banalya

Ugarrowwa

Ipoto

Fort Bodo

L. Albert

Aruwimi R.

Stanley Falls

Congo R.

L. Albert Edward

L. Victoria

Bolobo

Banana Point

Stanley Pool

Kasai R.

Matadi

ATLANTIC OCEAN

Congo R.

L. Tanganyika

Bagamoyo

ZANZIBAR

INDIAN OCEAN

L. Mweru

L. Nyasa

and 383 Africans, was to march with the greatest possible speed towards Lake Albert where they hoped to find Emin Pasha. The rear column, under the command of Major Barttelot with Jameson as his deputy and consisting of approximately 270 men, was to remain at Yambuya. Meanwhile, Ward, Troup, and Bonny were to bring from Stanley Pool the men and the loads left there. As governor of the Stanley Falls area under the authority of the Congo Free State, Tippu Tib had promised to supply Stanley with the extra porters needed. Barttelot was to resume the eastward journey as soon as these carriers were provided.[70] The advance column left Yambuya on 28 June 1887. Communication between the two columns was not resumed until over a year later in August 1888.

Conditions faced by the rear column proved extremely difficult. Supplies were grossly inadequate, the climate was unhealthy, and relations with the local population were distinctly unfriendly. It took nearly a year for Tippu Tib to provide the carriers, but instead of the 600 men originally promised, only about 400 turned up, while the number of Barttelot's party was reduced to 132 men wasted by famine and disease. Moreover, Tippu Tib insisted that the loads of 60 pounds (27 kilograms) were too heavy for his people. Having no other choice Barttelot had to ship some of the loads he considered unnecessary and superfluous back to Bangala. Troup fell seriously ill and had to leave Yambuya for England.[71] Subsequently, Stanley was intensely peeved to learn that eight boxes of his baggage were included in that transport. He never saw them again.

On 11 June 1888, Barttelot began his march eastward, but he only managed to reach Banalya, a mere 150 miles (241 kilometres) farther on. The column stopped there, incapable of any further progress. The situation continued to deteriorate. On 19 July Barttelot was killed when trying to impose silence on an African woman engaged in ritual song and drum-beating.[72] Barely a month later Jameson died at Lomami. It seems he was on the way to see the authorities of the Congo Free State in order to obtain permission for Tippu

Tib to lead a caravan to Lake Albert. Bonny, the only European who survived, was in charge of what was left of the rear column until Stanley's return from Lake Albert.[73]

Meanwhile Stanley's advance column marched along the Aruwimi River and then the Ituri River using boats and canoes whenever possible. This stretch of the journey was through parts of Africa not yet explored by Europeans. Innumerable cataracts and rapids prevented them from travelling fast. They were also considerably delayed by efforts to procure food as well as by frequent tropical rain storms. The caravan suffered from heavy human losses due to disease, skirmishes with the Africans, desertions, and shortages of food. Hunger became a real threat when the caravan reached the areas ravaged by the Arab ivory- and slave-raiders. On 13 August during a fight with the attacking villagers at Avisibba, Stairs was seriously wounded by a poisoned arrow. Dr. Parke's skilled care probably saved his life.[74]

On 18 September the advance column arrived at an Arab settlement commanded by an ivory-trader named Ugarrowwa. Here Stanley took advantage of unburdening the caravan of fifty-six men, who were temporarily left under Ugarrowwa's care. However, the number of the infirm and those unable to carry the loads continued to increase, so that on 6 October Stanley decided to leave the incapacitated men in a camp under Nelson's command and to move forward at a faster pace. On 18 October they reached another Arab settlement located at Ipoto and commanded by Kilonga Longa, a subordinate of one Abed bin Salim who was an ivory-trader of considerable importance. Those unable to march remained at Ipoto under the care of Dr. Parke. Meanwhile, Jephson was sent back to bring Nelson and his men to Ipoto where they, too, would have the benefit of Parke's medical attention. Having accomplished his mission, Jephson rejoined the column on 16 November.

As the advance column moved out of the Arab sphere of influence, food became more easily obtainable. Then, on 4 December, after 160 days of marching through the bush, the caravan entered open country. In another ten days they reached Lake Albert, but their initial enthusiasm was marred by the intense animosity of the Africans and the realization that discovering the exact whereabouts of Emin Pasha might present formidable problems. Stanley then proposed retreating some 60 miles (90 kilometres) westward and building a *boma* (fort) at Ibwiri. From that base he intended sending out expeditions to bring Parke, Nelson, and their men to Ibwiri, as well as the steel boat (the *Advance*) that was left behind because of the shortage of porters. He also intended to go back to Yambuya for the rear column.

The others were reluctant to return to the much-hated forest. Stanley argued that the expedition was not strong enough to stay in the open country and face all the dangers that threatened it there. Of the 383 Africans and 6 Europeans who had left Yambuya, only 169 persons reached Lake Albert. Accordingly, on 7 January 1888, the caravan was back at Ibwiri and soon busily engaged in constructing a *boma*. They named it "Fort Bodo"—the "Peaceful Fort."

Stanley assigned to Stairs the task of bringing Parke and Nelson form Ipoto to the fort. Stairs left on 19 January and six days later was at Kilonga Longa's where he found his friends in rather poor condition. Parke and Nelson arrived at Fort Bodo on 8 February, followed four days later by Stairs who had remained behind to take charge of the *Advance*. His next assignment was to march to Ugarrowwa's settlement. Leaving on 16 February, he arrived there almost a month later on 14 March. Of the fifty-six men left behind, twenty-seven had survived. However, their condition was so poor that only fourteen of them were still alive when Stairs's party arrived at Fort Bodo on 26 April.

Upon his return, Stairs was deeply disappointed to learn that over three weeks earlier Stanley, accompanied by Jephson and Parke, had gone back to Lake Albert in order to set up a camp at Kavalli's and attempt to establish contact with Emin Pasha. Stairs wanted to be with Stanley and to share the excitement of meeting the governor of Equatoria. Instead, his role in the expedition was now reduced to the despised routine of garrison life at the *boma* located in the unfriendly environment of the tropical forest.

In the meantime, Stanley had at last received news of the long-sought governor of Equatoria by way of a letter from Emin addressed to a "white man" of whose presence near Lake Albert he had heard. Jephson went in search of the governor and found him at M'swa. On 29 April the first meeting between Stanley and Emin took place when the latter arrived at Stanley's camp near Kavalli's.[75]

Over the next few days they discussed the future of Emin and his people. Stanley brought letters from the Khedive—the ruler of Egypt—and Nubar Pasha—the Egyptian prime minister—who advised Emin to return to Egypt but did not explicitly order him to do so. If he decided to stay in Equatoria, it would be at his own risk and responsibility, as no further aid from Egypt would be forthcoming.[76]

Stanley presented Emin with three possibilities. First, he could abandon Equatoria and return to Egypt. Emin's reply was that he would do this only if his subjects who were with him were willing to accompany him and this he very much doubted. Secondly, the Congo Free State could take over the government of Equatoria with Emin as governor. This proposal was made on the authority of King Leopold. Emin rejected it, mainly on the grounds that he could not undertake to maintain lines of communication between the Congo and Equatoria over vast and mostly uncontrolled territories. Finally, Stanley suggested a move to the northeast corner of Lake Victoria (Kavirondo), where Emin and his people could establish themselves in the name of the British East Africa Association. Stanley admitted that he had no authority to make this proposal but was certain that it would meet with the approval of the East Africa Association. Emin considered this the most feasible of the three proposals, and did not think that his subjects would entertain any serious objections to it.[77]

Leaving Emin to consider the matter further, Stanley marched westwards to Yambuya via Fort Bodo to see what had happened to the rear column. By the time Emin and his men had come to a decision, the East Africa Association would, Stanley hoped, have become a chartered company that intended establishing a British presence in East Africa.

Meanwhile, Jephson accompanied Emin Pasha on a tour of Equatorian garrisons. Emin did not suggest to his Egyptian clerks and soldiers a move to Lake Victoria (Kavirondo). Instead, he tried to convince them of the necessity to leave Equatoria in order to return to Egypt via the east coast. The soldiers were suspicious. The bad shape in which Stanley's expedition had arrived did not inspire confidence. Emin showed them the letters with instructions from the Egyptian government, but these they rejected as a forgery. Some of them insisted that the only road to Egypt was by Khartoum. On the whole, both clerks and soldiers opposed the abandonment of Equatoria. Rumours spread that Emin had betrayed the Khedive and was conspiring with the British. Stanley figured as an ogre who wished to take Emin's people out of the country and "hand them, their wives and children over as slaves to the English."[78] Some other old grievances still rankled. The soldiers rebelled and imprisoned Emin and Jephson on 19 August at Duffilé.

A few weeks later the Mahdists, prompted by the news of the arrival of Stanley's expedition, attacked Equatoria and captured the station at Rejaf. An attempt to retake it proved unsuccessful. At this point the Egyptian soldiers became disillusioned with their rebel leaders. Unwilling to surrender to the Mahdists, they requested the release of Emin and Jephson who, when freed, left on 17 November for Wadelai and then went to Tunguru.[79] A little later the Mahdist offensive lost its impetus and their forces withdrew to the north.

While Emin Pasha and Jephson were retreating from their tour of Equatoria, Stanley returned to Fort Bodo with 130 Madi carriers provided by Emin. On 16 June he began his march for Yambuya. Stairs was left in command of the *boma,* and once more had to face a long period of stationary life in the unfriendly and unhealthy environment of the tropical forest. Things were made worse by the lack of news from Jephson and uncertainty as to the length of Stanley's absence. This state of affairs lasted for six months until 20 December, when Stanley returned from Banalya with the remnants of the rear column and news of the sad fate of Barttelot and Jameson. Three days later they all abandoned Fort Bodo and marched towards Lake Albert.

On 9 January 1889, Stanley instructed Stairs to set up a camp at Kandekore where the sick men and some of the loads were to stay while Stanley continued marching to the lake. It was one more of the many disappointments Stairs had to face in his relations with the leader of the expedition.

A month later Stairs received an order from Stanley to move to Kavalli's. At the same time he received a letter from Jephson in which he learned about the rebellion in Equatoria. On 18 February he arrived at Kavalli's where he met Emin Pasha.

In the second half of March Stanley and Emin decided to abandon Equatoria and to leave for Zanzibar on 10 April. On 5 April a plot organized by some of the Pasha's men was discovered. Its participants intended to seize arms in order to prevent the return to Egypt. Stanley's prompt action saved the situation, but after an argument with Emin the relations between the two men became extremely cool. Stanley accused Emin of indecision and procrastination, while the latter suspected Stanley of having ulterior motives and felt that the expedition had failed to fulfil its purpose.[80]

Soon after this disturbing event, Stanley fell seriously ill and so did Parke. The departure of the caravan had to be postponed, and the march to the east coast did not begin until 8 May. When the column approached the Ruwenzori range, Stairs, weakened by recent fever, attempted to climb one of the snow-covered peaks. He also discovered that the Semliki River carried the waters from Lake Edward to Lake Albert—adding to knowledge of the sources of the Nile. During most of July Stairs suffered again from malaria. Towards the end of August, when at the Church Missionary Society's station at Usambiro, close to Lake Victoria, he learned from letters awaiting him there of his father's death in March 1888.

During the remaining three months of the journey there are only a few entries in his diary. After the strains and dangers of his exploits he might well have been in a state of psychological anti-climax. All were certainly in bad physical condition and probably preferred to look forward to their return to civilization rather than dwell on the recent past or the slowly passing present. At any rate, this seems to have been Stairs's frame of mind when writing to his brother Jack from Simbamweni in Usequa on 25 November 1889. He hoped, he wrote, to reach Zanzibar on 7 December, leave it on the seventeenth and be in Suez on New Year's Day 1890. He was full of plans for his four months' leave but doubted whether these would include a visit to Halifax. After three years in the tropics, winter in his hometown might be too cold to bear.[81]

THE ACHIEVEMENTS OF THE EMIN PASHA RELIEF EXPEDITION

The overt and "humanitarian" aim of the Emin Pasha Relief Expedition was to assist the governor of Equatoria and his Egyptian staff in their plight brought about by the Mahdist uprising. Today we might well question Emin Pasha's right to his position and look upon him as a representative of Turko-Egyptian colonialism imposed upon people of a different ethnic group. This point of view was, of course, alien to the Victorians in England and to contemporary continental Europeans.

In the light, however, of its original aim—to rescue Emin Pasha—and its undeclared goals—a combination of the design of Leopold II and the hidden imperialistic aims of some British financiers—what did the expedition achieve? When Stanley finally met Emin, it became obvious that the one who apparently had to be "rescued" was far better off than his would-be rescuers, for he managed to provide them with more useful supplies than they could offer him. The ammunition delivered to Emin, at a tremendous cost of human lives, was never used.

Also, as we have seen, the arrival of the expedition contributed to the deterioration of Emin's relations with his own people and to the eventual collapse of what was left of his province. Ultimately, upon Stanley's insistence, Emin was compelled to leave Equatoria. He had no desire to leave Africa and an accident at Bagamoyo, requiring a prolonged period of hospitalization, provided him with an excuse to remain there. Many of his people were not so fortunate. Of the six hundred refugees from Equatoria who accompanied him, more than half perished on the march to the east coast.

The expedition, however, could still boast of having evacuated them from Equatoria. Europe praised and applauded but without taking into account the enormous loss of life. Of the 695 men who had left Zanzibar only 253 returned. Those who did not die of disease and wounds perished from starvation or deserted. Members of the expedition wantonly destroyed many villages and shot an undetermined number of Africans. Of the eleven Europeans, two died (Barttelot and Jameson), while Troup and Ward had to return to England at an early stage. The remaining seven: Stanley, Stairs, Jephson, Parke, Nelson, Bonny, and Hoffmann managed to complete the expedition, but their health was seriously impaired.[82]

As for the hidden agenda of the expedition, neither imperialist Leopold II nor the trade-minded British found themselves further advanced. So Stanley's loyalty to one or the other was, fortunately for him, never really put to the test.

The expedition could, however, claim to have made some contributions to scientific knowledge. On the journey up the Aruwimi River Stanley collected information on the ecology of the unexplored great Central African tropical forest that stretches for some 300 miles (480 kilometres) to the east of Yambuya, and also gathered ethnographical data on its inhabitants.

As has been mentioned, Stairs explored the Semliki River flowing from Lake Edward to Lake Albert and revealed that the Albertine Nile has its source in the former of the two lakes and not in the latter as geographers had believed. It was Stairs, too, who led a party to explore the snowy Ruwenzori range, the legendary Mountains of the Moon, to which ancient geographers had traced the sources of the Nile. Although he failed to reach the snow line, Stairs managed to bring back many specimens of plants. Emin Pasha, who was an amateur botanist, gave most of them their generic names, noting that they were typical products of a moderate climate. One of them, thus far unknown, he named *Disa stairsii (Orchidaccae)* in honour of Stairs, and another one was called *Viola eminii (Violaccae)*—Emin's violet. (The Stairs's ground orchids are prolific on the northwest flanks of Ruwenzori and have five spikes of a deep purplish red colour.) Geological observations led the explorers to the interesting conclusion that the mountains were of volcanic origin. Stairs submitted a factual report of his ascent of Ruwenzori on 8 June 1889.[83]

In a pretentious address delivered by Stanley at a special meeting of the Royal Geographical Society in the Albert Hall on 5 May 1890 to an audience of over six thousand, he did not mention Stairs's name when boasting of the discoveries made in the course of the expedition. Stanley did, however, refer to Homer, Alexander the Great, Cambyses, Caesar, and Nero, just a few ancient celebrities, in whose company he obviously felt far more comfortable.[84]

In conclusion, one might somewhat unkindly observe that one undeclared aim of the expedition was definitely achieved: the satisfying of Stanley's craving for fame and fortune that came with publications and lecture tours. On one count, however, he was disappointed. As Emin Pasha's accident kept him in Africa, Stanley was unable to show him off on his lucrative lecture tours as a prize exhibit, a unique African trophy. For the second time in his life Stanley's plans were thwarted. The first had been when Stanley embarked on an expedition in search of Dr. David Livingstone, who was doing missionary and exploratory work in Africa. Stanley deemed it necessary to find Livingstone and return with him to England. Although Livingstone refused to leave Africa, Stanley's reputation was enhanced by this meeting and proved to be a lucrative proposition on his lecture tour circuit when he recounted his "rescue."

INTERMEZZO

We have little information as to what happened after 6 December when the members of the expedition found themselves in Zanzibar. Emin Pasha was in a German hospital, having fallen out of a second-storey window two days before while attending a banquet at Bagamoyo; the cause was poor eyesight, not inebriation. Dr. Parke stayed with him. Some days later Parke himself succumbed to an illness, but in spite of his grave condition, was carried from the hospital to the steamer so he could leave Zanzibar with his companions.[85]

On 13 January 1890 the members of the expedition were in Cairo being lavishly feted. From Shepheard's Hotel Stairs wrote a letter dated 21 January to the editor of the *Morning Chronicle* in Halifax. In this he asked the latter to convey his thanks "to many Haligonians who have so generously sent their congratulations ... on the successful termination of the Emin Pasha Relief Expedition."[86]

Stairs did not stay long in Egypt. On his way to England he visited Cannes where he sketched his father's tombstone. The drawing, which is included in his diary, bears the date 4 February 1890. In the same month he obtained permission to accept and wear the Medjidie Order (third class) given him by the Khedive of Egypt.[87]

On his return to England he was offered a post of adjutant with the Royal Engineers at Aldershot.[88] In recognition of his contribution to the Emin Pasha Relief Expedition the Royal Geographical Society made him a Fellow,[89] and he took part in the Society's evening meetings. He was also offered a fellowship of the Royal Scottish Geographical Society, an honourary membership of the *Société Belge de Géographie* and a corresponding membership of the Tyneside Geographical Society.

All members of the expedition were much lionized by London society. For example, Stairs was flooded with invitations to parties, dinners, and special receptions. He even attended a dinner at Buckingham Palace. Amusingly enough his most vivid impression was of the men's washroom. He related later on that it was situated in a "long corridor in the basement with wash basins on one side while on the other, as far as the eye could see, were hundreds of solemn, white thunder mugs."[90]

The receptions closest to his heart were those given in his honour by close friends and by fellow Canadians. The *Scottish Leader,* 3 March 1890, records a dinner held by the Merchiston Club in the Central Hotel in Edinburgh. This was presided over by Dr. Rogers, headmaster of Merchiston Castle School who, in his speech, emphasized the fact that Stairs was an old Merchistonian.[91]

Fame, however, left Stairs quite unspoiled. One of his intimate friends had this to say about him:

"After his return I was much impressed with his simple modesty, and his absolute reticence, even in fun or easy talk, about matters that have subsequently been the subject of so much painful controversy. He was absolutely loyal, not only to his chief but to every comrade, telling what was to their honour, and referring to nothing else. Of himself and what he had done he could hardly be got to speak. Another characteristic was the kindly way he spoke of the natives, and the high appreciation he had of their self-denial and devotedness."[92]

However, the expedition seems to have physically altered Stairs. On 12 July Stairs was present in Westminster Abbey as groomsman at the wedding of Stanley and Dorothy Tennant. The press report included a remark that Stairs "looked very weak and ill as, leaning on the arm of Count d'Aarche and walking with the aid of a stick, he slowly went up the nave to his place by the altar rails."[93]

Later during the summer Stairs visited his hometown, where he was royally entertained. The *Morning Herald* announced his arrival on 12 August, and on 11 September he attended a special meeting of the City Council of Halifax. The event, which was given

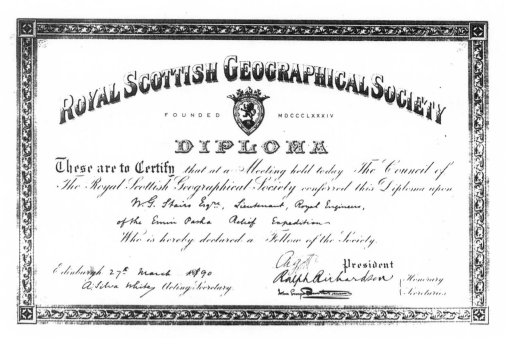

Royal Scottish Geographical Society Diploma of Fellowship

Tyneside Geographical Society's Diploma of Corresponding Membership

Societé Belge de Géographie Diploma of Honorary Membership

considerable press coverage, was attended by Daly, the lieutenant-governor of Nova Scotia, Mackintosh, the acting mayor, and the business and intellectual elite of Halifax. According to the local press report, at 3:30 p.m., the military band struck up "Here the conquering hero comes," after which Lieutenant Stairs entered in uniform and was received with prolonged applause. When the applause died down, Stairs was addressed by the acting mayor and presented with a commemorative silver plate. The reporter who described this event observed that Stairs "made his reply in a clear and distinct voice, though he was visibly affected and appeared to be considerably nervous."[94]

In his speech Stairs thanked the distinguished audience as follows:

Mr. Mayor, aldermen and gentlemen representing the corporation and citizens of Halifax:

"It is with feelings of the greatest pride that I have heard the address which has just been read. Of all the receptions that could have been extended to me in any way, and by any people, none could have been more gratifying or more appreciated by me than this one, coming as it does from people of my own native town, Halifax." [...]

Further in his speech Stairs attempted to justify the objectives of the Emin Pasha Relief Expedition that had been questioned by some its critics, and he emphasized the benefits that it brought to the British Empire and "civilization at large." He continued,

"To the openings that will be offered to the expansion of English and other trade in supplying new markets for the goods of the world, the improved condition of the native that will ensue, the suppression of the slave trade [sic] through the influence of the railway and telegraph lines, are only some of the benefits that will spring directly from such an undertaking as that of the Emin Pasha Relief Expedition.

Ladies and Gentlemen: Again [sic] I thank you for the gratification the presentation of this piece of plate and such an address afford me. They will act as incentives to future good work and will help me in other duties and positions toward success.[...]

As you have referred to Mr. Stanley, will you allow me on his behalf to express the gratification I am sure he will feel on hearing that one of his officers has been so honoured this evening."[95]

Stairs's speech reveals, in a clear and concise manner, the credo of an idealist who took literally the then current slogans of colonial propaganda. He had no doubts whatsoever that "civilization" as a whole would benefit from the labours of himself and his companions. Men of his stamp, ready to sacrifice their lives for the imperial cause, were of considerable use to colonial pragmatists whose motives were not as sincere as Stairs believed.

One interesting aspect of these numerous receptions and parties is Stairs's almost obsessive fascination with food: witness the collection of menus meticulously preserved in his scrapbook.[96] When starving in the tropical forest of Central Africa, he had fixed his imagination upon the pleasures of the table, conjured up images of truly gargantuan meals that he intended to consume on his return home. Now was his chance to indulge his wildest fantasies, for the menus collected display all the refinements of late Victorian gourmet cuisine.[97] Having known the excruciating pangs of starvation, he was obviously more than appreciative of fashionably sumptuous meals.

As time went on, the glitter and excitement of fame lost their appeal for him. Later, while reminiscing on the days spent in England, he expressed his disappointment at having made so few good friends from amongst three hundred London acquaintances.[98] He knew only three families at whose house he dared to present himself at dinner-time in town clothes and without being invited. Was he admitting to intense feelings of estrangement and loneliness? Was it hard for him to find a common language with society people and share their prevailing views.[99]

On 25 March 1891 Stairs obtained a transfer to the 41st Welsh Regiment and was promoted to captain. His new regiment had a close association with Canada dating back to the eighteenth century when it was stationed in the western part of the country.[100] It seems this transfer increased Stairs's chances of obtaining extended leaves of absence.[101] He had become disenchanted with life in the capital of the British Empire, and he wanted freedom to travel again. The routine of a provincial garrison did not appeal to him either, in spite of the fact that at Aldershot he was "in the company of the best comrades in the world with pleasant society, delicious food, and the town in the neighbourhood."[102] He felt that life was passing him by without his achieving anything worthwhile. He was becoming restless and yearned to return to the pursuits of an explorer, a discoverer of uncharted worlds.

If he did join another expedition, it would have to be as leader. This he had made clear in an interview given in Cairo in January 1890 on the return from the Emin Pasha Relief Expedition. Asked whether he would go on another African expedition he had answered that "the next time he would go as chief or not at all."[103] No doubt he had found Stanley more than trying as a commander, but being a leader was also for Stairs a matter of personal pride and ambition.[104]

An opportunity for realizing his dreams arose during the summer of 1890, when George Cawston, an associate of Cecil Rhodes and a member of the board of the British South Africa Company (BSAC), asked him to take part in an expedition to the country situated between the Congo and the Zambezi. Cawston intended to make an offer also to Jephson, Nelson, and Dr. Parke.[105] Before discussing the matter with Cawston, Stairs enquired about the starting date and the name of the leader.[106] We do not know what the answer was and to what extent it influenced Stairs's refusal to participate. He replied that there were many reasons why he should not go but did not specify any of them. Instead, he strongly recommended Nelson as leader.[107] One may suspect that Stairs was still having problems with his health.

In 1891 the *Compagnie du Katanga* approached Stairs and asked him to lead one of its expeditions. British investors with a financial interest in this Belgian company suggested Stairs's name—his previous experience of the Congo was a strong recommendation.[108] In fact, there were several expeditions going to Katanga. Why, we may ask, was there such interest in this part of Africa?

In the terms of the Berlin Act of 1885, this region had been incorporated into the Congo State; however, the "effective occupation" required in the agreement had not taken place. For this reason, some English circles believed that Katanga was open to "rightful" occupation by any foreign power. Such indeed was the point of view of Cecil Rhodes who saw in that region exciting possibilities for the BSAC. Rhodes's agent, Cawston, writing to Rhodes in March 1890, boldly stated that he was "very keen on securing this country."[109] What interested him was the region situated between the Barotse and the Nyasa, the Congo State, and the Zambezi—an area of roughly 700 mi. x 300 mi. (1100 km x 500 km), bounded on the north by the "famous copper country of Katanga" and on the south by the "equally famous gold country of Mashonaland." In the same letter Cawston strongly recommended Joseph Thomson, who was an experienced explorer, as leader of an expedition that was soon to explore these areas.

These imperialist aims clearly included Katanga, which had the richest copper mines in the world and which Cawston referred to as Msiri's kingdom. Msiri, the independent, wily, and despotic ruler of Garengaze, as his country was then called, had not so far signed any treaties with the European powers, and this made him a desirable prey in the eyes of potential usurpers of his kingdom. Future events would show, however, that he was far from being an easy prey.

The two expeditions sponsored by the BSAC failed to prevail upon Msiri to sign a treaty of submission. The first of them led by Joseph Thomson reached Katanga at the end of 1890 but did not enter Bunkeia—Msiri's capital.[110] The second expedition headed by Alfred Sharpe reached Bunkeia on 8 November 1890 and was also unsuccessful.[111] Not surprisingly, the interest in Katanga displayed by certain sections of the British press and even more actively by the BSAC alarmed Leopold II and prompted him to take measures to ensure effective occupation of this region. The king was not at all pleased to hear that representatives of the BSAC were making their way through Katanga. Nor did he appreciate that on a map drawn in October 1889 the company clearly defined the southern frontiers of territories under its control, but not the northern ones bordering on Katanga.[112] Leopold II decided to send several expeditions to the area. The first of these, led by Paul Le Marinel and sponsored by the state and the *Compagnie du Congo pour le Commerce et l'Industrie,* entered Bunkeia on 18 April 1891 and established a station near Msiri's capital. In spite of Le Marinel's insistence, Msiri refused to recognize the flag of the Congo Free State.

The second expedition, led by Alexandre Delcommune and sent by the *Compagnie du Congo,* arrived at Bunkeia some six months later on 6 October 1891. After spending five weeks there, Delcommune left for the south in search of minerals.[113] In the meantime, Leopold II initiated the creation of the *Compagnie du Katanga*—a Belgian counterpart of the BSAC. It was constituted early in 1891 with the purpose of opening up Katanga. Its capital amounted to 3 million francs and its shares were held by the state, by the *Compagnie du Congo pour le Commerce et l'Industrie,* and by English investors. These last were allowed to participate in the hope that they would not then press for British occupation of Katanga.

Among the directors of the newly formed company were Sir William MacKinnon and Sir John Kirk. Verney L. Cameron, the well-known African traveller, effected the amalgamation of the British and continental interests. The Delcommune expedition was to pass into the service of the Katanga Company, which was also to equip two other expeditions to Katanga—one led by Stairs and the other by a Belgian, Capt. Lucien Bia.[114] These expeditions overlapped, and in a sense, the one commanded by Bia continued the work begun by Stairs.

Stairs accepted the offer made by the Katanga Company in spite of his poor health, which had been severely strained by malaria. He was aware of the rashness of his decision and doubted whether he would ever come back.[115] The War Office granted his request for release from his military duties without delay.[116] The main goal of his expedition was to obtain the submission of Msiri to the Congo Free State. The other goals were to explore

Captain Omer Bodson

Marquis de Bonchamps

Dr. Joseph A. Moloney

Thomas Robinson

Captain William G. Stairs, R.E.

the mineral resources and to improve the knowledge of the geography of Msiri's kingdom—a formidable task as its area was approximately 57,000 square miles (150,000 square kilometres).

In the minds of some, Stairs's working for the Belgians and his subsequent behaviour raised doubts about his loyalty to the British Empire.[117] Stairs himself does not seem to have had any difficulty in reconciling loyalty to the British army with loyalty to the Belgian Katanga Company. Nonetheless, in the continuing competition for African territories there *was* a risk of international complications. For instance, what if a British army officer enlisted in the service of a foreign power were to collide with an Englishman serving under the flag of a British chartered company?

The national origins of the white participants of Stairs's expedition reflected the international nature of their employer—the *Compagnie du Katanga*. Capt. Omer Bodson, a Belgian, was second in command. Born in Antwerp in 1856, he chose a military career and served with the Belgian Carabineers. In 1887 he went to the Congo Free State as a member of the topographical brigade at Mateba. Bodson spent three years at Stanley Falls where he gave considerable assistance to the Emin Pasha Relief Expedition during its march up-country and presided over the court martial that tried the man who killed Major Barttelot. Eventually, Bodson was transferred to Léopoldville (Kinshasa), and then to Basoko. He returned to Belgium in 1889 where he took part in the suppression of the Liège riots.

Among others, the Marquis Christian de Bonchamps was a French cavalry officer. He was thirty-two years old when he joined Stairs's expedition. A keen traveller and sportsman, he had spent several seasons hunting in the Rocky Mountains. The expedition's doctor, Joseph A. Moloney, was of Irish origin. He practised medicine for several years in the south of London. His experience of African travel was limited to a tour of Morocco. Finally, Thomas Robinson—an Englishman, formerly a private in the Grenadier Guards—joined the expedition as carpenter and general factotum.[118]

THE COURSE OF THE KATANGA EXPEDITION

On 18 May 1891 Stairs left London and went by train to Naples where he boarded a ship for Port Said. He then sailed via Aden to Mombasa where he recruited some of his men. On 14 June he arrived at Zanzibar where he spent most of the time recruiting porters and putting together the loads. On 1 July—Stairs's twenty-eighth birthday—the expedition left for Bagamoyo, on the mainland, and by the fourth it was on the march.[119]

The choice of routes leading to Msiri's kingdom was very limited. Navigation along the river system of the Congo was out of the question in view of the long sequence of falls on the Lualaba. One could reach Katanga from the west marching from Benguela, from the east starting at Bagamoyo and continuing across Lake Tanganyika, or from the south by way of Shiré and Nyasa.[120] Stairs chose to take the eastern route via Lake Tanganyika.

Stairs followed the tradition of carrying cloth to exchange for food during the journey. He was careful to avoid Stanley's error of not providing enough of it. This practice, however, was useless in areas affected by famine, and as it turned out, little could be done

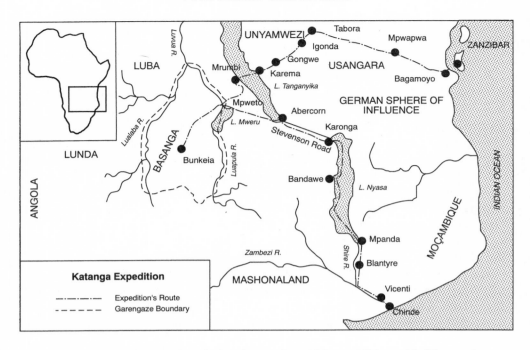

to avoid the threat of starvation. Stairs also equipped his expedition with fifty-one boxes of European provisions—far more than Stanley had provided for his ten white companions. Each of the whites had his own tent, a bed, a table and a chair, his own cook and servant, and adequate means of transport for his belongings. Bearing in mind the deprivations during the journey with Stanley, Stairs provided candles and books. He could then ask with some pride "whether ever officers of a caravan journeying into the African interior have travelled in better conditions than mine?"[121] In all, the expedition cost 186,531 francs, excluding travelling costs in Europe.[122] The original total number of carriers and askaris hired was 336.[123]

The expedition did, however, encounter unforeseen difficulties. For example, towards the end of the month the caravan entered mountainous country where the nights were chilly. The Africans, in their light clothes, caught cold and some developed pneumonia. Relations with the local people also presented problems. Frequently, upon seeing the approaching caravan, the Africans fled from their villages, which were then looted by the porters. It seems raids by Arab slave-traders had terrified the local populace making them wary of other caravans. Desertions were frequent and it was difficult to find replacements for the missing carriers. After passing through countryside ravaged by a disastrous cattle epidemic and a severe drought, the caravan reached Mpwapwa on 4 August. There it had to face a serious food shortage. Prospects were grim because ahead of them lay a country suffering from famine. Between 7 and 8 August the caravan crossed a waterless region known as Shunio Heath and reached Unyangaru, where they found a well containing brackish water. Having drunk it, many men fell ill.

Some other caravans seeking protection from attacks by local villagers or rapacious rulers joined Stairs's expedition. On 18 August the number of people under his command reached 1,950. The local chiefs often demanded a *hongo* (passage toll), and only large and well-armed caravans could avoid this form of taxation.

On approaching Tabora, Stairs was tormented by the fear of new and more numerous desertions. The caravan reached that town on 6 September, sixty-four days after having left Bagamoyo, averaging over 9 miles (14 kilometres) a day. At Tabora, an important Arab trade centre, Stairs met Captain Jacques of the Belgian Anti-slavery Society, whose caravan had caught up with him. From the discussions with local Arabs Stairs drew some interesting conclusions regarding the merits of various caravan routes.

After nearly a week's rest the caravan resumed its journey. Disturbing news arrived that Rumaliza, the Arab chief of Ujiji, had laid waste the northwestern part of the Lake Tanganyika coast and now intended to raid the south.

Near Karema, Stairs saw whole areas ravaged and depopulated by recent tribal wars. Food became quite scarce and water was hard to come by and often bad. They reached Karema on 9 October and began crossing Lake Tanganyika on the same day. Stairs met the local mission fathers who entertained him warmly.

A communication from Mr. A. J. Swann, who headed the Kinyamkolo mission station at the southernmost tip of Lake Tanganyika, advised Stairs to avoid a meeting with Captain Joubert of the St. Louis Mrumbi station, as Rumaliza would interpret such a meeting as collusion with both Joubert and Jacques in their anti-slavery activities. Instead, he suggested a meeting with the Arab chief himself in order to explain the real purpose of the expedition.

On 17 October Captain Jacques's caravan arrived. In the course of many conversations with the French fathers and Captain Jacques, Stairs discovered how strongly anti-Arab they were—a sentiment of which he disapproved. Stairs's expedition left Karema on 26 October en route to Mrumbi.

Between 3 and 6 November, the caravan passed through countryside ravaged by slave-raids conducted by Makatubu, a slave himself, who belonged to and acted for a Zanzibari Arab, Abdullah Shaash. As a result of this devastation the caravan once again found food very scarce. Hunger affected the health of the caravaneers and became a source of constant worry to Stairs.

On 8 November Stairs noted in his diary that he had a foreboding of approaching calamity. Events showed that he had every reason to feel uneasy. A letter addressed to Alfred Sharpe on Msiri's behalf and carried by one of the king's couriers fell into his hands. Written in English by Daniel Crawford, a missionary residing near Bunkeia, it urged Sharpe to return and protect Msiri against the Belgians. According to Crawford, Stairs took the letter and resumed his journey.[124] Msiri, it was obvious, sought reconciliation with Sharpe and possibly even contemplated signing a treaty with the BSAC. We need not be surprised that neither Stairs nor Dr. Moloney mentioned this not quite honourable incident in their diaries.

On the approach to Bunkeia, famine became rife because crops were not yet ripe. Had it not been for the abundance of antelopes, the caravan would have starved. Couriers, whom Stairs had sent to Msiri in advance bearing presents, now brought back letters welcoming him to Bunkeia. However, Msiri was under a misapprehension in thinking that the British had responded to his request by sending Stairs who had presented himself in his letter to Msiri as an Englishman. His disillusionment must have been great when his spies told him of the amicable meeting which took place on 13 December between Stairs and Lieutenant Legat, the Belgian resident who commanded Lofoi station near Bunkeia.

A day later, on his arrival in Msiri's capital, Stairs saw in piles of skulls and the "whitened skeletons fixed to stakes"[125] ample evidence of the ruler's extreme cruelty to his people and to those he suspected of being his enemies. Many Africans had fled the persecution, leaving entire villages abandoned. There was strong opposition to Msiri's rule among his Wasanga subjects, whom Stairs considered as potential allies in the event of conflict with the despot.

On 17 December Stairs met Msiri for the first time and reproached the chief publicly for his crimes. When Stairs exhorted Msiri to desist from barbarous practices, the enraged chief blamed the local whites for spreading unfounded rumours about him. This emotional interview ended with Msiri offering Stairs his friendship.

Two days later, in another stormy interview lasting several hours, Stairs asked Msiri to accept the Belgian flag. Msiri was evasive, so Stairs, on his own, decided to raise the flag that same evening. The following day, on hearing of Msiri's flight to a nearby village called Mayembe,[126] Stairs sent a detachment of askaris under the command of Bodson and Bonchamps with orders to persuade the chief to return to Bunkeia voluntarily or to bring him back forcibly. Msiri refused to return and threatened Bodson. In a brief but dramatic skirmish both Bodson and Msiri were killed. Stairs was thus placed in the difficult position of having to choose Msiri's successor and also to defuse the potentially explosive atmosphere among the chiefs. His first measure was to concentrate all his resources and efforts on constructing a fort at Bunkeia to ensure the safety of his own people. Food became more difficult to obtain—a cause of even further anxiety to Stairs.

Very early in January, he had to deal with the threat of a mutiny. The malcontents planned to march toward Lake Mweru, looting every village on their way and if offered resistance by the whites, to set Fort Bunkeia ablaze. Stairs fell dangerously ill. For the next three months he made no entries in his diary.

The Marquis de Bonchamps and Robinson were also stricken with disease. Only Dr. Moloney was active: he nursed his colleagues, completed the construction of the fort, received local chiefs who came to make their submission and tried to keep peace in the region. In his memoirs, Moloney gives a full account of those momentous days. Stairs's caravan diminished in terrifying proportions. The famine wrought fearful havoc, and not a day went by without their having to bury someone who had died of starvation.

By the second half of January the new crops had ripened so there was more food. On 30 January the Bia expedition, which had set off from Lusambo on 10 November 1891, arrived.[127] Captain Bia recommended that Stairs's caravan return immediately to the coast in the hope of saving the remaining half of its members. Dr. Moloney concurred, and the caravan set out on 4 February to return to the east coast by way of Lake Nyasa and River Shiré towards the estuary of the Zambezi. Stairs had to be transported in a hammock; he was extremely weak although quite conscious of what was going on around him. He only regained strength well into the journey—when crossing the mountainous regions between Lakes Mweru and Tanganyika.

By the middle of March he was able to take command of the expedition, and after 1 April resumed his diary. The entries are brief and laconic, dealing with the rather uneventful progress of the caravan through already well-known stretches of East Africa. He described his plans for the future and his general mood in a brief letter to Walter G. Jones, which he wrote on 19 May and despatched from Blantyre. He hoped to arrive in England by the middle of September. He viewed the expedition as a success and the only thing that made him regret that it was over was that he saw nothing else before him but "regimental work." As to his health he wrote: "I am now strongish again and able to do my work."[128] Stairs made the last entry in his diary on 3 June upon arriving at Vicenti. Two days later the expedition reached Chinde, at the mouth of the Zambezi River. Here Stairs had a fatal attack of malaria and died on 9 June, twenty-two days short of his twenty-ninth birthday.

ACHIEVEMENTS OF THE KATANGA EXPEDITION

The principal aim of Stairs's expedition was to get Msiri, the ruler of Garengaze, to submit to the authorities of the Congo Free State either by persuasion or by force. Furthermore, Stairs hoped to discover mineral deposits capable of profitable exploitation and also to engage in exploration leading to useful geographical discoveries west of Tanganyika.[129]

The main political aim was achieved through force in the fatal confrontation between Msiri and Captain Bodson. With regard to discoveries, Stairs managed to collect some valuable scientific data, which he presented in a series of reports published in the Belgian journal *Le Mouvement Géographique*.[130] In a communication dated 12 November 1891, and despatched from the village of Ngwena on the Luapula River,[131] Stairs listed observations made during the journey from Tabora to Karema (13 September to 9 October). These included the latitude, longitude, and altitude above sea level of some fifteen localities along that stretch of the route.[132] This was followed later on by a further list providing similar information on the places passed on the march to Bunkeia.[133]

In the report dated 15 December 1891, Stairs provided new data on the mountain chains and hydrographical systems especially on those feeding the riverine system of the Upper Congo. He also collected information on the periodic changes in the water levels of Lake Tanganyika and investigated the deposits of salt located northwest of Gwena, from where it was exported to the eastern parts of Urua.

Stairs's reports contained useful information on the agricultural potential of the parts of the continent crossed by his caravan. Many of the areas he visited had good soil and offered encouraging prospects for the cultivation of such crops as rice, various vegetables, maize, sorghum, sugar cane, and manioc. Moreover, he paid special attention to the suitability of the land and climate for the raising of domestic animals and for European settlement.[134] Hunger and disease, particularly during the stay in Bunkeia, prevented any further exploration and collection of scientific data. As has been noted, the plight of the participants precipitated an early end to the expedition.

Yet, in spite of what looked like a retreat, the Katanga Expedition, viewed on its own terms, achieved a certain measure of success. There is no doubt, in retrospect, that it played an explicit and unenviable role in the partition of Africa. Stairs felt that he had freed the people of Garengaze from the terrors of a reckless and bloodthirsty ruler whom everybody apparently hated. Nonetheless, it must be remembered that upon losing its independence, the country was taken over by the notorious authorities of the Congo Free State—amongst the worst, cruellest, and most predatory colonial rulers in Africa—whose domination over the Congo led eventually to a scandal on an international scale. One can only surmise that neither of these two systems of government was acceptable to the people of Garengaze. But, as is often the case, free choice was denied them.

From his own point of view, Stairs acted in perfect good faith, convinced, as he was, that he had the best interests of Europeans and Africans—humankind at large—at heart. It is one of the truisms of history that so often the well-intentioned know not what they do.

STAIRS: AN APPRAISAL

In conclusion, we may ask what sort of man Stairs was, given his ambitions, achievements, views, and attitudes. One answer that springs to mind is the well-known line from Gilbert and Sullivan's *HMS Pinafore:* "He is an Englishman, behold him!" Stairs described himself as a bluenose (and gave that name to one of his boats), as a Haligonian, and on many occasions he clearly expressed his attachment to the country of his birth. When abroad, however, he did indeed call himself an Englishman.[135] There are several explanations for this. He was, after all, born before Confederation and a Canadian sense of national identity was much less strong then than now. (Even now, the question, "What is a Canadian?" can lead to agonized debates.) Also, in Europe and in Africa, knowledge of Canada was limited and there may have been many people for whom "Canadian" was a vague term, whereas "English" was a notion with which even Africans and Arabs living in the interior of Africa were quite familiar. So Stairs's motives for calling himself an Englishman may have been entirely practical.

One cannot help feeling that, for people of British origin living in the British Empire, "Englishman" represented not only a quality of "Englishness" but also a certain ideal of manliness. It is this ideal that is celebrated in Kipling's famous "If," a poem that would have thrilled Stairs to the very core of his being. The code it puts forward is one that would have appealed to him not only as a gentleman brought up in British traditions but also as an officer in the British army and as an explorer in Africa.

Here it might be mentioned that the British army which Stairs joined was a far more professional body than it had been when Queen Victoria came to the throne. Post-Crimean reforms had led in 1871 to the abolition of the purchase system. This meant that commissions and promotions could no longer be bought by the merely affluent. Even though the army was still dominated by officers of the upper or wealthy middle class, it was now possible for men with ability to make their way through merit.[136] Self-possession, coolness in command, a strict sense of discipline—in short, *professionalism*—were qualities that Stairs's military training must have instilled in him.

We should remember, too, that he was a Royal Engineer. Even before the 1871 reform, officers entering that service did not purchase their commissions and were required to follow a course of training at the Royal Military Academy. Consequently, they represented a "scientific" group in the officer corps.[137] The knowledge Stairs acquired as a Royal Engineer gave him a practical and scientific background that was to prove highly useful in

African exploration. It was Stairs, for example, on the Emin Pasha Relief Expedition, who demonstrated the superior firepower of the newly-invented Maxim machine gun in order to inspire African and Arab notables with due respect for the whites. (This earned him the African nickname, "Bwana Mzinga," meaning, "master of the cannon.")

When Stairs was on the threshold of his African adventures, the British ideal of an explorer, missionary, or a colonial administrator was already well defined.[138] It emphasized character as a basic attribute of leadership needed when dealing with people who were to be "civilized" and educated. There was also a strong emphasis on personal probity and integrity, the capacity to inspire trust and to respond to loyalty. This high standard of conduct required one to be truthful, reliable, and to practice sexual propriety.

Such were the outstanding features of the ideal Englishman.[139] In noting Stairs's attitude towards others these were the criteria by which Stairs judged everyone. Among the virtues he most prized were energy and courage. He detested the routine, the boredom, and the idleness of garrison life which he described as "a slow death by inches" and loathed the contemptuous epithet "medal hunters" given by ante-room officers to those who preferred a life of action. When in action he regarded self-imposed norms of conduct—often difficult and extremely demanding in the African environment—constituting a vital part of the "white man's burden."[140]

For example, it was considered effeminate to be carried in a hammock; even when sick, one was expected to keep marching for as long as the legs would sustain one.[141] During his return from Fort Bodo to Yambuya, Stanley was apparently carried by his men all the time. Stairs observed caustically that one of the reasons for Stanley not taking any Europeans with him was his desire to indulge in this kind of unbecoming behaviour. Due to his consummate art of image-building, Stanley emerges—from his own writings—as the supreme embodiment of the virtues expected of a Victorian explorer.

Stairs himself possessed an enormous reservoir of energy. It was when weakened by a serious attack of malaria, but still full of enthusiasm for exploration, that he climbed the heights of Ruwenzori. Again, on his way back from Katanga, though exhausted by a prolonged fever, he was still thinking of new adventures. His companion Dr. Moloney commented:

"Not that he wished to return to a life of ease and quiet in England, though his constitution stood in imperative need of one or two years at least of comparative inactivity. On the contrary, he would have volunteered at once to go to the assistance either of Captain Jacques at Albertville or of Captain Lugard in Uganda. All the suffering and sickness at Fort Bunkeia he had completely forgotten, and his ardent spirit made light of fresh discoveries and achievements. Upon him the Dark Continent had laid her spell with an absolutely imperious influence."[142]

There can be no doubt that Stairs was a man of considerable personal courage and modesty, who never boasted of his feats or his ability to endure. (Modesty, too, was one of the essential qualities of the ideal Englishman.) His leadership was never questioned, even when he sent Bodson to confront Msiri in that last fatal interview instead of going himself. This decision was dictated by prudence. As leader of the Katanga Expedition he had to be in control, prepared to act should Bodson's party fail in its objective. It was a wise decision and did not reflect on his courage.

Stanley's glowing testimonial is proof enough of Stairs's reliability. The latter expected others to be equally dependable. A contract, whether oral or written, was for him sacrosanct. He intensely resented any breach of agreement on the part of his men to whom the European concept of legal obligation was alien.

He regarded himself as incapable of dishonesty. Yet his loyalty to England was questioned by Daniel Crawford. Crawford, a missionary resident near Bunkeia, and one of the reporters of Msiri's drama, wrote thus of Stairs:

"Fancy an officer with a delicate and scrupulous sense of honour waking up to the piercing realization that he had become the tool of a foreigner, drawing Belgian money to combat English pretensions! The truth is, this poor fellow was trapped into a very delicate position, not of his own seeking; and as the days advanced, the monstrous enigma of his anti-English duties became a nightmare to him."[143]

In fact, Crawford's imagination far exceeded his knowledge of the relevant facts. Stairs did not betray his queen or the Union Jack. He was on unpaid leave of absence from the British army and his supervisors knew his purpose. Above all, the British government had no interest in occupying Katanga, and Cecil Rhodes, who had an eye on it, did not enjoy the support of the Foreign Office. As we have seen, however, Stairs was not above intercepting a letter from Crawford (whom he could have regarded as a meddling missionary) to Sharpe. About this action he kept discreetly silent, probably excusing it in terms of expediency, a notion that is very important to the professional soldier.

On other issues, too, he could appear inconsistent. He strongly condemned Arab slavers and even planned on his return from Katanga to assist Captain Jacques in his anti-slavery campaigns. Yet, he was quite willing to hire slaves for the Katanga Expedition and was only prevented from doing so by the sultan of Zanzibar who refused to grant his permission.[144] Though on the whole he had a horror of looting, on occasion he could cynically admit that the enmity of local villagers was advantageous to the expedition for then its members could obtain food by force rather than by payment. He wished to be the Africans' friend, yet could inflict harsh punishments upon them. This he no doubt looked upon in the light of that well-known Victorian tenet, "spare the rod...."

As for that other major Victorian concern, sexual propriety, Stairs never really offends, though he made some unguarded comments. His few lines on young women in England are somewhat offhand. To him London girls were mostly "empty beings" who followed fashion in ideas and dress "like a flock of sheep." By contrast, the country girl was "far more interesting and also better educated."[145]

He was, however, very aware of African women, though he avoids sensationalism and never describes what happened when they were captured by men of another tribe, a frequent incident on the Emin Pasha Relief Expedition. He himself was quite susceptible to their charms. During his first tempestuous interview with Msiri he noticed that one of the king's wives "was really very beautiful, with regular pretty features, and certainly the most beautiful woman I have yet seen west of the Tanganyika."[146]

Even more revealing is the description of the girls who danced before him at Mazamboni's village. He was clearly impressed by their movements whose explicit sexual connotations prompted him to observe that "this would have made a great catch for the manager of the Alhambra, he would have full houses every night." In appreciation of their performance Stairs gave the dancers a cow, which they asked for, and made a highly significant comment: "[...] If these had been men I certainly should have refused, but being women they can wriggle anything out of an ordinary man."[147]

What is interesting here is the disarming candour with which he describes this highly erotic scene—none of the expected Victorian hypocrisy here. There is the same humour and absence of salaciousness in another passage where he describes women in Emin Pasha's entourage walking in the mud up to their knees: "[...] They do not mind the black men at all and will make a great demonstration of healthy-looking limbs, but should a white man appear, down go their clothes and they appear most grave and proper."[148] It appears these women were afraid of their husbands.

These passages, with their fresh ingenuousness, point up Stairs's principal quality as a diarist. He had no great literary pretensions, though he was occasionally moved to consider celebrating the African atmosphere in verse. He did, in fact, read Shakespeare and other poets, but his comments on them are embarrassingly naive: "Reading McBeth [sic] again. What a brute 'Mrs. McBeth' [sic] was and he himself on a par with Richard III, I think."[149] At Fort Bodo what he most regretted was the absence of manuals on gardening and other useful arts. When writing himself, however, he is more than merely informative. In recording his observations, attitudes, and moods with a certain frankness, he is sometimes gauche but seldom boring. His preconceptions and prejudices show he had no really original vision to express. There is nothing strikingly individual in his style. In so many ways he is the typical highly disciplined, conscientious "Englishman" of his times, convinced of his racial and moral superiority. Yet, his spontaneity prevents him from being a hardened type.

With this spontaneity went a sort of restlessness, a longing for adventure, a desire for fame. When dreaming of an ideal existence, he conjures up a rather stereotyped picture of life in an English country house "far from the noise of big cities with a fine grassy lawn as soft as velvet on which I could play lawn tennis under the shade of big green leafy trees smoking a cigarette and having as a partner some pleasant person with whom I could chat."[150]

Deep in his heart Stairs knew that this sort of life could not satisfy him. Recollections of life in Africa dominate his thoughts, for it was only there that he could achieve his much-desired freedom of action, be given opportunities to distinguish himself and exercise command over hundreds of men. When crossing the plains and the mountains on his way to Katanga, he had this to say: "I feel I can breathe and with the existence I lead here life really seems worthwhile."[151] There is little doubt that sooner or later Stairs would have returned to Africa—his first and last real love. In fact, he never left it; benign fate allowed him to remain there forever.

PART TWO

THE EMIN PASHA RELIEF
EXPEDITION DIARY

Emin Pasha and Captain Casati landing at Weré on Lake Albert

(contemporary illustration from *The Penny Illustrated Paper*)

CHAPTER 1
LONDON TO STANLEY POOL

20 JANUARY—28 APRIL 1887

Stairs leaves London on 20 January 1887 for Africa. Stopovers are made at Malta, Port Said, and Aden. At Zanzibar he joins six hundred Zanzibaris engaged by Stanley. The voyage continues via Cape of Good Hope. The expedition arrives on 18 March at Banana Point on the estuary of the Congo River. The long journey to the interior commences.

20th January   Left my lodgings in Moore Street 10:30 a.m., drove to Stanley's in New Bond Street and then left for the Fenchurch Street station. Bought a watch at Steward's (Strand West) £5 10s. Left London by the 12:08 p.m. train for Gravesend, saying goodbye to Twining, Nanton, and Duff.[1] Went down with Colonel J. Grant, an old African explorer.[2] Got on SS Navarino about 2:00 and said farewell to Colonel Grant.

The *Navarino* is a steel steamer of 3,400 tons, very old and uncomfortable. No smoking room and poor accommodation, belongs to the British India Steam Navigation Company.

We have about seventy passengers in the Saloon, mostly bound for India and Ceylon. On board are Jephson and Nelson of the expedition. The usual amount of smoking and talking goes on; most of the passengers are young fellows on their way to India—3,084 are in the army and some are in the civil (Indian) service.

21st January   Had a very calm night of it, slept well and got up 8:30 a.m. Passed the Isle of Wight just before lunch (1:00 p.m.). Put off our pilot opposite Bembridge and started off for Malta. Sea was very calm all day and apparently very little sea sickness on board. Our crew is composed chiefly of Lascars,[3] with a very few Europeans. The quartermaster and officers are mostly all Scotchmen. The crew seem to work very well together, but the stewards are very slow at their work, though willing enough. Passed a great number of steamers and craft of all sorts during the day. The wind has been from the SW all day and the weather fine, sea calm. Barometer rising at 9:00. Thermometer about 50°F and getting warmer.

The *Navarino* is a very poor sailer; we make on an average a little over nine knots per hour, our fastest today being slightly over ten.

Commenced reading Stanley's *How I Found Livingstone*. Had forgotten most of it as I read it about six years ago. Started a novel called *Violet Jermyn* by Grant. Finished it today. Set my aneroid to sea level this morning to test its qualities tomorrow and next day.

22nd January   Passed the day in the usual way, reading Stanley, smoking, talking, and walking. Run today was 234 miles. Passed several steamers homeward bound.

23rd January   Had service at 10:30 a.m. Passed a derelict barque at 1:30 p.m. within 50 yards name [sic] *Stormy Petrel.* Read Stanley and some papers. Had long talks with various passengers. Passed a homeward bound steamer very heavily laden. Should be off Cape Finisterre by midnight. Weather warm with SE winds, barometer 30.25 at 10:00, thermometer 60°.

24th January   Fine with heavy SE winds. Barometer rising till noon, then falling. My barometer keeps well up to the ship's and remains as good as I thought it to be. Passed several ships during the day.

Took Barttelot's dog for a run on the steering deck. Stanley's donkey is a first-rate traveller and stands well up to his feed. Saw the Spanish coast early this morning and afterwards left it. Made about eight and one-half or nine knots all day.[...]

Between 25 and 29 January, the Navarino *sailed along the coast of Portugal, passed Cape Trafalgar, the town of Cadiz, the Straits of Gibraltar and sailed along the African coast. On 30 January they passed the island of Pantelaria as they sailed towards Malta.*

31st January   Passed Gozo at daybreak and sailed into Malta about 7:30 a.m. Got up, had my bath and dressed and went ashore with Jephson and Ritherdon of the Madras Staff Corps (4th Pioneers). We walked up to the Imperial Hotel and had breakfast there. We enjoyed our meal very much after the bad fare we had on board ship.

After breakfast we sallied out, got a cab and guide and started off on the warpath. We bought excellent cigarettes on the Strada Reale for two shillings per 100 and good oranges—eight shillings for twelve dozen. We sent some cases home to England and [sent] a lot more on board ship. After making our purchases we went first to St. John's Church and saw everything to be seen there. Next we went to King and Co.'s to get a glimpse at the latest English papers.[...]

After leaving King and Co.'s we went for a short drive, but our time on shore was limited [so] we could not get into the country as we should have liked. We saw the Opera House, a very fine building, and listened to some ladies and gentlemen practising some of the music of Faust....

We got back about three o'clock, and shortly after this the *Navarino* weighed anchor and put out to sea, on our way to Port Said. The evening was glorious as we left the Maltese coast and everyone seemed to be in good spirits after their run on shore. The run to Port Said from Malta generally takes about four days, but probably we shall not get there till Saturday morning as the *Navarino* is [such] a poor sailer.

1st February   Fine, with slight SE winds and showers early in morning. Thermometer at noon 58°. Passed a very quiet day reading, walking. Am still reading *Through the Dark Continent* and got as far as where Stanley reached Uganda. Mtesa, the emperor, seems to have been an open-minded sort of man, ready to take in all the information Stanley could supply, though apparently his earlier days were spent in murdering his chiefs and creating general discomfiture to every one he met.

His successor, Mwanga, appears to be a bloodthirsty young man, but perhaps some day we shall meet his Excellency, and then find out more of his peculiarities.[4] Went to bed early. Barometer steady.

2nd February Fine with slight SE winds. Had a cricket match this morning between port and starboard, the port side winning amidst tremendous excitement after a hard struggle. We had a return march in the afternoon, the port again winning. Read *Thro' the Dark Continent* [sic]. The book gets more interesting as one gets on with it. Run 229 miles.

3rd February Very fine and enjoyable weather all day. Had some more cricket in the afternoon. Finished *Thro' the Dark Continent* [sic], this making the third book of Stanley's I have read on this voyage. At noon today we had 290 miles to run to Port Said, so that if all goes well we should get there by 7:30 or 8:00 tomorrow evening. The cigarettes I purchased at Malta are very good.

4th February Very fine day. SE winds. Passed several steamers in the afternoon. Were abreast of Damietta light at 2:00 p.m. Sighted Port Said light at 3:00. Steamed into Port Said about 5:00, and let go our anchor abreast of the New Hotel. Went ashore directly afterwards with Jephson, Simpson, Ritherdon, and some others. Made some purchases including cigarettes. Jephson and I then went over to the New Hotel and read the latest English papers till 7:00, when we had a very good dinner in the French style. The prevailing European language here is of course French. Here are collected Egyptians, Turks, Arabs, Italians, and all sorts of breeds of natives.

After dinner we went to the casino, stayed there an hour or so and listened to a French play. After this we went to the El Dorado Music Hall and heard a choice collection of French songs and saw some very bad comic acting. We went back to the *Navarino* and to bed about 12:00.

5th February Weighed anchor at 6:30 a.m. and shortly afterwards steamed into the canal. Got up at 8:00. We were then well in the [Suez] Canal which was about 60 yards wide at this point. Steamed along the canal all day, going about five or six knots. Ahead of us was a Dutch steamer, and just in front of her was the *Melbourne,* of the Messagerie Maritime Line. Had twice to allow steamers to pass us. Passed the *Liguaria* of the Orient Line and six other steamers. At 6:30 p.m. we came into the small lake at Ismailia and dropped anchor about a mile from this place. Some of the passengers went ashore, but the majority of us stayed on board and sang till 10:30 or so. The passengers on the *Melbourne* (anchored close to us) created a fearful noise with horns, drums, etc. Got to bed about 12:00. The last evenings have been very pleasant, clear skies and a very bright moon.

6th February Started from Ismailia at 6:30 p.m. and are once more in the canal. Shortly after breakfast we entered the Bitter Lake and steamed across it at full speed. Passed several steamers drawn up on the side of the canal. Sighted Suez at 1:30, and at 3:30 we were abreast of the landing stage. Shortly after we anchored, a steam launch with Mr. Stanley, Dr. Junker, and Dr. Parke (who goes with us) came off. Mr. Stanley had been waiting two days at Suez.[5] He looks very fit. Bonny, Hoffman [sic], and Stanley's boy, Baruti, also joined us here.[6] Took on board sixty-one soldiers for the expedition. They are chiefly Soudanese* and most of them know something about drill. They are a very fine

*Stairs was using the contemporary spelling of the modern Sudanese.

looking set of men—tall, well-knit and deep-chested; their uniform is khaki, armed with Remingtons and sword bayonets.

7th February Fine, fair winds from the north, set the square sails. [In the nineteenth century, some ships had both steam engines and sails.]

Started drilling the Soudanese soldiers. Some of them understand a little about drill, but the major part of them know almost nothing. It is a hard and trying job teaching them, as I have to use an interpreter to make known what I want done to the sergeant, who in turn gives the word of command in Arabic.

Started the men at cleaning their rifles and gave them another drill for an hour and a quarter in the afternoon, turning and forming fours. Gave them manual exercises in the morning. After a while I shall repeat the English word of command and use the short rifle drill of the English army. Am picking up already a few Arabic words of command. Read in the latter part of the afternoon and sang songs on the deck after dinner. Ran 209 miles from 4:30 yesterday afternoon. Barometer steady all day at about 30.5 [sic]. Thermometer at noon 66°.

In the Red Sea this afternoon. Passed several steamers and kept in sight the Egyptian coast.

8th February Very warm all day. Ship rolled a good deal. Had the square sails set all day and made 253 miles. The thermometer at noon registered 75° in the chart room. Cooler at dinner time. Gave the Soudanese soldiers an hour and a quarter drill in the morning and one hour in the afternoon. They are very willing and do their utmost to pick up the different terms. It is my first experience with native soldiers, but we seem to get on all right. All the movements have to be first explained [in English] to the instructor, and then [he explains] in Arabic to the men. At the end of the drills I give the words of command in English. The men were remarkably quick in picking up the words. They do not seem to understand the rolling motion of the ship and complain of being "giddy" in their heads. Some of the men are very well put together and will make good soldiers.[...]

Our soldiers are armed with Remington rifles and appear to take a certain amount of pride in keeping them clean. They also have a sword bayonet with [a] brass handle.[...]

The men are all Mahometans to all intents, though evidently not very fervent ones I should say. Very few of the men smoke pipes at all, but almost all are cigarette smokers. They will have to drop down to pipes though very shortly. Their pay comes to about one shilling per diem, with two-month advance; the head under-officers get £4 per month, the three next [in rank] £3 10s. each.

With the help of Assad Farrad, our Arabic interpreter, I am gradually picking up a little Arabic and can now give a few of the commands in that language. Our second interpreter is named Alexandre Hadad, a very nice looking boy.[...]

12th February Reached Aden roadstead early this morning. Got up at 6:00 a.m. and made the soldiers pack up and get ready. Mr. Stanley went ashore to breakfast with the governor, General Hogg. Nelson, Jephson, and I had our breakfast and then got into a steam launch and went on board the *Occidental,* our new steamer.[7] Left our things and went back to the *Navarino,* saw the soldiers safely on board the lighter, said goodbye to all and started for the *Occidental.* Got the men safely on board by lunch time.

The *Occidental* is a small coasting steamer of 1,200 tons or so, belonging to the British India Navigation Company and trading between Bombay, Aden, and Zanzibar; she is a slow boat and evidently not a steady one. We have now seven of the expedition in the saloon and have a table to ourselves.

We have also a German expedition proceeding to the German territory to the west of Zanzibar to colonize and explore. The soldiers are a bit seasick this evening.

Left Aden for Zanzibar about 4:30 p.m., the old *Navarino* starting for Colombo an hour before and giving us a cheer as she steamed out.[...]

13th February At sea. Making about eight knots per hour. Got vaccinated today by Dr. Parke. Vaccinated some of the Soudanese soldiers. They were in a great funk first and wanted the doctor to start on me first, so I bared my arm and the doctor waded in.[...]

When still at Aden, the expedition was joined by twelve Somalis who were to work as servants, cook, and tent pitchers. During the following two days the Oriental *rounded Cape Guardafui and sailed to the south. Stairs complained of the swarms of red ants, cockroaches, and rats aboard the ship. (During the voyage he made his acquaintance with the ship's doctor who attended the Merchiston School at the same time as Stairs.)*

16th February Fine with fair winds. Made 256 miles. Thermometer at noon 86°, at 10:00 p.m. 80°F. Finished *Tartarin on the Alps,* a French yarn.

The Soudanese give us a little trouble each day and seem unruly on shipboard. They will have to reform.

We sleep every night on deck now as the heat is too great in our cabins. We have not struck up much of an acquaintance with the Germans going with us to Zanzibar. Each party preserves its own secrets apparently. Most of them, however, speak English fairly well. Our crew on this ship is composed of Lascars as on the *Navarino.* They do their work slowly but well, but have to be handled with "firmness" as the captain says. We should cross the equator tomorrow night if the wind remains favourable as it is at present.[...]

17th February Fine. Very warm, favourable winds.[...]

18th February Passed the equator this morning at about 8:30 and saw the Southern Cross this evening....

19th February Sighted the coast at 9.10 a.m. and stood in for Lamu [an island off the coast of Kenya]. Met the steamer *Baghdad* just outside the roadstead and transferred our home letters to her. Got over the bar and anchored about 2:30 p.m. Some of the chaps went up to the village of Lamu about 2½ miles up the gut, but Barttelot, Parke, and myself landed just opposite to where we were anchored and explored the village of Sheila.

Quite near this place is the site of an old battle between the Somalis and Arabs. There must have been some hundreds killed as the bones and skulls cover the sand for 300 yards along the beach. We picked up a lot of bones, and I brought a skull and some bones on board. We had a long ramble through the village and got back to the *Oriental* about six o'clock. It is a very funny looking place from the water: the houses are built of mud and broken stone and are roofed over with some sort of leaf, evidently cocoanut palm. The natives speak Swahili and some of them also [speak] Arabic. We met one chap who could speak French "un peu."

20th February This morning Parke, Jameson, and the captain of the ship went ashore early and got a few partridge. They also fired at two gazelles, and though they wounded them badly, still the animals escaped into the jungle. Shortly after breakfast we weighed our anchor and put off to sea. We took on board at Lamu Mr. Wakefield, a missionary at this place. He is bound for Mombasa. He brought on board a very nice pair of elephant tusks of about 40 pounds each and worth from £30 to £50 in London. Reading up [on] Arabic words most of the day. The thermometer was 83° at noon.

21st February Sailed into Mombasa Harbour at 6:30 this morning. Landed a few letters and packages. We did not go ashore as there was nothing to see and no time to spare. Mombasa is a much better looking place than Lamu and appears to be a very important missionary station. Weighed anchor and put out to sea at 9:00 a.m. Steamed along in sight of the land all day and anchored for the night under the lee of Bemba Island. Caught a lot of small fish, which we had for dinner.

22nd February Started away this morning at three o'clock and got into the Zanzibar Channel about daylight. Sighted Zanzibar shortly after breakfast and pulled up opposite the town about 11:30. A lot of people came on board at once to see Mr. Stanley. Met Mr. McKenzie and Holmwood, the English vice consul here. Saw the sultan's prime minister. Had lunch on the *Oriental,* and went off to see our new ship the *Madura.* Got our light baggage aboard. We then started getting the small powder magazines out of the hold and took a couple of tons or so of powder from the *Madura* off to the sultan's magazine, where we housed it for the night. Got back to our ship about 7:00 p.m. in a perfect lather. It has been very hot all day, and one perspires frightfully. Zanzibar appears to be a very pretty place from the sea, but the illusion is dispelled on landing and moving up into the town.

23rd February At work all day at the sultan's magazine, loading up boxes of powder and caps. Loaded 4,500 pounds of powder and left 1,730 pounds in the magazine. Worked from 6:00 a.m. to 6:00 p.m. steadily.

24th February Very hot. Jephson, Jameson, Nelson, and I went on shore and looked over Zanzibar. Bought some books, etc., at Sousa's store. Went and saw the sultan's palace and some other sights. It was frightfully hot, the perspiration simply poured off us. At 12:30 p.m. the six hundred Zanzibaris commenced to embark on the *Madura,* and by 5:00 in the evening they were all aboard. The scene on the decks defied description: donkeys, goats, fowls, sheep, and seven hundred men all strewn over the deck in every direction.

The Soudanese look with disdain on the Zanzibaris but will have to knuckle down [sic] to them.

We all went on shore in the evening and dined with Mr. Holmwood, the English vice consul. We came off to the ship in one of the steam launches of the *Turquoise* [which was lying in the roadstead].

25th February Started today to organize the Zanzibaris into companies. Each European officer has 111 Zanzibaris to look after, to train, [to] drill, and [to] supervise as an English captain would do with his company. Mr. Stanley has the twelve Somalis and forty-three Zanzibaris as a bodyguard. These will be armed with Winchesters. Barttelot has the Soudanese to look after. I have very good officers in my company—as far as one can at present judge.

26th February Had the tower decks swept and disinfected this morning. Finished organizing the Zanzibaris into companies. Selected two little boys as my gun bearers, their names being Wadi Sadalah and Abedi. We issue rations each morning at five o'clock, ten men from each company coming up for them.

Tippu Tib has eight wives and sixty or seventy men on board.[8] He is a sagacious sort of chap according to Stanley's stories, and worth a great deal of money. His wives sleep aft, just near the saloon. He has the second-class saloon for himself.

27th February Today has been the hottest day we have had since leaving England; the thermometer stood at over 90° in our cabins for several hours. We apportioned the Zanzibaris to different parts of the ship today. I observed for latitude and longitude today and will do so now every day till I become perfect.

The names of my three chiefs are Rashid, Wadi Osmani, and Khamis Pari. Each of them has thirty-six men and under him one lieutenant. Khamis Pari speaks a little English, having been on the Congo before with Captain Elliott. We should be off Mozambique by daylight tomorrow morning.

28th February Observed for latitude and longitude today. Busy with the men in the morning. Read up [on] astronomy and a little Swahili.

We had very heavy rain showers this morning and head winds, which, however, went down about 11:00 a.m. Running down the Mozambique Channel all day, but do not see any land.[...]

On Tuesday, 1 March, the Madura *sailed down the coast of East Africa. On the eighth the* Madura *anchored at Simon's Bay, where Stairs bought some newspapers and discovered that nothing of importance had happened since his departure from England. In the afternoon the* Madura *passed by the Cape of Good Hope and steamed into the Cape Town harbour.*

10th March Got up at five o'clock, issued the rations to the men, had breakfast and then went on shore to get a lot of things for Stanley. I took Hassan, the Syrian, and Abedi, the Somali, to help me in getting and carrying the different things. We had a long and difficult job getting the right kind of clothes and boots and had to go from shop to shop, till we were quite tired out. I got back on board the ship by 2:00 p.m. having a splitting headache from being out in the sun, even though I wore a thick cork helmet. From the ship we get a splendid view of Table Mountain and the bay. The mountain certainly forms a splendid background to the town.

I went into the station when on shore and had a look at the engines and carriages. They are cut above those used in New Zealand and the gauge if 4 feet instead of 3 feet 6 inches. I believe the distance to Kimberley is about 650 miles. Connection is also made with Port Elizabeth—900 miles.

After lunch, a lot of people came down to the ship to see Mr. Stanley and Tippu Tib. They seemed delighted with Tippu and his wives. Weston and Phillips of the medical staff came down and we had a long yarn.

In the morning Perry of the sappers and some gunners called on us and we were asked to dinner at the R.A. [Royal Artillery] mess tonight, but of course [we] could not go.

Tippu Tib

The English mail due this morning has not yet come in, so we have been deprived of our letters, and thus missed the last chance of hearing from England.

We got the decks clear about 5:00 p.m., and cast off our lines from the wharf; soon after the audience on the wharf gave Stanley and the expedition three cheers, to which we responded. Half an hour later we steamed past the lighthouse and stood out for the open sea and for the Congo.[...]

The following seven days were uneventful, except that one of the Zanzibaris (of Nelson's company) died of dysentery. He was buried at sea. On 18 March the Madura *arrived at Banana Point.*

Stanley discovered that the steamers which were to take the expedition up the river were not ready because the Congo Free State functionaries did not expect them until the twenty-fourth. The cable communication with Europe was out of commission and Stanley's telegrams failed to reach their destination.

In the meantime, the expedition managed to secure the services of three steamers—the Albuquerque, *which belonged to the British Trading Company, the Portuguese steamer* Serpa Pinto, *and the* Heron *of the Congo Free State. Stairs observed that men at Banana Point seemed ignorant of the area above Stanely Pool. The loading of the cargo took place on the nineteenth.*

The expedition sailed up the Congo reaching Mataddi on 20 March, where the Portuguese had a trading station whose main activity consisted of trade in ivory and Indiarubber in exchange for hardware, merchandise, clothes, and gin.

22nd March   At work all day at Mataddi making up loads for the men. We despatched a good many loads by Ingham's hired carriers up the river. The river here is about 650 yards wide, runs about 4 miles per hour and is very deep. There are any quantity of crocodiles, though none of our men were taken off.

Two more Zanzibaris died today and were buried near the camp. They suffer a great deal from bad feet and ulcers.

23rd March   Left the Portuguese station early and marched the men over to the Congo Free State station and camped there for the night. Fired four hundred rounds from the Maxim.

24th March   Left Mataddi early this morning to march over to the Mposa River. One of my men died shortly before starting. We had little trouble crossing the river; [we] put together for the first time our galvanized steel boat and in three hours or so passed the whole of our force over the river swimming the donkeys beside canoes.

25th March   Marched the Mposa to Palaballa. At the start we had a very rough hill to climb, the men felling it very much. Reached Palaballa about twelve o'clock, but some did not come in till very late in the afternoon. Some of the fellows had grub in the mission house, but one or two of us stuck to our cook (a very bad one) and had some rice and goat stew. In the evening I sallied out and got a few limes from the garden. There were some nice looking oranges, but they were not ripe enough to eat.

26th March   Left the Mposa River camp at 6:30 a.m. and commenced our second day's march to Palaballa. Sickness among the Zanzibaris is on the increase; ulcers and bad feet are very common. Poor chaps, they have to struggle pretty hard to get along with their loads under a broiling sun. I reached Palaballa mission station at about 9:30 and started getting up the tent and making the men comfortable.

Today's march was very trying on the men; some of them did not get into camp till five in the afternoon, quite played out. We sent twenty men from each company back to the Umposa River to bring on loads tomorrow. The mission people here are very hospitable and kind to us. They appear to be very comfortable, having a couple of very good plantations to draw from.

Barttelot is back tonight at the Mposa with some of his Soudanese and 150 or so of Zanzibaris. I am writing this in our tent under many difficulties, though we are still very comfortable. Nelson, Barttelot, Parke, and myself sleep in the large tent. Jephson and Jameson have each one of their own. Mr. Stanley's is a most elaborate one.[...]

On Sunday, 27 March, the caravan camped at the Palaballa mission station (Livingstone Inland mission, or LIM). Two days later heavy rain made the track very slippery and difficult for the porters, particularly when they had to cross swollen streams. On Friday, 1 April, the expedition reached the Banza Manteke mission station where Stairs was entertained by Mr. and Mrs. H. Richards and met an American doctor named Small. A late start on Saturday morning was due to continuing rain.

3rd April Up and away early on the march, crossed two decent-sized rivers with very clear water in them. Today we passed a caravan with twenty-five tusks of ivory. We are continually passing these caravans for the coast loaded with ivory and Indiarubber. We passed another caravan under the charge of a Mr. Davey of the General Sanford expedition on the upper waters of the Congo.[9] Reached camp at 2:00 p.m. after a hard and trying march.

4th April Started away from camp at 6:00 a.m. and away on the march to the Kwilu River about three and one-half hours. The camp we have just left is the site of an old native village, now quite deserted owing to the action of the Congo Free State in punishing the blacks for hindering caravans. We had a lot of trouble today with the donkeys. So many bad crossings and bush patches always impede the advance of the column. We continue to pass native caravans every day. Some of them take down as many as fifty tusks of ivory. We reached the Kwilu about 11:00, Mr. Stanley arriving at 10:00.

We found that there was only one canoe at the crossing (and that not much of one), and that the natives had hidden the paddles. Just fancy passing nearly eight hundred men over a pretty swift river in one canoe!

We bent [sic] a long rope across the stream and started passing ten men and their loads each time, each round taking about ten minutes. The Somali boys worked with a will, and by 6:00 p.m. we had 425 across, some of the Soudanese swimming across above the canoe. We knocked up [sic] thoroughly tired out, made the loads all snug, had some grub and turned in.

Our camp today is in a small grove of trees on top of the hill above the river crossing. We hear plenty of guinea fowls near at hand, but no one has enough time to go an shoot a few. A great many of the Zanzibaris are suffering from the effects of drinking huge quantities of bad water. We Europeans drink nothing but boiled water or tea. The weather today was fine enough, but there is somehow a feverish feeling of depression after a few hours marching that is very trying. To stand still in camp near this river for any length of time would certainly cause very bad fevers and probably dysentery among the men. We still pass through the same sort of country, patches of bush in the gullies, grass (splendid for cattle) on the hillsides, and bare gravelly hilltops. On the whole it is fairly well-watered, though the water would knock over Europeans probably in a very short time.

5th April Up early and down to the Kwilu [River] to get the remainder of the men and donkeys [across]. Started at 6:15 a.m. and by 12:30 we had passed every man, woman and donkey over, except a few sick men following on a day's march in [the] rear. We passed over our donkeys very quickly: two at a time by the up-stream side of the canoe and held by the heads and tails by donkey-boys. My donkey Ned took the water very well. He is very small but active and good at getting over creeks and swampy places. We took all Tippu Tib's men and women over safely, though they gave us far more trouble than our own men. Last of all Barttelot, Bonny, and myself came over, and the eight hundred men had been passed without a single article of any sort being lost.[...]

It is a three-day march from here to Lukungu where the rice for our men is, and owing to delays, the men have already devoured their rations. Somehow or other they peg out all right, getting guavas, maniocas, and papaws along the roadside; at times they buy Indian corn from the natives and roast it in their fires or eat it raw. After passing all the men over the river, the rain came on and we stayed in camp, thankful for the rest afforded us. Our big tent cannot be called much of a success, the ordinary rectangular two-poled tents would have been much better.

6th April Away from camp early this morning, Barttelot and I bringing up the rear and getting along the stragglers. On the march one of my under chiefs, Khamis ben Athman, strayed from the track searching for food and was shot by some of the natives; one of Tippu Tib's men was also badly shot in the hand but killed his man with a bullet through the stomach. Khamis was a very good chief and his loss will be felt in my company pretty much. We reached Mwembi camp after eight hours [of] march[ing], the advance [column] only taking three and one-half hours.

7th April Left Mwembi at 6:00 a.m. and started on an easy three-hour march to Vombo. Camped in a deserted village under a fine grove of trees. Sun was tremendously powerful today, scorching one like the mischief.

8th April Started the head of the column away at 5:30 a.m., the rest following on in succession. Shortly after starting we had a very bad thunderstorm, the rain coming down in torrents, making the track very bad for the men. The march was 12 miles to Lukungu, but we did not reach this place till 3:30 p.m. when we camped on the square of the Congo Free State station, pitched our tents and had dinner in the station house and had a very comfortable evening.

9th April At Lunkungu all day. Barttelot started off with about 130 men for Stanley Pool to be one day ahead of us all the way. He took the Soudanese and all the "goe-goes" [sic] or lazy porters with him. I forgot to say that my stupid boy Abedi led my donkey over a bad place yesterday and broke one of its hind legs. I had to shoot it to put it of misery and so now am without a mount and will probably have to foot it across Africa. There are two officers of the Congo Free State at this place, both Belgians and very decent fellows.

10th April Left the station at Lukungu at 7:00 a.m. having first sent off the men for the boat at Manyanga; crossed the Lukungu River in a steel boat. Some of us walked over on a swing bridge, a very rickety affair. The first hour or two of the march was very good. Afterwards, though, we commenced to ascend a pretty steep range and the sun came out boiling hot, making it hard work. We got to camp early though as we had to stop to allow Barttelot's chaps time to get on. Our camp is on a flat under some palms and near good water.

11th April Our camp last night was chosen in a very bad place as we found to our cost. About seven o'clock the rain commenced to come down in torrents, flooding everything. Our tent was simply flooded. We stuck to it for a long time, but it was too much. I had about 4 inches of water round my bed. A Belgian officer who was sleeping with us in our tent got all his things soaked. We had a long talk about affairs in general. He is an officer of the Congo Free State and has been out on the Congo for two and one-half years; he is not of [the] opinion that the Free State is a success, as in fact not many of the officers are. He intends going on a three-month exploration trip of the frontiers of the Free State and the Portuguese territory; he expects good shooting. There are elephants, buffalo, and antelope all along here, but they keep well away from the track, and we never see anything of them.

Our march today was originally intended to be four hours, but after three hours [of] good marching we came to the Mpioka River, which was in high flood, and [we] had to stop to make a bridge to enable the loads to be taken over. This we did by felling three or four trees and stretching them across, lashing them where necessary. We took three hours or so to do this and so had to camp beside the stream. We killed a large venomous centipede in our tent this evening, quite enough to do for us all if he had got a chance [to bite us].[...]

By Wednesday, 13 April, the expedition arrived at the Lutete station (Baptist Missionary Society), where a French trading post was also located. One of the Somalis died of exhaustion after a bad attack of fever, which affected many of his countrymen. On the fourteenth the caravan camped at a place called Nzungi.

15th April Up before 5:00 a.m., but the last of the column had not left camp till 6:30. The march today was a five-hour one, but I was rearguard and took six and one-half hours to get all the men into camp.

Crossed two small and one fairly large river, the latter by means of a log bridge. Saw the Congo glittering in the distance, running between two walls of solid rock. Came upon some natives holding market on the side of the track. Most of them ran away as the Zanzibaris came up. They are very much afraid of our men and well so, for a greater crowd of stealing ruffians it would be hard to find. The natives had bananas, fish, beans, roots, and various things for sale for which they took brass wire and handkerchiefs as payment.

Close to the market impaled on a high pole we saw the dried up remains of a native who had killed one of his tribe in the market place and suffered for it by being impaled as we found him. We also saw a native bird trap set ready for use. This consisted of nooses made of fibres hung down from a vine, stretched between two poles. It was placed on the edge of a small patch of bush and about 30 feet above the ground. It is said to be very effective in catching doves and pigeons, and is very difficult to see against a background of bush.

We reached camp in the rearguard about 12:30 p.m.; the day being very hot we felt the march pretty much. Our camp is in a small village of about twelve huts called Inkissi. Mr. Stanley has one for himself, and four of us, Parke, Nelson, Jameson, and myself have another. On the outside of our hut the natives have all sorts of charms stuck up to keep away sickness and bad luck; there are fowls' heads, chilies [sic], feathers, rags, and all sorts of odds and ends, so we should be well protected. Unfortunately, however, these charms do not serve to keep away earwigs and ants of which there are any quantity.

Jephson is ahead getting the boat ready for crossing the Inkissi River tomorrow. Barttelot is camped with his men about 600 yards in rear of us. The Soudanese "bucked up" a bit today, but they still are very bad.

Old Stanley is getting a bit worked up now. He is a most excitable man, with a violent temper when roused, but it soon subsides. He says and does a great many foolish things when he is in this state for which afterwards he must be sorry. He is not a man who has had any fine feelings cultivated in his youth. I should say, outwardly and to strangers he is most polite and charming, but under this there runs a much different kind of strain. I only hope we shall all pull well together to make a success of the expedition, but he holds such a tremendous leverage over us, that for a single slip any of us might be put down as incompetent and dismissed at once.

16th April   Rained heavily during the night and on till nearly seven o'clock. We then made a start by companies for the Inkissi River, about 600 yards from camp, reached the river which was much swollen and started crossing the men over in the steel boat. Jephson had tried bending [sic] cables over, but the current was too strong and the weight of the boat parted the cables so Stanley decided to row the men over, which we did—about twenty-four men or forty loads at a time. We found it took about one hour to get each company over. We also have 150 Congo porters carrying loads for us. These we had to ferry over the river.

The Inkissi River is by far the largest and most rapid river we have yet crossed, taking down twice as much water as the Kwilu or Upozo, I should say. The steel boat is a great success and will be most useful to us as we get on and we encounter more rivers to cross. We hear that the steamers at Stanley Pool are all ready to take all of up-stream but seventy. This is very good news as we had been thinking the difficulty of getting steamers would be very great. I believe there are only four steamers all told on the river above Stanley Pool, viz., *Le Stanley* (stern wheeler) [and subsequently referred to as the *Stanley*], the *En Avant,* the *A.I.A.,*[10] and one steamer belonging to the General Sanford expedition [the *Florida*], which is now far away up some tributary of the Congo and cannot be got at.

I met a very nice chap today on the road, in charge of some of the Sanford expedition porters, carrying machinery and parts of the hull of a steamer up-river for trading purposes on the upper waters of the Congo and its branches. He asked me to breakfast and gave me two eggs as a present, which was a most acceptable gift under such circumstances as we are placed in. All these fellows and the officers of the Congo Free State travel from place to place like lords: they have the very best of tinned goods of all sorts—jams, bacon, oatmeal, tea, coffee, condensed milk, tinned fish, besides fruits, and whatever else the country yields. They generally have three or four native boys as servants, carry swell tents and beds, and generally do themselves up well. In fact, I know one of two officers of the CFS [Congo Free State who] get carried about by porters wherever they go. These Belgian officers are very hospitable to us as we pass by the different stations, but they appear to us to be the wrong sort of men to have as agents of a young state such as this is. They seem to lack energy and push, to be too fond of staying indoors at the stations and as a rule [are] very ignorant of the country above [Stanley] Pool.

The Sanford expedition is a trading company, organized by an American (General Sanford) for the purposes of procuring ivory and Indiarubber from the natives on the upper waters of the Congo and sending it down-country to Banana [Point] and thence to the Liverpool markets. They already, I believe, have one steamer on the river above [Stanley] Pool, and one more is now on its way up-country. I believe the manager is an American naval lieutenant called Taunt.[11]

Jameson gets some very pretty butterflies and beetles now. He must have some hundreds of beauties in his boxes by this time. We should be at Stanley Pool in five days from this, and are already six days behind time. On the whole though, we have not done badly. It must be remembered that our men on starting were very soft, that their loads were heavy—65 pounds—with blankets, rifle and fifteen days' rations besides, that the rivers have all swollen, giving us much trouble, and that the men have suffered greatly from dysentery and could not be pushed.

We camped for the day after crossing and got all the men over by 4:30 p.m., our camp being on a clear space just above the bush patch lining the Inkissi River.

17th April Left the Inkissi camp at six o'clock and started off on a five-hour march. My men going along well, we reached camp in five hours and ten minutes. The road was very good, the only obstacles being two small rivers and a bad hill. We passed through two small villages, one of which our men looted, taking all the manioca roots and driving off the poor frightened natives like so many sheep. I sailed in at last with a big stick and drove them off, but not before they had filled their blankets with *chakula*.

Tippu Tib's people travel and camp with us every day. We have great fun with the women on the march. They are a jolly laughing crew. One passes them every day, as they travel very slowly. We often lift up their loads for them and give them biscuits, and in return they offer us manioca roots—beastly things they are too. Tippu himself is a very good chap and so are most of his followers. There is one fellow, though, called Salim who speaks English, a proper brute. We all dislike him, he is such a sneak. There will be trouble with him some day unless he is nipped a bit by Stanley.

On the march I always keep my headman Rashid and my two boys close at hand to lift up the mens' loads onto their heads. This I find to be the best way. The other chiefs I send ahead with the men to encourage them on. Rashid is a splendid fellow, far away the best of the men. He is so quiet and yet when he likes he can use the stick very well. All the men like him and would do anything for him. I am very fortunate in getting such a good man for head chief. My boys are both fairly good little chaps, but they take a lot of teaching and get a fair amount of *fimto* (stick) every day. Our camp is on a hillside in some scrubby bush and close to good water. The distance form last camp is about 10½ miles.

Our grub on this expedition is very bad. In fact much worse then bushmen or surveyors in New Zealand or Canada get.[...]

18th April Up at five o'clock. Had a cup of tea and some biscuits as usual and away on the march by six o'clock. Jephson and the boat came along with us today; the heavy boat loads impede us a great deal at bad places. It would be better if they would march a few hours in rear of us, I fancy. Stanley told me this morning some news which may turn out to be very bad. He had letters saying that the *Stanley* was the only steamer available for taking us up the river and that the English mission had declined to lend their steamer to us. Now the *Stanley* can only take 200 men and loads, and towing two lighters she might take about 100 more, for a total of 300 men. He also showed me a letter from the American Baptist mission saying that pending instructions to the contrary, they would lend us their steamer the *Peace,* taking sixty men and loads. It is by no means certain that we will be able to get this steamer, as this mail may bring contrary instructions from America. To tell the truth, the missionaries are frightened to lend their steamer to an armed body of men, ready to fight any opposing natives up the river, as the natives seeing the *Peace,* might fancy it was the missionaries and so the "Gospel" would suffer.[...]

20th April Away from camp early, the morning being a good one for marching. Passed two native villages on the way and about 11:30 drew up in a third and camped for the day. An old chief called Makoko came to interview Stanley. Makoko has a beard 6 feet long and wears it twisted up into two short spirals of about 3 inches each. He is seventy-five years old and was in power when Stanley came down the river on his first trip. We reached a point 2,770 feet above sea level, the highest altitude between Stanley Pool and the sea. The name of this village is Makoko. There are about fifteen huts and the usual plantations of bananas and manioca roots. This is one of the few villages that the natives have not cleared out from; almost all the others we found devoid of natives. They had been scared by the advance of our men.[...]

The expedition reached Stanley Pool on Thursday, 21 April. A number of chiefs, officials, and missionaries came to the camp to meet with Stanley.

23rd April In camp and hot as the very mischief. Several lengthy interviews between the head of the Free State, Stanley, and some chiefs took place in the morning. Food is absolutely unobtainable here for the men; our rice is finished; we can get no manioca for the men; there is no meat; what are we to do? Can we leave two hundred or three hundred men here to starve and pillage? The missionaries have again and again refused [us] their steamer. Something must be done and we must get out of this as soon as possible to Bolobo where there is food. Today the CFS [Congo Free State] seized for us the steamer *Peace,* or rather requisitioned it, so as to avoid danger to the state and we have got her now for our use up the river.[...]

We have thus secured three steamers, the *Stanley* (220 men), the *Peace* (160 men and loads), and the *Henry Reed.* We also have got from Mr. Swinbourne[12] the hull of the steamer *Florida* of the Sanford expedition, our own steel boat, two lighters, and one of the mission whale boats will be towed behind the steamers. Stanley Pool has not been a station for five or six years, with the very best of rich land on almost every side, yet here today there is a famine. Acres of bananas and manioca could have been planted, but no, everything is ivory from morning to night; all are concerned [with] getting down the greatest quantity of ivory. The [the policies of the CFS] will never make anything of a state. The ivory soon will be exhausted, except far up the river and then times will get very bad, much worse than they are now. Things appear to have gone down very much since Stanley's time, from all accounts.

In the evening Jameson came down-river, having shot two hippopotami, only one of which he managed to get. We had the meat brought up to the camp and distributed as rations to the men. We took some for ourselves and had some steaks, which were very good.

24th April Had a general parade at 6:30 a.m. taking a list of hoes, axes, rifles, etc. Practised the men a bit at turnings and position drill. I afterwards cleaned up the Maxim and did some other small jobs. Nelson is away with fifty men cutting firewood some distance from here. Jameson is just going off on another hippo expedition to get meat for the men. He will be away for three days and will send meat back to camp every day. Had several visitors to the camp today, among them were two of the missionaries here—most cadaverous looking men.

I got five or six letters from home and England yesterday. I also had one from Mary from Port Said. She was on her way then to India and was expecting me to follow on by the next trooper.[13] It is now over three months since we left England and we have only got to Stanley Pool.[...]

For the following five days the men were kept busy getting firewood for the steamers and Jameson hunted for hippos, which continued to be the chief source of food. On 30 April the expedition was preparing to leave Stanley Pool and steam up the Congo River.

CHAPTER 2
STANLEY POOL TO YAMBUYA

1 MAY—24 JUNE 1887

The flotilla carrying the Emin Pasha Relief Expedition leaves Stanley Pool on 1 May 1887. Mechanical breakdowns and accidents slow down its progress. Encounters occur with the local villagers. Receptions are held at mission stations and government trading posts. Serious health problems begin. The expedition arrives at Yambuya and builds a fort. The expedition is divided into two parts: the "rear" and the "advance" columns.

1st May Started loading the *Henry Reed* with Tippu Tib's people and goods. At 8:30 a.m. we sent her off up-river and thus made a start on what will probably be a journey of forty days. We next loaded up the *Florida* with Jameson's and my men in her and made her fast to the *Stanley* and [the] *Peace* and the whale boat *Plymouth* and a state lighter.[...] There were the missionary and his wife, Mr. Greshoff, another German gentleman, Troup, Swinbourne, Casement, Baron Steinworth, and an engineer of the Dutch house. They gave us a vociferous cheer, which we returned. Soon after we left, the *Peace* followed and we lost sight of her after half an hour or so, apparently she returned to Kinshassa. However, a day or so will tell. At last we have started and all are glad, the men especially, as their rations of *matako* rods were not nearly sufficient for the famine prices at Stanley Pool.[...]

We are taking 606 men up-river, those with Parke and Barttelot amount to about 160 more. We should therefore have about 600 men to take up to the [Stanley] Falls and will probably leave 100 of these there in an entrenched camp we are to form.

We are very much crowded on the *Stanley*. The men simply cannot move but stay in one or nearly the same position all day.[...]

Going up the river we dodge about, crossing form side to side of the channel to miss the rocks and sandbanks. Just now we are not more than 10 yards from the bank, here covered with long grass and small bushes and infested by crocodiles. The mosquitoes are said to be very bad along the river banks, but we should be safe with netting rigged up. We landed the mails at the Kimpoko mission station and again landed and camped about 300 yards above.

Kimpoko is an American Baptist mission station, self-supporting to a great extent. There are no less than three white men, I believe. These shoot meat, cut their own wood, build their sheds, etc., farm, [and] in fact employ little or no paid labour on the station. We had a visit from some of them: long, tall, bearded Americans, all keen for news about the expedition. Some of them took a great deal of interest in the Maxim gun which we keep mounted, ready for action. We all slept on board and found it very comfortable and free from mosquitoes. The men camped within 200 yards of the steamer and as usual talked all night.

At 6:00 p.m. we started the men off for firewood, having forty-five axemen and others to carry the wood out. By eight o'clock we had about enough wood for the *Stanley,* and we lit large fires and split up our wood and stowed it away in the hold. The *Stanley* burns a tremendous quantity of wood every day. It takes nearly two hundred loads of sixty pounds each for twelve hours steaming. This wood-cutting will get to be very tiresome work, I should say.

In the dark one cannot watch the men as in daytime and so prevent them getting away. The men are hungry and want to cook their manioca. Then, too, wood is difficult to get and wandering about in the dark in bush is not healthy work for the shirt, as most bushmen know.

2nd May Up at five o'clock and started off forty axemen for wood, Jameson going with them. Shortly afterwards Nelson and Jephson took parties off to fetch and cut wood in. The *Henry Reed* is lying about 100 yards above us with Tippu Tib's people camped close by. We have heard nothing of the *Peace* yet. We suppose something must have fouled her screw and so delayed her. How Stanley must be swearing.

At 10:00 a.m., as the *Peace* had not yet turned up, the captain of the *Stanley* and I went down-stream in the *Stanley* to look for her. After steaming about 12 miles, we saw her in a small by-channel. Catching up to her, found that yesterday, soon after starting from Kinshassa, she had broken her rudder. We offered them help but they declined, so we came on, loaded up the men, took on some more firewood, and now as I write, all these steamers are on their way up-stream. We should get out of Stanley Pool by dark and camp for the night.

Nelson is a little bit seedy today. It looks like the commencement of a fever. After our start we steamed about two-and-a-half-hours more up-river and made fast to the left or south bank between the *Henry Reed* and [the] *Stanley.* As soon as the ropes were out, we disembarked the men for the night, cut grass for the goats and donkeys and then had a very comfortable dinner in the saloon, Walker and Bonny coming off to us in the steel boat.[1] We had a heavy thunderstorm during the night, but did not mind it under a good secure roof.

3rd May Up at 5:00 a.m. and started the men on board as soon as it got light enough to see. By 5:45 we had all on board an soon after the *Peace* steamed by with Stanley on board, giving us orders to go on to the Black River. Accordingly, we steamed off and soon left the *Peace* astern. The *Henry Reed* had just started after we got about half a mile up the river.

Tippu Tib's people are sadly wanting in discipline, as can be seen every day. They seem quite indifferent to the passage of time. I suppose they have always been used to take things easily [sic] and so now do not see the use of hurrying. Certainly now is the chance to make up time, if ever we are to do it. Our captain estimates that it will take nearly forty days to get to Stanley Falls loaded up as we are. This is nearly a week over Stanely's estimate. Stopped on the left bank about 3:30 p.m., and at once started cutting firewood. By dark we had got enough for fifteen hours, so we knocked off work and had our grub.

The men camped close to the steamer. While looking for wood I saw plenty of elephant's tracks evidently a week or so old.

4th May   Up at 5:00 a.m. and got all on board, steamed into the stream and drew up alongside of the *Peace* and handed over some rice and a goat. Soon afterwards, went on our way and left the *Peace* and *Henry Reed* astern. We are bound for Mswata now and hope to reach there this evening, or early tomorrow morning. I fired a few rounds from the Maxim this morning to try some ammunition that had fallen into a creek. The gun worked well and showed that very accurate shooting could be made with it. The ammunition was some of the thirty-four hundred rounds of R.L. 45 Gardner that we got from the English government just before starting. We pulled up for the night on the north bank about four o'clock. Got the men out and started cutting wood, but found it to be very scarce and so did not finish till nearly nine o'clock.

We split the big logs by the light of a large fire close to the steamer and got all the wood on board soon after. Some of the men went back to a manioca field two hours off and robbed the natives of their food. There were great rejoicings in camp when they came back as everyone had plenty of chakula and felt generally happy. The people here are the Bateke, apparently a quiet, docile set, otherwise I should think they would retaliate and attack us.

5th May   Up shortly after 5:00 a.m. and by 5:30 had all aboard. We found that the *Stanley* was fast in the mud and so had to get fifty or sixty men out to push her off. We started at once up-river for Mswata about two hours off, having seen nothing of the *Peace* or [the] *Henry Reed* since yesterday afternoon.

Jephson was a bit seedy yesterday, but feels much better now. We all thought it was another fever, but quinine and "Livingstone's" pills made him all right again.

One begins now to feel the dimensions of the Congo. Here the river is about twice as wide as the "Arm" at Halifax,[2] or say slightly over half a mile, but deep and swift, closed in on both sides with high bush-covered hills and grassy slopes, and stretching up and down till lost far away among the hazy blue hills. Far up from here at Bangala, the river widens and shallows and is studded with numbers of small islands, but here it flows on in one solid mass, hardly broken in its shape at all. We see plenty of natives all paddle standing up and not as the Indians do (viz., kneeling down). There are plenty of fish about here. I should say they would rise well to the fly as we see them jumping at moths and flies.

By 9:30 we reached Mswata, where we met Parke and Barttelot and their men. Stanley came along in the *Peace* about three hours later and the *Henry Reed* about two hours after the *Peace*. We put our wood on board and as soon as [the] *Stanley* came, issued *matakos* to the men and let them go off for grub.

Mswata was formerly a state station, but has now been abandoned, as many others have up the river. The people in this village are Batekes, quiet, harmless duffers they seem. Our men have bought large quantities of maize, bananas, plantains, manioca, and fish and seem very well satisfied with themselves. There are plenty of goats, fowls, and yams besides the above mentioned sorts of food, but the natives will not take *matako* for goats; they must have cloth.

6th May Up early and away by about 5:30 a.m. The *Peace* led the way at the start, but we soon passed her and in three hours were out of sight of both steamers. We passed Kwamouth about 10:30—saw some huts and the site of the mission station. The Kwa is the largest river entering the Congo; one branch, the Mfini drains Lake Leopold II, then the Kassai, which is largest of all, runs from the southeast and is fed by a great many rivers of good size. The *Stanley* has been up the Kassai for over 450 miles to the junction of the Luebo.[...]

At 4:30 in the afternoon we were going along splendidly, congratulating ourselves at the way in which we were leaving the *Peace* and [the] *Henry Reed* behind. We were all on the bridge talking or reading, when smash, bump onto firm rocks went the *Stanley*. The water immediately rushed into two compartments and things looked very bad. However, the Zanzibaris kept very quiet, and in about two minutes we had all the men on board the *Florida* and stood ready to cast her off. We soon found there was not much immediate danger as the rock we were on was of a flat table shape, reaching out over the stern and sides of the *Stanley* and having about 3 feet 6 inches of water at the stern.

While we were shifting the cargo aft and moving men to weigh down the stern, a very bad squall came up and blew us clean off the rock and probably proved our salvation.[...]

The men disembarked and the loads were removed. The captain with the engineers started the work of mending the holes in the steamer's bottom. In the morning of 10 May, *Le Stanley* was ready to resume its travel in the direction of Yambuya—the closest settlement to Stanley Falls on the expedition's route. The latter had been taken over by Tippu Tib in August 1884, and eventually he became its governor on behalf of the Congo Free State.

10th May Up before five o'clock and had the men all aboard before daylight. As soon as we could see we started off. About ten o'clock we sighted the *Peace* and [the] *Henry Reed* far ahead of us. We gained on them very fast, and at 1:15 passed them within about 50 yards. Something had gone wrong with the *Peace's* boiler and in an hour we had left her far behind. We had a very heavy thunderstorm in the afternoon with bad squalls of wind and rain.

At 4:30 we fetched the south bank and made fast for the night, the *Henry Reed* being about 75 yards astern of us. When we were out cutting firewood, we saw plenty of buffalo tracks and saw where they had been nibbling the grass shortly before.

11th May Away by 5:30 a.m., and after some difficult manoeuvring on the part of the captain to keep clear of shoals we landed our men at Bolobo without any trouble. Hibaka the king, is at present away in Lukolela buying ivory, so we could not see him. His son, however, came down to see us and shortly afterwards we drank palm wine with the head men.[...]

The following three days were uneventful, except that the boiler of the Peace *had broken down, which caused some delay in the progress of the expedition.*

15th May Up early and started organizing another company, loaded the *Henry Reed* with men and the *Peace*, and at 10:30 a.m. both steamers got away. After getting the donkeys and goats on board we put the Soudanese on the *Florida*, and shortly afterwards I embarked my men also on the *Florida*. We now have companies of eighty-five men each;

every man [is] armed with a rifle and all the sick, bad men and "goe-goes" [sic] picked out and left behind at Bolobo. We are now much better prepared for fighting than we where formerly.

At noon we started away up-stream leaving Bonny and Ward on the banks looking very sad, and in a few hours had caught sight of both steamers ahead of us.[...]

At this point in time, the expedition consisted of four companies of eighty-five men, each armed with a rifle. There were, in addition, eighty-seven Sudanese and Somalis equipped with fifty-nine Remingtons and seventy-six supernumeraries and donkey-boys.

At Bolobo we left about 125 men, with 50 rifles and 2,000 rounds of ammunition. We calculate on their being there for about fifty days. [The] *Stanley* will by that time have come down-river to [Stanley] Pool, will pick Troup up, come up to Bolobo and take Bonny and Ward on to [Stanley] Falls. It is to be hoped that Ward and Bonny have no trouble with the natives. We had great difficulty in getting any wood and on landing for the night at a small village, the natives ran away after first threatening to fight us. Soon after, our men commenced to loot in the dark and took a tremendous quantity of food and spears.

We had to knock off getting firewood very soon after eight o'clock and will have to get more in the morning. The spears our men took are very fine ones with long straight hardwood hafts and a broad blade, say 4 inches wide at the swell. They are bound with brass bands, lapping over each other for about 9 inches below the head.[...]

Between 16 May and 19 May travel up the river progressed smoothly, except for a minor problem with the boiler, which was soon rectified. Shooting hippos was the favourite entertainment although none of the animals' bodies were recovered. Stairs complained of the lack of sugar, soap, and candles, and the shortage of tea which was now being rationed at one-fifth of an ounce per day, per man. He blamed Stanley for this highly unsatisfactory supply of provisions.

20th May It is just four months today since we left England, and we have now been two months in Africa. Today there was a big row with Stanley, and after many high words he dismissed both Jephson and myself. Of course we are powerless to do anything or [to] retaliate and had to bear a great deal. After his anger had subsided he took us back, but [since] it was before the men and about them that the row took place discipline must suffer and the men think less of us and become incited to mutiny. I am awfully sorry this has happened as it destroys all harmony among us. At the same time, I will never admit being in the wrong, and consider myself fully justified in doing what I did, viz., throwing away food looted from a friendly [Zanzibaris] village. Of course, some innocent souls suffered, but they must blame the guilty ones for this. I threw away the looted food for two reasons. First, to show them that we considered it wrong to loot from friendly natives. Second, to serve as an example to the looters and to show them that if we could help it they would not profit one iota. I have stood more swearing at, heard more degrading things and swallowed more intemperate language from another man today than I have ever before.

We found plenty of food at Lukolela, and bought a lot of fowls at four *matakos* each. The men got five days' rations each, or one *matako* per day. With these they buy *chaquanga*, bananas, plantains, fowls, or fish. Here they get two small *chaquangas* for one *matako*. This bread is not very tempting to a white man but if cut into very thin slices and fried, it is not bad.

21st May Away from Lukolela at 6:30 a.m., the *Peace* and [the] *Henry Reed* getting half an hour's start [ahead] of us owing to our engineer not having steam up for us. Our wood supply being short, at one o'clock we landed and started cutting wood and soon after decided to stay for the night. We were cutting from 2:00 to 9:00 p.m. before we could get enough wood. I had to knock off as I felt a touch of fever coming on. It was petty bad for several hours, but the effects of the quinine soon showed themselves. After piling on all the coats and blankets I could get, the perspiration at last came out and I began to feel relieved.

22nd May Away from camp at 6:00 a.m. My fever has gone down a great deal, but still today my head aches horribly. Nelson and Jameson are now much better. The *Peace* and [the] *Henry Reed* camped nearly opposite to us last night, for what reason we cannot understand. Probably they imagined our boiler had gone wrong again. Stopped at 5:15 on the left bank, the *Henry Reed* lying close to us and the *Peace* opposite on the other side of the channel. Could not get any wood as it was pitch dark and the bush was almost impassable. Passed Ngombe about noon.

23rd May Away by 5:30 a.m. ahead of either the *Peace* or [the] *Henry Reed*. We shortly passed a large native village, all the people turning out to see us.

Had to stop at 11:00 on account of our wood giving out. In three hours we had got a fine supply and started on again, but in the meantime the *Peace* and [the] *Henry Reed* had passed us. We saw a great number of natives on the bank at Irebu, the junction of the Congo and Mantumba Rivers, which we passed about 10:00.

All the Congo natives stand up in their canoes to paddle and appear wonderfully skilful in handling them in the swift current. The Congo here remains very much the same as it has been all the way from Bolobo, namely studded with bush covered-islands with narrow channels. We generally keep to the left bank all the way up. In fact very little seems to be known even yet about the right bank just here. It is not known, I believe, whether Luker, Mantumba, and Leopold are connected in any way. Mr. Grenfell, the missionary, may however, have found this out; as yet he has not made his information public.[3]

24th May Today is the queen's birthday. This time we are under the flag of the Congo Free State. Our camp last night was on the left bank in a very good place.[...]

We reached the equator station in the evening, much to the astonishment of the Europeans here who had not heard from down-river for six months and of course did not know what to make of us. They at first thought we were a force coming to retake Stanley Falls from the Arabs. Equator is now abandoned by the state as a station and its buildings have been handed over to the Sanford trading expedition. There is also an Anglo-American Baptist mission station here, with two missionaries and a very nice earth house.

Though the state has abandoned this place, still an officer has been staying here for some time, looking out for Stanley Falls. Unluckily for him, he does not know as much about the state of affairs as we do as we brought news from Zanzibar that had crossed Africa about which he knew nothing. His name is Van Eile, a lieutenant in the Belgian service. There is a chap here called Glove, a young Englishman who formerly was in the service of the Congo Free State but now is in the Sanford company buying ivory from the natives here. He seems a very decent sort of chap. Quite a different cut from the usual milk-watery Belgian officer one meets on the Congo.

The names of the two missionaries I do not know. I suppose they do some work, but the natives are not of the right sort to take in Christianity easily. This is a bad place, taken all round for food. All that is used is obtained from villages some distance off. Some day there will probably be famine here, owing to the same reasons that caused one at [Stanley] Pool, viz., that no one plants roots or fruit here, or seems to provide in the slightest for the future.

25th May Barttelot, Jephson, Nelson, and Jameson went out with the axemen first thing in the morning to get our supply of wood, the missionaries kindly giving us permission to cut on their ground behind the houses. I issued rations of *matako* to the men and did some minor jobs, while Parke attended his sick. By noon we had finished getting our wood on board and we noticed that the *Peace* and [the] *Henry Reed* had almost finished with theirs.

Chickens are very dear here. One pays six *matakos* (brass rods) or their equivalent in shells for one small bird and the natives even ask as many as ten for a good fowl. *Chaquanga* is proportionately dear, of course, owing to the great demand and the short supply. We are once more in the northern hemisphere having crossed the line yesterday afternoon. This place [is] about 8' north latitude. It will be noticed that the Congo goes north a little more then bends back again to the south and crosses the line near Stanley Falls and then works away to the SSE and SE. The natives here are very much the same as those we saw at Bolobo, but seem to be bigger men than those down-river.

As we go up-river one notices that the spears, knives, canoes, and shields are getting superior to those down-river. All the full-grown men here carry a bunch of throwing spears and a shield made of webbed fibres. The spears are made very slight, with beautifully worked hafts, as straight as a die. One can get a good one for, say, eight *matakos* and a shield for about fifteen. The shields are small and light, just sufficient to turn a spear, but a slug or bullet would go through at least two of them. They are the most beautifully worked things we have seen on the Congo. If I had some *matakos* and had a chance, I would send some home.

The shield is about 5 feet long and 10 inches wide at the broadest part, made of basket work of several different colours and strengthened by two long ribs of black basket work surrounding canes.

We all went to dinner with Glove and Van Gele in a very comfortable mud and bamboo house of one story.[4] We had hippo meat, butter, palm wine, cabbage, bread, coffee, and tinned peaches, a regal repast after goat, rice and weavilly [sic], stale biscuits, and insipid tea. Van Gele has ascended the Mobangi River for some distance, but was stopped by the rapids. He also went up the Lulanga, a river just above the village of Uranga. This time he was in the *Henry Reed*. They came across a lot of very wild natives who would not allow them to land. After some persuasion and gifts of cloth, I believe he managed to land higher up and opened trade. These natives had never seen a white man before. The proper name of the river emptying into the Congo just here is the Rouki and not Mahinchu as Stanely has it in his maps.

Van Gele has also been up this river and also the Ikelemba [River] some distance.[...]

In the subsequent five days, Stairs admired the scenery and found it far superior to the famous Thousand Islands of the St. Lawrence River. He noticed that on Friday, 27 May none of the Muslim members of the expedition observed the fast of Ramadan. After a long reflection on the merits of the alternative routes which the expedition could have followed, Stairs appeared to have second thoughts about the wisdom of the choice of the Congo route, particularly in view of the four-hundred-mile stretch of an entirely unknown country which the caravan had to cross.

On Monday, 30 May the expedition arrived at the Bangala State station, where it was greeted with a salute from a Krupp gun.

31st May Up early, getting Barttelot and the *Henry Reed* off. Barttelot took forty of his Soudanese and all Tippu Tib's men and has rations for eighteen days. They go on straight to Stanley Falls, leave Tippu Tib there, try to quiet the country, and then Barttelot and his men come back to the mouth of the Aruwimi where we ought to pick them up. It will be an interesting piece of work, as the Arabs will of course imagine it to be an expedition of the Congo Free State for the retaking of Stanley Falls station and will probably attack, if they do not recognize Tippu Tib.

At noon, the *Peace* left amid cheers and at 1:30 we (in the *Stanley*) followed, having some trouble in getting all our men together.

Bangala is one of the biggest (collection of) villages on the Congo. The station at present is the highest one on the river, we, therefore, have said goodbye to everything that appertains to civilization, and in all probability none of us will see a white man again till we meet Emin Pasha.

We have now seen the whole of the working of the Congo Independent State. We have seen how it treats the different trading houses under its jurisdiction. We have also seen a fair portion of the country it governs and the natives under its charge. Our unanimous opinion is that the state, as [it is] now constructed, is one huge mistake. It was originally intended to be a *free state,* open to all, welcoming all honest trade, countenancing all open dealings with the natives and doing its best to establish postal and other communication between its different stations. Instead of this, what does really exist? A Congo *independent state,* open as regards its officials to all Belgians, is continually at variance with all the trading houses—English, Dutch, French, and Portuguese alike—hindering instead of aiding trade, and absolutely ignoring the importance of even a rough track with bush bridges on such a thoroughfare as that between Mataddi and Stanley Pool.

Certainly the Congo Independent State is a huge unwieldy mistake (as managed at present), worked purely in the interests of the king of the Belgians, who takes the best of care that outside influence is excluded and apparently imagines that some day this place will form a safe deposit for Belgian capital and manufactures. The officers at Bangala were all very good to us and invited us to breakfast and dinner, but underneath everything one could easily see there ran a vein of jealousy which required pretty strong effort on their part to conceal. They imagine, I suppose, that an expedition coming up *their* river [the Congo] in *their* steamers should be composed of Belgians, instead of Englishmen, as it is. This is only what one expects, as everywhere on the Congo the English are cried down and excluded from billets owing to the unpleasant fact that some day the English will control almost all the import trade to this [Congo] River, and also that the Belgians cannot help seeing that those English officers they have had out here have been far ahead of those of any other nationality in the way of managing the state and dealing with the natives.

The station at Bangala is fortified to a certain extent by means of a palisade and ditch. At the salients are placed gun banks, elevated above the palisade and mounted with Krupp guns (of which I believe there are two). The grass and scrub [have] at one time been charred in front, but now have been allowed to grow up again and will form very good cover should the Bangalas ever attempt to attack the station houses. They possess also at Bangala an excellent French brick-maker, who makes the very best of red building and fire clay bricks. He is a very decent fellow to talk to and well informed on most matters concerning his everyday life.

Of the other fellows little can be said. Lieutenant Baert of the Belgian service is outwardly a nice chap, but he has done some very nasty things here with the natives. The country about Bangala is very thickly populated, but none of the white men we met appear to have seen anything of it, [except] that part which adjoins the [Congo] River.

Captain Shakerston, our skipper, is a very amusing fellow in a quiet way. He has the funniest collection of Congo stories one has heard yet. He tells of an adventure with a hippo that occurred at Manyanga on the lower Congo. Some Belgians and natives had wounded a hippo on the river bank close to the station house and were all up quite close to the beast, plugging it with all sorts of missiles from rifles, muzzle loaders, and flint locks, when all of a sudden the beast charged them. Like rockets they all bolted for the house and clambered helter skelter onto the roof, just in time, for the beast kept straight on, burst through one wall, passed clean through the house and out the wall on the far side and escaped amid a shower of bullets to some bush close by. I should imagine it would be a very funny sight to see a huge hippo piercing the walls of a mud hut, with a lot of men perched on the roof like so many turkeys roosting.

After leaving Bangala we steamed till 6:00 p.m. and camped on the south bank in dense bush.

1st June Away from our moorings by 5:30 a.m. and soon caught up with the *Peace* and kept close behind her all the morning. Yesterday Stanley observed and I worked out the longitude of Bangala. It is in longitude 19° 32' E, latitude 1° 28' N.

What a subject of conversation that dinner at Bangala has been. How we have talked it over and laughed among ourselves and imagined again and again we were eating butter, meat, and vegetables and drinking Portuguese wine and champagne, but alas, it is farewell to these little comforts now for some time. I'm afraid the Belgian officers must think us all frightful gluttons, for certainly none of us spared the grub. We played havoc with their cigars and champagne at dinner and just as they were opening a fine bottle of brandy as a liqueur, Stanley rose and we had to adjourn. This was our farewell dinner with white men and Stanley, rising to the occasion, made a long speech exposing the dangers and adventures before us. Referring in "glowing terms" (that's correct!) to the king of the Belgians, [he] stated that it was owing to His Majesty that we were comfortably "roomed and dined" 800 miles up from the sea, and hoped that His Majesty would be spared many years of useful existence and remain the protector of the Free State (I hope the young man will).

The doctor recommends that we should get butter at least three times a day and advises the use of champagne in small quantities. His recommendations, however, do not carry much weight, as of butter there is none and the nearest fiz is at Bangala.

Camped on the left side of a small swampy island at 5:00 p.m. and managed by moon-light to get four or five hours [worth of] wood.

2nd June Away from camp at 5:50 a.m. Last night one of the Soudanese, who had been ill for some time, died in great pain. We buried him in the bush close to the steamer, giving him an eighteen-inch grave. At Bangala, Wadi Abdi, a Somali boy, died. He was one of the best of the Somalis, always ready when well to do his work, quick on his pins, and a good man in a boat or canoe. Abdi was one of the sort that we can ill spare. He died of exhaus-tion after an attack of some form of dysentery. Unfortunately the Somali boys all suffer very much in this country. The climate is too moist for them, used as they are to their dry arid Somaliland. They are constantly having severe attacks of fever and dysentery. In fact, since we crossed the Kwilu River, the Somalis have hardly done a stroke of work. To some extent this is owing to their not getting meat of any sort, and somehow the native food does not seem to agree with them. On board we have some nineteen of the Soudanese. The rest have gone on with the *Henry Reed* to [Stanley] Falls.

Of the nineteen, six or seven are suffering very much from ulcers and other com-plaints. They are very poor material for such an expedition as this. At making themselves comfortable in camp and in foraging for food they are not a patch on the Zanzibaris. Why, when we draw up to the shore at nights to camp, the Zanzibaris in fifteen minutes have their fires going, their shelters made and pots boiling, whereas one sees these Soudanese wandering aimlessly about, bemoaning their fate and cursing themselves for coming. In fact, [they] do anything but make themselves comfortable. Often I feel sorry for them in that they do not get the food they may have been used to in Egypt, but not for long, as one cannot sympathize with men who will not help themselves in a struggle such as this is.[...]

Travel up the Congo River continued. The routine of everyday life consisted mainly of naviga-tional problems such as avoiding the sandbanks and other obstacles and of cutting the wood for fuel during the stops. On 6 June Upoto was reached, where Stairs and the local head chief concluded blood-brotherhood.

In this part of the Congo, cowrie shells were used, instead of the matakos, *as a medium of exchange. The expedition lost two of its members: a Somali boy and a Sudanese soldier. Both of them died from what appeared to have been "debility and exhaustion."*

12th June Away at 5:15 a.m. Stuck three times on sandbanks. Passed the village of Yalumbo about noon, a very large village with great numbers of canoes. Late in the after-noon we [...] came to the junction of the Congo and Aruwimi, and turned up into the latter river. Stanley took the *Peace* into the bank at Basoko, a large village, and held a palaver with the natives, using his boy Baruti as an interpreter. The result was that we went across to the opposite side of the river and the natives promised to bring us food there in their canoes. They were distinctly averse to our landing and no wonder. Basoko has been twice burned, once by the state and then again by Tippu Tib's Arabs. Baruti, Stanley's boy who has been in England for some time, is the son of the chief of this village. Baruti's friends were there, but his brother failed to recognize him till Baruti had told him the names of his father, mother, and sisters; even then the natives were sceptical, but

Baruti said, "Here is the mark of a crocodile's teeth that I got when a boy here," and showing his brother the mark Baruti was welcomed by all, but not allowed to land.[...]

13th June Started at 5:20 a.m. Picked up the *Peace* and found that we were to stop till noon and thus get food from the natives. This, however, did not come off as the Basokos were too much frightened to venture [near] us. Some two small canoes, however, did come and were sent back to induce their friends to cut bananas and send them over to us. We waited till nearly eleven o'clock; Stanley's patience being then exhausted we got up steam and went up the river. Five minutes after leaving our landing place some twenty or thirty natives collected on the spot. This was done so quickly that there can be no doubt that they were in the bush all round the camp, watching our every movement.

The Aruwimi [River] at our camp is just about 900 yards wide and has three bad banks near its centre. The longitude of Karoko is 24° 12' E, its latitude is about 1° 15' N. It is a great change getting out of the Congo. One can now see both banks at the same time and one's eye takes in everything, whereas on the mighty Congo, distances are too great to allow one to see the river at one sweep. There are a few small islands in this part of the river and the usual number of sandbanks. We follow close to the *Peace* though [the] *Stanley* has been up-river about 96 miles when in the Congo Free State.[...]

Stanley, in his *Through the Dark Continent,* said that the Aruwimi is the same river as Schweinfurther Welle. He now thinks the Aruwimi runs from the direction of Muta Nzige. We steamed on till five o'clock and camped on the left bank at a small village, all the natives running away as soon as we came near the bank. We found no food of any sort as the banana trees had just been planted and the natives apparently had only just come there. All day long we passed village after village with scores of people. Sometimes we went within 10 yards of the banks. The natives all appeared valiant at first, but ran like deer as we approached their village and then came back again when we had passed.

A great many of the natives were painted with white and red clays. They all have distended ears caused by wearing small bits of wood stuck through the flaps. Most of them have their hair done up in different shapes, the prevailing one being much the same as the Bayanzi.

14th June Left camp at 5:10 a.m. and steamed across the river, then worked our way slowly among the sandbanks in a thickish mist. Towards the afternoon we came upon a very large village, probably one of the largest we have yet seen. Here we began to notice a change in the shape of the huts and for the first time saw the conical palm hut of which there are so many on the upper part of this river. For miles we passed this village, seeing hundreds of natives in hideous head dresses and gaudy with red ochre and white clay. They have most perfect paddles with handles of polished ivory. Some of their paddles also are made of bright red wood, which glitters in the sunlight, the effect being very pretty.[...]

15th June Away at six o'clock. This should be the last day we are to spend on board, as we hope to reach our destination this evening, if all goes well. This morning we noticed the banks generally got higher than those we have been passing. We stopped for the night just opposite to the village of Yambuya, where our entrenched camp is to be. The natives made a tremendous noise all night and canoes came close to us, the natives yelling frantically for us to go away....

16th June The natives would not permit us to land. We in the *Stanley* then came over, all our men being ready to land and my Maxim ready to murder them if they should dare to attack us. We made a landing soon after and frightened all the natives out and took possession. Unfortunately, they had such a long warning, that all the fowls and goats had been driven out.... We at once started clearing the bush behind the camp and by evening had cleared to a width of about 30 yards. This will give us some chance of preventing a rush on the part of the villagers....

17th June Up early and all hands occupied on different jobs. Stanley spent the morning in writing letters and held two palavers with natives who came in to sell food. Parke took some men to look for the manioc fields and came back with all his men loaded up. Jameson was unloading the *Stanley* and [the] *Peace* nearly all day and taking stock. I had about fifty men clearing the bush in front of the camp and finished about 4:00 p.m. I then got a lot of men with hoes and shovels, and having first traced the faces, we commenced digging the ditch for the palisade. The general shape of the camp is to be lunar or semi-lunar, with the river bank as a gorge. The palisade will be about 12 feet high [with] every thirtieth pole cut away to within 4 feet 6 inches from the ground. At the salients the banquette is raised 4 feet to 5 feet so as to give greater command. In the front face, to the right, is a high tower 12 feet 6 inches high which will hold six or seven rifles. From this point the ground on every side can be swept....

18th June All hands off to work early this morning. Jephson took his company off to get wood for the *Stanley*. Nelson and Parke ransacked the adjoining villages and brought in great quantities of firewood from huts, etc. Jameson doing odd jobs such as storing firewood, gathering poles, etc.[...]

20th June All hands off after wood again and by 10:00 a.m. we brought in our wood and stowed it on board the *Stanley*. Shortly before noon, the *Stanley* [set] off. We all stood on the bank and saw the last of her. Well, Nelson and I have spent some pleasant days on the old *Stanley,* with tables, chairs, and plenty of books.... One feels a pang at losing her and her jolly skipper, Shakastrom, and [her] engineer, De Manis. Good luck to them and may they return swiftly up-river again with the rest of our stores and men.

All went off in the afternoon again for more wood for the *Peace* and [the] *Henry Reed.* We got ten days' wood for the *Stanley,* a pretty large order. I have a slight fever.

21st June All cutting firewood. My fever is getting worse daily. This standing about in the manioc fields and out in the sun looking for wood is very trying. Wadi Mtete, one of our chiefs, came in with two fowls and some fish. This is all we have. This is the anniversary of the founding of Halifax, N.S.[5] What a day they will be having of it out there! How everyone will rush off trout fishing and then set fire as usual to the bush and burn up several square miles of good timber!

22nd June Wet and miserable. All still at firewood. I came into breakfast at 11:00 a.m., after a long talk with Stanley about the non-arrival of the *Henry Reed*. At last he decided to send me off tomorrow morning with the *Peace* and thirty Zanzibaris, ten days' provisions, and firewood and start down the Aruwimi and up the Congo to search for the *Henry Reed*. His suspicions as to the cause of delay were the following: (1) Tippu Tib might have seized the steamer at Stanley Falls and made the whites prisoners; (2) the Soudanese might not or could not cut enough firewood to keep the steamer going; (3) the Soudanese might have mutinied and shot Barttelot; (4) the steamer might have got on banks, rocks or been delayed owing to fights with natives.

I was to have gone as far as Stanley Falls if necessary. However, at 5:30 p.m. the *Henry Reed* rounded the bend below camp and came on and in half an hour was made fast and we learnt everything. They had trouble with natives, also with getting wood and were delayed half a day at [Stanley] Falls. Tippu Tib landed and was at first fired on. Soon, however, his friends recognized him and there were great rejoicings.

The Arabs have been burning and pillaging a great number of villages up-river, taking all the men and women as slaves to exchange for ivory which they take to Zanzibar. The *Henry Reed* brought down a cow, a present to Ngalyema, the chief at Stanley Falls. Our men were attacked once when cutting firewood and one boy was wounded. I believe Tippu Tib's men killed six or seven and the village was burned and manioc destroyed, so the natives learnt a lesson, I have no doubt. Slight fever today—temperature 103°.

23rd June All hands but the major and Jameson out after firewood. This is the last day's cutting for which all are most thankful.

24th June Both steamers (*Peace* and *Henry Reed*) got away between six and seven o'clock this morning. Thus we have seen the last white men till we reach Emin Pasha.[...]

MR. STANLEY AND HIS GALLANT COMRADES "IN DARKEST AFRICA"; MASAI WARRIORS IN THE REAR.

Stanley and his comrades with Masai warriors in the rear.

(contemporary illustration from *The Penny Illustrated Paper*)

CHAPTER 3
YAMBUYA TO
UGARROWWA'S

25 JUNE—18 SEPTEMBER 1887

The advance column proceeds up the Aruwimi River. The shortage of food poses complications. Frequent attacks are made on the column by the local population. Stairs is struck by a poisoned arrow at Avisibba. The advance column arrives at Ugarrowwa's settlement. Sick members of the caravan are left behind.

On the 24 June Stairs developed a fever and became so weak that he had to be carried when the column set out on its journey. Between the 25 and 27 two Sudanese died.

28th June All were ready to start at 7:00 a.m. and soon after this the order to march was given. We all said goodbye two or three times to Barttelot and Jameson and started off on our march of sixty days through the "unknown." I started very badly, having to be carried in a hammock. We made 7 miles today and camped in a small village out of which Stanley had just driven the natives. Two of our men were wounded. We made a *boma*, placed sentries and turned in.[...]

For the next five days Stairs continued to be carried in a hammock. The first of July was his twenty-fourth birthday and he recorded in his diary that at this time last year he was in Canada. Three days later we read that he felt "a good deal stronger."

9th July We left this morning at 7:10 in the boat and canoe. The pioneers left at 6:40. Nelson was in advance and Jephson brought up the rearguard. We in the *Advance* [1] went on up-river on our own account, stopping at five or six different places, looking for *mahogo*. However, though there was plenty, it was too small and we gave it up as a bad job. Stanely went far up the river exploring, and at 12:10 we met him on his way down and came down with him. We met the main column at 11:30. We then kept close to the column and stopped at 2:30 in the upper of three villages. I slept in one of the natives' conical huts and was very comfortable.

I am gradually getting stronger going in the boat every day, but my legs and arms are still very thin and my face bones are sticking out almost through the skin. In three or four days I hope to go on with my regular work. There is plenty of corn and *mahogo* in the village we are camped in, and our men have tremendous blow-outs every night. We whites have *mahogo* greens, *mahogo* cakes, and corn, and sometimes rice for grub, but no meat of any sort.

10th July Cutters left the village at 5:50 a.m., the main column following soon afterwards. Left in the canoe and [the] *Advance* at 6:30. Arrived at 10:00 at a large collection of villages and stopped till 1:30, when the column came up. I saw Parke for a few minutes. We then made up-stream for 800 or 900 yards and beached the boat, took out all her loads and marched on to camp about half a mile off in a large straggly village. The boats afterwards passed up over a baddish rapid. We saw three canoes with natives in them; evidently they were watching us, so Stanley fired half a dozen shots at them. They disappeared behind a small island and made for the shore.

The river is much rougher here. There are more islands; the rapids and rocks are more numerous and the channels tortuous.[...]

11th July Left village about 6:30 a.m. and marched half a mile to a village situated on a hill from which we got a good view of the river. We sent out men to capture what canoes they could. They came back after two hours or so with one fairly good one. Other men brought up the boat and canoes over the bad rapids between the two villages. I issued hoes and spades to my company and had a look at some of the rifles. Farag Ala, one of my boys, is suffering from a sore leg and is quite useless. He foolishly upset a kettle of boiling tea over his leg and in a day or so all the skin came off. Now the sore is turning to an ulcer as usual. Almost every Zanzibari has sores of some sort, while many have sore feet from treading on the *machongo* or sharpened sticks of the natives. I am feeling much stronger today. Parke shot half a dozen pigeons in the afternoon and we had a most excellent meal off them.

12th July Away in the *Advance* at 6:30 a.m. Stanley in one canoe, Somalis in another, and one other manned by Zanzibaris. The cutters left at 6:10 and the main column about 6:20. After half an hour's paddling we saw three canoes full of natives making for the village we had just left. We pulled up at 11:00 in a small village on the south bank for grub. Parke and Jephson came up and we had breakfast together. We left the village at 12:10 p.m. [sic] and made up-stream, stopping at 3:05 in the bush and pitched tents. The cutters came in about 3:50. Am gradually getting stronger I think day by day, though even yet I am pretty thin and weak. Strange to say we see no villages on the right or north bank, not one for miles below Yambuya. Made about 8½ miles today.[...]

The period between 13 and 20 July was rather uneventful. The progress of the column was often interrupted by torrential rains. On the fifteenth, Stairs noted that one of the soldiers had been put in chains for losing a rifle and was ordered by Stanley to be kept so for one month.

21st July We started off today about seven o'clock, Stanley going with the cutters, Nelson in advance and I in [the] rear. I tried to catch some natives by hiding twenty or thirty men in the village [which] the column had just left. We lay in the grass without stirring or making the slightest noise for half an hour when four canoes made for the village, and after a good look round three of them came ashore directly opposite the village. Presently three men well armed with spears and shields crept up to have a look about the village to

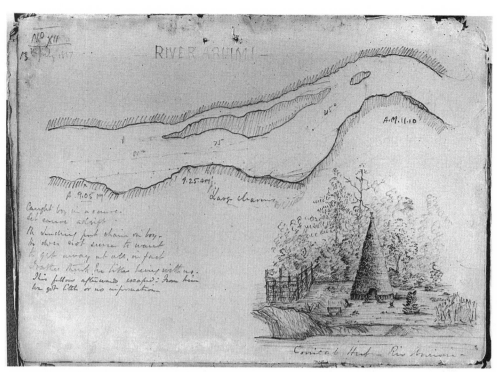

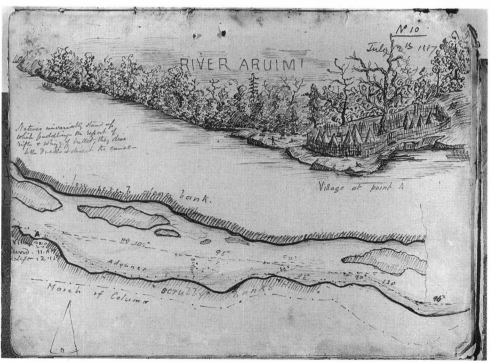

Sketches of the Aruwimi River and scenery by W. G. Stairs

find out if all was quiet. From our hiding places, we watched their movements and were almost making for them when one ass of a chief of ours showed his head over the side of a hut and a native, being quite close, poised himself for throwing his spear. This fool immediately got in a terrible funk and commenced to yell for help. Of course, the other two Washenzi heard the noise and made for the river like lightning. We dashed after them, but they dived into the river along with a lot of other natives who had just come up, and we lost them. We had a few pot shots at them in the water, but our object was to catch men to derive information from about the country ahead, not to kill [them]. One or two men who could tell us how far from the river the bush extends, what sort of country lies ahead, etc., would be invaluable.

Two of our men who went out early yesterday to get *mahogo* had not returned to camp when we left this morning. One of them, Charlie, belonged to Stanley's company, the other, Mousa bin Juma, belonged to Nelson. They both had their rifles with them, poor chaps, but probably had put them down on the ground to pluck the roots and were stabbed from behind by the natives who watch our every movement. This will be a lesson to the other Zanzibaris, who in future will go for food in bands of six or seven and thus run less chance of being surprised. The warning, however, will soon fade away I'm afraid, as our men are so reckless of their doings and have by this time acquired the most supreme contempt for the Washenzi.

We marched along the river bank for three and one-half hours and decamped in a village at a bend in the river ahead to the north. There are reports that an Arab caravan [is] ahead of us, entrenched in a strong *boma*. Certainly the Arabs may be there but not sitting still in a *boma*; this is not their way of going through a country such as this is, where the natives keep so far away from the noise of guns.

Late at night we heard shots and about midnight the three lost men turned up. They had been wandering about in the bush, scared to show themselves on the back track lest the natives should find them out.

22nd July The men that came in last night were punished and put in irons. We left camp about 7:00 a.m. and after marching about two hours, we came to five or six small villages connected up with each other by a good track. One of the villages the natives apparently had just left as a great many things had been left behind. Parke caught a native woman and child. I got a few odds and ends, but one finds it difficult to carry them along. From these small collections of huts, tracks led back into the bush, evidently to other villages. We saw plenty of tracks and fresh signs of elephants and also a good many pitfalls neatly set by the natives for elephants and deer.[...]

23rd July Left camp about 6:30 a.m. Jephson in advance, I in centre, Nelson rear, and Parke rearguard. Had good marching all the morning, passing several small villages. The boat's crew captured a good-sized canoe and four fowls, besides a long sword-shaped knife, some ivory, and one or two other things. We stopped for grub in a small village close to the river at 11:30. Stanley reached this place about one hour before. We had come 6 miles since 6:30. Stanley's donkey [and] Nelson's and Parke's donkeys all fell into elephant pits and had to be yanked out. Jephson also walked into one but did not hurt himself. They are covered over with bush very skilfully. We marched 2 miles after breakfast and reached camp about 5:35 p.m.—a grassy flat, the site of an old village. Placed sentries, had a big vegetarian blow-out and turned in.[...]

During the next four days the column made steady but uneventful progress.

28th July Just a month since we left Yambuya. Jephson led today, getting away about 6:30 a.m. My place was in the centre. We made about 6 miles by noon; had breakfast and went on till 3:00 p.m. Jephson had some adventures with Washenzi and captured a man and a boy. He had a spear thrown at him, but it went wide of the mark. Parke also brought in a native who will be very useful to us. He says the river goes away to the SE, and that the bush ends about two days (our marching) back from the river, and that the country there is all one large grassy plain, without villages or paths of any sort. Two days from here up-river he says a large branch river empties itself into the Aruwimi.

29th July Started away about 6:30 a.m., the doctor leading, Jephson in rear. We stopped at 10:40 for breakfast and then had made 4 miles, Stanley being half [a] mile ahead. We started off again at 12:00 and marched till about 1:45 when we came on Stanley who was clearing bush for camp. The rain came down in torrents soon after; luckily, we had our tents all up and were secure. A good many natives came to our camp to buy and sell, but they seem to have very few fowls and never bring us goats. Towards evening we issued *matako* (brass rods) and *cowries* (small sea shells) to the men: one *matako* for two days and three shells per man. Stanley intends stopping here tomorrow to allow the men to get food from the natives. The Aruwimi here seems to be about the same size as at Yambuya, or about 500 yards broad. Now and then we see grassy islands, signs of grass up-river. Almost all the villages are now on the other side of the river.

30th July Stayed in camp. The natives began to come to sell corn, *mahogo,* and fowls about seven o'clock. Very soon the prices ran up and they asked one *matako* for three Indian corns and soon after three and four *matakos* for one fowl. This, of course, we could not give. The men were giving clothes, buttons, empty cartridge cases, knives, anything to get food. Stanley went up-river in the boat to have a look about and came down to camp shortly after 11:00 a.m. Stanley made a plan to seize one of the natives, which was that ten men should offer cloth, beads, etc., to the natives and entice a canoe in and then grasp five or six healthy individuals and make them prisoners. The plan succeeded in that one man was caught. This fellow I put in chains almost at once and Stanley succeeded in getting a lot of information out of him. As soon as the men seized this unfortunate, all the natives commenced to yell with funk and rage and paddled about close to our camp for half a minute or so. All of a sudden Stanley fired a shot into the air. Like lightning, every man, woman, and child dived into the water and swam off in every direction down-stream like so many wild ducks. Besides the native, we captured two canoes. The specimens we have caught so far are very fine looking men of [about] 5 feet 8 inches, well shaped and with powerful muscles in the arms and back developed by the use of the paddle.[...]

31st July Raided the village opposite and got great quantities of corn, *mahogo,* etc. No fowls or goats. We got also three or four canoes. I got a spear from one of our men, some poisoned arrows, etc. I stayed in camp to look after things. All the others went. We gave our donkeys good feeds of grass and Indian corn and I husked three bags of corn for us to take on the road. We also got twelve tusks of ivory of all sizes and one ivory horn. Some of the tusks must have weighed 60 pounds. During the firing yesterday, some five or six natives were disabled and three were killed. Nelson followed the tracks of goats for a long time but with no success. The natives took off most of their things last night.

1st August A day of great rejoicing; all of us had good feeds of corn and *mahogo*. We made rather a short march, Nelson in advance. About 3:00 p.m. we pitched our tents in the bush and made ourselves comfortable. This morning I buried in the river the eleven tusks of ivory we captured yesterday.[...]

2nd August One of Jephson's men died this morning and was buried near the camp. Stanley went on in the boat and we caught him by lunch time. They had some bad water to pass through. In the afternoon he went on far ahead of us, and [...] we were left far behind. Parke was leading and kept us on the move till 6:30. We then had to stop in the bush all night without tents or boxes. Luckily, some of us had blankets. These we shared. Getting a fire started, we made some soup out of a soup tablet we had with us and then turned in. We were twelve hours today on the march, this through thick bush with very bad tracks is quite enough for most fellows. Late in the night we heard two shots in the direction we supposed Stanley to be. They seemed to be a long way up-river.

3rd August Away early and soon caught up to Stanley. Parke [was] in advance. I had a slight attack of fever and had a rough time of it getting along. We made camp about 4:30, and on nearing it were welcomed with the news that the boat had captured two goats.

Just fancy how pleased we must have been, gentle stranger, after marching long rough marches for thirty days without one mouthful of meat to at last sit down to a chop and some soup. Ah, those who have not been without meat for a month on hard work cannot know what its absence means. Today we are all smiles and full of hope. Yesterday we were grumpy, surly, and despondent—this all on account of the gentle goat.

Two of Jephson's men strayed away from camp yesterday. They came in this evening and got 180 each with good sticks. This is the only way to prevent our men straying away and getting killed by the natives. We lose the rifles. In this country our rifles are our lives. Our camp is opposite a large village. This we looted but only got a little corn and some odds and ends.

4th August A day of accidents. Soon after the flotilla and column had started, my double canoe upset in 12 feet of very swift water. Some fifteen rifles, fifteen boxes of ammunition, five boxes of *cowries,* three of beads, and a lot of sundries went to the bottom. We rigged up a canoe, got what good divers we could collect (as the column was far in advance of the canoe before we could do anything) and started to work. Hassan, a Somali boy, did splendidly. We tied a rope round his waist and he took another under water with him. This one he tied to the boxes. The men in the canoe then pulled him up and afterwards the box he had secured. It was perfectly astonishing to see the way he worked under water in such a swift current. One Zanzibari got up a box and rifle, but none of the others could do anything, though we tried as many as ten.

We knocked off work at 5:00 p.m. and had then got eleven boxes and five rifles. Darkness soon came on and we had a bad time of it. We were delayed an hour at a river through not being able to find the crossing Jephson had made in the morning. After crossing, which we did at nine o'clock, we lost the track several times and finally pulled up in camp at midnight. The cooks had some grub and we had dinner at once.

My fever was bad all day, several times I fancied I should have to knock under [sic] and go to camp. We had seventeen hours of rough work. Name of place Panga.[...]

5th August We are now a little over a third of the distance to Albert Nyanza. We have taken thirty-nine days to do this. A great many things have been against us. Perhaps first of all the difficulty we have had in obtaining food for the men. This has, at times, been very great and has delayed us ten days at the very least. The long time we have taken to do, say, 240 miles, however, is no criterion as to the time we shall be doing the whole journey as perhaps soon we may get into open country and be able to do 15 miles a day. Late in the evening I issued out a cup full of corn (Indian) to every man in the expedition. This is the corn we Europeans hoped to make many a dish of porridge out of, but our men were very badly off for food and so of course it could not be helped. Jephson saw a hippo and crocodile today—a wonder as we have seen no crocodiles in the river for 800 or 900 miles. To bed after a long chat and [a] smoke over a fire made between our tents.

6th August Away early. Marched to camp at the end of the track I cleared yesterday. As soon as we had made things a bit square we all started off to pull the canoes the rest of the distance and got all to still water by 10:00 a.m. Jephson and I then went back to yesterday's camp and brought over the *Advance*. We carried her over on the shoulders of fifty men, reaching camp soon after noon. Stanley went up-river then in the boat and was away three and one-half hours. He saw two villages, both on islands, but got nothing. All the natives had fled, as usual, taking everything with them. Nelson took fifty men from his company. I gave him 50 more and Parke took 100. They went out in different directions to look for food, but only got some *mboga* and wild fruit. Our men will starve soon, if food does not turn up. The river ahead looks smooth, but there is a large rapid 3 miles up.

Jephson and I got all the canoes ready for the water and pushed them in so that tomorrow we can make a start. As usual in the evening, I placed the sentries for the camp, and we all gathered then round our fire and yarned [sic] till pretty late on in the night. How, at times, we prospect [sic] as to what is going on at home, where our people are, and if any of them are dead, and so on. Arguments we, of course, have—and many.

Parke sweeps the tray for sheer bullheadedness, though Jephson pushes him closely. What surpasses everything, though, is the way in which we quarrel with the cooks. They are the greatest blackguards one could find anywhere. Marazonku, the head cook, knows little enough about cooking; all the under-sweeps fight him, we fight him, while he lies and grows fat on our miserable pittance of food. Truly, cooks are strange animals.

7th August Marched away early. I in advance with five *Rugga Rugga*. We marched 1½ miles by 8:30 a.m. and stopped opposite a village on an island. Here the loads were put down to wait for the canoes, which having struck bad water, were delayed. Unfortunately, Jephson's canoe got [hit] broadside on and striking a tree capsized. All the men were thrown into the water and had a rough time of it for about ten minutes. Eleven rifles went to the bottom. These Stanely decided to recover and put two divers to work. By 3:30 they had got up nine out of the eleven and Stanley and the canoes came on. In the meantime, at 11:30 I left with my cutters and marched up-river, the loads following as Stanley would not put loads in the canoes.

We reached the foot of the next big rapid by 1:30, being 4 miles above [the] camp of this morning. I put men to clear a camp and started all the cutters at making a road round the rapid for the canoes. By 5:30 we had cleared about 400 yards. Stanley and Jephson reached camp about 5:00. The rapid ahead is about three-quarters of a mile long, but perhaps we shall not have to cut all this distance as there is a small branch river up which we may be able to pass the canoes.

I wonder what they are doing at home now. Playing tennis, drinking gallons of tea, and eating cakes by the score as usual, I should say. Now is the season for the wily sea trout in the streams of Nova Scotia and New Brunswick. Many a fisherman will now be driving out to some farmer's house, away by the side of a sparkling stream as happy as the day is long, dreaming as he drives along of the many fish he has taken out of such-and-such a pool he passes by on the roadside. Oh, those are the times one feels oneself, nothing to think of but your rod and gear, with a good chap beside you of kindred spirit, yarning [sic] of old times and the different places you have fished together.

Gentle angler, there's nothing like being far away in the quiet bush beside a stream in which you know there are good fish. Upon my word, I would sooner be back far away in the Nova Scotia bush, camping out and trout fishing, than engaged in any single other sport or pleasure I know of. Look at the happy days Walter, Jack, and I have spent[2] at the Sambro Lakes, at Preston, at the Magdalen Islands, Musquodoboit, and scores of other places.[3] Why they are the best days of one's life, and ones we all will look back on with feelings of pleasure as long as we live. Well, enough of this, back to Africa and the gentle twistings of the Aruwimi and to our friends the Zanzibaris and Somalis.

8th August All started to work early this morning: I to finish the road for the canoes, Jephson to get the boat across, and Parke and Nelson [to get the] canoes [across]. We finished our road by ten o'clock and then started moving on some of the men to the head of the rapids to pitch camp. The other fellows had finished their work by three o'clock, the boat getting over by about 12:00. Stanley at once went up-river in the boat and returned late in the evening. He captured twelve goats and reported a collection of villages up-river with plenty of food for our now nearly starved men. He showed me some most curiously shaped knives that the men brought him, shaped almost as a sickle, with a very keen edge. They are most formidable weapons.

We were all tired with our day's work and turned in early. Stanley reports river ahead [is] smooth.

9th August We put the canoes all shipshape last night and all started at 6:45 a.m. to march on to the villages Stanley had visited last evening. Nelson was in advance, I [was] in rear. A sick Somali and [a sick] Zanzibari delayed us in rear for two hours, so that we did not reach the village till 2:30. Nelson and the others had been here some time and Stanley, arriving first, found some eight goats hidden about in the bush. These we issued to the men as rations, in addition to some bananas. There is very little food close at hand though tomorrow we hope to be able to get *mahogo* for the men and ourselves. *Mahogo* is the staple food of the natives all along this river and the Congo. With us it means everything: if we strike plenty of *mahogo,* our men feed up and march well; if we get none for five or six days, they go down at once.

The village we are in is quite different in style to those we have been passing for the last six weeks or so. The conical hut has gone out of fashion and the square or rectangular hut has come in. The village is surrounded with a strong *boma;* in addition to this, each hut has a strong heavy wooden *boma,* for what purpose I cannot say. In most of the houses (which are built very low) there are two rooms: one [is] for sleeping in and the other [is] a day room. I should say in this village there are about 150 huts and only one of them is conical.

The *Rugga Rugga,* while passing through a clearing today fired on some natives and killed one, a man of, say, thirty years of age. A goat strayed away from camp this afternoon and men were sent to search for it. These men found the goat with its head cut off and three Zanzibaris preparing for a feast. They were brought up before Stanley and got a very heavy dose of the rod.

10th August The name of this village is Uturi. Yesterday morning the natives sallied out to fight those in the next village [that is] a day from here up-river. The battle finished and having killed five of their enemies, the [natives] returned to seek their couches and have a good feed, but the white man in the meantime had stepped in with 350 fighting men; the poor native [sic] sheered off to make room.

I took 100 men, viz., 50 of No. 1 and 50 from my own company and started off back in the bush to look for food. After we had been away for three hours, or so, we captured a woman; with her was a man. This chap let fly two arrows at one of my men, one going clean through four thicknesses of tough leather of his ammunition pouch—one inch higher, and the chap would have been a deader [sic]. The native then ran and our men pounced on the woman. As she seemed to know where food was to be found, we brought her to camp and with the help of Binza (Mukir's old boy) we learned that no *mahindi* or corn was to be got here at all; that one day up-river there was plenty of food: *mahogo* and goats in any quantity. Of the big lake the other natives had told us about, this woman knew nothing, or rather she boldly affirmed there was no such thing as a lake anywhere near us and further that no large branch river entered the Aruwimi on either side. Some one of these natives has been lying on a truly grand scale.

Today gives one a good idea as to what life in an African village is like. The burning hot sun shooting down its rays into every nook and corner forces [everyone] indoors; some talk and smoke; mostly [everyone] sleep[s] away the hottest hours. On one side I hear the squalling of the baby of the captured woman, on the other, the infernal, incessant bleating of a nanny goat. All life, except that of insects, seems to be at a standstill outside the village. The very wind has gone down to allow the sun to work up to its full blast. The birds have all gone to seek the shades of some favourite tree. Everything is hushed. One often feels how dependent on our rifles we are at present: 1700 or 1800 miles up from the west coast, 1300 [miles] from the east, and right in Central Africa, with 1000 miles of bush on one side and the almost unknown on the other. A chap feels that rifles will play a very important part in the future.[...]

On 11 August the caravan passed a village called Ngwedi.

12th August Parke took 100 men, and I took 90 more and started off to scour the country for food. We went in the same direction for two or three hours. I then struck away to the east of a large track while he went straight on. We got plenty of bananas, a little sugar cane, some melons, and tobacco. We failed to find any traces of *mahogo*. The old woman, our guide, has turned out to be a liar. Parke threatened to cut her throat and give her to the men to eat. She was terribly frightened at this and then took them to a very good banana plantation.

Parke got back to camp about three o'clock and I came in an hour later. Stanley reached the camp about nine o'clock this morning and said that they had to pass thirteen rapids and had come 12 miles by water since yesterday. On nearing camp we passed on the track the body of Suedi Randani, one of my men who had evidently been foully murdered. The doctor brought the body to camp where we buried it. This murder has caused a great stir in the camp; all the men are keen on finding out the murderer. Stanley offers £100 reward for any evidence which will convict the murderer.

Another of my men failed to turn up in camp this evening. He was seen last on the march yesterday and complained of dysentery. This makes another gun lost to me. His name was Hassan Wadi Bakaran—a rather poor specimen of a man, one who was always sick when there was any work to be done. We were able to give each man tonight ten plantains and three pumpkins—not so bad. One of the Soudanese soldiers was lost on the march yesterday. He has not turned up as yet and most probably has been caught and cooked by the natives. We left a sick man of Jephson's company in a hut at Uturi. He was wasted away to nothing and would probably die in an hour or so. The pumpkins we got were quite small but very good eating.

13th August Left camp about 7:00 a.m. with the object of making a large village some 4 miles ahead. I was leading in place of Jephson who has a bad foot. On nearing the village we met some Washenzi, one of which we shot. After we had settled down in camp and made ourselves comfortable, Stanley sent off some men to search for food. While crossing a small river near the village (in the boat) these men were attacked by a large mob of natives armed with spears and bows and arrows. At once our men opened fire, but the natives stood. Hearing the noise, I rushed down with my rifle to try a shot or two. The arrows were being rained down on us, we dodg[ed] them behind trees and [behind] the boat. I had fired two shots, the second of which killed a man, when I was struck in the chest with a poisoned arrow, the arrow breaking and leaving about once inch of the point inside. The wound is just below my heart. The doctor says no vital spot has been touched, but perhaps the tip had entered the pleura. The sensation at first was that of a knife being stuck into one. Shortly afterwards my side stiffened and acute shooting pains set in in my back and sides. Of the evening, under morphia and opium, I remember nothing.

14th August Five men not turning up from yesterday's raid for food, it was decided to send out a party to search for them. Accordingly, Nelson took fifty men and went after them. They all returned to camp by 9:30, the lost men having wandered about in the bush till they struck the trail at the camp of two days ago. We then at noon struck camp and made [our way] up-river.

Once more I am travelling by river, this time in the big canoe. My wound is very painful today. Last night I got no sleep at all, owing to the shooting pains running through my back and chest. In the fight this morning and [in] that of yesterday, our men killed some fifteen natives. We, in turn, had about five wounded with poisoned arrows, some of the bad cases. The natives here have shown unusual pluck, even after they had learnt the hurtful power of our rifles. At first—at the time I got hit—they stood up in the open glade, fired their arrows and then would dart like lightning behind some bush or tree and then again emerge, each time taking deliberate aim at us and being exposed to our fire, every minute growing hotter. Gradually, however, they learnt, as man after man was wounded, that the rifles hurt as well as spoke [sic], and so [they] grew more careful in their movements.

The column marched off at noon, Jephson in advance, with orders to "halt on the river bank at 2:30 p.m. and wait for the canoe and boat," and then commenced what afterwards turned out to be the most careless piece of bungling that has yet taken place. With the

Lieutenant Stairs wounded with an arrow

(contemporary illustration from *Penny Illustrated Paper*)

column were many sick and weak men, while in the flotilla we had thirty-eight or forty. Well, we in the canoes and boat camped in the bush at 3:00, and by night no signs of the column were to be seen. I suffered a good deal while many hit with arrows are growing rapidly worse.

15th August Got ready to start off in the canoes by 6:30 a.m. but waited an hour or so to see if the column might come up. No signs, however, and on we went. We paddled on till noon, nearly, passing a largish village close to the river and then made camp in the bush, on a high bank close to some banana trees. As we passed along the river bank we watched closely for signs of the blazes on the trees, but no, the *Rugga Rugga* had not passed by. All afternoon we were anxiously looking out for the erring ones, but by night they had not turned up. What can be the matter? Have they lost themselves? Have they had a fight with the natives and got scattered? Where in the mischief are they? This is what Stanley and I said to each other as we talked things over in the evening. Our sick (of course, the very worst ones are carried in the canoes) are getting worse, the wounded men commence to experience agonies as the deadly poison from the arrow tips works this way through their systems. One or two with bad ulcers are doomed, I'm very much afraid, to early deaths. Across the river from our camp is a large village hidden from us by thick trees, but [it is] well marked and easily located by the infernal yells and horns of the savage inmates. I dread the night very much. I am tonight sleeping on ammunition boxes; my blankets and everything else are behind with the column. One consolation is that one can smoke.[...]

During the subsequent ten days Stairs spent sleepless nights sitting up in a chair suffering from acute pain. The health of those who were wounded with poisoned arrows rapidly deteriorated, and their final hours of agony were frightful. Two died on Friday, 19 August, and Stairs began to dread that the same fate awaited him because the head of the poisoned arrow was still buried in his chest.

The column encountered many bad rapids and the loads had to be carried overland. Its progress was also delayed by frequent torrential rains. Stairs's donkey died on the march because of the lack of sustaining food; the loss was a great blow to him.

26th August Had heavy showers early this morning and did not get away till after seven o'clock. Today the water was smooth and we made good time.[...]

27th August Stayed in camp all day. Luckily, we got a fine, bright sunny day, allowing us to dry all our clothes again. One's things are all mildewed from being so long in the damp bush. I cleaned the Maxim gun up thoroughly and fired some twenty or thirty rounds at some howling natives on the opposite bank.[...] This long dreary bush march now of nearly two months—day after day through rivers by scores and with food in scanty supply—is taking the very lives out of the men. One notices that every day the number of sick men becomes greater, and very few who get in poor condition survive. A few days' halt does wonders, especially if the halt is in a village, for there the men have a roof over their heads at night, food and firewood are near, and their general comfort is much greater than in a wet bush camp. One wet cold night in the bush takes it out of the men far more than a heavy day's march. The number of men with bad ulcers on their feet is astonishing. Why, I have eighty-three men in my company, and I should say quite thirty-five of these have bad feet. Five of my company have died or been lost since leaving Yambuya.

We have lost three donkeys, and now Nelson's seems [ready] to die. My boy, Farag Ala, who was scalded by upsetting a kettle of hot tea over his leg some forty days back, has had to be carried in the canoes ever since. The sore turned into an ulcer, gradually spread over his leg and made him a horrible sight. I have taken a Somali boy, one of the very few healthy ones left. His name is Hassan Miray, the chap who dived so well for us when my canoe was upset. He is a smart sort of boy and I hope will do well for me.

Late in the afternoon, some men carried into camp Juma, a very nice little chap of No. 1 Company, with a terrible wound in the foot caused by a bullet from a Winchester rifle some fellow had fired, accidentally or otherwise. All the ankle and foot bones were crushed to pieces. Parke found it necessary to amputate at the ankle joint. Poor chap, it must be a terrible blow to him.

Jephson got the big canoe as far as the top of the village by evening and had a very tough job as a lot of the men bolted away into some villages after loot and left him with only fifty-six men.

28th August Finished putting the big canoe down to the river where she was launched about 8:00 a.m. The column and flotilla then started; Parke in advance, Jephson in rear. Nelson was feeling very seedy and went in his canoe for a change. Just before starting, the rain came down in torrents, wetting us all through. It lasted till afternoon, then the sun came out and broiled us properly. At 4:00 p.m. we stopped for camp. We waited on till six o'clock without any signs of the advance guard turning up, when we heard a shot fired about a mile below us, evidently in the village we had passed about 3:00 p.m. We knew then that the column could not reach us tonight.

Nelson and I had only our wet rubber sheets and clothes to sleep in, and I, in addition, [had] a wet blanket. However, we got into the back part of Stanley's tent and somehow or other eked out the night. Moussa and some other canoe men who had wandered down to the village in search of loot returned about 7:00 p.m. with a note from Parke saying that he would make his camp for the night in the village.

Our food now consists solely of bananas cooked in different ways. The nicest way to my fancy is to roast them on hot coals, though done this way, they are not so good for one as those boiled. One eats eight or nine for each meal and then feels very much like a football afterwards. The absence of meat is more serious than most people would imagine.[...]

On the twenty-ninth an incident took place in which a native was shot after an unsuccessful attempt by Stanley to capture him. Next day, two of Stairs's men failed to turn up in the evening. Their disappearance was presumably not as grave in the eyes of the whites as the loss of the last box of biscuits that one of them carried.

31st August Struck camp by 6:30 a.m. Stanley took his company off up-stream to the head of a very bad rapid and made camp, the column following closely. The rapid turned out to be a very bad one. We found the canoes could just creep up along the opposite bank and then shoot across stream above camp and drop down to us. The boat, however, Stanley decided on taking overland. Parke brought her halfway and Stanely the rest.

My wound is much better, but still [I] can do no work and have a deadly pain at times under my ribs. Towards the evening we heard loud shouts in camp and rushed out to find what was the matter. We found some nine or ten Zanzibaris had been sent to us from one of Tippu Tib's parties fifty-strong [and] now camped some few miles up-river from us. It was a great surprise, this sudden meeting far in the interior of this huge forest. They told us they were of Balosi's caravan belonging to Tippu Tib, coming down the river in search for [sic] ivory. The party [has] fifty guns. They have been twenty days coming down in canoes and marching [for] thirty-six [days]. They came from Manyuema.[4] They made us a present of a goat, and after a palaver, [they] went back to their friends with best wishes. We shall meet them tomorrow we hope.[...]

1st September My double canoe failed to get over the rapid yesterday and had to be abandoned. The *baharia* all took loads this morning, and I expect [they] found this not so much to their taste as paddling their own canoe. Ten men went back again this morning to look for my man Juma and the box of biscuits—our very last box which we were saving till worse times came on us. We paddled on expecting to find signs of Tippu Tib's men but saw nothing of them, except where they had stopped for food in a village. At 11:00 a.m. we stopped at the foot of a bad rapid, and here Stanley decided to take the boat out of the water and travel overland, for what distance I do not know, or whether he will abandon the river for good. However, I expect his actions will depend on the nature of the river above this. It is hard to say what these eight or ten men that came to us yesterday are—whether they are runaways or not.

Nelson did not get in till late and was feeling very seedy; [he] had to lie down at once. It was found at night that three boxes of ammunition and one of salt had not turned up. As there were two or three suspicious signs of desertion on the part of two men, Stanley sent twenty of the *Rugga Rugga* back to look out for them and [to] try and capture them. I was at work all day—the first work I have done since 14th August—at lightening the Remington boxes by extracting sixty rounds from each. These will be carried by the men. Jephson was busy taking the boat to pieces. Nelson was so seedy that he could do nothing. We took all the rifles from the men as a precaution against desertion. All of us are more or less seedy at present; I fancy the banana has a great deal to do with it. Parke's amputation case seems to be doing well.

2nd September In camp all day. Late last night my lost man Juma turned up. His arrival was not reported to me, but Stanley merely gave him in charge of his camp-mate, a miserable wretched specimen of a man. Of course, this morning when we wanted to bring the men up to go back for the box, he was not to be found. We bound up the man Khamis who was charged with Juma's keeping, but Juma has escaped fearing punishment. I was at work all morning on the ammunition boxes; Jephson [was working] on the boat. Stanley was taken ill last night, but this morning was much better. He suffered from the same trouble as we did, viz., diarrhoea. Parke feels very seedy, his temperature was 104° today. The ten men returned with one man, a box of ammunition, three rifles, some hoes, and a spade that they found.

Late in the evening the *Rugga Rugga,* who were sent out last night to capture the deserters, returned having seen nothing of the men. At night, the whole four of us suffered from the effects of either bad water or improperly cooked bananas.

3rd September Struck tents early and had all the men fall in. We then found that two of Nelson's, three of Jephson's, and one of mine had not turned up. Most of them were sickly men, though probably some of them deserted. At 10:00 we made a start, after serving out the men with ammunition [and] up to twenty rounds per man. We marched on till 11:00 and then had our breakfast above the rapids. Nelson and Parke were in rear. The canoes and column went on and at 2:15 p.m., we pulled up for camp. Stanley marched all the way today, the first time for many a long day. Jephson started putting the boat together in the evening.

Our men are generally getting [in] very low spirit[s]. Already, waiting the last few days, we have lost eleven men through supposed desertion. Stanley has had all the *maniapara* up and given them long dissertations, and otherwise we have adopted every possible precaution. Still this state of affairs is bound to keep up as long as anything of the Arabs is to be seen. I have put no less than five men in chains—some of them [are] attempted deserters and others [are] men who threw down their loads.

4th September Had all hands up early, separated the effectives form the non[-effectives] and extracted the hammers from all non-effective men's rifles. We then started off, dividing the rearguard into two parties. Stanley went in the boat, I in [a] big canoe; Jephson in rear and Nelson in advance. About two o'clock we came to a baddish rapid and had to take the loads of[f] the boat and canoes. These were taken on to camp which was formed just above the rapids. A bag of No. 1 Company was missing this evening; some men were sent back for it.

The discontented feeling is growing among the men. No wonder: bad food, heavy loads, and then the long dreary marches through the bush, [with] the men doubting greatly that we shall ever get out of the bush. Placed another of my men in chains this evening for attempted desertion. He is rather a poor sort of chap and not the kind of man one would imagine a deserter.

5th September Struck camp and away early. All Nelson's loads in the canoes. Parke was leading. After an hour's march or so, Stanley halted the column and went ahead in [the] boat to look for a village. However, the only large village was too far ahead. Near us are two smaller villages and from these the men got a good many small bananas. We all did a few odd jobs about camp such as cleaning tools, rifles, and drying ammunition. The boat again went up-river to the large village and [the men] got two goats and a kid. Last night and this morning we only had two bananas each for our meals. These goats and new bananas will set us all up again.

The Somalis have broken down altogether; two are carried every day in the canoes and the others can barely get along from day to day. The Soudanese are very little better. They suffer very much from ulcers.

6th September Were delayed in starting for about an hour owing to the rain. One of Nelson's men died in the night. He had been carried for some time in the canoes. I marched today with the rearguard [and] Parke commanding. We had to carry three men and assist another. The heavy, cold rain made the men like so many flies. Jephson got into camp with the advance guard about four o'clock, whereas we did not [arrive] till six o'clock. The camp is just below a large cataract; over this we shall have to take the canoes tomorrow. The drop of this cataract would be about 7 feet, I should say, and the width 140 yards. One gets a very good idea of the river's volume from the cataract.

7th September Started getting the boat over the rapid after cutting rollers to place on the rocky bed, the distance the boat was, about 250 yards, and this the men did in about one hour. After this the canoes were all pulled over. The men are pretty badly off for food now; the bananas here are very poor ones.

My wound apparently is going to heal up altogether and leave the arrowhead inside. Parke thinks now there is no chance of it ever coming out. The way in which we are fed and looked after in this expedition is simply disgraceful. Stanley does not care a jot about our food as long as he is well fed. He never interests himself in his officers' behalf in any way. We come in wet after a long march [such] as yesterday and have then to pitch our tents—perhaps in the dark and rain—when all this time [Stanley's] men have been in camp, having come by river.

We were told in London that we should each have a canteen and candles at night. All nonsense and lies. Only one canteen large enough for three men was brought and one has great difficulties in getting a frying pan or pot out of this as over one-half of the utensils are used exclusively for Stanley. One never has a candle at night; for two months we have had just the light of a fire to sit by and smoke before turning in. Stanley has taken all the candles for his own tent. Why, there were not enough European provisions to last five men nine months. More fuss has been made about these, too, than the hanged things are worth. Fancy [a] one-pound tin of arrowroot being brought for the use of six people for six months! The committee of this expedition ought to be deuced for allowing so few provisions for six Europeans to be sent out and then not obtaining more at the Cape or on the Congo. Stanley, however, is far more to blame as he was far better aware of the state of affairs.

By noon we had finished getting all the boats and canoes over the rapid and launched them in still water above. Shortly after this, each of us—Nelson, Parke, Jephson, and I—took fifteen men from each of our companies and went up-river a bit, crossed over and went after bananas. After [a] four-hour search, [we] succeeded in getting a load for each man of very poor watery bananas. We passed through three small villages out of which the natives had decamped for some days. They were of the usual style, each hut encased in paling *bomas*. Nelson and I got some goodish tobacco close to one of the villages, but the average tobacco here is not worth curing. Nelson has finished all his English tobacco and now resorts to green native [tobacco] and biscuit paper for cigarettes. The boat's crew struck off up-river and brought in some splendid plantains. We secured a few good ones for the mess. Fundi Sudi, one of my men whom the rearguard had to carry yesterday, died this morning. He had one of the worst ulcers in his ankle [that] I ever saw. He had two others on other parts of his body and had wasted away to nothing. Salim Masoudi, another one of my men, failed to turn up last night. I am afraid he must have strayed off the path, intending to come on afterwards to camp and then lost himself or else become [sic] too weak to come. My loads [are] all in canoes.[...]

It was realized that the column had moved too far to the north, so it turned in the opposite direction following the course of the river, but had to cope with numerous rapids. The march was interrupted by frequent torrential rains. On 9 September a native woman was captured. In addition, some good bananas, a lot of cured leaf tobacco, and quantities of hemp (*ghang*) were found in a nearby village. The latter, because of its intoxicating effect, was promptly confiscated by the whites. A day later Nelson lost his donkey.

11th September The old woman Bim Juma caught is a most horrible looking hag. From her Stanley learnt of the cataracts ahead and also of the existence of high hills far ahead. I believe she also had heard that a party of Arabs was encamped some distance ahead. If this is true, I rather fancy we may leave some of our many sick with these people and thus relieve the expedition to a great extent.

We go in greatly now for smoking native tobacco. Sometimes we get it green and cure it ourselves. At others we get it already cured in the huts of the Washenzi. Bye-the-bye, "Washenzi" is the term given by the Zanzibaris to the cannibalistic natives of the interior. "Wangwana" is the term they give to free men, and "Watumwa" [is the term they give] to slaves.

12th September We started off as usual but much later owing to an inspection of the sick by Stanley. I started from Yambuya with a company of eighty-eight strong. This morning I had forty-nine men capable of carrying loads. Nine men have died or been lost. The other companies have suffered equally.[...]

On 13 September Stanley and Stairs shot two Africans and wounded two others who were quietly sailing in a canoe. The following day was spent in camp. No entry had been made for 15 September.

16th September Last night the rain came down in torrents for hours, flooding up every hole and cranny the water could find for itself. Nelson's and my tent was on the path in a hole. About midnight I was awakened by Nelson wandering about the tent in the dark in 24 inches of water and then found [that] everything was floating about in the tent and the water [was] within 2 inches of my bed. Luckily the water soon stopped rising and we just waited patiently till daylight to collect our scattered things. My watch was under water all night and is done for completely. My aneroid is very sick and two compasses refuse to turn on the pivots at all. Every book, knife, all my small things and clothes have been soaked. I lost some things in the water too, I'm afraid.[...] At ten o'clock [we] started off.

We are now 141 geographical miles from the point on the lake that Stanley intends striking. Our latitude is 1° 24' N and we want to make 1° 22' [N] on the lake. I was rearguard today and had fever all the time.[...] This fever is a frightful thing to take it out of one. One is strong and active in the morning and by night [one] may have to be lifted into bed, almost senseless. One of Nelson's men evaded the rearguard and escaped with a box of ammunition.

17th September Made an early start [with] Parke leading. Had a fairish track in the morning but bad towards afternoon. About 3:00 the rearguard came up to a fairly large river of, say, 40 yards wide. Over this we were ferried by Sua Tatu's and my canoe. Here we could hear the sound of much firing a short distance ahead and on coming up to the noise found it was a detachment of Arabs in our camp having a parley with Stanley. We had a long pow-wow of two hours or so and found out a great deal [about] the country we should have to go through ahead.

The name of the chief is Ugarrowwa;[5] his camp is one day up-river from here, on the other side of the river. Here he has about fifty guns and a good number of women. This is the headquarters of those nine or ten fellows who came to our camp some seventeen days back. They called it a twenty-day march and we have taken seventeen. The chief presented Stanley with three goats, 20 pounds of rice grown up-river, six fowls, and a lot of very fine ripe plantains. He went off to his camp in a very fine canoe, amidst the beating of drums, singing of women, blowing of horns, and the excited yells of his fat followers. Everyone seemed pleased; we had rice for dinner and turned in.

From this fellow we learned that another detachment of Arabs had occupied a village permanently some four or five days up-river and were occupied in getting ivory and improving this village as a standing camp. Twenty days farther ahead of this, was stationed a very large body of men with six hundred guns and [a] rich supply of cloths and goods. This party is on the edge of the bush and grass country, and game abounds in plenty, so we should be right for food when we get there. If Ugarrowwa speaks truly, then in thirty days we should once more see green grass and breathe fresh air after (by then) over 100 days, almost what may be called imprisonment in the bush. Reached [a] spot opposite Ugarrowwa's camp.

18th September Call [sic] all the men in early, weeded out the sick, took away their guns and prepared them for deposit at the Arab village. Stanley paid a state visit to Ugarrowwa, and William presented a clock later on. Everyone seemed delighted, except myself. After some work on repairing boxes, I put up my Maxim gun and got her ready for the formal visit Ugarrowwa was to pay us in the afternoon. About 12:00, just as we were having breakfast, we were startled by a loud report and then all of a sudden the Arabs burst forth from their village, letting off guns, beating drums and yelling like fiends. Presently the canoes stopped and the women commenced a very pretty chant keeping it up till they reached our landing place. Ugarrowwa then led the way to Stanley's tent and a long palaver ensued. They all then came down to where I had the gun mounted on the riverside and I fired 150 or 175 rounds off for their edification.[...]

Ugarrowwa was once a *pegasi* or porter on Speke and Grant's expedition up from Tanganyika to Victoria Nyanza. He is a great admirer of Speke's and says he was one of the finest hunters he ever met. He has the reputation of being very cruel, but most probably this is what has made him what he is at present. He can now muster three hundred guns, I believe, and is gradually working his way up to become a white-bearded old father whose name will be well known over all Central Africa.

In the afternoon, I took over to the village the fifty-eight sick men we are leaving behind us. I had a palaver with Ugarrowwa again, shook hands all round and started back to camp. I left at the village five Somalis, five Soudanese, and forty-six Zanzibaris. What a great relief this getting rid of the sick will be to us. All the old crawlers with rotten limbs who took six hours to do a two-hour march are gone.[...] Thank heavens, we who toil along day by day through rivers, swamps, and mud will have a little work thrown off our shoulders, and perhaps the column will make better marches to the promised land, "the grass country."

CHAPTER 4
FROM UGARROWWA'S TO THE "OPEN COUNTRY"

19 SEPTEMBER—3 DECEMBER 1887

The expedition leaves Ugarrowwa's camp. Nelson and fifty-six incapacitated men are left behind. The sick are left under the care of Parke upon the arrival at Kilonga Longa's. Jephson departs to bring back Nelson. The caravan leaves the sphere of Arab influence. The food situation improves. Jephson rejoins the column at Ibwiri and reports on the terrible plight of Nelson and his men. The open country is reached on 3 December.

19th September Farewell to the Arabs.[...] I was leading today and had very bad luck meeting big rivers and for three hours cutting my way through vines and scrub without any sort of track whatever. About 3:00 p.m. we got to a bad river and had to hail the canoes and get ferried across. We [...] camped at 4:30 having only made 5 miles. The flotilla came up shortly after this. The Arabs paddled 1½ miles up-river and said goodbye to Stanley there. Three of our men ran away today, went back to camp, were caught by the Arabs, got fifty each, were brought on to us and I made them fast to a tree for the night. Their names are as follows: Mabruki bin Ali, No. 3 Co., Johandu of my company, and Osemi of No. 4 Co. Desertions have been so numerous and threats of death so common, that if anything is done to these fellows it will be the rope.

20th September [...] The three condemned men were brought out, and Stanley addressed the men, telling them he would hang one today, one tomorrow, and one [the] next day. The men then drew lots and Mabruki's lot was cast for today. Accordingly, he was tied up and run up with the help of the prisoners in charge. He died without a struggle in two or three minutes. This is the first execution we have had. The example will prove of great value in preventing further desertions. All the chiefs agreed that it was good and of use.

This finished, we all started off on the march [with] Nelson in advance. The road being good we made 7 miles and camped as usual close to the river.[...] I made the remaining two deserters fast to trees for the night, placed the sentries and turned in. We had a violent thunderstorm towards evening, making us uncomfortable and [making] the men wretched in their miserable shelters.

21st September Osemi, one of the doomed men, escaped during the night. I at once put the soldier in charge of the man under guard and tied him to a tree. We all fell in again.

Mohandu the other man was brought out, tied, and the rope made fast round his neck. The men were all ready to hoist away when Stanley started away on a fiery speech, treating the great number of desertions that had taken place, the many times he had threatened to shoot men for losing loads, and the great importance it would be to us to have a large body of men to repel attacks in the open country: "I have come here not to lose men and ammunition, but am sent by one queen and two kings to rescue the *Muzungu*. Don't think I'm afraid to go on, even if you desert me. Said Barghash and the sultan of Egypt will say I have done well to kill this man," and so on.

The *Maniapara* then went in a body and asked him to forgive the wretched man. Stanley spoke a bit longer and then ordered the ropes to be cut. I'll bet this was the nearest shave Mohandu ever had.

Marched till 11:00, crossed the Lenda and camped.[1] We found a very good place for camp on a grassy bank overlooking the river, some men went off on the almost hopeless chance of getting food![...]

22nd September Off early this morning, all with empty stomachs and low spirits, Jephson leading. Probably never since we have left Yambuya have the men been so hungry and in such low spirits on the march. All along the road the same cry *"Njaa"* (I am hungry), or *"apana chakula"* (no food). Not a shout to be heard, just the slop-slop of the men's feet and complaints of being hungry and tired. We are little better of today, not having anything but a small bone for breakfast. This with three days before us. However, at 1:00 p.m. we met Stanley and camped. [We] learnt that there were a few bananas to be got on the other side of the river.[...] We got a few and cooked them at once and felt much better. Gentle stranger, perhaps you are not aware how it feels to be properly hungry, or still worse, to have men under you hungry and played out, with hard work to do every day. Well, it is not a pleasant sensation, I can tell you.[...]

23rd September Got away by 6:45 a.m. I, in advance, had very bad cutting for the first hour through a banana plantation, then struck fairly good tracks and made very good marching. About 11:00 we came to a small rapid and here met Stanley [... who] told us to go on to a village ahead. This we did and finding it deserted, [we] came on ahead. Soon after this I found a canoe and paddled up to camp at the foot of a very big rapid over which we shall never be able to get the canoes. The *Rugga Rugga* came in shortly after this.[...]

24th September Today we fell in as usual but did not march. Almost all the men were sent back to a banana plantation some 2 miles away to get bananas—poor chaps, they need them. The canoe crew and boatman we kept for work [to get] their canoes over or around the rapid. Stanley started by cutting a track round the rapid and making a rough survey of the channels. The fall of the rapid from top to bottom must be quite 40 feet, and this, say, in half a mile. A small rocky island lies about in the centre, dividing the water into two large channels. On each side of this the water tosses and tumbles in all directions, making a very pretty sight.[...]

Ulcers on the ankle bones soon take it out of the men. To add to this there is always the trouble and uncertainty of getting food. Men suffering from dysentery, of course, rarely get better, as there is no proper means of treatment provided, and the coarse rough food soon acts on their raw stomachs.[...]

Jephson and Stanley, who had been cutting the track for the boat and canoes, returned to camp about 10:30, having had an easy job as they found the Washenzi had been taking canoes over from time to time, and so had formed a track over which our boat should pass easily.[...]

We are now about 112 geographical miles from Kavalli on Albert Nyanza. I have made a rough map of the most interesting part of Africa, at least most interesting at present, and perhaps on it [one] will be able to trace the course of the Aruwimi; almost all this portion is in the Congo Free State, though in another twenty or twenty-five days we should have got over the border.[...]

25th September Got up early.[...] Some fate seems to be against our getting on; obstacle after obstacle comes in our way. First it is the almost total absence of food, next it is the rapids, then perhaps bad rivers to cross and masses of densely tangled brush to carve our way through. What is it that is acting against us? People in England no doubt are now supposing that we have long since arrived at the lake, relieved Emin Pasha perhaps, and started to take him out to the east coast. Why, even Stanley himself thought we should arrive in Wadelai by 16th July, and gave his thoughts expression in London before starting. But look how it actually is: we have taken ninety-odd days to get here, and have still thirty-five days [of] marching to do, supposing we strike open country in twenty days, as we hope; this would bring us to the end of October. According to all Arab reports we are still some fifteen days from the edge of the bush. From this, ahead there are five days of bad marching through some sort of cane brush, then we are told we are to reach grassy open rolling country abounding with game of all sorts. May these reports be true is the prayer of us all.[...]

On 26 September the march was again slowed down by several bad rapids. The gnawing pains of hunger were temporarily relieved when the column came across a small banana plantation.

27th September Picking five good men with billhooks and rifles I started off early to go up-river and report on the nature of the rapids and see if any food was to be got. I told all my chaps to be quiet and only blaze a tree here and there when necessary, as we might get a shot and perhaps return amid shouts to camp with some hippo or elephant meat, and [...] we nearly did.

While we were marching along quietly and quickly and had gone perhaps 1½ miles from camp, we reached a large elephant and hippo wallow quite close to the river. Mirabu who was behind me, gave a low whistle and beckoned violently to me to look in a certain direction he pointed out. For some time I could see nothing, but gradually, high over the small scrub, the shape of a very large elephant caught my eye. There he was—the big brute—not 15 yards from the track we had just passed over, standing perfectly still and watching every movement we made. I had only my .07 Winchester and a Remington military rifle. To use the Winchester would only tickle him, while the Remington, though of greater penetrative power, would do him but little harm unless a vital spot were hit. However, I took a Remington and sneaked up close, but he saw me and trotted off, turning his head around for an instant. I hit him slap in the side of the head and he bolted like a shot. I put one more bullet between his ribs as he disappeared. This was the first elephant. The next gave more trouble and nearly finished this child.

We found a herd of four or five feeding in the bush about a mile form where I fired at the first one. I sneaked up to one huge black chap busy feeding on the tops of small trees and got within 10 yards of him. I could see him from head to tail, utterly unconscious of my presence. Kneeling down, I put a Remington bullet slap into his side just below the tip of his ears and where the lungs and heart should be. For a few seconds he staggered a bit and then rushed into some thick scrub and vines and stopped. I again sneaked up to this spot to get another shot at him, but could not see him properly and was just moving to one side to get a better view when he gave out a fiendish yell and charged straight at me. I ran like a shot behind a big tree and had my rifle ready, but he stopped on his side, and I on mine [kept] quite still. He did not seem to know where I was and simply stood looking about with his huge ears straight out like a schooner coming down wing and wing [sic].

After ten seconds or so, in which I nearly died of funk, he turned sharply round and bolted into the bush and got away. It was a deuced near shave as he could have very easily put his trunk around the tree and squashed me flat. He must have been quite 12 feet high, and [he] had huge yellow tusks. The men ran like deer with the exception of Mirabu who also got behind a tree close to me, but for some reason or other did not fire. We marched on till 1:00 p.m., seeing fresh signs of elephant, hippo, deer, pigs, and buffalo but did not get a shot at anything else, though we heard buffalo crashing through the bush close at hand.[...] We got into camp at 5:40 and found the men had been most successful in getting bananas.[...]

28th September Away by 6:30 a.m., the canoes only taking the same number of loads as they had sailors. We on land had had a fair time of it, the only obstacle being the foot holes of elephants which, being filled with water, made the marching in places bad. In the canoes they had a regular field day of it: rapid after rapid had to be passed, [and] in places the bush along the bank had to be cut away to allow the boats to pass. They were in one place for three hours or so [and] had to fight for every inch they advanced. At 11:00 I, who was in advance, stopped for breakfast and went on in forty minutes.[...] About 3:30 we heard the natives pounding their cloth and bananas, and shortly after this we caught sight of some huts and saw the natives peacefully at work. We had no canoe nor could we find one. Stanley was far behind us and could not get up by dark. If the natives saw us, they would bolt taking everything with them. We had thus no means of cutting off their retreat from the opposite side of the island. I sent word to Stanley to send a canoe, if possible quickly, up the eastern channel to attack. The natives would then rush out on our side with their goats and everything while we, hidden in the undergrowth, would grab everything. For three hours we waited, till darkness was coming on.

At last, seeing no canoes could reach us today, I decided to fire on the village from three places: one at the top of the island to sweep the other channel, one at the bottom for the same purpose, and one directly where we were hidden. I opened the game by shooting one chap through the chest. He fell like a stone and was seen next day, stiff as mutton. Immediately a volley was poured on the village. At first the natives ran, but rallying, they peppered us well with their iron-tipped arrows [though] without effect. For some minutes we took pot shots at heads as they appeared above the grass and huts and [we] managed to drop a few more.

Gradually they made off one by one till all was quiet. At the bottom of the island, the doctor managed to drop two as they were making off in a canoe.[...] After all was quiet, some men swam across the channel, [that was], say, 75 yards wide, and ransacked the place. The only things they found were some spears, dried bananas, and smoked elephant meat. Stanley and all the canoes could not reach us and camped far down-river.[...]

It was most interesting, lying in the bush and watching the natives quietly at their day's work. Some women were pounding the bark of trees preparatory [sic] to making the coarse native cloth used all along this part of the river. Others were making banana flour by pounding up sun-dried bananas. Men we could see building huts and engaged at [sic] other such work. Boys and girls [were] running about, singing, crying; others [were] playing on a small instrument, common all over Africa—a series of wooden strips, bent over a bridge and twanged with the thumb and forefinger. All was as it was every day until our discharge of bullets, when the usual uproar and screaming of women took place.

Some must have reached the other shore by swimming as we only saw four or five canoes making away from the island. Our men shot very badly—one could see the splashes from the bullets in the water not halfway across the channel. It is a wonder no accidents occurred, as men were shooting when directly behind others. Pitched camp in the dark and turned in early after a feed of roast bananas.

29th September About nine o'clock Stanley turned up with the boat and landed on the island opposite to look at the scene of the recent battle. They found some bodies in the grass and saw a lot of blood in the canoes.[...]

30th September We had a great streak of luck this morning. I had just left the track with the intention of trying to get a shot at a hornbill or some other large bird and had gone perhaps 10 yards or so, when I saw a native elephant pitfall and looking down it saw a fine bush doe. We speedily cut her throat, dragged her out of the hole and cut the shoulder off for Jephson's and my breakfast. This was a great stroke coming as we are all almost starving.[...]

About four o'clock Jephson and I heard firing ahead, and after twenty minutes or so [we] came upon the camp and found that five Arabs had come down from their village some four days off to meet us. From them we learned something of the country ahead and found this information to tally pretty much with what Ugarrowwa's people told us. We are four days off from their camp, which they say is many days from the big Arab camp on the edge of the bush.[...] From their camp onward they say there is plenty of food to be had, and beyond the big camp, rice, *mtama,* and plenty of cattle and game.[...]

The Arabs brought a few bananas to sell, but no present for Stanley. They would only take cloth, of which we had none, so I got a man to give cloth while I gave him tobacco for the bananas. Stanley never bought one for us, though we are practically starving on one meal a day. After I had bought the bananas, the doctor went to Stanley and told him that the other three fellows were under an obligation to me for having used my own tobacco for food when Stanley himself should have bought it. Stanley offered Parke tobacco and told him to give it to me, but William, who was near, told him that I had plenty of tobacco, on which Stanley withdrew the tobacco and said, "Oh, then it's all right." Just fancy what a caddish thing to do. His not buying bananas for us at a very critical moment shows his meanness of character and is a breach of our agreement with him, viz., that he would provide us with a "due share of the native produce of the country." All along this has been disregarded by him, and one has to give shirts, tobacco, etc., to allay one's hunger.

For fellows working ten or eleven hours every day, trudging through mud and bush, wading over rivers, and urging on spent men, forty bananas of the sort we are now getting are none too many. Instead of this we get, on an average, twenty-five wretched little things with nothing in them. Of course, one cannot stand this long and has to buy bananas out of one's own tobacco or clothes. To people living, say, in England and used to big ripe yellow bananas, they would say, "Oh, thirty bananas should be quite enough to keep up a man's strength." Not at all. The average banana is almost 7 inches long with little or nothing in it and [it is] green, besides their having very little sustaining power. The expedition has treated us all disgracefully, both in the matter of native and European food. What we have got so far has been mainly owing to our own exertions.

Once more we find that Arab reports are not at all to be relied upon. They told us yesterday it was four marches to their camp ahead and after that many days on to open country. Today the chief coming in says it is four days right enough to his camp, but only five or six marches on to grasslands and game. Just fancy, if this be true, we should reach open country in 10 or 12 days from now, after over 100 days in the bush. To those who have worked in the bush for any time, this blessing will be apparent.

We must have made about 4 English miles today, after a heavy tramp through wet boggy elephant holes, and [we] were fairly well tired out on reaching camp.

Great numbers are suffering from bad ulcers on their feet, some of their feet are simply rotting away, the toes being easily pulled out by the doctor with a pair of nippers. He says it is gangrene.[...]

On 1 October Stairs made a nostalgic comment that on that day the pheasant shooting season began at home. The subsequent entries deal with comments on the increasing hunger. The situation was somewhat alleviated when a small banana plantation was discovered. By the fifth, no food was left and none could be found. The river navigation became impossible due to swift currents and a mass of dangerous rocks.

5th October For ninety-two days we have possessed a flotilla on the river. Today it seems as though it were coming to an end. Of course, there is every chance of our being able to place the boat once more on the river, but the canoes will be sunk here and probably we shall not be able to procure any [more] higher up, owing to the absence of natives.

The condition of the expedition is becoming deplorable. This route has turned out to be the most difficult one that could be chosen. For two and a half months, our people, though at times getting plenty of bananas, have not had three days running in which they have had enough food to eat since we left the Nepoko River village. Nelson's feet are getting worse, though every possible care has been bestowed on them. We have, say, ten men who cannot stir. These will certainly have to be left behind to die.[...]

6th October This morning things came to a crisis. Our sick men could not march and keep up with a hungry column in search for food. Our loads were too numerous to be carried by the men we possessed, so Stanley held a *shauri* [with] all the men and chiefs present. His plan was to leave a white man here with the sick [men] and what boxes we could not carry, press on with the column to the Arabs, or to any place where we could get food, load up men with food there and send them back to bring on the boxes and what sick [men] they could. To this the chiefs added consent, and Nelson proposed that five or six men should be sent on quickly ahead of the column and try to communicate with the Arabs. This was at once done; five *muniparas* started off with orders to press on.

Nelson, being unable to walk, was ordered to stop. We left about eighty-one boxes and, say, fifty-four sick [men]. With Nelson we left what little European food we could, a tent, and five or six good men to procure what food could be got in the bush. Parke left him a supply of medicines and of ammunition—he had about fifty or sixty boxes.

In the morning the canoes were all sunk close to the camp and the boat sent on in pieces. Stanley marched on at about ten o'clock and told us he would cut ahead as fast as he could. We (Jephson, Parke, and myself) did not get off, however, till noon or after owing to the boat not being ready. After a goodbye [to] Nelson, we started on a march to get food for these fifty people we have left behind. What is in store for us nobody can say. Nelson is in a very tight box where he is. We will do our best to get him out of it. Food is what we want. We travelled on till dark, could not catch Stanley and camped one hour behind him, in one tent, without blankets.[...]

On 7 October the march continued with only bush fruits and berries for food. The level of exhaustion among the men reached a danger point.

8th October This is the day one will not forget in a hurry, I should say. To start with, our boatmen, who are now in a pitiable state, almost refused to work; some intended to abandon the boat altogether and march on quickly up to the front. They all feel their position [so] far in [the] rear of [the] advance [column] is a bad one, and so it is, as they, poor beggars, have not the same chance of picking up food as their brothers in advance have. After speaking to them and telling them we could not get across to the Arabs without the help of the boat they started off again. In three-quarters of an hour or so, a man came down to us with a note from Stanley saying he had marched on ahead and camped, had taken a small village on an island here but found no food, and that yesterday he had shot an elephant [that] had got onto a small island near his canoe and probably would die there. We were to put the boat together, search for the elephant, bring him on to camp, and come on with the rearguard to camp.[...]

[After reaching his camp,] I had a long talk with Stanley about the condition our men were in and the chances of food. It certainly looks very black, especially with Nelson behind us. If only Jephson could bring the elephant, all would yet be well, the men then would get two good days' rations and we would be saved. All waited with open eyes and ears for the boat to come. At last, about nine o'clock, we heard the oars, and soon after the boat came up. "Have you got the meat," we yelled. "No," came the answer. We all felt sick, and quietly, one by one, the men left the landing place and, with hardly a word, turned in for the night.[...]

Between 9 and 12 October vain endeavours were made to procure food. There was scarcity of game and fishing produced meagre results. Captured blacks were unable to indicate sources of food as they themselves were on the verge of starvation, subsisting merely on wild fruit and meat obtained through hunting. By the thirteenth four men died of starvation. On the same day Jephson captured two baskets of Indian corn from unsuspecting Africans, one of which he gave to the men and the other was divided equally among the whites, providing each of the latter with twelve small cups of corn. No comments were made on the equity of distribution of this unexpected and ill-gotten prize.

13th October To give an idea of how things stand, I left Yambuya with a company eighty-eight strong; eleven I left with the Arabs, seventeen have died or been lost, twelve I left with Nelson, and today I have only forty-eight men and five of these are sick.

14th October Waited for the boat which turned up about 5:00 a.m. The men looked quite played out, and before starting to work again they got an hour and a half [of] rest, and then Stanley went across the river in the boat and found a camping place. Returning, all loads were taken over in five or six trips and we finished this job by 4:30. Parke went over some time before this and got up our tent and started the dinner. Farag Ala, the doctor says, will die; he had meningitis.[...] We are all very much exhausted tonight though little work has been done by us. Baruti and some five of the company were sent off by the boss to try and find some signs of the Arabs.[...] The chances for food on this side are much better than on the other, according to native reports, but then again, we have so often been deceived by these people that one [comes] to take their stories as lies.

15th October [...]I found I had thirty-seven men in my company, Jephson said he had forty-two in his; Stanley then held a long *shauri* and let the men have their say. As usual with these things, a great waste of time ensued and it was ten o'clock before we marched off and very little result was obtained.[...]

Some men from Baruti's party turned up about 2:00 p.m. and said they had found an Arab track leading NNE. This they had followed some distance and then turned back another way and met us. This is good news, supposing it will take us on to the Arabs, as three more days without food will probably mean the abandonment of the whole expedition.

Stanley stopped at 5:00 and made camp and soon after killed his donkey for food. We divided [it] up and distributed rations to all the men, keeping a leg, liver, and heart for ourselves. Each man's share should be about one half to one pound, not bad at all. As soon as we got ours, we made soup, stew, and roast. These, with bush beans, gave us the first fill up we have had for fourteen days. Oh, the blessedness of being able to sit down after dinner at night with a good pipe and feel full. The men, too, seemed more cheery in their camp—one [was] even heard singing.[...]

One of my men, worn down with ulcers and starvation, died on the road this morning. Poor chap, he had worked well up to the last few days, and then suddenly wasted away and died. Omare, a man of No. 1 [Co.], while searching for fruit up a very high tree, fell to the ground (60 feet) and sustained [a] concussion of the brain and injured two men who were underneath the tree. He will recover in a few days, the doctor says, and in fact can walk fairly well now.[...]

Stairs suspected that the lack of food was mainly due to the fact that the Africans, being driven away by the Arabs, failed to cultivate their fields. On 17 October the expedition set out on the Arab track, which was previously discovered by Baruti.

18th October This morning started off with hopes of hearing or seeing something of the Arabs. Stanley left camp, say, at 6:45. We three in rear did not get away till one and one-half hours later, holding a sort of court martial over some boys who had been stealing our supply of corn. Stealing is now the order of the day—no one can be trusted. Even William, Stanley's white servant, was flogged the other day for stealing his porridge. Hunger plays the devil with everyone.

Just as we were leaving camp we heard shots, horns, and a bugle mingling in confusion ahead, and then knew that Stanley had struck the Arabs. Hurrying on, we soon came up to them, and found that they had settled in a large clearing three hours from the river. We had a long yarn with the Muniapara [a title for a headman] in his house of meeting, the headman Abed bin Salim being away.[...] Stanley was given a house, and we three got another with three rooms and [a] verandah; [we] should be very comfortable.

The Arabs came here about seven months ago, took the village from the natives, enlarged the clearings greatly, planted rice, beans, and Indian corn, and weeded out and planted more banana trees. On the whole, [they] are in a fair way of having a very fine station. The name of the head Muniapara here is Khamis, an open chap with a pleasing face. He is helped in his work by five or six others. They have come right through the bush from the Lualaba above Nyanza in five months and have only got twenty tusks to show for it.

They have captured, however, a great deal of ivory in the shape of slaves. One sees them in all stages, from the newly taken one who has to be watched to prevent running away, to the fat jolly wanderer who speaks his Swahili with just the slightest tinge of Washenzi intonation. One sees great numbers of different bush people gathered together from different parts, those with disfigured lips from far away Mamgunu, those from the huge forest between the Aruwimi and Upper Congo, and lastly one finds the Washenzi of these parts.

The Arabs attack and capture a village, kill the grown-up men and make prisoners of all the boys, girls and women they can. These they can carry with them on their marches, selling women where they can for ivory, and bringing up all the boys for raiders and the girls for their harems. Their system is a good one, though one which destroys the country they pass through; this has been one of the causes of our suffering so much from hunger.

Unfortunately for us, the rice they have planted has not yet had time to bear fruit. Indian corn they have in great quantities. Bananas are scarce as yet.[...] We are absolutely without money of any sort—a most dangerous position to be in. So far we have taken anything we could see owing to our strength, but here, where we are friends, we must pay for things. Our beads, wire, and necklaces were all lost by the upsetting of a canoe, and we brought no cloth for trading from Yambuya. In fact, our only money is *matako*, or brass rods, which really are not currency in these parts. Now that we have passed through the desert and got to food, Stanley will find the problem [of] how to buy food a difficult one to solve. To add to this, food will have to be got to send back to Nelson, [who is] now in a desperate state, and food for eighty men who will have to be sent back to him for the loads.

Greatly to our satisfaction, five of the boatmen turned up in the afternoon, saying they had worked the boat up-river to a point opposite to us some three hours away. This relieves us of a great load.

Went for a stalk after some birds in the cornfields in the afternoon, but was stopped by the Washenzi Arabs, who imagined that I was trying to shoot fowl. Rather than offend them, I turned back and got to camp just in time for a huge feed of goat, corn porridge, *mboga,* Indian corn, and tea. By George, how good everything tasted and how one's spirits rose with each successful spoonful of porridge or bite of meat. One cannot realize the satisfaction it is to get one's stomach full after fifteen days or so of gnawing hunger.

We had a talk with Stanley, and afterwards sat by our fire for a long time thoroughly satisfied. The only thing to mar our pleasure is Nelson's critical position in rear.

19th October Slept till nearly seven o'clock in our comfortable house and once more feel this morning that life is worth living. We had a good breakfast of porridge and meat, corn and beans, and all felt better for it. As the men had a holiday today, we also took one. Directly after breakfast the people came to us with splendid looking corn flour, beans, corn, fowls, etc., to sell. We have nothing to buy these with, but I gave a kommerbrand[3] of red flannel for two baskets of beans, about ten cups full. For a small tin I got nine heads of green corn, for three empty brandy bottles we got thirty cups full of beans.

Stanley, who is supposed to feed us, has sent us nothing, barring giving us twenty-seven heads of corn each and our share of goats. It is simply scandalous the way in which we are treated. He, for his meals, has fowl, goat, porridge, beans, corn, and bananas, while whatever we eat we pay for out of our own miserable supply of necessary clothing. The men got no rations today at all, and consequently have been stealing the Arab corn and been tied up to trees. After being promised quantities of food on their arrival here, they have so far only got four heads of corn apiece, a beastly swindle. Stanley may say he has no money to pay for food; well, then he should give ammunition and rifles. Jephson had a long interview with him in the evening, the result being that he is to go back to relieve Nelson with seventy Manyuemas and ten Zanzibaris to carry food and bring up the loads. He will, in all probability on getting back to this place, remain here with Nelson. He is to start the day after tomorrow and will be away, say, fifteen days. Stanley in the meanwhile [sic] [is] going on.

Our position is critical in whatever light one looks at it. There are at least seven days with no food at all ahead, our men will not get any here, and will thus have to start with empty stomachs. Faith in Stanley [has] lessened tremendously. Stanley proposes to return from the lake [...], pick up Barttelot, then [travel] up [the] Aruwimi, and perhaps then strike direct[ly] across to the lake. The expedition is now so frightfully cut up that I doubt if these plans will ever be realized.

20th October Showery. Rifles [are] being lost or stolen to give to the Arabs for food; took all rifles away from the men. The men were again given four ears of corn—a mere drop in the ocean. Mofta Myaiga was badly wounded by one of the Arabs for stealing corn. He got a spear through the back [that goes] into [his] pleura. One could hear the wind rushing out when he talks.

Discontent is [more] rife than ever. One heard the men complaining bitterly today. One Jephson heard saying, "What use is there [in] going on? We are told again and again that there is plenty of food ahead. We never get any of it; all is finished."[...]

In the evening I went down to Stanley's tent and had a long talk with him. At first he was despondent to the very lowest degree, "the whole expedition is broken up now, there is nothing for us to do but return. Perhaps we may make [it] back to the Nepoko, follow up its course some distance and then slant off eastwards. But we must be prepared to lose one half of our men. These Arabs have wrecked us. Had I known them to be on the river I should never have come this way. I can come to no terms with the Manyuema. They are playing a destructive game to us [sic]; by not giving us food, they are inciting our men to selling their guns for corn and gradually will work our men over to their side. To go ahead without fixing terms, we cannot, or they would steal every load we left here."

He looked very bad over it and has had a rough time since reaching here: The men have had no food. Tonight all that we had for food from the expedition was *tea;* everything else we purchased out of our small store of clothing. I suggested returning as far as Ugarrowwa's, send back for Barttelot, bring him on, then strike NNE for a while, afterwards true east, and work on to Kavalli or some place north of this as before. [Stanley] would then be out of the radius of destruction caused by the Arabs and at the same time would not lengthen his course. To go up the Nepoko would perhaps be easier, it certainly would be a month and a half longer.[4] We also would have to pass through the wilderness between Ugarrowwa's and the Nepoko, which would prove fatal to a great many of our men.

No entries were made in the diary for 21 and 22 October.

23rd October   Nothing much to say. Stanley changed into his tent from his hut. He is looking seedy and says he has [a] bad fever ever since he has been here. This is bosh and one of his funny ways to enlist sympathy. He has been arranging all day with the [word illegible] about food and leaving our sick [men] here, and says he has at last arrived at a satisfactory termination. He came to us at dinner and made the remark, "You don't appear to be starving, at any rate." We all jumped at him and exclaimed that he had given us nothing we were eating, barring the tea. He at once shut up. Upon my word, it is scandalous the way he is treating us. We have averaged two corns per meal from Stanley here.

An Arab caravan came in from the north today after eight days [of] marching. They brought home some twenty tusks and there was plenty of food where they had been.

24th October   Fell all hands in, weeded out the sick to be left (twenty-eight) and formed up all the strong into companies. Stanley made his company seventy-two strong, picking out fully 70 percent of the best men. No. 2 Company, which is to be mine, is also seventy-two strong but consists of thirty-four men who were not willing to go on with Stanley and of the others the scum of 160 men. I suppose, when my poor sickly chaps begin to die on the route, [Stanley] will jeer at me for having such scum and slang me on the state of my company. Ahead of us is ten or twelve days [of] wilderness, our men are weak, and I should say that fully ten of my men are not able to start on the twenty-seventh, even supposing plenty of food existed. Stanley is forcing me to take men that Parke rejected as unfit to go, men who were in the very extremes as we reached this settlement.

In the afternoon I issued two corns per head per man. We were all called into Stanley's tent in the evening, and then he divulged his plans to us. In substance they are as follows: Jephson is to go back to the relief of Nelson (as arranged before) with our people and Manyuemas; Parke is to remain here with Nelson [when the latter arrives], look after the sick ones, and afterwards, when a caravan comes here from the lake, either of Emin's or our men, he is to go on to the lake. Nelson will, however, remain in this place till two and a half bales of clothing are in some way delivered by Stanley to the Arabs to pay off the debt incurred by the expedition staying here. (Thus Nelson is simply a hostage and may remain here for years, a most cruel proceeding and only necessary on account of Stanley's failing to bring more monies.) Jephson, after leaving Nelson here, will take the boat to pieces, store [it] here and come on after Stanley and myself with the boatmen and some fifteen others. I am to go with Stanley to the lake with a company of seventy-two men. Other plans are not yet decided on.

The marching plans are: 50 percent [of the men] unloaded [that is, one half of the carriers would not carry loads, allowing them to rest every second day], seventy-two men carry one day, and seventy-two the next; Stanley in front, I in rear. For fifteen days or so we are shown a good route through the wilderness. Deserters are to be apprehended and handed over to Nelson or Parke.[...]

Parke—in fact, all of us—were rather staggered on hearing that he was to be left here. Stanley had, we fancied, decided on Jephson. It is perhaps useless to try to estimate how long he will be here, but giving two months to the lake and two and a half to communicate, organize a caravan from Emin Pasha and reach here would make it four and a half months. But should the head of the expedition descend to Nepoko, bring up Barttelot to the lake, then send to relieve Nelson and Parke with the cloth, they would both be here quite twelve months. Fancy a deadly existence of twelve months in a place like this.

Now take the question of food. Stanley has shown himself a cur on this. He has simply arranged with the *Maurezuma* [5] that his men should, as soon as they get well, work in the fields and receive provisions. They are to receive no meat at all, and on the doctor's asking Stanley about this, he said the *Maurezumas* had no goats or fowls and told him to try and win them (the *Maurezuma*) over with smiles. This is all the money he has left the doctor—smiles. No *matako,* no right even to claim meat and with a clause in his agreement, I hear, that the *Maurezuma* have a right to punish our men who offend, instead of the white man alone possessing that right. The result will be that some of our men will get their throats cut for stealing corn, as this is the unalterable custom here now. [Stanley] has left it to the chiefs to provide food for Nelson. This will amount to something quite insufficient, I have no doubt.

As the caravan for Nelson does not leave for some days, no doubt I shall be able to write more about these arrangements.[...] I feel a sickly sensation at parting from Parke. He is a ripping chap to get along with: always cheery, ready to help one, a great chap to have on the march to brighten one up when things are going bad, and lastly of course, the danger of sickness is much increased by his absence. We shall have no one who knows anything about treating wounds, perhaps for another year.[...]

25th October Parke and Jephson got their instructions this morning. They are the same in almost every detail as those imparted to us by Stanley last evening.[...] I bought some flour and beans for the road, but Stanley should be sure to make some provision for me for the road. I am going to try for some fowls. We all surmised at dinner (our last meal we three will have for some time together) as to the whereabouts of Nelson. I said he would be there. Parke and Jephson said no.

26th October Fell all hands in, took twenty men from each company to go back with Jephson, gave them thirty heads of corn each and sent them down the river to be ferried over by boat.[...] I bought four fowls for the road, but expect they will be stolen from me. Parke made up a medicine chest for me, or in fact for us, as Jephson will catch me up after, say, thirty-five days. Parke and I had one last meal together this evening, and to me, going on through a wilderness, it will probably be the best one for some time. We had soup and meat, fried liver and kidneys, a stew of goat, beans, corn, bananas, and tea.

After dinner we sat by the fire for two hours talking the whole thing over. At last I produced some whisky from a small bottle I put up when we were on the Madura and we drank [to] each other's healths [sic] in a good stiff nip. Poor old Parke felt very sad over being left, and no wonder, as the conditions under which he stays are by no means understood by him.

27th October Up by 5:00 a.m., dressed and had a good breakfast of things bought by my pyjamas and shirts, and then fell into our companies. After some talk, gave out rifles, then loads and made a start about 12:15. Parke and I had lunch for the last time, and then getting my rearguard together and boys ready, we said goodbye. He walked a bit with me, and together we quelled a row about stealing ammunition pouches. Then again we said goodbye.

On the march again now, only I am the only white man in rear till Jephson comes up. I felt very lonely at times, especially so after just leaving Jephson and Parke and starting as we are through the wilderness. Saadi disappeared and [word illegible] with two rifles and one box of ammunition from my co[mpany]. Reached camp at 4:30, having gone, say, 3½ miles. Sent men back to Parke to try and get hold of Saadi and the other man. Had a good but lonely feed and turned in.[...]

On 28 October Stairs noted that four months previously the advance column left Yambuya. Next day the caravan passed several plantations plundered by the Arabs. After one day of rest, the column resumed its march moving towards a village where, according to the rumours, food was plentiful. The constant preoccupation with provisions found its expression in the following remark which ended the entry in Stairs's diary on the last day of October.

31st October I wonder how they are getting on at home? By this time tennis will be cold windy work and any outdoor pleasure will have lost its charm. How a good cup of coffee and some bread and butter would be these mornings in England, but how still a greater treat it would be here. Fancy sitting down to a breakfast of bacon and eggs, coffee, toast, and good butter with some honey or marmalade, or a good chop to finish off with. Oh, ye gods.

1st November Left camp about 7:00 a.m. Everything promised a bad march. Last night we had heavy rains and I fancied the track today would be bad. Luckily, it led, however, along a bridge through light bush and we had very little trouble. By 11:30 I caught up to Stanley just having grub. We had then gone, I should say, some 5 or 6 miles. After grub we went on for about an hour and a half and then struck a series of clearings, then some tents occupied by friendly natives who gave us pipes of tobacco, and lastly we came out on the large village we were expecting to reach today. It is the largest village seen yet and consists of the ordinary streets with a few detached huts at each end. Shortly after reaching here the chief of the place came and presented Stanley with a goat and some corn. [...] We made some 8½ miles today.

Upon my soul, the way I am treated is disgraceful. To get food I have to ask several times for it and then [I] get a few bananas thrown at me. Last night it got dark owing to the storm at 6:30. I had simply to lie in the dark with no light or comfort of any kind till it was time to go to bed. While all this time, there was Stanley in the front part of the tent, with a big candle burning and comfortable as a bug in a rug. We were told we should be supplied with candles before leaving, but Stanley has taken every one for his own use and we never got a single one. The name of the village is Ibussa and the Sultan [is] Momungu.[6] There seemed to be plenty of food about here if one could only get it.

2nd November We did not march at all today but simply stayed in camp to give the men a rest and a chance to pick up a bit of food.[...] Ulcers play the mischief with our men. One breaks out, say, in a man's ankle, gets worse day by day till he cannot carry his load, he goes downhill and has hard work to keep up with the column at all, and at last has to be left behind to die or perhaps find shelter with the Arabs somewhere. This is a constant occurrence.

The natives here have made the same mistake as we noticed down the Aruwimi. They make huge clearings of, 1 or 2 square miles. [In] these they plant a few bananas trees, corn, and tobacco, and then leave nature to work out her own results. The consequence is that in about two years the scrub springs up all over the clearings, chokes out a great many banana plants, and makes an almost impassable "piece of cultivation." No attempt at burning is made after felling and all the large trees are cut down—a great mistake.[...]

By this time Jephson should have reached the spot where Nelson was left and have found out whether he was there or not.

3rd November Off at the usual time and had our usual tightrope walking in the shape of [sic] fallen logs in a large clearing. Nothing of event occurred beyond the fact that Hamid Matamusa skipped and has not since been seen. He belonged to my co[mpany] and very luckily I had not given him a rifle.[...]

4th November Off early with a wet slippery track, passed a small deserted village and afterwards, for half an hour or so, had bad travelling through a large clearing. About 10:30 we came on another small village and here the men got a lot of small bananas. The Manyuema guides had gone ahead yesterday and were to bring us some food today at the next village. We reached this about noon, Stanley getting here at about 10:30. We found that our guides had been successful in getting one head of corn per man; this is merely a drop in the ocean, but with the bananas the men stole this morning, they should have a pretty fair feed tonight. This village is a very tumble-down affair with two streets in the shape of a T with here and there irregular detached huts. The hut I am in is very small though comfortable enough. On the whole, I would rather sleep in a tent detached from Stanley.[..]

5th November Again off on the march, which proved probably the worst one we have had yet. By lunch time we had gone I should say 6 miles. All day long the track was very slippery. Every now and then a man would come down with his box and perhaps injure his leg or arm and one would have to give the load to another man.[...] We struck the hills about noon and from then till we reached camp it was up hill and down dale over a very bad, tiring track. We got to camp about five o'clock, just in time to avoid a thunderstorm. Everyone seemed perfectly played out. Personally, my knees felt as though they would not work, and every muscle in my legs fairly ached again.[...]

The Manyuema again persuaded the Washenzi to bring us in food, and today we were able to give every man and boy eight good fat bananas, the sick men sixteen each, and the white men twenty each. Stanley also got a present of a large basket of dried bananas and some eggs, every one of which turned out to be rotten. The natives about here—or in fact the Arabs—never go in for eating eggs, they allow the hens to lay the eggs in the bush and then hatch them. What eggs they ever do give you are fierce [sic]. Two of my men did not turn up till 11:00 or 12:00 at night, they had gone off the track to steal bananas and got lost. The bananas here are much superior to any we have yet seen since we left the Nepoko. It does one's heart good to get hold of a good big yellow char roasted with its coat on. On every side of us we can see plenty of fine bunches, but as we are friends with the natives, it does not do to let our [men] steal right and left.

This is Guy Fawkes Day.

6th November Off early for a short march, passed two clearings, a small but well-occupied village. After going 4 miles or so [we] camped on top of a high hill from which we get a view of the surrounding country. Reached here [at] 10:30, Stanley [at] 9:30. Plenty of sweet potatoes, corn, and bananas. Again we gave each man eight bananas, even better ones than yesterday. Khamis, the chief of the guides, gave me two very good bunches of bananas—a most thoughtful and welcome gift, as I should only have got twenty or so from Stanley. As it is, I am able to put forty or fifty away to get ripe or use on the road ahead. From the back of my hut, which by the way is a very good one of the circular type, I can see for 20 miles[...]

The country is broken up by hills of 300 or 400 feet high, all bush-covered, and far away one can see the [many] clearings of the natives showing that there is a good number of people in these parts. The men are building themselves good huts as the chances are we shall have to be here for several days. We must be quite 3,000 feet above sea level now.

Here we heard from the natives rumours of a big wide river running ahead. This is in all probability Albert Nyanza. We also heard of cattle being ahead; some said in seven days, others, not till the next moon should we reach them. The natives ahead are reported as being cannibals and very fierce. These people here eat their own kin should one be killed in a fight. Their bows are much larger and more forceful than those of [the natives of] a week back. Their salutation is given in a most peculiar tone: *Shambu Bordu,* then followed by *Butenda.* This is repeated six times, the person saluted also repeating it.[7]

7th November Stayed in camp all day; did a few odd jobs about camp. We are 3,200 feet above sea level here and 60 miles from the Arab settlement we left on the twenty-seventh, and have 62 geographical miles to go to get to the lake. The natives again brought bananas, each man getting seven. As usual had a heavy rainstorm just as the sun went down. Gave Khamis a pair of pyjamas today as a gift. In the evening he returned with a fowl and Juma brought me another. It will pay, I fancy, as they have brought me sweet potatoes and a goat.[...]

The march was continued on 8 November. The column passed several deserted villages and towards the end of the day was out of the country controlled by the Arabs. On the tenth they reached a village where they found a large quantity of dry Indian corn. This was the first time since the expedition started that food could be obtained in any quantity. Stairs got a hut which proved quite comfortable. A decision was made to wait in that village for the arrival of Jephson and his men.

11th November We have made good marching again during the last two days. Today when Stanley had worked out our position we had come 13½ geographical miles in the right direction. We are now only 39 geographical miles from the lake. Again in camp all day. Early this morning some thirty-eight of our men went off with Khamis to sack another village. They had poor luck yesterday as the natives had moved everything out of the village some time before their arrival. The natives here this morning said that [after] two days [of] good marching ahead there is a patch of open country owned by natives owing large herds of cattle. The Manyuemas say they could reach it in one day.

One [man] of No. 1 Company named Jume Wazuri killed yesterday, to his own cheek [sic], seventeen fowls. These he decapitated and concealed in his hut but was found out by some of the men who told Stanley, the result being that I tied him to a tree and distributed the fowls among the sick men.

I had Marazoon at work all day pounding corn meal. It is a most laborious and tedious job; then, he eats about as fast as he pounds. The corn is boiled, say, for an hour to make it soft. It is then put into a *kinu* or pounding pot. After this is finished it is put into a flat basket or plate and tossed up, the chaff being blown out and the unpounded corn coming to the surface. This is skimmed off with the hand and the finest flour which is below is put into another vessel, and so on. Of course, the corn must be ripe and cured, though at a pinch, one can make a sort of mash out of green corn, but his preparation ferments if left for a day or two.

Some of the pounders are on a most elaborate scale of ivory, cut and scratched with all sorts of devices. The *kinu* is made of a hard wood and is generally plain without any ornaments. The fleas are numerous here in the huts. In mine one has only to bare one's arm and in a minute or so one can count five or six great whoppers hard at work. In Stanley's hut they were so bad that he had to decamp and pitch his tent. Cockroaches, beetles, and ants also infect all these places. As for the rats in my hut, they move simply in droves, being attracted by the quantity of corn stowed in it.[...]

Stairs's entry, made on Friday, 11 November ends with a list of seventeen men from his company whom he lost since leaving Yambuya. Thirteen of them died of disease and starvation and four were murdered by the local Africans. The subsequent two days were devoted to the much needed rest, and pillaging of the neighbouring villages took place. As the result of pillaging, the sultan of the village of Ibwiri, in which the column temporarily stopped over, decamped with all his people, goats, fowls, and so on in spite of formerly given assurances of friendship. Finally the sultan was caught and brought back.

14th November Our enemies the fleas and rats were again hard at work last night doing their best to keep us awake. As it was much cooler, however, we all managed to get a little sleep. Stanley had apprehensions that the natives might make some attempt at an attack on the village last night; these proved to be false though, and all of us survive this morning as fit as ever. Our friend the sultan, whom we have as a prisoner amongst us is a most sour looking brute. He objects very much to the hard cords he is fastened up with and would like very much, I have no doubt, to be loose.

From him we learnt that the Ituru and Eturi Rivers approach each other closely a short distance ahead and then separate, the first going north, the second south.[8] On the other side of the lake he says there are men (good men) who wear clothes the same as ours and use guns to fight with. Perhaps this is Casati the Italian who is now imprisoned on the eastern shores of Albert Nyanza. More likely it is that the old man lies.

Just a month ago today we crossed the column over the Aruwimi to try our luck in finding the Arabs. Then we were all weak, despondent and in grave doubt whether we should be able to go on or not. Today, a month later, our hopes are high and our stomachs much fuller, and though we do not know what has happened to Nelson and his men, we 115 [men] in advance feel that after all, life is worth living.[...]

Books are things that would now be worth their weight in gold. Stanley is so mean that he never offers the loan of any of his, and does not like being asked for them.[...]

15th November Yesterday morning we got some more information out of the old sultan. He says on the big lake [there] is a canoe as high as the houses in the village, only very long (probably a steamer). Also he says, "Ituri and Thuru Rivers joining here run up high hills and then when they get to the top, fall straight down over the lake." Pretty good this, rivers running uphill and then over onto the other side.

The maps that Gessi got up for Gordon places Kavalli in longitude 30° 12' E, whereas another map that Stanley drew up puts it in [longitude] 30° 30' E, [an] 18-mile difference.[9] I fancy Stanley's is the more correct as Gessi, I believe, worked only with the compass and other men's data to get up his maps.[...]

16th November About 3:30 Jephson and some more Manyuemas reached our camp. Everyone was burning to hear of Nelson and his men, and for some hours Stanley and I plied Jephson with questions of all sorts. Nelson, thank heaven, was alive when he reached the camp where we left him—just alive though, and no more. He had only four men left out of the fifty-six. Nelson had simply been living on fruits that his two boys had gathered for him in the bush. He was in a desperate state of despondency and fairly broke down on seeing Jephson and his men. All the rest of the men had died from starvation and sickness. Jephson said no one could realize the privations we had gone through until one returned over the track we had come and saw the numbers of skeletons on the roadside. In one march he counted six, and many others at different times. On reaching Nelson, one of the first things he did was to throw the bodies of four men who had just died into the river.

Nelson, of course, had formed all sorts of conjectures as to what had become of us, and finally decided that the column must have been delayed through hunger, as in fact was the case. Day after day, with his [men] dying around him, and nothing but a most scanty supply of food of the most wretched sort, Nelson must have been in a terrible state of mind, especially with such a man as Stanley for a leader, who thinks far more of his boxes than of his officers. Jephson made a very smart job of it, leaving the Arab camp on the twenty-seventh and reaching here on the sixteenth.[...] Nelson's feet were very bad when he got to the Arabs, and he could not sleep at night on account of anxiety. Fifty-six men and boys were left with him, of these only four reached the Arabs. This is a catastrophe that ranks pretty high in African travelling.[...]

On Thursday, 17 November Stairs set off with fifty-six men in search of the open country which, according to the local people, was a two-day journey away. On the eighteenth the caravan crossed the border of the Congo Free State. Stanley allowed Stairs only two days to reach his goal. The latter, unable to find a way out of the forest, turned back, and on the twenty-first returned to the camp.

Meanwhile, the captured sultan, who served as a guide, managed to escape. On 24 November, after two weeks of rest and good feeding, the advance column resumed its march which continued for the next five days. The open country was sighted on the thirtieth.

30th November Got off about 6:15 a.m. and soon struck plantations and had very bad marching over fallen logs and scrub. We sighted and reached a village on a high hill about 10:30, and there, away to the ESE, we could see the open country. By Jove, how our spirits rose and how good we felt after nearly two hundred days of it in the bush with nothing to see but sky, and then to see open country makes one feel a different chap altogether. Tomorrow we shall reach it, I hope, if all goes well.

The appearance of the country (about four days' march from here) is very much like that of Kent, undulating and hilly with here and there patches of bush on the tops of hills and gullies. The grass from here looks just like wheat within a fortnight or so of ripening; in places it is quite green though, looking from the distance like English grass fields in spring.

We made our camp at 11:00 a.m. in this village. From our hut Jephson and I can feast our eyes on the welcome scene, running out now and then to have a glimpse and make sure it is a reality. The men got plenty of hide here and other things, showing that cattle are near. I got a wooden cow bell much the same as those used by the Suris. The bows are much larger than formerly and bamboo is used for arrow shafts instead of wood.... Our course today was nearly south and we made about 4½ miles, I should say. Some men under [Chief] Rashid went off in a southeasterly direction to see what the country was like there and to try for goats. Stanley afterwards named this hill "Mount Pisgah."[10]

1st December Got an early start on a NE track leading through a newly felled clearing, having passed this we passed off the east and then to the south over a high range of hills. From the summit we could see far back over the bush some 15 miles in the direction in which we had come. One is not able to pick out the villages in the bush except from a very high hill, but generally one can see where the clearings are and so judge of the number of villages. We caught Stanley about 11:45 and had lunch in a large but broken-down village, having gone this morning about 5 miles. During lunch time Stanley got the sun for latitude. Marched one and three-quarters of an hour after grub and then made camp in a small collection of huts where we found water very scarce and far away. Here the men caught some goats and as usual slew a lot for their own use. We notice the bows and arrows are getting much more like those used by the natives of the plains, the arrows being bamboo and much larger than the bush ones. The shields, too, now are mostly made of cattle or buffalo hide instead of grass basket work. The track all day has been leading very badly, and we only made about 2 miles.

2nd December   All left camp this morning with the certainty of reaching open country today, as last night, one of the men had reached the edge of the bush and reported it was a short distance off, and so it turned out to be. We had lunch in a village where we got the most splendid bananas, some fowls, and a few goats. Stanley again got the sun [for latitude]. Leaving about 12:00 we marched for an hour and three-quarters and then struck a long patch of grassy country; we are now out of the bush. There may be more patches of bush to go through, but I fancy we have left the main bush behind. We have thus been, since leaving Yambuya, 158 clear days in the bush—a dose quite sufficient for most men, I should say.[...]

3rd December   Left camp early and followed the track out of the village in a NE direction of a mile or so. We then came to a deepish looking river of about 30 yards broad which the native woman said was the Ituri. The *Rugga Rugga* tried for a ford in several places, but

Emerging from the forest

(contemporary illustration from *The Pictorial World*)

the water was too deep to allow our loads to get over dry, so Stanley retired to the village we had just left, the men unloaded and Jephson, with twenty men, went on the back track some 3 miles or so to see if he could find a track leading down to the Ituri at a practicable ford. This, however, he failed to find, and returned about three o'clock having done nothing but wander from elephant track to elephant track. Jephson and I then went out with some men, and after less than an hour's work, by following a small stream, we found the Ituri, and what was better, a very good crossing.

We stripped, and I took my rifle and a man and crossed over. On the far side we found a belt of about 400 yards of bush. Passing through this [we] at last reached real open country. No mistake this time. Short jolly green grass rolling away to the east and northeast, far away to the blue hills forming our horizon. The bush ends quite suddenly and very much as the native women described it to me, viz., on the west side of the Aruwimi the bush comes close up to the river's edge and on the other side it is all open country.

It would have made an excellent group for a photographer to see we three out on the grass dressed as we were. Baruti Uledi, our man, was stark naked but wore my white helmet and carried my stick, Jephson had his shirt on only, and I had a shirt and rifle, and there we were, stalking about this grass, talking to each other like mad and feeling ourselves once more where one breathes free air and can see more than trees and sky. Game seemed plentiful by the number of fresh tracks we saw. We returned to camp and had a good feed and talk [sic] over our bush experiences. We had been 160 days in this almost interminable graveyard and now to get out of it seems more than one can realize.[...]

CHAPTER 5

LAKE ALBERT, FORT BODO, AND JOURNEYS TO KILONGA LONGA'S AND UGARROWWA'S

4 DECEMBER 1887—26 APRIL 1888

The column moves towards Lake Albert. The lake is reached on 13 December. The search for Emin Pasha is temporarily abandoned. The decision is made to return to the forest and to build a boma. *Ibwiri is selected as the site of Fort Bodo which is then constructed. Stairs leaves for Ipoto, returning during the first half of February with Nelson, Parke, and the other survivors. Stairs marches to Ugarrowwa's and brings the survivors to Fort Bodo. Stanley leaves for Lake Albert before Stairs's arrival.*

4th December Made tracks about 1:30 from camp. Soon afterwards struck the Ituri where Jephson and I had crossed yesterday and passed all the people over safely. Stanley and the *Rugga Rugga* gained about an hour over the rearguard here, I should say, and on reaching the open saw plenty of game.[...] By 11:30 we made 7½ miles to the NNE and had lunch in [sic] a small stream in a bush gully. After this we marched on another 2 miles and camped in another patch of bush where water was plentiful.

The whole country to the south of us today was one huge English scene: rolling hills divided by patches of bush in the gullies; every shade of green that one could imagine is to be seen. Here and there one sees the patches of burnt grass that have been burnt by the natives. As game country, it appears to be all that one could wish. We saw fresh signs of different animals and actually fired at buffalo and eland and saw spring buck. The only sign of natives we saw was a village to the south of us on a high hill. To the NE is a range of high hills that we could just dimly see through the haze. [In] back of us to the NW is the dark green bush graveyard we have passed through and left so many men's bones in. I only wish Parke and Nelson were here to enjoy the pleasure of being out of prison, in fact, [I wish] the whole expedition [were here].

5th December Started off early and had bad marching. After going for about an hour, heard cocks crowing and other signs of a village ahead. The *Rugga Rugga* reached this and drove out a few remaining natives capturing two women and a boy. Stanley waited here trying to get information out of some of these people, but it was of little use as none of our natives or the Manyuema boy could understand them at all. We got quantities of very

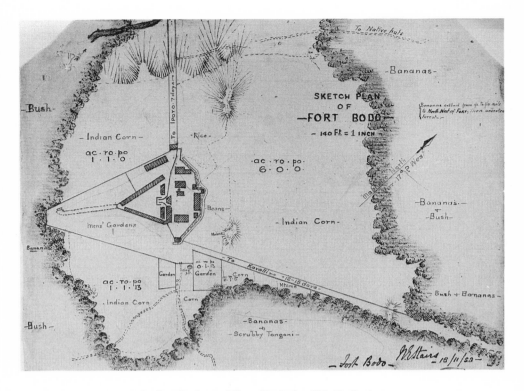

A sketchplan of Fort Bodo by W. G. Stairs

(Public Archives of Nova Scotia)

good ripe bananas and sugar cane, and some fowl and goats. I don't think I ever saw such quantities of splendid bananas.[...]

The natives here build their houses in groups of three or four among the banana trees, and not in one big village as the bushmen. Their plantations are beautifully kept, and as a result the beans and bananas are very fine. In appearance they look very much like the bushmen we have recently caught, but they have not the peculiar intonation in speaking that the others have.[...]

We left the village about half an hour after I came up with the rearguard.[...] We again came on some more plantations and in one of them a chap called Yakuti in my company was shot through the loins and in the side by a native concealed among the bananas. Shortly afterwards I saw one sneaking along the edge of some long grass and fired at him twice, the second bullet hitting him as he partially stopped in his running and turned off into the long grass at once. The arrowhead passed clear through Yakuti's wrist into his side, but [it] was not a poisoned one. Half an hour after leaving this village we came upon Stanley and found he had made camp also in another plantation.[...]

On 6 December the column crossed a river and a camp was set up. Security became a prime consideration in an open and populous country where an attack could be expected any time. Next day

Ituri River was reached. Attempts to make friends with the local people proved unsuccessful. On the thirteenth Lake Albert was approached. The descent to the lake was hampered by frequent attacks on the part of the local warriors.

13 December [...]After a short stop to feast our eyes, we commenced the descent and then began our worst piece of fighting ever since we landed in Africa. Every inch down this desperately steep hill the natives pushed us. From behind the huge granite boulders they would shoot out, rush down to shooting distance and let fly their arrows. Again and again I took back the rearguard and pasted [sic] them, but still on they came, and not till we had reached the plain below and crossed a largish river late in the evening did they give us any peace. Shortly after this we made camp in a village and surrounded ourselves with a *boma*. Never shall I forget this day's work as long as I live: my feet swollen to almost bursting with marching, then the anxiety lest we should be cut off from the main column, and to add to this the hot sun and jagged rocks—I tell you, at night I was fairly well done up. We had only one wounded, but it was a miracle as the arrows kept flying about in all directions. At 11:00 we drank water which run[s] into the Aruwimi [and] finds its way into the Congo and on into the Atlantic. Forty minutes after, we drank from a stream running into the Albert Nyanza and down the Nile to the Mediterranean. These two streams are not more than [a] twenty-minute walk from each other. We should be somewhere near Kavalli as we see the river running into the south end of the lake.

14th December Got away early, all anxious to make for the lake shore. After two hours' marching towards the lake and within half a mile of it, we struck a large path leading to a village, and following this were soon close to the huts. Here we sent Fetteh, the interpreter, out and managed to talk with the natives. For two hours we sat in parley doing our best to obtain their friendship. At first, it seemed as though they were afraid of us and desired friendship, but afterwards they became bolder, and at last we said we should retire. All we wanted was a canoe, we said, but this they refused, so we moved and marched along the grassy plain northward along the lake shore. Here for the first time, we saw game of all sorts in any number: springbok, hartebeest, eland, and buffalo, besides the signs of leopards and other large animals, making it a perfect paradise for sportsmen.[...]

At 3:00 we camped on the plain about three-quarters of a mile from the lake to give ourselves breathing space to form plans as to future actions. In this huge park, though game abounds, still there is no food of any sort; not a square yard of it has been turned over by the natives for planting—no *mtama,* no corn, no bananas, nothing. The natives all along the shore live on fish and make salt which they sell to those living high up on the plateau and in turn get corn, beans, bananas, etc. This absence of food makes it quite impossible for us to build our fort close to the lake.

Then there is the canoe question. To buy a canoe we twice found [to be] out of the question. To take a canoe means making enemies of all the natives north to Nyamsassi and south to the end of the lake. This Mr. Stanley says we are not strong enough to do. Both Jephson and I, however, think we are. How then, now that we are at the lake, are we to communicate with Casati who is at Kibiro across the lake?[...] Jephson advocated marching up the west side of the lake till some good food-producing district was reached and then seize a canoe and build our *boma*. To this Stanley replied that it would be impossible, first, as we should lose half our men fighting our way up, and second, as no canoe could possibly cross over the lake there and reach Casati in safety.

My plan was to at once seize the biggest canoe we could find close at hand, send a strong force—seventy men, say—back up the hill to collect food for ten days and then start the canoe south to [the] end of [the] lake and up to the Unyoro shore to Casati. When the canoe was dispatched, retire the whole column to [the] plateau, build [a] strong *boma*, collect plenty of food, and then set to burn all the natives' huts, destroy—where it would not hurt ourselves—their property, raid their goats and cattle, endeavour to draw them into some position advantageous to ourselves and then kill as many of them as possible.[... Or,] to send the canoe up the west side of the lake for two days or so and from the natives perhaps learn something.

We did not possess sufficient men to do this, [Stanley] said, and could not afford to make enemies with the natives. (It afterwards turned out that they became bitter enemies.) Second, to meet the arrival of the boat we must have a *boma* and possess the shore at some favourable point. Third, we had [sic] not sufficient men to watch the canoe and at the same time send out a force upon the hills for food.

To these objections I say, first, that we are already enemies of nine-tenths of the natives of Kavalli, or of that part we have marched through. Second, we could easily arrange that signals should be made by the boatmen, say, by lighting fires, and that by the time they return the natives on the lake shore will have had their stomachs full of fighting and will keep off at a safe distance. To the third [objection] I simply say that we have enough men.

Are we to return again to the bush from the goal without having a try at communicating with Casati after five months of starving, fighting men and rapids, after fevers, ulcers and rebuffs of every sort, [and] after passing the Manyuemas, the destroyers? By George, no! I say let us have some sort of a shot at it by all means, let us fight and starve here a bit longer if we shall then be masters of the question. Is Emin Pasha still alive and at Wadelai? [It is] a question that all Europe must be bursting to know by this time. No, Stanley must have more men and the boat, he says, but again tomorrow will try to talk to the natives of another village close to camp—a fishing town. Now is the time for a short bold dash for Kavalli, win or lose. If this flood is not taken, ten months may elapse before we can get our entire force within striking distance of the lake shore and Emin Pasha [may] be a dead man.

At night we heard hyaenas and leopards close to camp, but no damage was done to the sentries placed far out from the camp in the grass. Heavy rains at night made Jephson and I very uncomfortable in our fly.[...]

15th December Today I took some men out to the village of Kavalli and endeavoured to shout across the channel to the natives on the island, but it was no use. After two hours, we returned to camp sickened.[...] At night we thoroughly thrashed out the question of what could be done to get news to Casati, and it was then, I fancy, that Stanley fully made up his mind to retire back to the bush and bring up more men. Stanley stood Jephson and I a couple of bottles of fiz [champagne] and we drank success to our return to the lake.

We all felt pretty sick at having to go back after such trying work getting here.

16th December Started away from camp about 11:00 a.m. up the plain and marched past a huge track leading to the hills to delude the natives into the belief that we were going to continue our march north. After three-quarters of an hour past this, we halted until 5:00 p.m. in a very paradise for sportsmen. On all sides of us were game of all sorts: eland, hartebeest, buffalo, springbok and several other sorts of deer. Stanley managed to shoot an eland and Sua Tatis got a hartebeest. Both of them were cut up and given to the men, though we had the livers of both and found them first-rate eating. At five o'clock we started back again till we struck the big track just mentioned and followed it up in the dark towards the mountains till about 10:30 when we bivouacked in an open space without fires, and keeping very quiet all night. We had several goats in rear close to where I was marching, and for quite an hour a leopard followed us keeping close to the goats all the time but out of sight in the grass, so that we could not get a shot at it. Once or twice I thought it would spring, but it seemed to think better of it and at last we lost its peculiar "chin" [sic] and our goats remained unscathed.

17th December Away before daybreak, struck the foothills in three hours, sent on an advance guard to clear the hills, and had breakfast. We were so early that the pioneers met with no opposition from the natives, and soon afterwards the whole column passed up the hill without firing a shot. Never shall I forget this march up the hills: for five blessed hours I toiled in rear to get the goats up the hills, cursing, beating, imploring—everything. On reaching the top I was perfectly done up. We marched westward another 5 miles and made camp. We got our last sight of the lake from the top of the hill and with sad hearts turned our faces westward, perhaps not to see Albert Nyanza again for ten or twelve months. People in England will wonder why, after coming so far, we did not make a dash for Casati. Stranger, so do I now; I think a greater mistake was never made. It is all very fine to say, "Oh, when we return we shall have plenty of men and the boat." Perhaps so, but all the same, it may then be too late. This is not a caravan; it is an expedition and should be expeditious.[...]

On 18 December efforts to procure some meat were crowned with success when thirteen cows were captured. Between 19 and 22 December no entries were made in the journal. Information relating to events on the twenty-third was written on 1 January 1888, and Stairs confessed to having forgotten the "little things that may have happened."

24th December Left camp at 6:30 and made a short march down-river to where the native bridge was. We found that the bridge had been cut very badly by the natives and was simply a floating tangled mass of vine. To untangle this, set it up, and repair it took us all day, so we pitched camp in the afternoon for the night.[...] We had a bad storm in the afternoon lasting about half an hour; the stones must have measure about three-quarters of an inch in diameter, I should say.

Well, here is Xmas Eve, and all day long, nearly, I, Bill Stairs, have been sitting out in the grass watching the rear and guarding the flocks of the Emin Pasha Relief Expedition, now returning to the bush graveyard to pick up the stragglers and Barttelot's column far away down the Aruwimi. Here in Central Africa, sitting under my mackintosh [which is] spread over the tops of three spears stuck in the ground to shade us a bit from the sun, [while] around me are the cattle and rearguard, nearly all lying down in the long grass trying to get away from the scorching sun. Jephson is at work on the bridge. At lunch we meet and talk over our last Xmas Eve's experiences. This time there are no plum puddings, no mince pies and brandy, and no Xmas cards and "merry Xmas to you"—nothing but work. Happy enough we might be though, were it not for the bitter thought always coming up that we are returning to the terrible bush without having accomplished anything of our mission to Emin Pasha. This at times gives us the blues.[...]

This time last year I was in Portsmouth staying with my sister, and two years ago ten or twelve of us had a very lively dinner together at Monico's in London. One's thoughts, of course, go back to home and all one's people at this time, as 'tis is the thirteenth Xmas running that I have spent away from my own home. One has merely dim recollections of what it used to be.[...]

25th December Xmas Day. Well, here is Xmas 1887, at last. Many a time have we wondered where we should put in this day, and here we are today crossing our force over the headwater[s] of the Aruwimi [with] all hands hard at work all day. No doubt our people are thinking of us and wondering where we are and what we are doing as they go to church or drink our health at dinner.[...] Our stay now in Africa cannot be much under three years.

Stanley watched his company over the bridge to the island, then I sent mine, then put over the cattle, getting all over to the island where Stanley had pitched his tent at 5:00 p.m. By nightfall all my company, thirty of No. 1, and four goats were ferried over. Finally I was taken over and we made camp in the village, Jephson and I. Stanley remained on the island with forty of his company.

Our hut is a very good one and bananas and corn abound close at hand. Jephson and I sat down to our dinner, hungrier than we would often be at home at Xmas, but we had pretty plain food to masticate. We had one small help [sic] of goat meat each, left from this morning's breakfast, green corn, bananas, coffee, and goat milk. For a long time after dinner we talked together over old Xmases and what our friends would be doing. I produced my small bottle of whisky and we each had one nip and drank [to] a speedy return to the lake and [to] good luck to our friends in England and elsewhere.[...]

The 26 December was an uneventful day, but on the twenty-seventh, when the local villagers had wounded a man from Stairs's company, Stanley decided to retaliate by destroying several villages—a mission which was executed under Stairs's command. During the next three days the expedition passed Mount Pisgah and entered the bush once again to face starvation and poisoned arrows.

30th December One realizes plainly on the march this morning what a backward move we are making in thus retiring without having done anything to find out whether Emin Pasha is still on the Nile or not. Supposing Emin Pasha has decamped, then we are here slaving our very lives out in the bush to get ammunition up to the lake absolutely for no purpose. Then again, suppose he is there, then shall we not be too late? Here is New Year's Day almost upon us. How long are we to spend in Africa? As things turn now, in all probability we shall see two more New Year's Days before we leave the country.[...]

31st December Made a fairly good march today, had a little trouble with the cattle and goats passing fallen trees. From every one of the four or five villages we passed through, the natives had decamped. In the afternoon we took a more northerly route than when we were going east so as to avoid the spur of Mount Pisgah. We made camp in the bush but are close to villages as the men can get bananas and return to camp in an hour or so. The *Rugga Rugga* captured a woman and child, though what use they are now to us, one cannot see.

Just fancy, this is New Year's Eve tonight, and here Jephson and I sit yawning over the fire with hardly a thought of it, our conversation being mostly about Jephson's schoolboy and tutor life.[...]

This time last year I was orderly officer at Chatham and Broghton Barracks, and I remember in the anteroom at the former we had three huge bowls of rum punch and some of the chaps had pretty sore heads next morning. The year before last at this time, I was also in Chatham, and then two years before that in New Zealand. Next year on the first, we shall still be in Africa, I expect, with something done towards the relief of Emin Pasha.[...]

During the first three days of January 1888 the column made good progress. The villages along their path were abandoned by their inhabitants who had left almost nothing behind. The heat in the bush was very oppressive. Stanley had an attack of fever, although at the same time, he had an excellent appetite. He behaved in a way that suggested self-pity or hypochondria and a desire to attract the attention of his companions. The 4 January was a day of rest during which Stairs had time to reflect and to write down some of his rather uncomplimentary comments regarding Stanley's personality. During the next two days the caravan continued on its march passing villages burnt down by their inhabitants in order to prevent the expedition from occupying them.

7th January Started on our last march to Ibwiri and at noon reached the site of the village and found the natives had burnt everything to the ground. This will be a great loss to us as we had been counting on using the materials of the houses to build our *boma*. In the afternoon we got about 500 pounds of corn [which] the men found hidden in the bushes and started building the *boma* of boards 10 feet high.

8th–15th January We started today getting quantities of stores such as boards from the adjacent villages, [and] poles and rods from the bush, and all sorts of things necessary to build the fort. I was at work with sixty men bringing in loads of corn from a collection of huts we found the natives had fled to. We got 240 loads today and 240 loads on the next day.[...]

Every soul worked from before sunrise to after sunset. Out in the broiling sun all day, Stanley, Jephson, and I slaved, directing the building of towers, houses, sheds, *boma,* men's huts, and everything connected with the defence of the place. Not till the evening of the fifteenth—just one week's work—did we stop to draw breath. On and on through the hot scorching sun, which is terribly powerful just at present, we toiled, hailing sunset and the trumpet every evening with pleasant feelings. During one day I went back to our old fourteen day's camp [sic] keeping at a safe distance and found it burnt to the ground and everything cleared off.

The natives have so far given us very little trouble, keeping at a safe distance and only daring to venture into the huge plantation for bananas.[...]

All the houses were made of clay with roofs of dry beams. The houses are all capable of being connected by barriers and thus form a line of defence perfectly proof, even against bullets. The outer *boma* is, of course, only as a protection against arrows, though in many places it is bulletproof.

I am to go back with ninety men in a few days and bring up Nelson and Parke with all the loads to this place. This is Stanley's orders, but how it is to be carried out is hard to see. Mind you, we are in debt still to these people for food supplied by them to us. The loads of rifles and ammunition there are our pledge that the debt will some day be paid off—it is three and one-half bales of cloth.[...] What other guarantee Stanley is to give, I cannot see nor do I think it possible he can give any. The statement that we are soon to go down to Barttelot and bring him up will not wash with these people. They are the most infernal liars and swindlers themselves, and so believe everyone else capable of the same things. Once we [got] Barttelot's column and the beads and cloth up, there would be an end to the matter, but this is very far from being accomplished yet.[...] Stanley has given me twenty days to go back to the Arab settlement, make up the loads, and bring them and the boat back here. I want twenty-seven days to do this, as the track for seven days out from the Arabs is very bad, being in places a tangled mass of fallen logs and scrub, over which the heavy loads will take a long time to pass.

16th January Today two foraging parties were sent off in a SW direction to stir the natives up a bit and prevent them [from] thinking we had gone to sleep.[...] I had my boys, Farag Ala and Abedi, washing and mending my clothes all day, while myself patched up my boots as well as I could. All of us are very badly off for boots. Our stock is quite exhausted by this time.[...] No sign of the foragers by nightfall; they have evidently gone far afield.

17th January Worked nearly all day at my clothes, mending and changing one garment into another as a makeshift. Really, Jephson and I are in a desperate way as regards boots and clothes, and there are yet many months to go before we can get any addition to our bags of rags. The work on the fort still goes on, done by those who are to remain here.[...] Today Stanley started the poles for a granary he is to build in the square in front of our houses. This is to do away with the rat nuisance. Jephson also was building towers and putting on roofs all day. Later this evening the *Rugga Rugga* returned having captured some native women and seven or eight goats. They said they had been a very long march off and had seen plenty of signs of the natives, but everything indicated that they had moved off a long distance and taken all their portable stock with them. No signs of corn were seen at any of the camping places they passed on their way out. Two natives were shot by them. I am to leave for the Arabs' the day after tomorrow.

18th January Today I got my instructions (verbal) from Stanley: if the worst comes to the worst I am to fire on them in case they should refuse to give up our loads. This mission I am going on will be full of risk should certain events come off [about] which I have no doubt. I am the bearer of a letter to Ismaili, one of the chiefs. [It is] written in Swahili.

19th January Got [up] about 7:30 a.m. for the Arab settlement, Stanley saying we should be back in twenty days. I said twenty-nine days to Jephson last night. I have eighty-eight men, six *Manyapara* (headmen). All told we are ninety-seven. I hope there will be no trouble of any sort with the Manyuema as it would lead to most unpleasant after-results [sic] at Zanzibar and elsewhere. Should Kilonga Longa be there, I do not expect much trouble, but if Ismaili be [sic] in charge there I am very much afraid we shall have trouble.[1]

20th January Left camp early, lost the track several times as the elephants had obliterated all signs of it in places by tearing up trees and messing up the vines in such a way as made [sic] it a difficult job to tell which was the traffic path and which the elephant [path]. Rained about 11:00. At 2:00 p.m. we drew up at Vilimani [feeling] cold, wet, and miserable, made a camp there and soon got comfortable in the huts. Washenzi have all fled into the bush. Just one year ago today Jephson, Nelson, and I left old England thinking we should be about fifteen months in Africa. We shall be two years more before we see the last of this country, perhaps more than this. When shall we stroll down Regent Street again or have another fight with the War Office people, or when shall we join the festive dance again, or the still more festive mess supper? Oh, ye gods, just fancy grilled kidneys, snipe, salmon, ices, jellies, fiz, and the many other luscious things one gets at home. At present my diet is corn and bananas.[...]

21st January Many time[s] as one trudges drearily along close to the back of some wretched ulcerous creature striving hard with his load, one forms menus by the score that one intends to have on reaching England again. Even coffee and tea are now things of the past, though I have a little I am keeping till some rougher time, perhaps in the rainy season.[...]

The march continued along a trail where the branch paths leading to the villages had been blocked by the Africans who were fleeing at the sight of Stairs's column.

23rd January Marched very fast this morning. Passed one of Stanley's camps [at] 12:50. Our camp is the past habitation of the Monbuttus, or race of dwarfs that live in the bush here. How far north or south these little people exist I cannot say, but I know that the Manyuema met with them [...] south of Ipoto. These people live altogether by their prowess in the bush, killing elephants with pits and spear [word illegible], catching birds and other animals. These and the elephant flesh they smoke and dry, and then sell to the natives in return for corn, bananas, and sweet potatoes. Sometimes these little men steal the bananas off the trees. It was when doing this that one of our men saw one. Should the natives catch one stealing, they kill and eat him at once. Otherwise they are friends. I have measured many footmarks of these men, and 7½ inches is the biggest on record. Their arms are bows and arrows (deadly poison) and spears. [They have] circular huts from 5 to 8 feet in diameter, fire outside.

24th January Made two and a half of Stanley's camps and got within one hour of the Manyuema. Marched fast all day, must have gone 20 miles by 4:00 p.m. Should reach Arabs tomorrow. Men in great spirits. Should Manyuema be unwilling to give load[s], we will fight them and give them a deuced good licking. I hope this will not be the case as I have verbal [orders], [but] I have no written orders, and great trouble would afterwards arise with Zanzibari people. Then Stanley would be sure to say I had disobeyed and some other such things.

This book being now finished I go on with another one, almost the last, yet there are probably two more years to record. This one leaves off where I reach the Manyuema settlement at Ipoto and find Nelson and Parke well but having passed through a rough time of it.[...] Four months of our wanderings are written in this book [...], but not as one would have liked to have put them down. The terrible days of starvation through which we passed and the many men we have lost I have got notes of.

Trusting that some future day I may open this again, myself in Old England, I "shut up shop."

25th January Reached the Manyuema settlement at 11:00 a.m. Met Parke and Nelson both looking well but still suffering from poisonous sores brought by the poison inoculated by the flies. The place I found a reeking mass of filth, and Nelson and Parke squatted right down just where the filth was worst. They have had a regular hell on earth of it with these brutes of Manyuemas. At every possible turn they would be frustrated by some paltry excuse of Ismaili's or some other equally brutal chief. Nelson, to get food, had to sell his 500 express [rifle], his field glasses, his sword, [his] watch, and [his] gold chain, and nearly all his clothes. For these he received paltry supplies of food. No arrangement of any sort had been made by Stanley for Nelson and Parke. They were told that when Nelson came up he would pay them well as he was a big man.[...]

Nelson had been ill from the time he crawled into Ipoto with Jephson. He is terribly irritable at times, almost driving one mad [with] slanging his boys and swearing at everything in general. I was glad to see old Parke again and feel that once more he was to be one of us. Shortly after arriving held [a] *shauri* with Kilonga [Longa], the chief, and was successful in getting the loads from him.[...] I was very much afraid we might have trouble in getting the loads, but everything turned out all right.

Could not agree with Kilonga [Longa] as to the payment to be given him for looking after loads to be left (sixteen) but at last closed at three rifles and three hundred rounds of ammunition.

26th January All ready by 2:00 p.m. and made a start. Uledi I sent off early this morning to the Ituri for the boat. At 4:00 we met and went on together, making camp just outside the cultivations. Of the twenty-three sick men at the settlement, some thirteen elected to come on with me. The other ten were away on *Rugga Rugga* with the Manyuema.

Starvation exists to a terrible extent at Ipoto, and all those able to move at all have gone off into the bush to raid native villages and thus get food. Those in the place simply exist on *mboga* and are as thin as the pictures we used to see in the *Graphic* [magazine] of the famine in India. Some of our invalids will never be able to reach Ibwiri. One's spirits rose at once on getting out of the hell Nelson and Parke spent so long in.

27th January Off early, Parke leading with Heri as guide. Made camp at 10:30 a.m. I stayed behind with the boat and had great difficulty in getting the rear section along. Changed the men several times but with no advantage. Reached camp, the men quite done up, at 4:00 p.m. I had to shoot Parke's donkey on the road today as we could not get him over the *gogos* (logs) and had no time nor men to make a track for him. Poor Neddy, he was the last of the donkeys we brought from Yambuya; the bush is too much for these brutes. Food is very scarce along these roads, the Manyuema having eaten everything up.

28th January Nothing of event occurred today except that we had trouble more than ever with the rear section of the boat. From this on to 4th February the days went by, food scarce, work hard, men tired. On 3rd February we reached the big village east of Mabunza.

4th February The doctor left this village today with all the odd loads and boxes and reached Stanley at Ibwiri on the eighth without mishap.

5th February I halted today to give the boatmen time to collect a little food; they got some bananas and flour for two days.

6th February I started off the boat, reached Kilimani on the seventh and Stanley on the twelfth, thus being twenty-five days out from the fort. I found then that Jephson had gone away with some men foraging [sic]. I was very glad, of course, to get back to comfortable quarters, but all the same one enjoyed being on the march, [being] one's own boss, and [being] away from the constant naggings of Stanley.

12th February Reached the fort at Ibwiri at 1:30. Found Jephson away with *Rugga Rugga*. During the month I had been away great improvement had been made. Jephson and Stanley had cleared 4 acres and planted corn and beans. Nelson's feet are still very sore. He and Parke have got their systems thoroughly poisoned from the filth at the Manyuema camp. The next question is, are we to go on the Nyanza, or to go back to pick up the major? There is a lot to say for and against both plans. I am for going on to the lake as fast as we possibly can.

All the men who remained at the station are in splendid trim—as fat as butter and cherry.

Slept for the first time in the officers' house which seems very comfortable in the daytime, being nice and cool. Nelson says, however, that the roof leaks a bit.

13th February Men at work. Boat carriers [have] a holiday. I cleaned and packed up all the bolts and nuts of boat (211) and handed them over to Stanley, cleaned five rifles I brought on, and oiled eighty-three breech locks. Parke and Nelson indoors. Nelson spends all day lying in his bed and shouting to his boys. Stanley has built a long sort of a walk fenced in on both sides; this he calls Avenue Nyanza. It is not of much use except to give us safe exercising room. The huts are whitewashed with a wash made of whitewood ashes. The men's quarters look first-rate. The one bad fault of the place is the tops of the houses—they are made without pitch—and in these heavy tropical showers [they] leak like the mischief.

The grain has been all stowed in a granary in the centre of the fort raised about 8 feet off the ground, thus rats are avoided. We fly the Egyptian flag, one of the rottenest flags we could possible fly. Nothing good ever came out of Egypt; their ammunition was bad, the boxes bad, powder caps done up in rotten boxes, the men useless to a degree [and] the boots that the men wore were bad.

14th February Yesterday we had a lengthy *shauri* about our next move. He [Stanley] is evidently determined to thrash every side of the question out. His last scheme is that I should take twenty men and go through to the Ugarrowwa's, send on the twenty men with [a] letter to Barttelot, bring back the men who were left there as invalids, come on to him [Stanley] somewhere near the edge of the bush, then, united, go on to the lake. One officer and a garrison of, say, thirty men [are] to stay here.

I am against this on account of the following: first, I don't believe that twenty men can be trusted to make their way down the river even as far as Yambuya. Second, I don't think Ugarrowwa will give over the men and rifles *to me*. Third, I don't think that a month's delay is worth the few men we will get from Ugarrowwa—really fifty-six, but only thirty of them would be fit to fight.

Whether I should ever catch Stanley or not I do not know; the journey for at least ten days would be through unknown country as, on account of the famine, we never dare go back by the same roads we come. Jephson will be for going on to the lake. Today is St. Valentine's Day.

This day last year the expedition passed Cape Guardafui on the Africa[n] coast. Then we had good cigarettes and not too bad grub and were generally happy with books, chairs, etc., now, however, things are changed.[...]

15th February Got my orders to go back to Ugarrowwa's. Jephson came in last night with ten or eleven goats and other loot. I am to take twenty-five men down and twenty of them go on to Barttelot. I have to join Stanley by 25th March. Can't do it.

16th February Started off from the fort, amidst cheers from those remaining, on our long dreary trip back to Ugarrowwa's. In one's heart one knew the thing could not be done quickly, and one felt very much incensed at Stanley for the limit he imposed of thirty days to go and [return]. Though now it is nearly three months after this date that I write this, still in my rough notes I remember putting down that I told Stanley that there would not be thirty men below fit to come on. He said, "Nonsense, why I expect fifty."

My spirits are high, though, and one cannot tell whether the rope is going to put one [forward] or draw one back. I am ashamed of this book as it is such an eyesore and certainly looks as if it would break up soon like the ice in the Canadian lakes in April. Made Stanley's camp in the bush about 4:30 and camped. Men heavily laden with corn for the road got in one and one-half hours afterwards. My escort is twenty-three men, twenty of which go on to Barttelot, my two boys and self, total twenty-six.

17th February Here is Stanley's timetable, all nicely [laid] out and dried and [with] beautifully worked-out marches, accompanied with a rough chart showing the route I am to take! Very nice to sit down in a comfortable room and tell one to go 250 miles or so downriver and [to] return, sixteen days or so of which [travelling] would be through unknown country, and [to] return in thirty days to the fort. In his letter to me he has either not considered or absolutely ignored the following very important items: first, has the rainy season commenced down there yet? (It had.) Second, was food to be got on the traced routes he ordered me to follow? Third, are the men at Ugarrowwa's now quite strong, or are they weak from disease and famine? Fourth, will there be canoes ready for us to cross the Ituri, or will there be delay in crossing? No, I was to go ahead without a break, marching the 250 miles in 15 days, or an average of 16 ⅓ miles per day through unknown bush tracks to a great extent—not forest, mind you, but tangled, vine-bound bush. Is this generalship? Is it rational?

Camped at Vilunari and had a lot of corn. No natives.

18th February A desperate day.[...] Marched very fast NW, WNW, and W till 10:30 over this very large track, passing three old villages from which natives had fled. At 11:30 had gone, all told, some 10 [miles] or 12 miles, then difficulties commenced. The big track struck north and we wanted west, so followed a track leading in that direction for nearly two hours, then lost track.[...] Made all together four attempts. By evening had walked 25 miles and at last struck blazed road which natives said led to river. Decided to camp and follow tomorrow. Found an occupied village and got plenty of tobacco and bananas.

This blazed road turned out next day to be a failure, only going as far as some deserted huts and then stopping.[...]

19th February   Off again but blazed track. Stopped at some old huts and had to retire. Began to dread we should go on in this way till we had wasted four or five days. Held a *shauri* and after much deliberation decided to follow an old road to Ipoto and then get guides for some short road on to Ugarrowwa's. Off we went and by nightfall had reached the second boat camp west of Kilimi and made camp.[...]

Stairs reached Ipoto on 20 February leaving it again on the twenty-fourth with a group of Manyuemas. During the remaining days of February, the caravan continued its march assisted by guides procured in the local villages. By 9 March the column reached a place named Upper Masumba which was under the direct management of Kalunga but really under the control of Ugarrowwa. Here, large quantities of rice and corn had been planted.

9th March   All this will be abandoned, though, very shortly, as, owing to the scarcity of ivory Ugarrowwa has decided to move both of his Masumbas [settlements] and will locate somewhere down the Aruwimi in quest of more elephants. Kalunga is found to be a first-rate and most agreeable manager.[...]

The Manyuema have been here nearly two years now and have exhausted all the supply of native goats in their raids, and as the Manyuema men never breed goats or fowls, the supply of meat in the Masumba is very small. Here there are two cattle (*su*), the remains of a former raid to the open country.

It is sixteen camps to open country and three to Ugarrowwa's, though it has been done in one. In a former trip eight days down Ituri, Kalunga told me that he got over 100 splendid tusks. Certainly they have a splendid collection here now, and some eight months ago they had cleared out every tusk and sent it overland to Ugarrowwa's. The master or owner of this Masumba, of Ugarrowwa's and Nyangwe of Ipoto is Abed bin Salim, a rich Arab, now on a visit to Muscat. He has been forbidden by Seyyid Barghash [the sultan of Zanzibar] to return to Nyangwe and will live in Zanzibar. All Ugarrowwa's and Kalunga's ivory will now go down the Aruwimi in canoes and thence up the Congo (or Lualaba). Thus it is seen that we have been the means of opening up a new road which these people have availed themselves of. Who can tell, this may alter in time the importance of the Ujiji country and end by the ivory going down the Congo to Banana Point instead of up-river and then across the continent to Zanzibar.[...]

Bad reports reach us from Ugarrowwa's: twenty-six or twenty-eight out of fifty-six said to have died and the remainder very weakly [sic]. Kalunga sent a fowl and some rice. Long yarn with all the chiefs. Decided to stop tomorrow and go on next day with some of Kalunga's men. Gorillas here very plentiful but very wild. Natives here all fighting against each other.

10th March Arranged to go tomorrow morning and only spend two days on the road. Lenda is two days from here.[...] Have a slight though troublesome fever, cannot keep down the quinine.

11th March Left the Masumba at 6:30 and marched for six hours without a break, camped on site of destroyed village and made 12 or 13 miles. Ivory caravan with us, about twenty tusks, some good ones, one of four *frazilahs,* 140 pounds.

12th March Got off early, and shortly after starting, rain came down in torrents. At 1:00 p.m. I came upon the Manyuemas seated down in a large village (deserted) and as everyone was nearly dead with wet and cold, decided to stop and make camp. [...]

13 March Marched till 4:00 p.m.[...] My bag, food, [and] tent did not come up by nightfall. After thoroughly exhausting myself in the cold wet bush, my fever became much worse, and by midnight the attack was very violent.

14th March Fever bad. Waited for men to come up and then gave them a deuced good flogging. At 2:00 made our old camp opposite to Ugarrowwa's and, crossing over, were soon talking to Ugarrowwa and his chiefs. Ugarrowwa I like better than any of the other chiefs of all the Manyuemas in these parts. He is a Zanzibari and knows the ways of the white men as witnessed by his taking bills of exchange on Zanzibar to the tune of £900, as we afterwards arranged. The place looks much the same as it did before except a few new houses have been put up. Rice and corn in plenty but not fully grown.[...]

Found twenty-nine men out of the fifty-six we had left were dead, and some fifteen of the remainder were away on *Rugga Rugga.* Cannot possibly catch Stanley now as I shall have to wait here at least four days for the absentees. What a tough blow this is. Fancy now I shall have to stay at Ibwiri and do [word illegible] work and miss the very cream of the expedition and what one has looked forward to during one's many weary months of toil.[...]

I found that all the Somalis except Duallah had died, two having been speared by natives while after bananas. None of the Soundanese had died, but two died the first day after leaving Ugarrowwa's. Juina, the man with the amputated foot, was able to walk about quite briskly with the aid of a stick.

For two months, while the rice and corn lasted, our men fed up [sic] like lords. After this, however, starvation ensued and many died from disease and famine. All food, nearly, was got by *Rugga Rugga* and brought into settlement. Some of the men I met were in poor order through laziness, but most were in good trim for short marches. Our men were quite differently treated to those at Ipoto. I made Ugarrowwa terribly disgusted with Ismaili and Kalunga by telling him of this, and assured him Abed bin Salim and Seyyid [Barghash] (the sultan) should hear every detail.[...]

15th March Fever raging. My head is almost bursting. One cannot keep down food or quinine and I am suffering also from bad diarrhoea. I must have lost a good many pounds in weight during the last few days.[...]

Visited the graves (twenty-eight or so) of all those who died and were buried here—a most melancholy sight. Just 50 percent of those left here. Deaths more from sickness than starvation: ulcers, fevers and chests [?], took off this number.[...]

16 March Sent off Abdullah and other nineteen men to search for the rear column and carry off letters for different officers in it. All went off cheerfully. Hope they will find the major soon and bring us news. Vomiting, diarrhoea, and fever all day, spent time in bed.[...]

17th March Closed with Ugarrowwa's for £870, being pay for twenty-nine men at £5.00 per month for six months. (Two men away [on] *Rugga Rugga* I did not close for with him.) Gave him bills of exchange in Arabic, Swahili, and English, payable at the English consul's at Zanzibar. Each was signed by Rashid and the English ones have my signature attached. Gave Ugarrowwa a letter to send or deliver to the major to give Ugarrowwa 100 [pounds of] ammunition. Gave Ugarrowwa two rifles and about fifty rounds Rm. [Remington?] cartridges. Two more men, Uledi Ferahani and Saburi, came into camp about 11:00 a.m. Also told major to give Ugarrowwa £60 if got the two men now absent.[...]

On 18 March Stairs commenced his return journey to Ituri. Between 19 March and 8 April, Stairs's entries were brief and laconic. His main preoccupation was to obtain food. Also he complained of frequent attacks of fever and increasing weakness.

9th April Am perfectly played out with this constant fever. No one helps me on the road at all. There is no one fit to carry me, so I have to walk. Quinine will not work as one cannot keep it in one's stomach. This lonely helpless feeling depresses a chap terribly. [Add] to this the disappointment of not getting to Stanley and the lake, and you can form some idea of the time I had. Reaching camp, I fall on my rubber sheet already laid on the ground by Abedi, and then crawl into bed. Rashid is the only one who helps me at all with the men. He is a good fellow, Rashid, and one who obeys what is told him.[...]

Reached Ituri and made camp. What a welcome sight this old river is again after such an absence, though all hope of seeing Albert Nyanza this time is destroyed. What a state of weakness my men are in; it is terrible. We left with twenty six men and I have only got sixteen now—ten deaths. Found no canoe and had to wait in camp. How is Kilonga Longa to know we are here unless we send a man to swim over? Two men tried in evening but failed.[...] Lay on my back all night in agony simply burning up.[...]

10th April Got Kapaporo, a Manyuema, to swim the Ituri River early this morning. He reached Masumba and re-swan river at night saying there was [a] canoe one hour lower down. I am simply burning up inside. One's heart and pulse go like race horses. No thermometer. Toothache again

Between 11 and 26 April Stairs's entries continued to be very brief. Obviously he suffered intensely from fever.

26th April Started off early and at 4:30 reached Fort Bodo. Here I found that Stanley, Jephson, and Parke had started for the lake on 1st April. (At once I felt all the old disappointment again.) Nelson was left in charge of the fort. Stanley, in a letter, was to follow our old road and make his fort on the small island near Kavalli. Jephson was then to go on as far as Wadelai if necessary, and Nelson tells me that Stanley gives him fifteen days to do this. Rot! Parke will be of great use to them all. Stanley was very ill for over a month, after

I left, with gastritis; he seems to have suffered a great deal. I believe he was very mad with me when he heard from Peringania that I had followed the Manyuemas instead of crossing the Ihuru, and [he] swore terribly.

By George, after all my hard work and after deuced near getting left with fever, I reach here and only find that I am to remain and do Masumba [settlement] work. It is a terrible blow. I would have given anything to have gone on with the safari. I only brought fourteen men into the fort of those from Ugarrowwa's, and all these are weak and tired. Nelson is living in Stanley's house; I will live in the officers' house which I now call mine. We agreed to mess apart as this would undoubtedly save many a row. Fancy plantation work right on the equator. We work here from 7:00 to 11:00 a.m. and from 1:00 to 4:00 p.m.–plenty long enough under such a hot sun, but one hour and a half shorter than Stanley's hours. Stanley, before they left (and Jephson), built more houses and planted great quantities of Indian corn. The beans we planted are a failure. Fortunately, Stanley left some of his books to while away our spare hours. I found some eight or nine goats left here, but five are only kids. Killed a large goat for my men, and Nelson gave all some very good meat from a kid he had just killed. There are four fowls, two of which lay eggs. I suppose one must just go in for this work with a light heart and try and do the most possible, but at present one's feelings are anything but pleasant. Corn, beans, and tobacco are the only things worth growing, as we have no seeds of any sort.

"The Pasha is coming..."

(contemporary illustration from *The Pictorial World*)

CHAPTER 6
AT FORT BODO

27 APRIL—22 DECEMBER 1888

Stanley fails to appoint the commander of the boma *before his departure. He returns on 8 June bringing back the long awaited news of Emin Pasha. Stanley leaves for Yambuya on 16 June, accompanied by Parke, who goes to Kilonga Longa's to recover the loads previously left there. Stairs assumes the command of Fort Bodo. The remnants of the rear column return 10 December. Fort Bodo is abandoned. The expedition resumes its march to Lake Albert.*

Stairs spent 27 April resting, eating good meals and investigating the changes that took place during his absence. The plantations were being ravaged by local villagers and invaded by elephants and buffaloes which destroyed the banana groves.

28th April What a miserable set of chaps we have become.[...] No clothes, no boots, no pens, no pencils, [no] ink, our knives lost or broken, no candles, or anything in the way of food except what we can get out of the country, very few medicines. To make things worse, Stanley has taken almost all the quinine. Nelson only left ninety grains–just three good doses in a bad attack. Mind you, this quinine is not Stanley's but Parke's, some that was given to him at Cape Town by a surgeon. Here we are then, without quinine; I have a couple hundred grains left of my own. Of all the old women that any of us have seen in the way of secretary, oh Lord help us, old De Winton sweeps the tray.[1] Utterly ignorant of African life, he recommended this and that and scorned other things, and we, taking his advice like fools, have been badly left. We have one cooking utensil [each] on an average.[...] We were told expressly we should have candles and a small canteen each. What a preconcerted lie this was.

Old De Winton knew there were forty boxes of grub for five whites. When he afterwards knew there were twelve whites going, why didn't he order more boxes? *Secretary!* What the deuce does an old R.A. [Royal Artillery] officer know about this business? Stanley, of course, would join in and say in quite an offhand manner, "Oh, they'll manage in some manner, don't order any more, tra-la-la." Then, when we have been out fifteen months, the quinine, brandy, and ulcer medicines are out. After this, let no one run down military expeditions; they generally allow their officers medicines when sick, and light to see by at nights. What fools we all were not to inquire into these matters before leaving England. But no, we begin to think of this in Central Africa when right on the equator, as far as possible away from salt water.

Stanley treats his officers like dogs, and himself as near like a prince as he can in this country. It would be splendid if we could only march to Zanzibar in company with Emin Pasha.[...]

This day last year we reached Kinshassa.[...] We have lost over 210 men from Yambuya till now. Of these, at least twenty have died of arrow wounds.[...]

From the end of April to 4 May, the men were busy building a granary and planting tobacco. The work on the granary continued, while Stairs and Nelson suffered from intermittent attacks of fever. On the eleventh Stairs noted with deep regret that he had finished his English tobacco. However, he enjoyed his spare time by engaging in some culinary exploits.

13th May   I made a great discovery today: finding that the juice of fermented bananas before reaching the *pombe* stage was very sweet, I thought sugar could be boiled down from it. We then filled a *chungu* of partially fermented liquor and boiled it down, when at last a thick sweet syrup of delicious taste was the result. This we used on our porridge with great success. I also made a little jam which is grand.[...]

One's feelings as to what Stanley and others are doing, and one's thoughts as to when they will return are almost constantly coming up.[...] They should be back here by middle of June. Abdullah should also have returned by that time, unless the major is still at Yambuya.[2] One cannot help feeling that it will be two years before any of this expedition every sees Zanzibar. We are now four months beyond the time Stanley said he should return to the major. Is the major's safari still extant?[...]

The routine work of construction, clearing and hoeing fields continued during the subsequent four days.

18th May   My supply of ink is just about finished; again and again I have added water to it, until it much resembles American public picnic lemonade. How to make more, I am at a loss. The Arabs make *fari* ink by burning the stalks and husks of rice in an earthenware pot and then boil[ing] the residue down and us[ing] this as ink. I have seen some of it but, it seemed to be rather watery looking stuff.

Nelson and I are going to try our hand at distilling whisky from corn and rum from bananas. So far we have made or prepared a good many new things, but the want of a book on the subject places us completely on our own resources. We have made banana beer, banana syrup, and jam which is splendid, tasting like crab apple, or quince if very strong. We also have made salt, soap (in a sort of way), red pepper, Indian corn, beer, and some other things. Then we make banana and corn meal, puddings, cakes, toast, fritters from ripe bananas (when we have fat, which is very seldom), and a lot of minor dishes.

One often forgets almost that on every side of one are enemies, and that we are liable to attack at any moment.[...] There are now no inhabited villages within 15 miles of this place, but still the natives have built here and there rough bush camps generally near some source of food [such] as a plantation for bananas. The women, of course, carry the loads. Often our men, also looking for food, encounter these parties, and then the rifle speaks up and drops perhaps one or two, the others all running. Then again our chaps sometimes get an arrow which often enough does for them [sic].

No attempt at friendship has been made here by any side, nor in fact do we want to be friends with these people as one feels sure that under the cloak of peace these cunning devils would play back on us and perhaps get the best of it. No, an open enmity is far and away the best.

I have on guard in the towers of the fort some eight men every night and two sentries by day. Zanzibaris make the poorest of watchers, though, and constantly one ha[s] to be out in the night to see that they keep on the alert. We make them shout from post to post every hour, and every night I visit them three times. The Washenzi seem to know the difference between us and the Manyuema well enough; they say the Manyuema take women and ivory while we only take goats. The Manyuema kill many more natives than we do and are much crueller. In the ramble from Ugarrowwa's I just had, the Manyuema stabbed four of their women slaves to death and cut off the hand of another, letting her go into the bush to die.[...]

On 19 and 20 May some ripe corn had been stolen by the local villagers. No entry was made on 21 May. On the twenty-second men were at work planting the fields, and on the twenty-third they were harvesting corn. Thursday, 24 May was recorded by Stairs as the queen's birthday. On that day Stairs completed a plan of the fort. He also noted that his attempts at making ink had failed.

During the subsequent two days, skirmishes with local people led to the death of one man. Stairs noted that the harvest proved a success and 7 tons of corn were stored.

27th May The average yield per acre from the big field was 60 bushels. I don't think it will be safe to put more than 10 tons into the new granary. Today I got about 100 more Wasongora words from the captive boys we have, but it is very difficult work. Plurals, genders, etc., one cannot possibly get for some time. In our expedition of a few days ago I got a small brown and white native dog of the regular Washenzi breed. I should like very much to get her home or cross her with Stanley's dog. I have named her Mtoro— the runaway. Read a lot of Wolseley's pocket book. What a godsend a few books would be here.

Between 28 May and 6 June the time was spent mostly on clearing the fields and planting. Houses for Stairs and Nelson were constructed.

6th June Rashid and men finished hoeing at 11:00 the piece in front of the ditch. I put them then onto the old corn field near the tobacco. The others work same as yesterday. Killed the big black goat having two other ewes and a ram. Nelson has bad fever (105°) again, and today is in bed. Stanley should be back in ten days to [sic] his calculation.

This book now is simply a source of insanity to anyone writing it. To start with, one has just to pick up and collect the many scraps lying about on one's board table, putting these together they form the book. Then one gets quite lost shifting these about till they assume a proper form for writing on. Truly we are in a pretty bad way as regards our supply of the many little necessities every educated European travels about with. I have not a single pen and only one miserable little lead pencil, (none of the others have ink), and very little paper. The use of this book for a journal shows up pretty fairly my need for another one.

I had often wondered what it would be like to be left in a detached fort in some black man's country far away, even [from] any of the comforts of the backwoodsman. By Jove, we have it now in good earnest. On the march one does not mind the absence of tea, coffee, sugar, salt, etc., so much, but in a fixed position with one day [...] just the same as another, one feels the want of salt [...] especially, very much, and tea would be positively a godsend.[...]

7th June Same as yesterday. All at work.

8th June About 2:00 p.m. heard shouts and shots and soon after Stanley and the safari came in amidst great excitement. What is the news? [...] Yes, the white man is there; we have seen him and fought side by side with him; we had very little fighting; all our former enemies are now our friends, Jephson left in boat and in six days brought back news that he [Emin Pasha] was alive. A letter had been left by him with the natives, and Stanley, getting hold of this, knew all would be well.

Parke looks rosy and Stanley fit. Jephson remains behind and will go the rounds of the stations with Emin Pasha. Casati was alive and with [Emin Pasha] in his camp.

9th June Stayed indoors yarning [sic] nearly all day with Parke and Stanley. They have discovered a snow mountain to SW of lake, perhaps Gordon Bennett.[3] Emin Pasha and Casati both willing to come out and in six months are to be ready at south end of lake.[...] Emin Pasha has suffered very little from sickness and has made an enormous collection of insects, snakes, etc., and has discovered old spades and tools buried away for centuries in the earth. Mackay, the missionary in Uganda,[4] is safe and sent letters on to Stanley and Emin Pasha.

The pasha was very much pleased at seeing the white men and made great presents of honey, cloth and tobacco, vegetables, cattle and goats. He lives very well and appears quite happy, rather objecting to leav[ing] Africa. His followers number six thousand, including two drilled battalions [that are] well armed. Stanley brought 105 natives with him to this place as porters. They are of the Madi tribe at the NW end of Lake Albert. Stanley this time made friends with the Wazamboni, our old enemy, and advanced on and drove away an unfriendly tribe.[5] He had fifteen hundred of [the] natives working for him. He, Stanley, looks very much pleased at the success he has achieved. Parke, Jephson, and Stanley sent letters through Uganda. There is some doubt yet as to whether they will get through or not, but if they do, people at home will hear of us about August or September.

Letters from Zanzibar had reached Casati, but not forwarding them to Emin Pasha, they were burnt with his home when Kabba Rega, the king of Uganda, drove him out. When Casati was relieved he had nothing on but a loin cloth. These Madi people will go down by Yambuya with the column and carry loads. They say the bush is a bad place.[...] Many of them are bound to die on the road. They gave us a dance in the fort at night, a very clumsy affair, not at all like the Somalis or the South Africans. Poor devils, they have no clothes and don't know how to build quick shelters in the bush. [They] will suffer terribly at night in the bush and, if there is much wet, will die off like rats. They will be of great help to us though, as our men can go empty-handed. Who is to go with Stanley yet, we don't know.

Emin Pasha gave Stanley and Parke each a donkey, first-rate little beasts. They will be left here. He has promised to give us all one. He has two hundred of these and a trained elephant. The report of Stanley's arrival with a big army has, I believe, frightened the king of Uganda very much. Now with the major's people and, say, fifteen hundred of Emin Pasha's we could do some pretty good work if any big tribe should attack us.[...]

10th June Still yarning [sic] about Emin Pasha and talking to the men who all look very fit and bumptious as they always get with full stomachs. All want to stay here, dreading the bush journey through mud and water very much.

Emin Pasha sent Nelson and myself honey, tobacco, and salt in good quantities—a perfect godsend. He also gave Stanley quantities of honey and potato whisky, but he has not given us a drop of it yet. The latter is very good stuff though a bit smoky. Parke brought also a present of a basket of tobacco from Emin Pasha for each of us. It is mild and very light coloured and not bad smoking.

The newly arrived men were preparing to leave in five days' time with Stanley, and indeed on 16 June the column, 211-strong with 14 men under Parke, left in the morning. Stanley hoped to be back in about three months bringing with him Emin Pasha and Jephson.

Stanley left Stairs in charge of Fort Bodo with Nelson as second in command. The garrison numbered fifty-nine. During the subsequent three days the time was spent mostly on gardening. They planted seeds—onion, watermelon, pea, and eggplant—obtained from Emin Pasha. The neighbouring blacks often plundered the fields.

20th June Coronation day?[...] Last night I fully expected a raid on our corn by the natives. Just about dusk we heard them shouting in the bush quite close at hand and afterwards heard other signs of their presence. Nothing definite could we hear or see, though I watched in the towers till nearly ten o'clock.[...] I half-believe the donkeys scared them off by their braying in the yard near the ripe corn.

Poor old Randy, Stanley's dog, died in my room last night. He had been left under my care by Stanley on leaving for Yambuya, and here now, he only lives four days. I feel certain he died of a broken heart.[...] Stanley will be in an awful way about it and will think I either starved him or beat him to death.[...]

21st June We have been eighteen months out from England. It was originally to have taken us only eighteen months to reach Zanzibar. Now we are about halfway. In a few days we shall have been absent from Yambuya a year. Gardening, making fences, cutting leaves. Wound chronometer.

22nd June Nelson is up today for the first time since Parke left. He was up for morning parade.[..] He is simply maddening, though I should not say so. He is the biggest grumbler I every saw.[...] His only talk is about grub, which he bolts with the speed of a hungry dog. Among the men he is an utter ass, too, and pick[s] holes about men insulting him. I can hardly speak civilly to him now; it's either grub when he answers or, "I've got a pain in my big toe" or something after that style.

Am making a pair of veldt shoes. They require a lot of patches to make them wearable and will not stand the wet very well. We make them of untanned leather.

23 June [...]Yesterday and today we weeded all the roads and cleaned out the drains, and by this evening should have the place shipshape. I am now certain I was never built for sitting down to this sort of work, it slowly drives me wild, generates a temper fit for an old Indian curried [sic] general, makes me notice every little weak point in my neighbours while at the same time one forgets one's own.

Here life is the same day after day almost without a break. The only way to make the days pass pleasantly is to work yourself with the men. I cannot talk cheerfully now with Nelson. Firstly, he is a chap now I begin to despise on account of his loafing qualities. Secondly, if we do attempt to talk, the subject always ends in food. Not a bright life is it? Perhaps I had better not talk any more of this. [When] one [is] alone all the time [and] hardly ever speaks one's own language [one] gets to notice all these things.[...]

How great a pleasure it would be here to know something of botany, all the innumerable shrubs and plants are simply unnameable by us.[...]

24th June Parke should be now on his way back with the loads from Ipoto. Sunday here is always a dreadful slow sort of day, one has nothing to do much but write up one's journal, and see that the goats and sheep do not go out into the garden. This is a most trying job and one which no amount of supervision seems to have any effect.[...]

25th June Terigua, Juma, and Anami ran away yesterday on sentry and have not returned. [They] were under punishment for sleeping on sentry. Tingue [sic] had a months' rock drill. My punishments are as follows: flogging up to 100 strokes and in addition one month's stone drill, then, of course, any combination of these: tying a man up till he is repentant; standing in one position up to two hours with a heavy stone on one's head–this they dislike most of all. Stone drill means marching up and down in the square four hours per day with a 50-pound stone on a man's head.[...]

Between 26 and 30 of June, Stairs was ill with a bad attack of fever which left him very weak. Once again he complained of Nelson's laziness and indifference and his failure to supervise the men's work.

1st July My twenty-fifth birthday (1863) today. One is getting old and feels one is doing nothing in this place, locked up from all the world. On my last birthday I was near Yambuya and bad with remittent fever; thank heaven it is not so now. Second birthday in Africa. I hope the next will be near Zanzibar.

They must be having a good time of it in Canada by now: sea trout, with trout fishing, tennis, and strawberries and cream, and ice cream. By Jove, how good strawberries and cream would go now–hush, don't speak of it.

Yesterday to "save her life" we killed the only calf and gave rations to our men, keeping as much as we wanted for ourselves. She was badly on the wane, poor thing.[...]

To turn to fever, I believe that there is no greater mistake made by medical books when they say do not eat large quantities of meat in hot climates, if so the liver becomes torpid, the bowels clogged, etc. Don't believe this at all. Eat as much meat as you want, do not gorge yourself, but to prevent violent fevers when doing hard work, keep up your system [sic] to full power [with] plenty of good meat and other food–if necessary, meat four times a day.

The cause of a great many fevers is weakness in oneself, I mean poorness of condition. Every time on this expedition that I have walked and worked hard for, say, ten or fifteen days at a time with poor food, I have been attacked with bad fevers. Once I got to food and got rid of the fever, I never get [sic] another till once again my system becomes weakened by hunger. No, meat and other good strong foods are the things to work on in this and every other country. I know that fever itself wears one down violently quick [sic], but what I say is that the primary cause of that fever [is] weakness, perhaps combined with a chill or effects of the sun. Those coming strong and healthy—built up with good English beef—to this country, are rarely troubled with fever for the first six months for the reason that their systems is well able to knock off malaria, etc.[...]

Drank [to] my own health in evening and had the best dinner I have had for many a long day: soup from the heifer we killed, cold tongue, a steak, the undercut joint, bananas, corn, *ugari,* etc., and then half a cup of Emin's whisky to finish up with.[...]

2nd July Made another change and tried to dry the corn we pulled last week. For myself I think the best way is to husk the corn—not shell it—and then dry it for a couple of days in the sun, and then put it into the bins. The natives leave the husks on it, but dry it over fires.[...]

Parke ought to be somewhere near the Kilimani today or perhaps leaving it in three days; then he should be here. I am moving the *boma* out some 6 feet on the SW side to give room for a large house, should Emin Pasha come here. I also will build another for his officers.[...]

3rd July Settled down to stationary life such as this place affords.[...] Often I wish I could tear away from here and once more get on the march. Once on the move, one's spirits rise and one feels one is doing something. Here, ever so hard though you work, ever so much you may think, there is still that buried away feeling which at periods comes up from its grave and lets you imagine you are doing nothing [for] your own or anyone else's good.[...] The very greatest comforts are smoking and looking after the garden. I feel I am becoming like my father, who, in seeing a dandelion blossom, invariably cuts it off with his stick. I, in turn, on seeing a weed on one of the trucks [sic], stop and root it up. One says one hardly speaks a word of English, I omitted to state that one swears in English.[...]

4th July Men constantly bring in reports of the boldness of the natives in coming close to the fort for bananas and potatoes. We are helpless till Parke comes to have a slap at them.[...]

5th July This is Parke's twentieth day out; he must be near.[...]

6th July Had a weighing match: doctor 154 pounds, Stairs 155 pounds, Nelson 150 pounds, Abedi 170 pounds, Farag Ala 95 pounds, [and] Mufta 95 pounds.

About 11:15 a.m. the doctor and his carriers turned up a the fort. One of his men, Khamis Sururan, died on the road for want of food really. Parke has been twenty-one days absent. He brought up a good sized [word illegible] unhusked rice for us to plant. This will be a great godsend should Jephson be four or five months in coming. Stanley, he said, was very mournful about the long journey ahead. I rather fancy he would have liked it better had he taken some white officer with him. He did Parke out of a goat with usual meanness. Kilonga Longa and the other few chiefs who were there were in good lying form. Ismaili actually had the guts to say to Stanley that he gave Parke and Nelson food every day during their stay at Ipoto—a most confounded lie. The road, Parke said, was very bad. Stanley was carried in a chair all the way to Ipoto! Note this!!!

What were Stanley's reasons for going to Yambuya alone? Undoubtedly they were the following: so that afterwards in his book he can say [he] alone braved the terrors of famine and the bush, found [his] way down the river and by [his] skill and nerve, saved Major Barttelot; he knows he will have all the goats and food to himself. (Don't think this paltry; it is not. On the subject of food Stanley is a perfect glutton; he eats more than even Nelson.); he wants to get out of paying the Manyuema, and does not want us to see the affair.[...]

7th July The rice will make a good crop I hope. Today I went over the crop of beans and put in seed where it was wanted; we also planted some fresh beans.[...]

8th July Showers again showing that now is the time for planting corn. This, that I am now writing, is with the ink just made. It would run much better from an ordinary pen; this is a stylo and the thick ink catches. If used thin, [this ink] is of no use. This makes another manufacture turned out by Fort Bodo.[...]

9th July Upon my word some of the things Dr. Parke tells us about Stanley in his dealings with Emin Pasha astonish even me. His petty meanness and selfishness crop up on every possible occasion. He and Emin will have a big row [one] of these days; he, [Emin], is not a man to have anything to do with one who practices anything underhand. When two big men meet 'tis seldom they can work together peacefully for long; each wants his own way in a matter. Emin will not be ready for Stanley when he comes up, and this will incense *Bula Matari* very much.[6] Egyptians and such ilk take a long time to act. It's an open question, too, whether this is not the best policy in such a country as this.[...]

10th July Nelson got in his crop of tobacco, plenty of it but poor quality being second leaves. Stanley must have heard by this time news of the major; if he has not yet met Abdullah, then things are black.[...]

11th July The Zanzibari is no soldier, and when rough times come up, he shows the coward [sic] to a degree: his trustworthiness and pluck desert him at the same time, and he wants then to be off. As the porter, though, in quiet countries, I should say very few other natives could come up with him—our loads are all over 60 pounds and many [are] 68 pounds. These the men will carry all day on very poor food and remain cheerful.

Besides this load, say of 65 pounds (an average), he carries a Remington (9 pounds), his blanket or mat (say, 5 pounds), then, say, 4 pounds of food (for they rarely carry much more), then the hoe, axe, or spade—these are nearly all gone now—(say, 3 pounds more), and the total would come to 86 pounds. Not a bad load![...] Though these fellows can carry this amount, I say 50 pounds should be the limit.[...] Their pay is £5 per month.

As a sentry, where protracted attention to every little thing going on around him must be given, the Zanzibari is an utter failure. I have lectured a man for sleeping on sentry at the same time giving him 50 strokes and 30 days stone drill, yet on his next guard that man was asleep and got 100 lashes. Sentry with us is not play; *we must* be on the alert, especially towards dawn. No, they are not of the right stuff for sentries. Here at night the very slightest snap of a twig or the faintest spark from the native fire stick must be heard and seen; both times the Wasongora have come, white man gave the alarm.

12th July Planting and hoeing.[...]

13th July One becomes frightfully exasperated at the old one's [Stanley's] doings at times and vows all sorts of things. But then, what can one do, he is a despot of the worst sort. Eaten up with pride, vanity, and arrogance, he is incapable of seeing anything good in the doings of others, his own [doings] occupy so much of his thoughts. A meaner more selfish (especially concerning his stomach) man, one has never seen, nor did one think man descended so low. He will borrow food when one is starving and then not repay it. He will borrow or ask for anything that his eye lights on and when asked in return for the same thing he will say he has not got it, when all the time it is sticking out before one as [if it were] a sign board.

To show the utter rottenness of the expedition, *we received* more from the man we were *going to relieve* [Emin Pasha] than the expedition ever brought from England—more in clothes and food. Of course, more cloth was brought, but for eighteen months *who saw any* of it? By utter stinginess and false zeal for ammunition, not a bag ever left Yambuya. So far, not one officer has given him a word of praise: his generalship, in spite of all his *own* praise, has been of the poorest; he let three hundred native porters slide through his hands at the lake through sheer pride in not listening to Emin Pasha's word to tie them together.[...]

It is interesting, though not very amusing, to go over the number of lives we have lost since leaving Yambuya. We started with 389 souls and reached the lake twice; on the return of Stanley to Yambuya, he had 117 men of those that walked out of Yambuya eighteen months ago, and we were left 58—a total of 175 men out of 389, making 214 deaths, desertions, missing, etc., in eighteen months. This is about 53 percent. Most of these deaths were from privations in the way of food caused by bullheaded plugging through the bush [and] not stopping for food when it was to be got.

At times when one thinks of the hard work one has willingly done for Stanley, of his petty and great meanness one has endured, of the four months [of] starv[ation] one has passed through, of the crushings one has got in being called [a] deserter and other choice epithets, one's whole soul burns again to think I [sic] ever had anything to do with such a man. One's good feelings for everyone at the start and for him have been swept away as clean as a corn broom sweeps a marble floor, and in their place, feelings of the bitterest, the most intensely acute, have crept in and take[n] the place of the former. What is the reason [for] this? Why, every day, seeing this man jealous of any popularity his officers get; jealous of any petty little thing they may do which will bring them up in the eyes of the men; every day seeing him secretly talking with his men against some officer and breaking down discipline as he would break down his officers hearts; every day hearing his constant bickering really about nothing; seeing his paltry borrowing fits; being treated like dogs and not getting a due share of provisions; hearing his false voice in his conversation on official work; seeing his bullheadedness in not taking the advice of such a man as Emin Pasha—these and the many other qualities he possesses, all tending in the way of petty mean jealousy, kill one's good feelings, [...] and make one's inner feelings bitter as gall. Examples one could give by the dozens but it is doubtful if such would do any good.[...] "Ingratitude is treason to mankind."[...]

14th July It is very strange one is forgetting all the tunes or snatches from operas one knew in England, for instance, *Patience*. Slowly but surely the airs from this are fading away as well as those of the *Mikado, Olivette, La Mascotte,* etc. One is constantly whistling the same few old stale things and has forgotten other[s] more recently come out [sic]. Fever again today (102°).[...]

On 15 July one of the men died of a wound inflicted by an arrow during the march with Dr. Parke from Ipoto to Fort Bodo. The subsequent five days were filled with hoeing, sowing, and all sorts of household chores. Stairs reminisced on the pleasures of life in England and speculated on what his friends there might be doing at this time of the year.

21st July Hoed up field in rear of corn. Gave rations of ten to each man. In afternoon, when giving rations, Shaban deliberately walked up the line out of turn and was going to snatch up a bunch of corn. I stopped him, he replied in an insolent, insubordinate manner, and I punched him. At once he ran out and got a thick stick to hit me I suppose, but I sent him off again. This is the second attempt made by some of the worst characters here to stir up the loyal men to a general desertion of we [sic] white men and march away onto the plain and [to] Emin Pasha where they will get better food and plenty of beef. Long before I punished Fatheela W. Hagi, I knew that some ten men were trying to poison some good men into desertion en masse and leav[e] us and the loads. In both cases did those two men act badly so as to try and draw the sympathy of their comrades to their side. Felteh, Msungesi Idi, and three or four others are also prominent. No wonder they want to go away: here the work is irksome, the food [is] poor, and the hope of getting out soon [is] very thin. On the plains they would have good food and little work—the Zanzibari idea of a true heaven.

What this will come to [in] the end one cannot say. I am quite ready to reason and talk with reasonable men, but to talk to a lunatic like Shaban is madness. My every effort here has been to make the men's lives happy and as easy for them as possible. Food I cannot give, as what corn we now have must be kept for rations on the march with Emin's men. The sentries I have punished severely when caught asleep—a proceeding any even, rational-minded savage must see is advantageous to all. If the sentries sleep, why, then we are in the hands of the Washenzi.

My blood boils at times over a thing like this, as it is all owing to Stanley's conduct, every bit of it. His lack of treatment [sic] of his officers in every single detail tended to lower them in the eyes of the men. If one of the officers *justly* beat a man and that man went off and complained to Stanley, he would take the [first] man's part to a certain extent, or at least sympathize with him, and so the officer lost [sic] prestige. In a thousand ways he [Stanley] has tried to belittle his officers in the sight of his men and so atone to them in a measure for his *own cruelty*.

I want to stick, through this expedition, a comrade of the men, not their enemy. I should like to bring my company to Zanzibar and be able to say [that] well I know there is not one man in it who dislikes me or thinks me capable of any brutal or unkind act. If so, I should be happy.[...]

22nd July Stanley knows not what this word "discipline" means. His method of enforcing obedience is solely with the rod; he reigns by terrorizing his men, not by expostulation, reason, and then force. Anyone of us could teach him lessons on treating men.[...]

23rd July Addressed the men this morning. Told them how mad they were in thinking of running away from here, how they would get eaten up on the plains, etc., and said if they would only play fairly towards one [me], I should do the same towards them. After this I gave them a holiday for today. No work done at all today. Felteh has been the *chief* instrument I have now in working up men's feelings.[...]

Stairs had another attack of fever and his temperature rose to 103°; it subsided by the twenty-eighth. He blamed his sickness on the unhealthy situation of Fort Bodo, which was in the proximity of a swamp. On 1 August the building of Emin Pasha's home was completed and his arrival was expected shortly.

5th August I hear people like Stanley saying they are splendid fellows, heroes, models of virtue, faithfulness, courage, etc., yet [no] man ever born up to now hates Zanzibaris from his inner heart as much as H. M. Stanley. One judges by his constant venomous imprecations and his sorry dry treatment of them. It is easy enough after reaching home to publish in one's book splendid fellows, martyrs, heroes, tigers!! But let me hear the white man say all this [...] here, far away from anyone else, with poor food and bad lookout [sic] all this talk will then be altered and the most patient, godfearing Englishman, who at home never utters anything worse tha[n] "the gracious" will become [so] adept in the art of swearing that the tallest blasphemies on a Canadian or Yankee canal [sic] would turn green with envy and import a few Zanzibaris to work up his declining talents.[...]

The week between 6 and 12 August was rather uneventful. The villagers had been cutting Stairs's tobacco, and the loss was considerable. The camp was also plagued by rats.

13th August Food is getting scarce and I am very much afraid there will yet be trouble with the men. Some day I fully expect them to move off on their own hook and make towards the plain. Consider our position: all the loads left here, deserted by the men who would tell all sorts of stories, and perhaps we should never be relieved at all. Bah, the whole expedition has been trampled up right from the start to [the] finish till one is sick of it.

14th August At home yesterday. Nelson's men for potatoes. Caught dove.

15th August At house.[...] Two men for potatoes and two for bananas. Men loaf terribly when out for potatoes.[...]

On 16 August Stairs observed that two months had elapsed since Stanley left for Yambuya. Most of the time was spent on cultivation and various household chores. Health problems, such as ulceration and fever were becoming increasingly acute, and Stairs felt that the whole basin of the Congo was nothing but a pestilential prison, unsuitable for colonization.

20th August Men away for bananas.[...] It no doubt would seem strange to English people that here in 1° 20'[N] lat[itude], all of us have fires going every night. We have them partly as lights to go to bed with and partly to keep off the myriads of bats.[...] We find that the nights are rarely warm. In fact, the only heat we experience at all is that from the sun about noon; constant thunderstorms and violent rains cool the atmosphere almost daily.

21st August Last night the same gang of Wasangora who stole my tobacco returned with the object of looting more. This time they also found us awake and ready. The moon, though almost full, was partially hidden by drifting clouds when Ali, one of the sentries, came to my hut and told me he and his companions on guard had spied natives in Nelson's tobacco. I at once seized my Winchester and went up into the watchtower in search of the intruder[s]. From there we could dimly distinguish some twenty Washenzi all busily engaged in plucking Nelson's short new tobacco crop. At a signal we all three fired, reloaded, and gave them three rounds each. Like men possessed with the devil they ran, dropping bows and arrows [and] baskets half-filled with tobacco and ma[de] for the bush like deer; we only heard one yell from them.

In an instant all hands were ready and out [they] sallied. We found one dead in the tobacco, shot red-handed with his tobacco close beside him, another boy [was] wounded and was quieted with a bullet through the head—[a] most horrible looking wretch, a regular man-eater. This made two dead. We also feel certain that the one who yelled so much was badly wounded but managed to get away into the bush. Bows, arrows, and baskets we picked up. (All told, eighteen baskets.) This morning, also in the bush, we found their hiding place [...]. All sorts of wild roots, etc., were brought in by our own men this morning.

This will be a most salutary lesson to them, I hope. The sudden surprise at night when fancying we were all asleep and harmless will have great effect on the savage's brain. This morning I cut off the heads of the two men and placed them on poles, one at each exit from the bush into the plantation. This may prevent further attempt of the sorts [sic] for some time and so save life [sic].[...]

22nd August Weeding corn; blocked up with clay [on] west part, south side. Swept up, cleaned out houses.

23rd August What does the Zanzibar [sic] chief conversation consist in? Exactly the same topics as I imagine all natives talk about: food—of how much food they had at such and such a place and how little they get now.[...] Always the same, on the march, on sentry, in their huts, everywhere, it is food and *pombe*. Should they get plenty, it is all the same, delicacies then are talked of. Civilization has done him a lot of harm; he knows just sufficient [of] the white man's ways to be impudently saucy. In a standing camp, the Zanzibar [sic] is impatient to get away, frets himself if there is move not [sic] the same day by day, magnifies the slightest injury, while on the other hand likes to become bumptious and troublesome. If discipline has not been installed thoroughly into him beforehand I am confident it cannot be done.[...] He likes excitement, change, looting, and other such pleasures, delights in capturing a woman or two and giving her immense loads to carry besides making her a slave to his person.[...]

Out of our fifty-four men and boys I hardly think more than twenty-three will be able to carry loads on the march. Seven or eight more might take loads of 20 pounds, but that is about all. *Ugari,* made from green plantains of a bad type, and greens is the now [sic] only food of the men. Many slowly fade away under this diet, especially if they [are] attacked by bad ulcers. To tell the truth, for the men, and to a great extent for ourselves, it has been one long starve ever since we left Yambuya thirteen months ago, only relieved by short sallies on the plains.[...]

24th August Men our far in the bush after palm stalks to make brooms; others weeding.[...] I have a presentiment that Jephson will be here in a few days! I hope so.[...]

25th August This morning about nine o'clock, after a great deal of suffering, Anamri died. He had wasted away to a mere skeleton from pain caused by his ulcer. The diameter of this ulcer, the worst I have ever seen, was about 5 inches, all his foot bones and sinews were attacked to within 10 inches from the sole of his foot upwards.[...] The flies are very dangerous here, they rest on men's ulcers and there carry the poison about injecting it perhaps inside some other unfortunates's system. One cannot be too careful about keeping the place clean.[...]

26th August Killed one last sheep this morning. Two days and we will have no more meat.[...]

27th August Men have been stealing our onions.[...]

28th August Now we have peas, onion tops, beans, and corn out of our garden.[...] We have been out of England nineteen months and seven days. From Yambuya, exactly fourteen months. When leaving England, Stanley expected in nineteen months to have finished the work and again have returned home.

29th August Men at the same work as yesterday.[...] One understands thoroughly well by this time why it was that nearly all the Belgian officers on the Congo looked pale and unstrung, many indeed appearing asleep all the time. It is the heavy atmosphere and want of something attractive to the mind. To pursue pleasure out of doors there must be hunting or fishing; to most men this is absent. To the keen, there is botany or entomology, of course.

30th August At same work as yesterday.[...] Slight fever in the evening.

31st August Fever all day. Tremendous hurricane last evening, destroyed the roofs of nearly all the sentry towers and those of some of the men's huts. Also damaged a lot of corn and other crops. A great many trees blown down flattened out the corn. Had all these removed and the men's huts repaired today. It will take a week's work to get everything straight again. Bridge again destroyed.[...]

1st September Another month and Jephson not here yet. Repaired roofs of towers and granary. Corn is springing up by itself well. Fever much better. Oh how one wishes Jephson would come quickly. I am desperately tired of this sort of life and long once more to be on the move.

2nd September Men all away after bananas. Khamis Feredi, the sick man, is now worn away to a shadow. I have never seen such a skeleton in my life: he weighs about 70 pounds now, formerly would weigh quite 140 [pounds].[...]

3rd September Men away getting bananas.[...] Today Stanley estimated he should reach Yambuya; in reality I expect he reached there, though, some time ago and is now on his way east again.

4th September At work again on the wretched roofs.[...] In evening Ali Jimba came to me and said *the men* had asked him to come to me and say [that] food was getting scarce and Jephson had not yet come; men were gradually losing their strength and that day proposed two *shauris*. [First,] that fifteen men and the white man should go to the edge of the bush with a letter. If natives appear ready then these men would work through to the lake and give the letter to Jephson. This letter [would] say that food was giving out and that a safari should come down soon or we could not hold out. [Second,] if natives were unfriendly then men return to Fort Bodo, move all loads on and build ahead somewhere. I dismissed Ali telling him I would consider the matter.

Now these things I know: that though *all* want to get out this place, including we [sic] whites, yet only some eight or ten would persist in their complaints should I speak to the men and tell them the utter madness of either [of] these propositions; that [...] they are tired of bananas and *ugari* day after day without change and want new food; that there are bananas enough here for every man to have two big feeds of *ugari* or porridge every day; [and] that there are some very bad eggs among the men who, at a pinch, would abandon loads, white men, and everything for the sake of feeding.

If Stanley hesitated to pass through the Wazamboni country with 120 strong men, well armed and elated with late successes, how much more so should we with fifty wretched men and boys, only twenty-three of which are effective. The rest [are] all "ulcer" boys, none of whom have ever seen the open country natives in a fight. No, to neither of these propositions can I give my assent. Stanley's words to me while having breakfast before leaving here were: "For God's sake don't leave this place till you are relieved. Kabba Rega [the ruler of Unyoro] will hear of your coming and you may walk straight into his arms. Then where is our ammunition? If Jephson does not come, wait for me!" My own opinion is that it is *death* to everyone of us should we leave this place.

The storm we had the other day has knocked over hundreds and hundreds of banana trees, which of course makes the outlook worse. With the bananas I hope we can stand out till the end of September or middle of October, then I should begin to give the men a little corn out of the bins. This would tide us over till the new corn came in, about the fifteenth or twentieth [of] November. We could plant again, but then *it is the dry season,* and we should get very little yield.

Between 5 and 9 September little was happening except for some tendency to mutiny or desertion by those who wanted to return to the open country. Stairs took great pains to explain to the men that such an action would be sheer madness as they would all be killed by the inhabitants of the plain.

10th September This is the territory of that most "Rotten of Rotten" concerns [sic] the Congo Independent State. You are welcome to your vast extent of wastelands dear Leopold! You have about the finest empire of water and sand that the world affords: bush from Myangwe to the Niger, from the Atlantic to the thirtieth meridian east.[...] No doubt there are still fools who will extol this mismanaged concern, but if I ever live to reach England it will be my duty to state exactly what exists between Banana Point and Basoko, and Basoko and the thirtieth E longitude [sic].

Do you know the Arabs (Manyuema) are working north and west, gradually invading your territory and draining every single tusk of ivory out of it? Do you also know they meditate taking Basoko or perhaps by this time ha[ve] done so? Are you asleep? If you are wise do one thing: abolish the state and once more throw the river open to the unhampered trade of the Dutch, English, and French houses. Waste no more money out here.[...]

I am afraid the present state of things cannot exist long. The men, impatient at our long stay, are becoming more anxious to get on to the lake. I have a little corn, but to give it to them now is madness; we must wait till the next crop is nearly ripe. We have thirty men disabled from ulcers; we have close on [sic] seventy loads. To start means the abandoning of these loads of which some thirty are ammunition. This lost, we can scarcely hope to cross Africa, through unknown savage tribes.[...] It is not for ourselves that all this anxiety is caused; it is for the men and the *loads*. If Emin Pasha does not come out with us through the fighting country and we lose these boxes of ammunition, we are helpless and our cause is hopeless. Stanley has told me this: "I will drive my way through to Zanzibar if the devil is in front," and I, knowing how bullheaded and determined he is, feel sure he would attempt it. With a small force you must have ammunition and ours is going to be a small force.[...] If Emin comes we could do with less ammunition in proportion to our numbers. He would, say, bring 600 fighting men, or even 850. This is a big force and, with all the camp followers and our men, would inspire the natives with fear. Truly, in this country, "in numbers there is safety."

To anyone who says "Ah, but you lay far to much stress on the importance of plenty of ammunition and too little on what cloth would do," I merely answer with a question: "By what means have we travelled over 730 miles of country from the Congo to the lake?" Why, by *rifle alone,* by shooting and pillaging. About the cloth I merely say Stanley is not a "cloth giver." He prefers [a] leaden method of securing respect and food.[...]

A small party that was sent for food did not return. The efforts made on 11 September to find the lost men failed. By the twelfth Stairs lost all hope of seeing them again. He was afraid that, had they fallen into the hands of the Washenzi, they were bound to meet with a horrible death.

13th September Planted my old tobacco plot with beans. This planting makes the men's spirits go down terribly as they then say, "Oh the *Muzungu* intends making a long stop here, we shall all starve!"[...]

14th September Planted small plot of bananas. It is most amusing to hear the men talking about *dawa* (medicine or charms). Many of the men who doubt the efficacy of the doctor's medicines, walk quietly away to one of the scribes in camp and from him get small extracts from the *Koran* written out on a dried banana leaf. These they neatly fold and sew up in a small piece of cloth. These then are tied to the affected joint or limb and trusted as an absolutely certain cure for the disease. [Then] they will go up to Parke and again get medicine, this time believing that it will do them good. *Dawa* with a Zanzibari, as well as, I suppose, with an Arab, means almost anything in the shape of medicine, charms, fetish collections of bones, teeth, etc. They have *dawa* for leopards which simply kill the leopard [on] sight, no force trap or stratagem of any sort [is] used, merely this *dawa* or charm.

The Manyuema smear their faces with banana flour before proceeding on a safari, to protect them from evil spirits and the enemies whom [sic] they may have to fight. They build small houses on reaching camp and in them place little fires which are kept up till morning; these houses are the *Magumba Shetani* or "houses of the devil." [The devil] wanders about the camp promiscuously, and would feign sleep with the men in their shelters, but on seeing these nice warm little huts, lays himself down by the fire and sleeps comfortably there till morning. Some of the Manyuema also look with dreadful superstition on fire. To allow a fire stick, once lighted in their houses, to be thrown out means that some evil [will] happen to them. All sticks lighted, fires made, or even ashes of a lighted pipe thrown down are to go out by themselves in the hut and never [to be] thrown outside. The greatest care is taken not to throw live coals into the ash heap when sweeping up the house.

Meat (beef) in any form is refused by the tiniest and most starved Zanzibari should he be suffering from an ulcer or venereal disease. Even the bones from chicken soup made by Nelson were refused by his boys on account of [their] having an ulcer. This, I have no doubt, has some connection with *dawa*. On the other hand, they will eat goat meat at all times. Abedi, my boy, tells me that in Zanzibar his father will beat him severely should he hear that the boy had been eating either beef or fowl of any sort when he was sick, or had sores of any kind.[...]

During the thirteen days between 15 and 27 September, the preoccupation with food continued. The absence of meat from the diet was felt intensely and some efforts were made to catch fish. It was not only the carriers who complained of the diet. Stairs shared their complaints and conjured all sorts of fantastic menus he would like to have upon his return to England. He also regretted that he did not have garden seeds and a book on botany and zoology. This would have helped him to introduce some variety into the diet. The time was spent mainly on repairs to the fort, planting and procuring bananas which, apart from the vegetables obtained from the garden, were the main source of food. On the twenty-seventh both Stairs and Nelson were down with fever.

28th September One does not mean to be so low-spirited or down in one's luck at having to stay here. Far from it. It is our duty, and all of us know it—to stick to this place to the last. But one puts down every side of the question in one's journal, so that perhaps on looking over these days a true story will be depicted.

Returned African travellers appear, as a general rule, to praise the country they have been through without much regard for the truth. This, to my mind, is far worse than those pessimists who run down tribes, climates, etc., *in toto*. In the first case, money may be invested and the investors "fooled"; whereas it is a speculator's own look-out [sic,] should he invest in the second case. Besides, *one forgets* one's troubles to a certain extent after a relief from them [while] beside a fire after dinner in England, with a good cigar and a whisky and soda; the pleasant side of affairs only occurs to one, and perhaps listeners do not hear an absolutely correct account. Then I know and know thoroughly—never believe that *any* man as you know him in *civilization,* will be the same man in mid-Africa. Let success go as it may—no fighting, plenty of food, spare porters, everything—and man will be as different in disposition in every way, as day is from night. A promise, I find, made in Central Africa is very much like a cloud: you may catch at it a thousand times without success, and at last you see this thing dissolving before your eyes and stand cursing the one that ever induced you to believe there was any substance in it.

29th September All of us have now become confirmed gluttons could the food be provided. Not gluttons [for] this sort of food here, but for good solid English food: beef, mutton, goose, ducks, spuds, vegetables of all sorts, turkeys, gamepies, oysters, beer, stout; these are the sorts of things one pants after. By George, how I should like to be in the Criterion, or the Bristol, or at so and so's. Just for one night would the grub fly. When one gets in this state it shows that present food can not be up to much. Read *Henry VIII*. Five or six of our men will never reach Zanzibar—Fenaghi, Sudi, and Uledi are going down the hill [sic] very fast, so much so that they now cannot go for food to the *shamba*.[...]

30th September Another month gone and still Jephson [has] not come.[...]

1st October Since leaving the Madura I have lost 21 pounds—my weight now is 142 pounds. On 6th July it was 155 pounds so that since then (three months) I have lost 13 pounds. Both Nelson and Parke have also lost on this grass-feeding.

The men's gardens are getting on in fine style: it was my idea to give the men ground and seeds and get them to till these and make gardens, as I thought they would have some further hold in the place and perhaps forget a little their desire of absconding! To show the zest with which this has been taken up I may say that I have given some twelve of fifteen men seeds. The fish baskets have also awakened an interest in the men, every man having now two or three or more baskets and getting fish sometimes twice a day—generally the small sort, but even these form a relish to their otherwise dry *ugari*.

2nd October Though we three whites have gone down in weight, as I said yesterday, still our boys have kept up or even put on flesh during the same time, showing that the food certainly agrees with them. What in the mischief are Emin Pasha and Jephson doing? What has happened? Are we to be relieved at all by them or wait till Stanley comes up? Stanley's estimated date for this place is about 18th December.[...]

Between 3 and 9 October the inhabitants of the fort looked for some new activities to break the monotony of life. For example, Stairs decided to cut up a big and "clumsy" tent and make two smaller ones because he badly needed a tent of his own when on the march. The men, in their spare time, made baskets for catching fish which appeared to be a very desired addition to their diet.

10th October At this time last year we were right in the very focus [sic] of starvation.[...] We have now been over six weeks without a bite of meat; it is telling heavily on the three of us. The men, I fancy, look much better than they did. Sudi, the sick man, cannot live long. Won't Stanley be mad when he hears of all these deaths. He never thinks for one instant that here, as at Ugarrowwa's and Kilonga Longa's he ha[s] left [any]thing but the wreck of the expedition and, of course, will go for me like the mischief. But what of it? Is it not to be expected from a man who has called a faithful, hard working officer of his a "deserter," and who has threatened to *crush him under water* with his Zanzibaris and also to tie him to a bush in the forest and *let him die*.[...]

Not one of we three whites miss a single week that we do not have an attack of fever which leaves us as weak as cats and robs us of a pound or two of flesh which *we cannot* make up on the food we have. Perhaps anyone reading this might say, "Oh, but you talk far too much about these things, your trials." I answer, "Not one whit." What good are we doing here at all?[...] We are just simply farming in mid-Africa under bad conditions, waiting for the time when we shall be relieved. All this time we should be on the Nyanza; then our men would have a chance to get strong and ready for the road and we should then be doing *some* good. If there were no strong tribes in the road we should pack up and be of by stages tomorrow, but the Wazamboni are ever there and we should not be justified in moving one step across the plain.

11th October A most unforeseen and unfortunate affair happened today, tending very much to depress everyone in camp.[...] About nine o'clock this morning when all hands were at work, I took three men and went into the bush to cut some poles of a particular sort which the men, by themselves, would never be able to do. We have [sic] finished cutting our poles and were ready to start back for camp when suddenly we heard several long shouts some distance to the south of us accompanied by reports of two Remington rifles. We naturally considered that our men had met with natives, fired on them and caught a woman, for the yells resembled those of a female, exactly. On our way back, however, we found that two of our men had been fired on by natives and had run towards camp and that one of them, Msungesi Idi, a very hard working chap, had been slightly wounded in the right breast. We laughed and chaffed about their running away and soon after reached camp. The very first words I then heard were that "Msungesi is dead." Dead, and not fifty minutes from the time he was hit. The arrow merely entered the flesh and muscles; no vital part was injured in the slightest. Death then, according to all of us (Parke included), must have arisen from either [one] of two causes: from apoplexy brought on by fright and nervousness (he was terribly excited Parke says, and in addition was a short, thick, heavy man), and consequent death from some blood vessel bursting in the brain, or from the poison on the arrow which must have been a wooden one.

We were all very much depressed over this as Msungesi was a regular character about the place, always ready for work; [he was] noisy, cheery, and contented with his lot. One never forgets either that any unfortunate occurrence such as this creates a gloom over the camp for several days. During this time a great deal of loose talk goes on among the men and the old question—my bugbear—of going to the lake is once more on the tapis. Parke held no post-mortem as, after questioning the men a bit, I found they did not fancy the idea. These natives must have heard our fellows in the bush, sneaked up to them and then fired a volley of arrows after which they ran, as soon afterwards others of our men came up and explored the bush but found nothing but fresh tracks.

The Wasongora bowmen are as certain of their mark, if they get a careful aim, as one of us would firing at a big barn 20 yards off. The more I see of these natives the more certain I feel that the "wooden, poisoned arrows" are used for human warfare only, the iron-tipped ones being used either for game or men. This reduces our men now to fifty-two.[...]

12th October Buried Msungesi yesterday afternoon.[...] I must try and make this book do till the end of this year if I can manage it.[...]

13th October Parke's state today gave both Nelson and myself great anxiety. He has *bilious malignant remittent,* a very bad type of fever. Recollect [word illegible] stranger, our position should one of us get really bad. We have *no proper medicines,* we have no fowls to make chicken broth, no meat to make tasty soups, no beef tea, no sugar, [no] flour, not a drop of tea or coffee; once a man's condition gets down very much, and a fever attacks him, it is the very mischief to build him up again, even with good food. Think how much greater the difficulty must be when there is nothing for him but preparation of Indian corn, which in a great many cases his tired and weakened stomach will refuse. Think of this and then anyone can realize our position: when healthy, each of us eats five cups of Indian corn, *flour* (not meal) per day; this to us now has absolutely no taste and very little [word illegible] fattening power.

I gave rations of ten good corn to each man. [I] am trying to make a decoction to tan leather. I put great quantities of bark into a large *chungu* [of] 8 or 12 gallons, and am boiling this for two days, then will soak the hides a week or so in this decoction; I hope it will be of some use in the making of thongs [from] the donkey's hide, though perhaps it is doubtful.

14th October   Parke very bad yesterday afternoon, this morning better, though, and was able to get up and go out to the men's quarters and lance Khamis Pari's bad leg. Men off for bananas.[...]

These bush natives must be great snake-meat eaters if they all go in for it at the same rate that the Monbuttu woman does. The last snake we got, which [word illegible] Farag Ali caught in one of my traps, we had cooked. Of this she ate out 2 pounds at night, about the same next morning, and still some more during the same afternoon. Interlarded with this slippery feast were huge *chungus* of banana *ugari* and roasted bananas. To finish up with she also made away with about 3½ pounds of the roots of *mayuba* plant, and still she lives. I fancy her legs must be hollow a bit, or she could never make away with all this. This is not all either, for shortly afterwards, she sneaked to Parke and quietly asked for *mahindi* (corn). None of the Zanzibaris would eat this meat though I feel sure their mouths were watering[...] One chap took a little "just to make some oil from."[...]

15th October   Men our for bananas. This time last year we had just crossed the Ituri and were within three marches of the Manyuemas though, at the time, we were not aware of it. We were then all in desperate condition and sacrificed Stanley's donkey to keep up our strength for a future try. A year afterwards (today) we are not much in advance although it is true Emin Pasha has been found.[...]

16th October   Sent men out to look after the elephants—the brutes were gorging themselves last night on the fattest *migomba* (stalks of bananas) they could find. The men built several fires, these, with the smell of the men, may scare off these proboscidians for a week or so. They are a thousand times more destructive to our food supply than the natives. *One elephant* in *one night* will clean, I should say clear and destroy by trampling under his feet from 3/4 to 1½ acres of corn, and I should think quite 3/4 of an acre of bananas. The beasts, after this heavy feed, move into the thick bush, during the day, and then scavenge during the following night and repeat the performance if not stirred up. Parke moved into Emin's hut today; we feel certain it will do him good. I don't believe the old "barn" he has been living in is at all a healthy place. Should Emin come, Parke will go back, of course, to his old quarters.[...]

During the subsequent three days the main problem was the elephant devastation of the banana plantations. On 19 October Sudi, who had been ill for a long time, died. He was buried the same day.

20th October There is a great deal of talk going on now among the men about going to the plain: one or two would appear to want to throw over the white men and male in toto; others wish to have another *shauri* with the white men and endeavour them to give consent.[...]

Among the Zanzibaris in a camp, say, where three or four men are living together, should one get sick and [be] unable to go for food, the others unanimously will hunt him out of their mess. What then becomes of him, I ask. *Ah ta cufa pekiaki* ("Oh, he will die by himself.") People may not believe this, but it is absolutely true.[...]

Between 21 and 26 October Parke's health did not improve and the situation was made even more desperate when Stairs also succumbed to fever. In order to frighten off the elephants, fires were burned at night. This proved to be successful as no more elephants entered the fields.

The fortnight between 27 October and 9 November was spent mostly on hoeing and planting. It was discouraging to realize that the crop of corn was expected to yield barely one-quarter of what it was previously. On the twenty-eighth Stairs commented on the fact that meat was absent from their diet for over two months. Parke was better, though very weak, and his health continued to improve.

In contrast to these prosaic preoccupations, much time was spent on reading poetry and plays, which prompted Stairs to observe that "if we stay here much longer we shall all be great authorities on Shakespeare and Tennyson."

10th November This morning Parke and I were debating as to whether or not I should take chloroform tomorrow and he [would] make an incision to try to get the arrow out of my wound. We went into his hut to go through some preparatory probing just to make sure where the arrow was. After about thirty or forty minutes with the probe and tweezers, who would think it but by Jove, out came the arrow! It had struck one of the ribs and the point had been broken, then it lodged across the hole which has been open for fifteen months and constantly suppurating. The piece we got out was about 6/10 of an inch and about 4/10 [of an inch] had broken off and the hole [was] about 1 inch long.

It was an ordinary native poisoned arrow, made of *mwali* palm just as the natives about here make, but owing to its long confinement, it is in places eaten away. The relief at getting this out is very great and anxiety now, I hope, will go altogether to the winds!! Fifteen months it is since I was hit. Parke says he is very glad he did not make any incision as he intended. The position of the wound was so dangerous—just over the heart and lungs. I must say it was a narrow squeak; had the arrow just missed this rib I should have been a dead man many day[s] ago.[...]

Nelson is going down in condition again very fast; he lies on his back nearly all day and will not be persuaded to move about and take a little fresh air.[...]

The raising of crops remained the preoccupation. The entires in the journal between 11 and 20 November include many remarks on the growth of the plants and the quantities harvested. During 13 and 14 November some 242 baskets of 200 corns each were collected. On the following day, planting of corn and hoeing of the new fields was resumed. On the sixteenth Stairs had noted that it was already five months since Stanley left for Yambuya. He also observed that, in retrospect, the time seemed to have gone very fast.

21st November Dr. Washenzi got some leaves, etc., to concoct poison with.[7] Planting big field where former corn did not take. *Rugga Rugga* saw nothing, but reported natives had been cutting bananas yesterday at end of NW plantation.

I am heartsick to the very core at having to stay at this place, utterly disgusted with the rotten way in which everything has been done in this expedition, tired of working with such a lot of brutes as we have here and boiling over with rage at them. Upon my word, I often feel like going away into the bush and not coming back again. To keep one's temper down day after day in working with these men is more than [an] ordinary mortal can do. I have acted squarely and fairly with all of them, have eased their troubles as much as I possibly could have done. What is the result? They do not thank one in the slightest, in fact they take everything for granted in the way of helping them; behind one's back they swindle one; lie about one; try and frustrate any little plan one makes about getting birds or fish, and so many other "endearing trifles" too numerous to mention. Sick of them I am utterly. I also feel that some day one or two of these beauties will smart of it, if I know my name; this is the only consoling part. I am speaking of a clique of some ten or twelve men only. The rest are all right.[...]

22nd November Today the Monbuttu made some of the poison for us that the natives use on their arrows: both Parke and I have got specimens of the different plants, etc., used, and when I know a little more about it I will try to describe the several plants and [the] method of making the poison.

Planting west field and started hoeing up the old south one. Finished re-roofing old granary. Hoes are nearly all done for; the roots play the mischief with them. We use three native hoes now to help a bit, they are but poor, clumsy things. Those made in Unyoro are far superior though perhaps not so for very rooty ground. Showers every afternoon for last ten days or so.

23rd November Hoeing SE field, cutting pea sticks [for pea plants] and doing odd jobs. Poison made by native [is] ready.

24th November This morning about 9:30 Parke made an incision about 2/5 of an inch long close to back bone [sic] of my dog, and together we introduced a quantity of the poison, to see if it will have any effect. We preferred this way to prodding him with an arrow as lockjaw might supervene. We await the result with much anxiety. If this does not do for him we will make him swallow a lot as well and [see] what effect that will have. This poison is a dark green, whereas that made by the Wasongora and Monbuttu in their villages and camps is of yellowish-brown colour (like dirty yellow sealing wax, such as is used to stop the corks of wine bottles).

Sent out *Rugga Rugga* [to] hunt out elephant last night—an elephant came within 170 yards of fort, making great noise, cracking the branches and banana stands; I fired a shot as near him as I could [word illegible] and after some horn blowing he ran off. They are much more difficult to distract at night than in daytime. Nothing made them go off so quickly as the smell of men or fire.

Some of the men saw a leopard the other day, or said they saw one. Perhaps it was only some large type of bush cat of which there should be a number judging from the skins on men in villages. Whether or not the leopard comes this far into the bush I cannot positively say. At Ugarrowwa's one [carried] off a child in sight of some women and children.[...]

25th November   Jephson has now had six months to come here; what can be the matter with him? Is he so wrapped up in the comforts of Emin's country, the good food, and easy travelling that he has forgotten his promise to come here? Or is it worse? Is there something more formidable in the shape of obstacles?[...]

26th November   Men again off for bananas. Boys got a good catch. Peas for dinner yesterday. The dog died yesterday from the poison.[...]

27th November   Sent out four men to look after elephants, saw only tracks.[..]

28th November   The leaves Parke and the native woman got yesterday for making the antidote have been collected and dried. Tomorrow the woman will make it up. The antidote is applied through the skin.[...]

29th November   With six men I went through the plantations looking for marks of elephants. We saw a great many plants broken down near the bush.[...]

30th November   The dry season is upon us, too, I think, and I am rather afraid the want of rain will damage the crops very much. The rice is getting ripe very quickly. Next week we should be able to take some of it in.

1st December   Cutting pea sticks and roding [sic] up the peas. Sent out *Rugga Rugga,* followed up natives but could not catch them. Sent out four men for bananas. Weeding corn near bush.[...] Have two men at basket making—one Sultani, a Zanzibari, and a Madi chap. We are sadly in need of baskets and *chungus.* Parke has made a very good grid iron out of some old wire, the "irony" of it though his [sic] in our having no meat to grill.[...] We have now been over twenty-two months our from England. It is doubtful if we shall reach Zanzibar in another fourteen. Everything now seems to be hanging in mid-air. We know nothing of the whereabouts of Stanley or Jephson—for all we know Stanley may have gone gaily off down [the] Congo and left us here. We simply go plodding along day after day, planting, keeping things in repair, fighting natives and elephants and trust that soon someone will turn up. Issued the usual weekly ration of ten corns each to the men.[...]

2nd December   Fortunately had a shower last evening and also one this evening.[...] Farag Ali has fever and a swollen foot.

3rd December   Parke lanced Farag Ali's foot.[...]

4th December   Parke off with ten *Rugga Rugga,* came up with six or eight natives to NNW of fort 2 miles in the plantation. They were sitting round a fire near native hut on the track. Killed one and caught two children.[...] Monbattu woman says natives here eat those caught belonging to Kilimani.[8] The ordinary way is to cut up the body, dry the meat thoroughly over a fire and eat when required. The bones are roasted on the coals and the marrow eaten. The native *Wasangora* sultan at Kilimani is named [blank space left] and the native name of the place is Tnimanba.

Started getting in rice; am afraid of locust or locust-like insects who greedily eat the green rice. They are the same as destroy the rice in Zanzibar, the men say. Weeding garden. Farag Ali better. Peas we get now are very good—much better than last crop.[...] Rained heavily last evening, good for crops.

I am glad to say Christmas will soon be on us with the almost certain prospect now of having to spend it here. We have been puzzling our heads what to have to eat. I am saving a poor, tiny, miserable pittance of salt as a present for the other two chaps; a funny Christmas box this—an egg-spoon full of salt! If we could only shoot a bird or monkey it would not be so bad. Perhaps we shall have some fish. Got in eight baskets of rice.

5th December Re-sowing where corn failed. Weeding garden. Four men on basket making. Getting in rice in afternoon. New moon last night. Perhaps the natives will come this morning to cut our young corn. Being the dry season I am taking account of the rainfall as well as I can, though we have no gauges or instruments of any sort—[...] all are lost or destroyed. The bush march was too rough to get anything fragile through unless special carriers were in charge of it. This, of course, we could not get with Stanley.[...]

This time last year we were getting close to the lake, going strong and with a tremendous supply of spirits. Personally, I cannot say I feel in the same mood this year as I did last at this time. Reading *McBeth* [sic] again. What a brute "Mrs. McBeth" [sic] was and he himself about on a par with Richard III, I think. The men are eating great numbers of the locust, or rather grasshoppers, that have been attracted here by the rice fields. I had a few last evening; they are not bad and serve as a relish or *kitiweo* for the men.[...]

6th December Weighed ourselves: Parke 148[pounds], Nelson 138 [pounds], [and] Stairs 131 [pounds]. Nelson weighed over 12 stone in England. I weighed 11 stone 10 pounds when at Chatham.

Taking in rice and dry beans. Doing odd jobs about the place. Two baskets finished. Abedi off for fish.

7th December Finished picking the rice this afternoon with exception of a little not yet ripe.[...] Zanzibaris are poor farmers: everyone has his own idea about things and these ideas all differ so widely that one can depend but little on the information. We planted this rice too closely by 6 inches on the information of Khamis Pari.[...]

8th December Went off SSE with twelve *Rugga Rugga,* shot two natives and wounded another. Found their camp about 7 miles SSE from here. Do not appear to come into plantation near camp but turn off to west, just at margin of bananas. Very bad travelling. Found a brass rod, one of those we use for trading purposes. This must be one of those that Stanley gave to the sultan of the village west of here last year. Abedi off for fish. Last time the boys were off they saw a lion, at least so they said. I do not think the lion comes so far into the bush as this. Drying the rice. Weeding the corn. The total rice yield was 100 pishis (1400 cups).[...]

9th December Men off for bananas. Slight showers in evening.[...]

10th December Boys off for fish, again saw the lion![...]

11th December If we have many more of these dry scorching days a great deal of the corn will die off. All that is young now is looking very poorly. Have fever today; first time for over six weeks. Side where was wounded still pains; there must be a bit of decayed bone in the wound yet as the suppuration is constant. Had a little rice today of the new crop; it was very good, quite a change form the endless corn porridge. It will be a great help to make the corn last out.

It is wonderful how quickly fever prostrates one in this country. If one is doing some work in which one's whole energy is employed and one's nerves strung up, perhaps a fever can be warded off, but sitting down to it with ordinary work is quite a different matter. It is then impossible almost to fight it off. A man at 6:00 a.m., will be strong and cheery and happy with himself and all the world; at noon he feels slack and tires to fight against this feeling; by 3:00 p.m., he has three or four swelt[ering] hours of wrestling and gets up after this feeling perfectly washed out and incapable of doing anything that entails bodily and other labour. I hope these attacks will not come on one when in England.

12th December   Nelson went out with ten *Rugga Rugga,* saw nothing. Fever again today.

13th December   Fever again. Oh, how heartily sick I am of this place. Jephson now can never come and Stanley probably a long way off. Fever baddish.

14th December   Went off with some men through bananas looking for some good ones for Christmas.[...]

15th December   Yesterday just one year since we reached Albert Nyanza, and here today we are sitting down in Fort Bodo unable to do anything except try and get our men strong. Stanley, heavens knows where he is. Jephson has been over seven months at the lake doing what heavens only knows. Upon my word, at times, I feel utterly sick of this waiting.[...]

During the subsequent four days the inhabitants of the fort were mostly engaged in their usual daily activities.

20th December   About 11:00 a.m., heard shots and soon after this Stanley and the safari from Yambuya arrived from the west side. The only other whites were William and Bonny, the sole survivor to us of the Yambuya garrison. The story of this most disastrous affair I leave till later. I only add here that we were all shocked to hear of Major Barttelot's death. Stanley had sent off letters to England which would, of course, put an end there to the reports of his death which we have read in scraps of papers sent out. Bonny gave me two letters, one from Father and one from Mother. The dates were 7th February 1887, nearly two years ago.

Only thirty-six [word illegible] of the Yambuya garrison ever reached here and twelve Soudanese [...] and one Somali [makes] forty-nine. All the Somalis have died with the exception of one. Upon my word, I have never heard or read of such heart-rending stories as Bonny brings up—deaths, desertions, sickness, wholesale swindling and robbing on the part of the Manyuema make up a story that completely hides itself in a mass of such complications that at first one can grasp nothing. All the whites seem to have fought against each other. Later on I give more details.

In England great interest seems to be taken in the expedition. The news that we reached the lake had got to England. Reports of Stanley and all our deaths were rife. The Conservatives have again got in in Canada and the Nova Scotians [have been] beaten on their cry of separation from the Dominion. All were well at home. Georgie appears to get on well among her friends in New York. From Mary I got no news.[9] All of us were delighted at seeing Stanley and the smiling faces of the [word illegible].[...]

On arriving at Banalia, of course, Stanley was stunned with the news—the Major dead, the goods gone, Troup invalided [sic] home, Ward stopped on his way down-country, probably at Bangala, and Jameson somewhere on the Congo between Stanley Falls and the [Stanley] Pool. A horrible story of cruelty, misery, and death was then told by Bonny to Stanley, the same as he told us.

I abstain from making many remarks as I think B[onny]'s story wants confirmation. We must hear Jameson and Troup speak first. The major was shot dead by a Manyuema from a loophole in a hut not 15 yards off the [word illegible], alleging that the major intended to beat a woman of his. This man was afterwards shot by Jameson, Tippu Tib, and the white men at Stanley Falls station after a trial. Jameson was away when Stanley arrived at Banalia going down [the] Congo after answers to dispatches. Over 130 men died at Yambuya alone.

Getting his men together and those he could scrape up from Bonny after a stop at Banalia, of three days, Stanley started off up-country. It must have been a terrible blow to Stanley to have his base so demolished as it was. All he brought is simply the wreckage of what was originally left, both in men and goods. All of us are shocked and horrified at what has gone on down there and for some time I am afraid we shall not get over it. On his march up-country the column suffered three terrible periods of starvation. At one time they were eight days in a hole with absolutely nothing to eat. This was close to the Ihuru River, only three marches from Fort Bodo. Stanley reached us today, 20th December. We will be able to issue to twenty-four thousand corns—this will give every man about sixty-six.

Accompanying the expedition in the hope of collecting and getting ivory from Emin Pasha is a force of Manyuema. They number 76 souls under a chief called Saadi, 19 under Fundi, and 12 under Kibobora. Of the 110-odd Madis who left us and went down-country to carry our loads, only 21 returned; thus 90 of them have died. Chama is the last and only surviving Somali. Out of over 60 Soudanese, 12 reached here.

The major had shot one Nubian for continual thieving. Whether he was justified or not one cannot as yet say. The Manyuema have played the mischief with all the country within, say, 250 miles; new settlements have been opened up, slaves by the hundreds taken, and, of course, the ivory all collared. Tippu Tib has men as far north as the Oubauni River.

The force Stanley brought into the fort [...] totals 298. Our total loads now number 280, our carriers only 222, and we have reduced everything down to its lowest as far as loads go. In consequence of this we shall have to make double trips as Stanley, this evening, decided to abandon the fort. Of the stores of European provisions that were left at Yambuya, we officers up here who have been one and one-half years without anything in this shape get 6 tins [of] condensed milk, 3½ pounds of tea, 4 pounds [of] butter, 165 lumps [of] sugar, 1 tin [of] biscuits, 1 bottle [of] brandy, a tin [of] arrowroot and 1 of sago among 5 of us, also 1 crock of beef-tea each.

21st December Today all the new arrivals at the fort received a day's rest, well deserved. Many are very sick and feeble and the ulcers of the Manyuema are most horrible to look on. Several are suffering from other sicknesses, of course, but ulcers and wounds from pointed sticks swell the list most.

Nelson and I were at work making up loads. Stanley had decided to remove all hands from the fort and march on by easy stages to the front. Tonight Bonny told us a lot more about the Yambuya affair. The whole thing seems more like a horrible dream than anything else. Bonny's story, I am inclined to think, must be taken with a grain of salt. In his whole story he is most even; one thing he says tallies exactly with another. Barttelot appears at first to have gone hand in glove with Jameson. Afterwards, however, he would appear to take Bonny into his confidence. Now Barttelot, from Bonny's own story, did everything he could to please Bonny. Yet Bonny says he was a most disagreeable and cantankerous chap. It is very hard to make anything at all out of it. Bonny arrogates a great deal to himself that he has no right to. What I want to hear are Jameson's and Troup's story [sic] on getting to England. Such grave and serious things are said about Jameson and Barttelot that I will not even put them down here.

Ward and Troup fought among themselves; the Major and Troup and Ward fought. Jameson, it would seem, was the best liked by the men and did his best for the expedition. Till I get absolute particulars from Bonny, I abstain from making any further statement. One only hopes the lower English papers have not got hold of a lot of this and are publishing them. It will be [a] long time before they can be contradicted and a lot of mischief will be done.

Poor old major, it will be a great blow to his father who I believe was very fond of him. Besides, he was a most lucky chap and had a grand chance before him had he only not been murdered.

22nd December Issued sixty-six corns to every man and woman in camp. Packed up and did some odd jobs. Had a long chat with Stanley and all the fellows in the evening. Bonny again repeated his story and told us more about what had happened. Stanley gave us some cuttings from English papers. Reports had been circulated that Stanley and all of us with the advance column had been killed, these, of course, were contradicted by my three and other letters. They have for some reason (probably thinking Stanley was dead) sent on almost all the provisions to Bangala. Everyone had most positive opinions that Stanley and all of us would never come back. Stanley's maps and a whole lot of things belonging to different fellows were sent down to Bangala.

By the Halifax papers I see that at last the ferry boat company intend getting a new steamer. A cathedral is to be erected and electric lights increased in the city. The Liberals have been badly licked in Nova Scotia, but in the whole Dominion their cause has brightened. Uncle Alfred has been elected as Liberal and Mrs. J. E. Kenny as Conservative. J. F. Stairs has been beaten.[10] It's just what I always said: the Liberals have only taken up the cry of separation from the Dominion to get into power. Once they get into power I fancy they will be remarkably silent [in] Ottawa on this point.

CHAPTER 7

KANDEKORE TO WADELAI
TO MAZAMBONI'S

23 DECEMBER 1888—7 MAY 1889

A fortified camp at Kandekore is set up. Stairs stays behind with those unable to march. Stanley sets off for the lake on 11 January. Stairs learns of the revolt against Emin Pasha. The Kandekore camp is abandoned on orders from Stanley and Stairs's party marches to Kavalli's where he meets Emin Pasha. Serious frictions develop between Stanley and the pasha. An agreement is reached to set off for the east coast on 10 April. The departure is delayed.

23 December This morning about 8:30 a.m. the safari left the fort, leaving Nelson, Bonny, and some forty or fifty men who leave the day after tomorrow. For many a long day I have not felt so light-hearted.[...] At the small hill, just where our own plantations ended, I turned round and had a last look at the place. I, of course, felt sorry at leaving after having worked so hard at putting [sic] the crops onto the state they are now in, but this was quite outweighed by the thought of once more getting on the march and onto the plains and out of the bush.

Nelson and Bonny (who is very thin) will leave on the twenty-fifth. We go ahead, camp, send men back and then all behind come on. We have to do this as we have nearly 100 more loads than men and so have to make double trips. The men, as a body, are all in the best of spirits but in poor condition; it is a case of the spirit is willing but the flesh weak. The Manyuema people suffer quite as much if not more than our men but get along well with the short marches we are making. I reached camp with the rear of [the] column about 3:00 p.m., the distance gone over being about 9 miles.

Stanley['s] plans as to what he will do on reaching Mande are not yet settled; I fancy it will end in the sick people and feeble ones being left in camp just beyond the Ituri River, and Stanley and perhaps another officer [will] go on to the plains, find our news of Emin Pasha and afterwards return back and pick up the sick.[...]

During the subsequent ten days the column moved slowly forward coping with the problem of transporting the loads whose number exceeded that of the porters. On Christmas Day the men, under Stairs's command, were attacked by the villagers, but they managed to drive off the attackers taking revenge, in turn, by raiding several villages. On 30 December Ituri River was reached. On New Year's Day (1889), after a long fast, some fowls and goats appeared on the menu for the first time, and Stairs commented in his journal that the "men completely lost their heads" at the sight of meat. The whites, on the other hand, enjoyed tea and other provisions brought from Yambuya. The immediate task facing the expedition was to set up a camp where a detachment was to remain for some time. In the meantime, efforts were to be made to re-establish contact with Emin Pasha.

3rd January Took some eight or ten men across the river and cleared a place for the new camp we propose shifting to tomorrow or next day.[...] Stanley intends leaving a force behind with the sick and a lot of the loads and then take [sic] a strong body on to the lake to find out what is the matter there. Should all be right, he will at once send back, but should Emin Pasha and Jephson be detained there, then he will not run the risk of losing his loads at the hands of Emin's Nubians. It is very hard what to think is the reason [sic] [that] no news has reached us from Emin Pasha.

This site would be a first-rate place for such a station as I have just spoken of, except that I feel sure we can never keep out the elephants. Judging by former experiences, elephants are always numerous near the rivers, and here they seem especially so.[...]

4th January Sent Umani and eight men across river to build a hut for the goods [to be] ready for us when we cross. Stanley ought to be here [between] 8th [and] 10th. Hope to be able to move over tomorrow, but the men are poor hands in the canoes.

The *Rugga Rugga* came in this morning bringing me four live fowls and three kids. They had gone north and east until they cut our old track to the lake at the village near where Jephson and I found a crossing of the Ituri. They got a good supply of goat meat for themselves and their comrades which I let them keep.

5th January Started early this morning at crossing the column over the river. By 9:20 had got all hands over in the two canoes—108 loads and about 75 people. In the river here there are quantities of the most horrible looking crocodiles.[...]

Today Stanley should have started on his way up to [word illegible]. In the evening, as Umin bin Brahim was going to bathe and [was] just entering the water, I saw the head of a huge crocodile appear about 7 yards down-stream from where Umari was. I yelled out, *"Mamba Maluba!"* ("Crocodile, crocodile!"). Umari was just in time to get away.[...]

6th January Men want to go off on another *Rugga Rugga,* but I would not think of it as Stanley may come any day now and perhaps send me on to the plains.[...]

7th January The soldier ants came into the kraal last night in millions. All through the night, till 2:00 in the morning, we fought them with fires, brushwood, and every other means we could adopt.[...] By midnight the fight was general; all hands turned out. At last we turned their line of march and gradually got peace but very little rest.

8th January About 1:30 p.m. twenty men with each a load turned up on the other side of the river. Stanley is camped at Mande waiting for Parke who is a day behind with the sick. I sent back twenty men empty-handed according to directions from Stanley. These are, I suppose, to help along the sick and weakly [sic] ones.[...]

9th January Stanley came up to the river with the rear column about 10:15 this morning. Parke got in about 5:00 p.m. and behind Parke [by] two days were sick men straggling all along the road. Uledi and his twenty men had gone back from the Mande camp to try and pick these people up and bring them on to camp.

Stanley's plans are fairly well matured.[...] He will leave all the sick and weakly [sic] ones at the village of Kandekore on the hilltop about twelve minutes east from here. From this village he will take on the strongest men, say 90 or 100, and go on to the lake, taking, say 2 white men and leaving 2 at the village. Here will be left most of the expedition loads; those of Emin Pasha [will be] taken on. Parke will be left, of course, to look after the sick and I to look after the fort and men. Nelson is unable to march, I feel certain, but I had to tell Stanley otherwise. I am simply broken-hearted at being left behind this time. Not because of the fact that I am left, but because I know Stanley did it for certain reasons which I must refrain from giving and because these reasons are absolutely unjust and unfair.[...] No man knows better than Stanley himself that he has not got one white man who does his work more willingly and cheerfully than I do. In the evening Parke, Stanley, and I had a long chat. Stanley decided that W[illia]m Hoffmann, his servant, should be left here.[...]

10th January I give about sixty days as the length of our stay here. Knowing the Zanzibaris as I do, I expect some will try to desert me. The position is a fair one as regards defence. The water is about 900 yards off. I am as yet unacquainted with the vicinity but perhaps later on will have a look about the place. Stanley takes about 110 Zanzibaris.

11th January Stanley went off this morning to the lake for the third and last time. I hope originally it was intended that Nelson and Bonny [should] go, but Nelson's ulcers prevented him walking, so Bonny was the only other white man. I have not yet made up the numbers of those with him but will do so in a day or so. I am again left in charge of this place and the garrison. This time I have over 130 men or lot of slaves, boys, girls, the whole forming a regular second edition of the Tower of Babel.[...] We are on a hilltop and on a clear day can see the open country. Mount Pisgah lies about 3½ miles west of us [with] the Ituri River between. As yet I have not decided what precautions I shall take as regards defence, but the men's huts will go to form the outer defence and inside I shall make an inner ring with the goods and a tower inside.[...]

12th January Today the men were again occupied in building their houses. About forty of our people are in a very bad state; it will be months before some of them could [sic] be expected to recover well [even] if in the very best hospital in England. Some three or four will die in a very short time Parke thinks. We are both determined to do our very utmost to get every man well and strong as quickly as possible. The sick get goat soup, Indian meal porridge, and other foods and have all their water supplied to them. Those very bad are in a hut by themselves with a man constantly looking after them.

This is the largest command I have ever had; the responsibility is very great and I only hope everyone will try his best to help them on. It was a great disappointment in not getting on to the lake, but I see that perhaps it is for the best that I should stay here. As a result of Nelson's idleness at the fort and consequent soft feet, the march up [here] gave him six ulcers and he could not go on to the lake. He now is laid up in bed just at the time [that] there is so much work to do.

13th January Building *boma* on W side, am making this of upright boards 4 feet high, with pointed sticks, giving a total of, say, 7 feet. Terribly hot winds and in scorching sun. The atmosphere is directly charged with the smoke of the plain fires. The sun has the appearance of a crimson ball but has the orthodox Central African power nevertheless. The houses are the coolest places one can get into.[...]

The following two weeks were devoted to the construction of towers and huts. The daily routine resembled that of Fort Bodo. The presence of the neighbourhood villagers continued to be a constant threat. On 19 January Parke became gravely ill and remained so for the next three days. Meanwhile, the mortality rate was high among the men with seven deaths, mostly from ulcers and dysentery.

28th January Stanley has been away eighteen days now and no news from him. If we get no news by next Sunday then I shall feel sure Emin is not at the south end of the lake, that he is not ready to come out, and that perhaps he does not intend doing so.[...] Put the goods into the store today. My brother Jack's birthday; he must be twenty-seven years old today, if I am not mistaken. I often wonder if he is married yet, and my sisters Anna and Hilda. The gap of three years will seem very strange to one on getting back.[...]

29th January Nelson and I all day doing up loads in sacks. These afterwards we weighed and put into old powder boxes. The loads average about 54 pounds.[...] Up to the hilt [sic] with all sorts of work now, good for us, though, as it makes the time pass by and all are healthier and happier for it.

30th January Finished re-doing the beads and cowries this afternoon. At work on the new tower. The view from this tower is a very fine one: the bush on the S can be seen stretching away till one loses sight of it some 25 miles off at the crest of a range of hills. Mount Pisgah in the mornings, when low banks of clouds seem to stick about halfway up its side, is a very fine sight. The plains at their nearest point to us are about 4 [miles] or 5 miles off. Wadi Khamis, the chief, has fever.

31st January Finished the new tower this morning. Sewing up damaged covers of the bales of cloth.[...] Parke gave me a state today of the Nubians and Zanzibaris. By "fit" we mean absolutely free from sickness or sores of any sort.[...] William's ulcer is still irritating, but he does not give it a chance; he will not walk about or take exercise at all. There are five Madis fit and six with ulcers or other troubles.[...]

1st February Went on with my survey of the place till the afternoon, traversed the road to the plains to about 1½ miles east of the fort. Saw two native elephant spear falls and set one of them off.[...] Some men I [had] sent out for corn encountered nine natives and shot one, bringing in the hand; the others ran dropping some bows of the open country pattern.

2nd February Went off on track to SSE some 2 miles and made a prismatic compass traverse. Started on map of the place. Been sweeping up the place and removing rubbish. It is twenty-three days now since Stanley left here. Life here is very much the same as at Fort Bodo only that there are more men, and they are a much livelier lot. Not a day passes but the drums are going and [there is] always a dance in the evening. Some of the men are very graceful in their movements in these dances. Then there is no scarcity of food here as at the old fort, and in consequence one does not have the same complaints and whinings about food.[...]

3rd February Mending boots and shirts. Long ago my boots have given out. I am now using those of my own manufacture—a wretched substitute as the skin is untanned or unprepared in any way. Nelson gave me an old pair of his boots. These I have patched and sewn up quite out of shape. Every time I use them, though, my feet suffer. I don't see what I am to do; ahead are nine months of a march and I have no boots to march in. I only hope I will not get ulcers. One's feet in this country are the most important part of one and to be unable to use them means, perhaps, death.

4th February Took four men early this morning and went on to the plains to try and get a shot at something. Reached plains in one hours's easy walk. Fired at a buffalo but missed and saw nothing else.[...] The African buffalo is one of the most dangerously active animals [for] charging. A single beast, if wounded and away from its comrades, almost invariably charges; on the plains there are no friendly trees one can slip up and so avoid a pair of sharp horns.[...]

5th February Great sport was caused in camp today by a Manyuema woman. This woman got herself up in feathers and flowers and with a native rattle went all about the camp singing to the devil. About ten o'clock, though, the sun got very fierce and she strolled back to her hut having been unsuccessful in calling up "His Majesty!" I believe she is quite mad at times; at night, all of a sudden, one hears the most blood curdling yells and imagines about forty thousand Washenzi are coming on against the camp. After a few inquiries it generally turns out to be this woman.[...]

A girl belonging to Katembo (one of the Zanzibaris), who was sleeping outside one of the gates of the fort and suffering terribly from gangrene in the foot, was taken off last night by a leopard. This morning with some men I followed up the tracks for some distance but lost them there in the bananas. The beast is certain to return in a night or two and make another try.[...]

6th February Sent off a party of *Rugga Rugga* today in a SSE direction.[...] The road from the plains [by which] I returned to the fort a few days ago is a bit larger than that of Stanley's.[...] On this road there are three large banana plantations.[...] When I use the word "bananas" I really mean plantains, that is, the big coarse sort with corners. The real banana, such as one eats in England or gets from the West Indies, is very scarce in this part of Africa.[...] The natives about here have small crops of corn but of an inferior kind. Of tobacco there is a great quantity.

7th February Collected a lot of castor oil beans to make oil for the sick and also for our rifles. In all, got three large *chungus* (clay pots). Wadi Khamis and I started on a trap for the leopard. It will have two ordinary Remington rifles loaded and a goat as bait. A Monbuttu woman was out getting firewood yesterday, and when [she was] only a short distance outside the fort gates, was sprung upon by the leopard and had arms and back scratched. She escaped, however, and came screaming into the fort. Last night I sat up outside the fort with a rifle till midnight. At this hour I had to return as the moon set and I could not see the goat I had tied up as a lure to "His Majesty."[...]

I often wonder what English people would say if they knew of the way in which we go for these natives; friendship we don't want as then we should get very little meat and probably have to pay for the bananas. Every male native capable of using the bow is shot.

This, of course, we must do. All the children and women are taken as slaves by our men to do work in the camps. Of course, they are well treated and rarely beaten as we whites soon stop that. After three or four weeks with the men they get to be as happy as clams and gorge themselves with food, almost to bursting. It always seems very funny to me to see a native woman, who yesterday was running wild in the bush, come to the doctor with the rest of the men and slaves for medicine for her ulcers. They all, of course, have heard of the white men from our former trips to the lake, but still all appear very much astonished on actually seeing the *Muzungu* (whites).

8th February   At the castor oil today, should get about 1 gallon of good oil.[...]

It is a great thing on coming to a new place, where one is likely to remain for some time, to make a sketch of the different roads, valleys, and hills and to explore in every direction for 5 miles or so the country on every side of your [sic] position. Of course, all books recommend one to do this, but it is only now that I fully see the real use of it. Now I know nearly every road, crack, village, and hill for some miles from the camp; the satisfaction and comfort one feels after making this rough survey more than atones for the work. I can never rest now for a day unless I know just what exists on every side of me.[...]

9th February   Swept up. Sent out men for bananas for making flour for the load. In the afternoon the *Rugga Rugga* sailed into the fort absolutely laden with loot. They brought me six goats and some fowls, beans, corn, skins, spears, shields, and arrows and bows, bead dresses, and what I have not seen for 700 miles: an idol, or rather the head of an idol or god that is solicited when rain, success in war, or anything else is wanted. It would be very interesting to know really what form of worship these people have, if any, as I should like to get some of these curios home, but there is absolutely no chance as every man is wanted to carry ammunition. At every camp I get splendid collections of skins, bows and arrows, shields, pipes, pots, knives, billhooks, baskets, and hats but have always to leave them behind.[...]

10th February   About 12:45 p.m. today Rashid came into the fort bringing 35 Zanzibaris and 100 Wazamboni carriers from Kavalli's village.[1] I got two long letters from Stanley, one from Jephson, and a note from Bonny. Stanley is camped near Kavalli's village being [in] good now with all the natives from here to the lake. On his way east at Mazamboni's village he heard of Emin Pasha and Jephson. The news was conflicting, but still he was able to make out that a revolt had occurred in the Egyptian Equatorial Provinces and that the pasha, Jephson, and Casati the Italian were all prisoners. Stanley received definite news of them at Mpinga's village about two and one-half days later this side of the lake.[2]

Kavalli had sent a packet to him [Stanley], and on opening it, I found one letter from Jephson dated Dufilé, 7th November 1888. A "PS" was added: Wadelai, 24th November, and another, Tunguru, 18th December 1888. He also got two brief letters from the pasha. The general thread of Jephson's letter was about as follows. The letter warned Stanley to be very cautious as a revolt had broken out. A meeting of Emin's officers instigated by his chief clerk and a lieutenant of No. 1 Battalion was formed. This assembly deposed Emin Pasha from his position and on the 15th August both Emin and Jephson were made prisoners. This was about the time we expected Jephson with relief at Fort Bodo. It was the doing of the discontented [No. 1] Battalion.

Soon after this, however, the "old crowd," the Mahdists, [...] sailed up the Nile in force and landed near Lado. Their head, named Omar Saleh, sent dervishes to the commander of Rejaf demanding the surrender of the garrison. These [dervishes] were seized and the garrison [was] prepared for resistance. In a few days Rejaf fell, five officers and many soldiers being killed. Rejaf is the pasha's northernmost station. A panic then was the result on all sides; and three stations—Bedden, Kirri, and Muggi—were abandoned. The ammunition at Kirri was seized by some natives.

At Dufilé Jephson says "we are like rats in a hole and unless you come very soon you will be too late and our fate will be like that of the rest of the garrison of the Soudan." The last words of Jephson's letter are doleful enough: "If we are not able to get out of the country please remember me to my friends."

Emin's soldiers, especially those of No. 2 Battalion, were so angry after these stations were abandoned [by Emin's troops who were supposed to have defended them] that they declined to fight unless the pasha were set at liberty which was done. The pasha and Jephson were thereupon sent to Wadelai but not reinstated.

The Mahdists have sent down to Khartoum for re-enforcements. All were anxiously looking out for the expedition's arrival at the lake and appeared to be dreadfully afraid of the Mahdists.

Stanley says there is a report about a second relief expedition being at the north end of the lake. The men of this are said to be armed with rifles like ours, to carry their loads just as our men do, and that they are led by white men, not Arabs. Can this be Joseph Thompson?[3] Not at all unlikely.

Kabba Rega has been again thrashed by the Waganda. Someday I fancy Unyoro and Uganda will all be one territory under one sultan, viz., that of Uganda.

The Wazamboni Rashid brought, as a rule some fine fat looking fellows, but they are unused to load carrying and many of them are mere boys. I expect by the time we reach Mazamboni's four days off most of them will have [had] enough of it. Jephson was well. I fancy now Emin will have to come out. He is now making his way south collecting whom he can. Both steamers were seized by the rebels and our boat the *Advance* [was] destroyed. It would seem now, though, that Emin has possession again of at least one steamer.

11th February Tomorrow we shall make a start, and by next Tuesday 19th I hope once more to see Mr. Stanley and Jephson. Stanley's orders and directions are very explicit.[...]

12th February Off again on the march. Up go one's spirits like the mercury of a thermometer plunged into boiling water. By 8:00 a.m. all hands got off. Carried two sick men—Takadiri and Khamis (boy).

13th February Our camp last night was in a small patch of bush almost 4 miles east of the forest. How pleasant it is to once more get out to the plain and feel the breezes.[...] Our caravan is about three hundred, all told.

14th February The track we are marching on now is about 10 to 15 miles south of that by which I went to the lake before. The Wazamboni are not bad carriers, but every day there are squabbles and loud talking between our men and them. They complain bitterly that our men push them on the road.

15th February Left camp and in one hour came upon parties of Wazamboni who had come out from their villages to meet their friends. Soon these increased and our men got their loads carried by these most obliging people. Soon afterwards we sat down in a village for half an hour, and then after another hour's march, into Wazamboni's. [Stairs is using the name incorrectly here when he refers to the village.] At once the chief, Mazamboni, came out to see me and brought a jar of milk. We had a long *shauri*.[...] He promises to have plenty of carriers ready the day after tomorrow, and will give my men food tomorrow.

All day long a regular fair day in camp. Our men selling and buying and the crowds of natives made the camp quite lively. Our men gave twenty cowries for one fowl, quite twice too much. A letter from Stanley awaited me. Emin Pasha now will come out, there is no doubt. The first lot of those willing to follow us have already come down by steamer and another lot will shortly follow. The whole of the Equatorial Provinces will be wrecked and many lives lost and work undone. Stanley wants me to get along as fast as possible. I sent off couriers to him with a letter telling him we were coming along well.

The women here are really very pretty and the men handsome looking fellows. The dress of the women is a little sprig of green bush which is renewed every morning. These ladies therefore are provided with a brand new gown every day—a thing many white ladies I know would be proud of.

In the evening Wazamboni warriors gave a war dance. These are the same lot of howling wretches who, fourteen months ago, howled and yelled at Stanley, Jephson, and I enclosed in our *mimosa boma* on the hilltop just behind this camp. For three days we stayed there trying to make friends, but it was no use, and Jephson and I burnt down at that time every house, granary, cattle kraal, destroyed their crops and bananas and punished them in every way we could. Now they are our best friends.

It was very amusing watching the young women dancing with the men—the peculiar wriggle they give [is] very "fetching." The young girls and women yell at the tops of their voices in the wildest excitement. One woman I noticed with a baby under her arm [was] frantically wriggling about in and out among the crowds of men. She appeared to quite forget her baby which was squalling most horribly.

These people value cowrie shells more than any other article of trade, except perhaps cloth. They also value arrowheads, long straight sticks for spear shafts, axes, and things of this sort. Billhooks, too, they are very fond of. We whites are absolutely without any means of buying anything, so that we are in some cases solely dependent on the native chief's charity.

17th February Left Mazamboni's after some trouble about getting enough carriers; travelled over a very good road N of our old one and reached Mpinga's about 3:00 p.m. Here a year ago we had a big fight. Mpinga is not nearly such a fine looking man as Mazamboni. His [Mpinga's] people speak the same language as the Wazamboni. The women are very much disfigured by the way they do their lips: the upper lip is pierced and a large ring inserted, periodically increasing this ring. The lip protrudes quite 4 inches in many cases.

Soon after arriving Mpinga sent me a small jar of milk—a most acceptable gift. Then I tackled him about food for the men. He sent us some *mtama* flour and potatoes, but here his bank appeared to stop payment. First I asked him to send some goats. After a desperate [word illegible], a blind goat with a stiff neck and a small kid were brought. The

Brisk encounter at Mazamboni's village
(contemporary illustration from *Penny Illustration Paper*)

appearance of this blind goat created intense amusement to our Zanzibaris, and though I tried hard to keep a stern look on my face, it was of no use and I burst out laughing in Mpinga's face. The far away sad look in that goat's one sound eye and the generalized [sic] appearance of his limbs was far too much for me. He [Mpinga] at last added to the show by bringing up a small calf. This was too much, and I told him then to go off to his house and set the whole "cattle show" up as he would very easily be able to do it. He then went off and late at night sent up another cow and two goats, but I refused them.

18th February Started away early from Mpinga's and reached Kavalli's about 12:30 p.m. Met Stanley, Emin Pasha, and officers, Jephson and Bonny. I think now there is no doubt Emin will come out with us and Stanley will give his officers time to return to Wadelai and bring out their men. I think the danger is very great to us should two hundred guns of Emin's come out. All were well. The camp is a good one near Kavalli's village. Jephson has had a lucky escape. The people in this country have apparently no idea of the importance of time. Most of them would as soon die in this place as not. We want to get out; they seem to not care much what they do.

19th February Did some odd jobs about camp. Had [word illegible] with the pasha. He, of course, feels very keenly having to leave the country he has been governor of for so many years but is very glad that he has such a good excuse as that of the Mahdi invasion.

The pasha is a very spare little man with, I fancy, not a very strong mind. The difference of discipline between his men and ours is very marked. Ours at once spring to an order like shots, whereas his men have to be coaxed and asked to do any work. Here there are some ten or eleven clerks and officers who joined the rebels but afterwards asked forgiveness and expressed a desire to go out with us. At least two of these beauties were sent up from Egypt to undergo a period of seven years confinement for *murder*. One of them also desired very much to have the pasha shot only a few weeks back. These people will go back to Wadelai and try and persuade their men to come out; some, I fancy, will never return. Jephson told me his story which is very interesting.

20th February Put up the Maxim and explained the mechanism of it to the pasha and his officers. They were all very much surprised at the rate of firing possible. Emin had two mountain guns which are now in the hands of the rebels and I believe there is very little ammunition for them. Emin tells me that if he gets out safely with us he will go to England and thank them first, then he will urge the English government to take over that part of Masailand east of Victoria Nyanza and the kingdom of Kavirondo. He says he has not yet finished with Africa and someday will return.[...]

The period between 21 February and 1 March was filled with various chores. The men were building huts for the pasha's people—an activity which they disliked, considering it beyond the range of their rightful duties. Friendship established between themselves and the Africans changed methods of securing the supply of food: Stanley's expedition was authorized to levy taxes in kind. Stairs complained that this was hardly enough. If the villagers failed to pay, taxes were collected forcibly. In this way Stairs and his men procured 127 head of cattle which he described as "a most acceptable piece of loot."

On the twenty-eighth Stairs left camp with 122 porters and went down to the lake to bring up the loads which were left there. A day later he was on his way back carrying 100 loads and bringing some of Emin Pasha's people.

2nd March Reached Kavalli's and Stanley at 1:00 p.m. Feet very sore. Nelson laid up with fever. Everyone else well. One of the women gave birth to a child on the road with the utmost unconcern of her surroundings. She marched on again quite cheerily.[...] What a caravan we made up today. Women, babies, parrots, beds, chairs, every sort of odds and ends to be found in the Soudan must have been represented. Casati is a captain in the Italian service; he was formerly ADC [Aide-de-Camp] to General Soldeve. He is quite grey now.

3rd March Signor Casati arrived in camp. One has, now and then, talks with the pasha about the state of affairs. Felkin and Junker are to blame about the ideas Europeans have, or had, of the pasha's country and people.[4] For years, a smothered rebellion has been waiting for wind to fan it into flames. The proposition of the pasha's that he should leave the country afforded them their chance. The pasha's, Jephson's, Casati's, and Vita Hassan's lives, for some time, were merely suspended on the slightest threads.[5] They were insulted, disobeyed, jeered at and at last told to clear out of the country. The second advent of the Donaglas or Mahdist will bring these beauties to reason, I have no doubt.[6]

I feel very anxious, and I'm sure Stanley does, about what is now going on at Wadelai. It is true we have the pasha, but what if Selim Bey,[7] who has gone up to Wadelai, should return and bring a lot of cutthroats with the name of soldiers here? Might they not seize our powder and ammunition? They are quite able to do it. Everyone knows our Zanzibaris are no fighters against guns and determined men. The apathy, the indifference with which these people, including the pasha himself, seemed to look upon our relief expedition, [and] their absolute helplessness in acting promptly are simply appalling and to us quite beyond understanding. That we, who have for two years partially toiled through forest, dangers, fevers, and sickness of all sorts, should be met at last by people who will not help themselves (let alone others) is so maddening [as] to almost make one say, "Well! Go then and be hanged. The Mahdis will cut your throats and serve you right." When people consider us their slaves I fully believe we will be your servants for some little time but never your slaves.[...]

The entries in the diary covering the thirteen days between 4 and 16 March are generally short and refer to the repetitious daily activities. The food situation had improved after the raids on the villages which failed to pay the "tax." Stanley became ill which prompted Stairs to observe that the locality of their camp was unhealthy in spite of its high elevation above sea level (over 5,000 feet). Between 13 and 16 March Stairs made a trip to the lake to bring more loads, during the course of which he had an attack of fever.

17th March   Went up the hills on a picnic with the pasha, Jephson, Parke, Nelson, and Bonny. Spent the day in collecting birds, beetles, insects, etc., for the pasha. The highest hill I was on was 5,500 feet odd [sic]. We had a capital lunch and enjoyed ourselves very much. This must be remembered as a great day to us all as it is the very first of its kind we have had since the expedition left England.

Bonny shot a good specimen of a plantain-eater which delighted the old pasha very much. He is a tremendous enthusiast of things botanical, zoological, entomological, etc. He is such a funny looking little man with his crooked nose and spectacles peering over some insect, that one always feels inclined to laugh at him. But he is such a good old soul, so kind and generous and so sympathetic—one can see he never could make a governor.

18th March   The pasha and Stanley have agreed together about the length of time we are to give the officers who went to Wadelai. It is fixed as the 10th April—on that day we move from here.

Today we reorganized the Zanzibaris into companies. N[o.] 1, Stanley's company, and [the one] which Jephson will look after, numbers sixty-one. All the Winchester rifles are into this company which will generally be the advance guard. My company, No. 2, had [sic] fifty-three men; I have pretty good chaps this time and I hope we shall give a good account of ourselves. The names of my chiefs are Muini Pemba, Saat Tatu, and Abdallah bin Juma—Abdallah is an old favourite of mine. Nelson has No. 3 Company with about fifty-five men.

The pasha was delighted with the survey I made for him from the lake up to camp. I am also making a section of the mountains with aneroid for him. He has given me some maps of his country, two pairs of new cotton trousers, a notebook and pencil, and [a] paint brush. He is a most generous person.[...]

On 19 March Stairs told the men that a decision had been made to depart on 10 April. They were very happy to learn that a date for leaving had definitely been fixed.

The main event between 20 and 24 March was a very successful foraging party led by Stairs and Jephson. It brought in 290 head of cattle. When it was discovered that some of them were previously stolen from a local chief, it was decided to return them to him. Nonetheless, the expedition retained about two hundred head of cattle and twenty goats and sheep. According to Stanley's records of the same event, Stairs and Jephson captured 310 head of cattle, of which 40 belonged to Chief Ruguji. It is impossible to determine whose version is correct as Jephson's comments are missing.

On the twenty-fourth Stairs noted that Captain Casati suffered from leg ulcers which took a long time to heal.

25th March Today letters came from Shukri Agha and Selim Bey.[8] The steamer arrived yesterday from Mswa. The letters from Wadelai came in a canoe to Mswa and were forwarded by steamer. Selim Bey's letter, rather the letter from the officers and clerk at Wadelai, asks the pasha's forgiveness and states that now all [are] desirous of coming out with us to Egypt via Zanzibar and that already large parties have been sent off by land and water.[...] Shukri Agha stated he would wait [for] further orders from the pasha.

Stanley, after getting the letter from Selim Bey, called Jephson, Parke, Nelson, and myself into his hut with the pasha to talk over matters. Emin Pasha backed Mr. Stanley, what[ever] he decided upon. Stanley then asked me if I thought we should be justified in leaving here on the 10th April or [whether we were] taking everything into consideration: the way they had rebelled and taken their governor and some of our officers prisoners; [the way they] had insulted them [and] threatened their lives; how already we have waited nearly a year for them; how slow and dilatory in their movements they are; and a score of other things. Of course, I answered that the 10th April was ample time, and that those really desirous of leaving and joining us would be readily able to do so. The other officers answered in the same way.

The pasha, one could see, had hoped that we should extend the time beyond that date, but nevertheless he promised for himself that on that date he would be ready to march. Stanley spoke to the pasha very strongly, and at times I fancied there would be a split. Luckily, things blew over.

Among those from Wadelai will be some six hundred men of the 2nd Battalion, at least so the pasha says! Say three hundred of these will come. Several times these lambs have expressed a desire to settle down in the country to the south of the lake and follow us a few days then leave us, but before doing so they openly said we "will rob them of every round of ammunition possible." I feel certain that this is just the sort of thing they are capable of doing. This Stanley expressed in very strong terms to the pasha and stated he would never allow these men to come into his camp armed.

What a strange man Emin Pasha is when matters of common sense are concerned. In conversation socially, and in many ways, I believe there can be few more pleasant and more entertaining men than the pasha. Leave these scenes and start on any business matter or affair where it is a question of duty, and the pasha is entirely incapable of seeing things in their true light. Have not some of his people rebelled at least three successive times? Have they not even threatened to hang him, to chain him up? Yet he will say *"No they will never rebel again."* How stupid; how mad it is of him to speak like this. Fancy trusting these low blackguards.

I hope it will never be said of Stanley or any of his officers that they trusted these brutes one jot. They are just as ready now to do mischief as they were before, and to tell the truth I earnestly hope that when we finally leave this place on the 10th April *not one* soldier from Wadelai, or one of their split-tongued officers will put in an appearance. About Shukri Agha and his irregular soldiers from M'swa, according to all accounts they would be a very valuable addition to our strength. These people, however, not having any idea at the value of time are pretty sure to put off coming by that date and [will] so miss us.

At the end of the *shauri* both Stanley and the pasha decided to write strong letters to Shukri Agha to move on this place at once. Stanley's letter will be all right, but that of the pasha will "not be straight" and as a man should write. The pasha cannot *order* anyone to do a thing, he requests them, always.[...]

In the subsequent eight days, preparations continued for the approaching departure towards the coast. A strong urge to be on the march, characteristic of the Zanzibaris and other men belonging to Stanley's expedition, was in sharp contrast to the indifference and lethargy of Emin Pasha's people. On 1 April Stairs left with a party of porters for Mazamboni's village and arrived there the following day.

3rd April Sent a note announcing my arrival to Stanley. Mazamboni's people sent me some food.[...] Hawash Effendi, immediately on reaching here, plagued me to get carriers for him to send on to the pasha.[9] Today it is the same thing. If left to work on his own will, he would soon break this existing friendship between us and Mazamboni.[...]

4th April I have arranged with Mazamboni that two hundred of his people start on the sixth for Kavalli's to bring back loads to this place—probably thirty will turn up. Conversation between Hawash Effendi (a major) and myself today. First, let one say that the pasha told me at Kavalli's that Hawash Effendi would build the pasha's house here. Hawash Effendi was present and said, "Of course." The following then may show up the ways and wiles of these yellow-bellied Egyptians:

Hawash Effendi: "My men have already built two houses and tell me there are no poles to be got in this valley and so I shall have to build a house like those the Zanzibaris build."

Stairs: "Yes that seems to be the best thing you can do."

Hawash Effendi: "Now will you give me some Zanzibaris to go out and cut the necessary poles and rods as they know best just what to cut?"

Stairs: "No, I can't do that as it will establish a precedent. Besides, the pasha distinctly told you in my presence that you were to build his hut."

Hawash Effendi: "Yes, I know, but can't you just lend me these six Zanzibaris to fit and tie on the poles? My men do not know how to do this."

Stairs: "No, I cannot even do that."[...]

I then turned round and walked off. Do these beauties imagine us to be their slaves—men who number murderers, rebels, and thieves in their list?

Why, only yesterday one Effendi stole salt from another and threw it into the river to avoid detection. I told this lamb I would fire him out of the camp with his wife, babies, and all if he tried any more tricks of that sort. By the Khedive's orders we are only to "escort by any route Mr. Stanley may choose, such persons as are desirous of making their way out to the coast and Egypt."[...]

Between 5 and 7 April efforts were made to mobilize some more carriers. In the evening of the sixth Stairs came down with fever once again.

8th April The time is drawing near for Stanley's appearance. The carriers I sent off the day before yesterday should leave Kavalli's today and with them some Zanzibaris.[...]

9th April This is the eve of the pasha's leaving Kavalli's. Poor old chap, he will be in a terrible state of uneasiness all day—the more should Shukri Agha not have turned up.

10th April At last the day has arrived when the Emin Pasha Relief Expedition is to move off from the Nyanza camp and start on its long march to the coast (all well) and home. We of the expedition, who have for weeks and weeks past looked forward to the 10th April as a red letter day and as one which would give us our deliverance from that huge monster, the Soudan and all connected with it, now feel in great spirits, that at last the day has arrived. Emin Pasha, on the other hand, who twice got the date of final departure postponed, cannot but feel sorrowful and disappointed. If Shukri Agha has not arrived by this time at Kavalli's, it will only add to the pasha's bitter disappointment, and also be detrimental to us.

The chief personages, or those whom we would wish most to get out of the country we have secured. Heavens alone knows even yet if we shall be able to secure the pasha—his ways are so strange. Now let us be off and away from any influences this blackest of countries may possess over the pasha's mind; let us swing away east and southward [sic] to the snow-capped mountain of Ruwenzori and far across the central plains to Msalala and the Central African Sea [also known as Lake Victoria]. There we shall see our white brothers and learn the news from the busy European world. Then we shall know what we all have been burning to know for the last two and one-half years.

How are our friends? (For there will be letters for us there.) What is the state of affairs in England? Has there been another European war? What is happening in America? in Canada? Then to me there is the all and ever important question about my service for pension and promotion being counted or not. If these three years I am out here do not count of pension and promotion, then there is nothing for it but I must leave the service. At present one does not know what the state of affairs will be when we reach home, but I hope I shall not have to leave the service on account of three year's work in Africa.

Why the native carriers did not come in from Kavalli's yesterday I cannot imagine; perhaps they will come tomorrow. Will Stanley keep his promise and come tomorrow, or will he listen to the pasha's pleadings for more time and give in to another postponement?[...]

11th April The natives had another big drinking bout last night. All night long we could hear them blowing horns and shouting to each other. They must have got through a great lot of *pombe*.[...]

Springtime at home now. In Canada the ice is losing its iron grasp on the lakes and streams and the dusky trout begins to move about, ready for the season. In Scotland the fishing now should be good.

Yesterday I got a present of a goat, five fowls, and a lot of flour and bananas from the chief of a village about 1 mile from here. Strange to say this very village I raided in December 1887 and took seventeen goats out of it. In return, I killed a cow for him and gave it to his men and himself and pleased old Mazamboni by giving him the shoulder. These people are as bad as hyaenas for meat.

Some natives came in this morning from Mpinga's with the news that Stanley had arrived there last evening with the pasha and all hands. They stated that Kavalli had also moved with them and that the old camp at his place was burnt down on leaving. He and all hands will be here tomorrow. Stanley might have at least sent a note to me.[...]

12th April The first lot of Stanley's people came in at 10:00 a.m., the others at all hours, up till 4:00 p.m. Stanley was carried and does not appear well. Nelson had to wait with Parke at Mpinga's till nearly noon as Mpinga's carriers ran away. They threw away some twenty loads of the pasha's people amid general swearing, and then came on here, bringing Mpinga a prisoner. A great row had taken place at Kavalli's between Stanley and some of the pasha's people.

It appears from Jephson's account that some of the pasha's soldiers, at night-time, went in among the Zanzibari quarters and endeavoured to seize some rifles belonging to our men.[...] Next morning Stanley went down to the pasha and endeavoured to reason with him. Either he, the pasha, must pull his men in and investigate the case, or Stanley must take matters into his own hands.

Stanley proposed two things to the pasha, both of which the pasha declined to follow. One was that the pasha and Stanley should move off at once, or that a camp should be formed some 2 miles off and the pasha move one there and let Stanley clear out the people on the tenth. When the pasha had answered Stanley in his aggravating dilly-dallying way, Stanley jumped up and swore he would then take everything in to his own hands. He rushed out, fell in the Zanzibaris, had all the Turks and Soudanese driven into the square and with his rifle loaded and ready asked for "those who dared to say they would stay behind. Stand out here and let me see you, you dogs."

The pasha, I believe, chased Stanley all about the yard imploring him not to do anything rash. All Stanley answered in his rage was, "I am resolved. I am resolved." He made the culprits lay down their arms and had them all bound up. He then gave all the clerks, servants, and soldiers to understand that everyone present must follow him, those that disobeyed would be shot. This was a most wholesome lesson to these people. They will now perhaps see that they cannot play the same game with us as they did with the pasha; they will know now who are their masters and will see that we will stand no nonsense from any of them.

Most of the trouble has been caused by the Egyptians in the country, not directly by the soldiers. When the soldiers have acted badly they have invariably been instigated to do so by the Egyptian clerks and other officials. One thing difficult for any white governor in the country to contend with, of course, must be religious fanaticism. The Muslims look with the greatest contempt upon a white dog of a Christian, no matter however great that Christian's abilities may be, and no matter how infinitely superior in every way he may be over themselves, he is a Christian and cannot but have ideas counter to those of Islam.[...]

13th April Last night some fifty-seven people of the pasha's—chiefly those belonging to Hawash Effendi—took it into their heads to desert, taking some four or five guns, food, tools, clothes, etc. It is only what Stanley told the pasha they would do.

Stanley was taken very ill during the night with vomiting fits and cramps in his stomach. Today he is really very bad. Stanley's camp is about 100 yards from mine. Jephson and I occupy my hut, all the other fellows living up above with Stanley.

14th April I am very much afraid our stay here will be a prolonged one owing to Stanley's illness. We must all try and wait patiently and get him well as quick as we can, though the stay will be torturous to all of us.[...]

15th to 21st April From 15th to 21st Stanley has been in various stages of illness, at times being really bad, and now today, the twenty-first, he is much better and able to sit up.[...]

What a poor patient Stanley is; how inconsiderate [of] others and how selfish for his own ends. Poor Parke succumbed to the constant night watching and now has a severe attack of bilious remittent fever. The pasha's slaves and people continue to run away nightly in spite of our cautions to him. Jephson is sickly today.

21st to 29th April During this time we we were all waiting for Stanley's and Parke's recoveries. Now, twenty-ninth, it will be yet some six days before we shall be able to start.[...]

The pasha's people—men, women, and children—have been deserting for the last ten days at a terrible rate. A report has been spread that we intend to return to the sea by bush route. All have heard of our suffering in this deadly bush, and getting frightened, run away.

We held a court martial the other day and sentenced, among many other sentences, one man to be hanged. He was afterwards let off through the shilly-shallying of the pasha. Yesterday I sent thirty men and some of the pasha's people down to the Nyanza to see if they could catch any of the fugitives. Stanley is rapidly getting better, while Parke may be said to be well but weak. All of us are burning to get on the march and see the unknown land ahead.

1st to 4th May Nothing much goes on in camp from day to day. On the second the party under Shukri Agha returned from their search for deserters having caught two men and some women. Among these was a deserter of ours, Rehani.[10] Stanley ordered us to hold a court of inquiry into his case. He had induced about forty of the pasha's people to desert, but we found out the plot and disarmed all those intending ones. After hours of careful investigation of the case by Nelson, Parke, Jephson, and I as president, we found him guilty, and Stanley sentenced him to death. All hands were fallen in, and in half an hour after this, we hanged him on the nearest tree leaving his body suspended in mid-air all night.

This will have a wholesome effect on any others who may have intended to desert. The pasha and Stanley hate each other now to an extent almost incredible. We officers all hope another outbreak will not take place as the pasha feels he is being treated very badly by Stanley and even now has suffered enough to make him leave us at Msalala, a proceeding very much to be regretted should it occur. It is impossible to get any straightforward answer from the pasha, even in small matters; he is too long a resident of the Orient for that (twenty-four years or so).

There is only one course that can be adopted to prevent the breach widening and that is that the pasha should hand over to Stanley all his people, and he, the pasha, [should] have absolutely nothing to do with them. Let him then come and live in our camp with his household and all will go smoothly and cheerfully. This, though, I'm afraid he will never do and it will perforce have to be done by Stanley. The result will be a violent storm on both sides. This state of things existing is a great misfortune for all of us and should it continue, many damaging things about the expedition may be made known to the European public.

No entries had been made for 5 and 6 May.

7th May   Getting everything ready for the start tomorrow.

CHAPTER 8
EPILOGUE:
THE MARCH TO ZANZIBAR

8 MAY—5 DECEMBER 1889

The march to the east coast commences on 8 May. From the fourteenth Stairs is down with fever for over a week. On 30 May the men of Kilonga Longa's kill, by mistake, several members of the caravan. On 6 June Stairs attempts to climb one of the Ruwenzori peaks. He also discovers a previously unknown source of the Nile. The column crosses the equator on 20 June. On 18 August Lake Victoria is sighted. Ten days later the Church Missionary Society station at Usambiro is reached. Stairs learns of the death of his father. The journey is resumed on 17 September. The expedition reaches Mpwapwa on 19 November. The arrival at Bagamoyo marks the end of the journey.

8th May At last off on the march [with] our faces towards the southeast. All the Zanzibaris are wild with joy at getting away on the road again and so, of course, are all of the whites. Marched to Balla-Balla. I was in rearguard; the pasha's people gave a great lot of trouble. Stanley reached here (being carried) in three and one-half hours. Saw the last of Mazamboni. He hates the pasha and his people.

9th May Got away early from camp. The confusion at first was indescribable: all tried to push forward at the same time. Our regular order of march was completely broken up, and instead people and cattle were huddled together four or five abreast pushing and cursing each other heartily. All the [sic] morning the road was bad. About 11:00 a.m. Stanley stopped at Bujungwa for camp.

The pasha's people as yet are poor marchers; of course, they are soft and unused to the road and no doubt in time will improve, but still they will give us endless trouble before they become drilled into the thing.[...]

We are going in a south and SE direction following a deep valley by keeping along the east slope. This, of course, makes the marching bad. Across the valley about 6 miles is the edge of the great forest we had to pass through and [where we] lost so many lives. It reminds one of a great big devil with outstretched claws, ever on the watch to catch passersby and draw them into its fathomless bosom, never afterwards to be heard of by man.

Stanley will have to be carried many days; his legs are very thin, though he is picking up. [Travelled] 5¾ to 6½ miles.

10th May Away before the sun showed itself. Camped at Vurumbi. I had great trouble with the women and children, and at times thought I should go crazy with the broiling sun, the endless nagging at the people to go on, and the steep slopes. Our column now beggars description. Ahead is Stanley and his company, behind him generally come the pasha, Casati, and one of our officers, then follow all the pasha's officers and their wives, children, and slaves—the most motley crowd to be found anywhere. They are awful people to fight among themselves and the noise of shouting sometimes can be heard quite a mile away, I should say. Behind all this crowd come the cattle, say 150. These, of course, mix with the people and add to the confusion. Behind these come the weary and [the] sick and [the] stragglers, and driving them with curses, shouts, and sticks comes the rearguard moving like a snail across a garden path. Nelson and I take turns day by day at rearguard duty.[...]

On 11 May as the column approached the Semliki River, which runs into Lake Albert, it was attacked by Kabba Rega's people who were armed with guns. Stairs, with a strong detachment of askaris, went to meet the enemy who ran away; no shots were fired. Between 12 and 16 May Stairs and Jephson succumbed to a very bad attack of malaria. Skirmishes with Kabba Rega's warriors continued. During the next three days the column crossed the river using one canoe: 1,168 people had to be ferried across, the majority of them were the pasha's people, mostly women and children. On 23 May Stairs was able to walk again and acted as rearguard. By 26 May the big mountain range Ruwenzori was approached.

27th May Halted. Sent out No. 3 [Company] to find road ahead. Never in my life have I seen such quantities of bananas as there are here; on every hillside and hilltop there are plantations of splendid bananas and plantains. Look wherever you will along the edge of the bush and plain, and you will see these fine plantations.

Boiled thermometer and found height of camp to be 2,942 feet above sea [level]. Also found height of range opposite the camp to be 9,147 feet and distance 3½ miles off. I should say by comparing this height with Ruwenzori that the latter will prove to be about 15,500 feet.[1]

Since coming here we have not caught a glimpse of the snow mountain now 10 miles off owing to the masses of clouds which hang constantly over the mountains at an altitude of 6,000 [feet] or 7,000 feet. We know, though, that a great part of Ruwenzori is covered with dense bush. In another march or so we should be abreast of the mountain, and then perhaps some of us will try and make an ascent.

The pasha's people are very weary of the bush even though we have been such a short time in it; the mud, streams, and twigs have done up a great many of them about the feet. They are poor stock, these people, with very little life or go [sic] in them.

28th May Today's march was a very trying one to all, but to those in rear it was especially fatiguing. From 6:30 a.m. till 3:30 p.m., we in rear plunged along through mud, up and down slippery hills, every few minutes receiving a check as some one of the pasha's people would go down with his or her load and block up the road. At times I thought we should not reach the camp, so obstinately stupid the people seemed to be in stopping at every hilltop and village we came to. About 2:00 p.m. we came to open country, but such open country I never saw before—just one mass of ups and down[s] covered with grass.[...]

Some of these women from the north are very plucky load carriers, but their brutal masters load them down cruelly, so much so that on a slippery hilly road they can hardly get along at all. We have, I should think, some twenty or thirty Egyptian, Coptic [a Christian sect in Egypt], and half-bred women—the wives of the different clerks and officers. It is most amusing to see them on the march walking through mud up to their knees; they do not mind the black men at all and will make a great demonstration of healthy looking limbs, but should a white man appear, down go their clothes and they appear most grave and proper. They are terribly afraid of their husbands I fancy. With us they will scarcely say a word.

Stanley got in about 12:30.

29th May Marched again and at 9:30 camped in a series of villages near the mountains. Here an old man was caught out of whom some information was got. The country we passed through today was fairly level and covered with long tangled grass. We marched parallel to the mountains at a distance of about 1½ miles from where the big hills spring up. Nelson, who was in rear, got in early. The huts here are round, roofed with grass.[...]

30th May A most disastrous day. After Stanley had reached camp about 11:00 this morning and things had been made busy, some eight or ten of our men, Manyuema, went off as usual prowling about in search of loot. At a short distance from camp they were fired at by some persons hidden in the grass only a few yards [away]. Uledi Sadi had his elbow shot away. A boy of Sadi, the Manyuema chief's, was killed. Poor little Farag Ali, my old boy, was terribly [sic] shot in the stomach and chest and died at night. Khani Unyamwezi was badly wounded and two others slightly wounded.

Of course, our men replied, thinking the people in ambush must be those of Kabba Rega. After some time, however, it was found that instead of them being Kabba Rega's people, they were Manyuema of a party of Kilonga Longa's ivory hunters camped only two hours from us. They had come up here from camp after bananas and hearing us, had taken us for Wanyoro raiders and so had ambushed themselves and fired on us. Our men killed three of their party.

It was a most disastrous affair and one feels quite sad at Farag Ali's death; he was such a bright cheery little soul—the life of his own camp and always had cheery "Mornin' Master" for me every day as I passed him. This is the second safari Kilonga Longa's men have made out onto the plain and now they are settled just at the foot of Ruwenzori for the purpose of collecting ivory, though I should think Kabba Rega's men have already taken most of that article out of the country.[...]

31st May Halted. had a visit from the Manyuema chief, Khamis, and his men, accompanied by Bukoko and another native. Bukoko is the chief of this district, a small sparely built man.[...] From Bukoko we got some information about the country ahead; it is said to be [a] three days' march from here to the Usongora country. There are two lakes, the larger of which is Muta Nzige and the smaller [is] Usongora.[2] The first is fresh water the second saltish [sic] and it is from here that the Wasongora get their salt and sell it to the natives about here for corn.[...]

1st June Halted again to allow our people time to prepare banana flour.[...] In two days' or three days' march we hope to be able to turn the corner of the range and slant a little more to the south. Some streams from the mountain passing near camp, for instance, the Rami, are very cold.[...] The height of the mountains opposite here is about 11,000 feet. The Manyuema again came into camp and appeared to drive a good trade with the pasha's people. Uledi Sadi and the other sick men are doing well.

2nd June Made a fair march of 7 miles and camped once more in the bush. All along the foot of the mountain range which now runs SSW, is very broken country covered with scrubby bush. In many places the ravines are 100 feet deep and create a great deal of trouble for the pasha's people, who are only accustomed to open country and make a poor show of it in the bush. Many of the plants and trees one used to see in the big Congo Forest one notices here, and one also notices many of the same birds throughout the bush, though there is one great distinction, and that is the presence here of the prickly acacia which is absent in the forest between the Congo and Albert Nyanza.

The effect of the Manyuema's residence in the country is most plainly marked by the numbers of deserted villages and ruined plantations we passed today. The paths also are grown up with grass, showing no signs of native traffic at all. We have now turned the corner of the range, as it were, and ahead of us on our left appears a huge broken mass of precipitous mountain cones, all separated and defined by deep rocky ravines. The lower spurs and gullies are covered with dense forests of large trees, making an ascent anywhere about here impossible.[...]

3rd June Marched 4½ miles through the bush. Can from here see snow on the two peaks. Scenery most wild with huge broken mountain masses ahead.

4th June Sent out two parties to find a road ahead; one of these under Uledi was successful. From time to time we got glimpses of the snow-capped peaks, but on the whole we could see very little of the upper mountains, owing to masses of vapour which shrouded them.[...] Every gully appears to have its banana plantation and every coign of vantage its huts. Many of the huts present a very strange appearance perched far away upon some cone-like hill, with desperately steep tracks leading up to them. Almost all the bush natives, I should say, have fled up to these mountain villages, many on hearing of our approach, and many on account of the Manyuema.

5th June After an up- and downhill march of only 3 miles, reached camp. Plenty of food. Stanley and I had a talk about going up the big mountain.

6th June Started off with forty rifles up the mountain. I knew it could not be a good place for trying an ascent—the bush was too thick by far. Well, I went on and on and camped at night at 8,570 feet among the heather. Next morning I reached 10,617 feet at 9:00 a.m., but here I had to stop. The men had no food. It would take us one and one-quarter days yet to reach the snow. I had no time to do this and to go on would end disastrously. I therefore ordered the men back. I took two aneroids and a thermometer. The above elevation is with all corrections made. As I have made a long report of this to Stanley, and as it will someday most likely be printed, I do not write anything else about this ascent.[3]

I was able to give Emin Pasha thirty-seven specimens of different plant, two of which are new to science, I believe. At 10,000 feet I found blueberries and blackberries, and lower down, violets. I am sorry I could not have gone onto the snow and brought some down, but this was out of the question as we were with no food.

7th June Reached Stanley in the afternoon. He was greatly pleased at our getting even as far as we did. The pasha was also delighted at getting the plants.[...]

8th June Gave our men another day to prepare food. I am exceedingly glad I brought down the blueberries and plants for the pasha. The pleasure he evidently feels far more than compensates for the trouble.

9th June Camped in forest. I, in rearguard, got in at 5:30 p.m., being just eleven hours on foot, driving along the weak and sickly ones of the pasha. It is terribly trying work, this— both [for] body and mind. On the road we passed a hot spring. The water, though quite clear, had a taste of sulphur. Its temperature was 102° F [sic].

10th June Marched 6½ miles. Were attacked by natives, but after two hours in camp they came in to make friends. This is a great gain to us, as we shall now be shown a short road and will not lose any sick who may have strayed off the path. The natives are Wakongu. They have no cattle. One notices huts perched high upon the mountain sides. Here the forest ends and ahead is nothing but open country.

11th and 12th June March SSW and SW 12 miles, under the guidance of natives.[...] Here the natives report a large river coming out of Muta Nzige.[...] Does this go into the Nile or Congo? The long vexed question in England.

13th and 14th June Took sixty rifles and went to examine river. I returned on the fourteenth to Stanley, and in my report to him I say, "I have now not the slightest doubt in my mind but this is the Semliki running into the Albert Nyanza and on to the Nile, and that therefore the long vexed question to all geographers is now definitely settled and the Muta Nzige helps to swell the Nile. From camp to this river was 16 miles. The river was 42 yards broad, 10 feet deep, running at 3 miles per hour. [It] was salty and of dirty colour. Here the natives call it Engezi. It comes from the Nyanza of Unyampaka and goes on to the Nyanza (Albert).[4]

15th June Reached the boundary of Usongora.

16th June Crossed the Mpondo River, captured thirty-six cattle of Kabba Rega's and camped at village of Kisaho, whose chief was Kikambo. All natives had fled. Immense numbers of cattle have been driven off from here quite lately. Saw the Nyanza for first time.

17th June Crossed the Nyamagazani River [...] and reached the village of Katwa at the western end of Lake Muta Nzige. Natives came in from island.[5] Immense quantities of salt. This was Kakuri's old village.

18th June Remained camp.

19th June Remained in camp. Water in Lake Katwe [also known as Salt Lake] is intensely salt.[6] I have managed to get a pair of boots out of Vita, the apothecary. The are not up to much but may help me on a bit.[...] The lake is in a basin 250 feet deep. It is 1½ miles long and 43 miles round. The big lake is about 500 yards from camp. It appears to run to the ESE, though perhaps this may only be part of it. Jephson and I went down to the Salt Lake this afternoon and saw some of the most marvellous sights I have ever seen in my

Ruwenzori from Karimi
(from contemporary engraving)

life. The water of the lake is of a blood-red colour.[...] That of Salt Lake City would only have the one-twentieth part [sic] of salt in a given volume of water that this has.

The method of making the salt is as follows: pans of 20 foot diameter are made in the mud on the flat shores and quite close to the water. This is then allowed to run in and the pan is dammed up. In a short time the sun causes the water to evaporate, leaving a thin coating of ice-like salt on the top. This soon sinks and more is formed on the surface. The salt sinking to the bottom forms the most perfect crystals on a strata of pink salt whose crystals are smaller. The natives then come, and with their hands, take out these cakes of salt. We got some of these cakes 1 inches thick. An enormous amount of salt must be taken out of this lake which Kabba Rega's people have deemed politic to take. The country for many miles about, even as far as Ruanda [sic], is supplied from this source alone.

Stanley took some men and went out on the lake for a look about in the canoe I got the day before yesterday. They went along the eastern shore some 7 miles, but had then to come back as the canoe was such a poor one. Some of the Wahuma natives say one can go to the far end of the lake in one and one-half days in a canoe; others say it takes as many as nine days paddling.

I am very much afraid that Stanley will never be able to circumnavigate this lake. The duties of looking after the pasha's people, fighting natives, etc., have made this expedition more like a small army fighting its way through the country than a geographical expedition. We have no time to sit down with eleven hundred people; food cannot be got for them. Kabba Rega's people, too, are ever ready to cut off any detached party of ours that comes in their way.[...]

20th June Made a very fast march of 18½ English miles and reached the shore of the Nyanza at Hamkonga, a village belonging to Kashisha the Unyampaka chief, and opposite to Irangara Island. We are today exactly on the equator. This is part of Unyampaka, though tomorrow we will enter Toro and after passing through it [we] will again enter Unyampaka. From Irangara Island opposite to us, Kabba Rega took in one haul—ten thousand head of cattle; they had been congregated there by the Wahuma for safety. The Wanyoro crossed over at night, surrounded the villages and took men, women, children, and cattle, with scarcely a blow on either side. All were then driven off in a body to Unyoro.[...]

The mosquitoes are terrible here. For two nights the men have had no sleep at all. They simply sit up and talk and yawn all night over the fires.

21st June Made 5 miles.[...] Passed along within 2 miles of the lake, but the country was so flat we could see very little of it.[...]

During the subsequent eleven day, malaria was rife and those affected by it included Stanley, Parke, Bonny, Jephson, Stairs, Emin Pasha, and his daughter Ferida. Constant alertness was necessary because the caravan was frequently attacked by the Wanyankori tribesmen. On 1 July Stairs noted his twenty-sixth birthday. Two days later a decision was made by Stanley to follow the Ankori (Ankole) and Karagwe route toward the coast, which appeared to him to be superior to the three other alternative routes, namely: to the west and eventually south via Ujiji; through Rwanda; or, to pass around southern Uganda and cross the Alexandra Nile (the name given by Stanley to Kagera River).

4th July The glorious fourth. Marched from Chikombi, our camp by the lake SSE 7 miles and reached Kitete on the uplands. We are here about halfway up the mountain range that bounds the lake on its eastern side. Many natives came in to see the white men and their caravan. [They] thanked us for opening up Katwe, the Salt Lake, to trade again by driving away the Wara Sura.[7] This stroke will, I fancy, make our journey through Ankori a simple one. From here we get our last view of the Nyanza. Stanley's old camp must be north of us some 5 miles.[8][...]

5th July Today we reached Kiwiga. The natives are strolling about camp in numbers. We are firm friends. I bought a very neat pipe from them for some meat. Our peaceful passage through Ankori is now fairly assured, I fancy.

6th July Kiwiga to Busimba.[...]

The writing of the diary was interrupted by illness and 11 July an entry was made, as Stairs explained it, on the twenty-fourth when his health had improved somewhat. From 18 July until 19 August (with the exception of 4 August) the diary is complete.

11th July I write this on the twenty-fourth—from the eleventh onwards I had so many attcks of fever that I could not muster up enough energy to write even a few remarks each day. These fevers have made us all look like many spectres; we are all pale and thin with pinched faces and miserable bony appendages for legs. It is most exhausting in this state to march even a few miles and one arrives in camp and flings oneself down praying that nothing will come to disturb one's weary rest. Oh, for a temperate climate. This cursed fever will ever be a drawback to colonization in Africa.

18th, 19th, and 20th July Remained in camp, I with a bad fever and Stanley also knocked over. Goodness only knows how these continual attacks of fever are likely to end. All of us are subject to them. They leave us quite exhausted and feeble as cats. The causes Parke has drawn are bad water, cold winds, and extremes of temperature between night and day. Ankori is very badly off for water. The usual supply is from [a] filthy stagnant hole where men and animals drink alike.[...]

Oh, for a Canadian summer and the woods and good food. How one's spirits and strength would go up and how one would again think life worth living.[...] Yesterday Umari, one of our chiefs, came back from Antari's village[9] where he had been on behalf of Stanley. He says Antari is very fat and eats nothing but milk and meat. He sends [sic] Stanley some spears and skins.

21st July Marched. Weak with fever. Made 6 miles.

22nd July I, in rearguard, was attacked by about two hundred natives who tried to capture my ammunition. We drove them off with a volley and killed two of them. Antari's son came in to see Stanley and make blood brotherhood–the "prince," as Stanley calls him.

23rd July Stanley made blood brotherhood amid firing of guns. I fired off some sixty or seventy rounds against a hillside much to the admiration of the natives, who sent us a jar of beer and a goat–not bad. The son of Antari is a very nice looking boy of about twelve years old, he had plenty to say and one would like to punch his head, but then he himself has nothing to do with the general uppishness and meaness [sic] of the Wanyankori. We have heard from some Wanyamwezi who were staying at Antari's that Bagamoyo had been shelled and burnt by the Germans. This is most likely true enough, and is in revenge for the Germans who have been killed up-country. This must have happened over a year ago, I should think. It is hard to say what the Arabs will do. They could make it pretty hot for whites.[...]

24th July Marched 6 miles south.

25th July [Marched] SSW 10 miles. Fever bad; had a hard time of it to get along. Luckily, Parke sent some men back from camp to meet me and these helped me along greatly. Reached the Kagera River.[...]

26th July Very weak–still the accursed fever. Marched to the crossing, crossed over No. 2 Company and the pasha's people.[...]

27th July Finished crossing all hands over the river. The Kagera or Alexandra Nile is here–a well developed stream 70 yards broad and 8 feet deep, banked with papyrus and running along at 2½ miles per hour. The water is fresh and unlike that of Muta Nzige in taste: its sources of supply must be the papyrus swamps in Ankori and Mpororo.[10] It is of a reddish brown colour and a great improvement on the filthy liquid we have been drinking for some time past.

We are now in Karagwe and four or five days from the capital.

28th July Five miles south. Water bad. I was carried today in a hammock, I was so weak. A terrible comedown: I can only walk 200 yards without a rest.

29th July Again carried. Reached the hot springs of Mtagata, these are about four in number in a shady bit of bush in a gully surrounded on the south by hills and open to the north. At one place the water rushes out of the earth in a goodly sized stream whose temperature is 120° about [sic]. This stream is perfectly tasteless and is excellent water for washing and cooking. When it gets cool it is also good for drinking. The other springs are pools of warmish water. It is in these that the natives delight to loll about and wash their troublous sore. They say it effects wonderfully quick cures on ulcers and other sores. But most probably it is the exchange from dirt to cleanliness that works the cures.[...]

30th July Arrived in camp. The meaness [sic] of these natives surpasses anything one has ever seen. For a little flower they want a doti of cloth, just fancy the sharks. The Arabs, it is said, have all removed from the king's capital and gone to Unyamyembe; for what reason I can't make out. Perhaps there is no ivory to be got here now. We rejoice in having plenty of hot weather always ready–a great blessing. All of us drink the waters!

31st July Marched. I in rearguard. Weak.

1st August Marched.

2nd August Ditto.

3rd August Reached Kafurro the old Arab trading establishment of Karagwe.[...] Kafurro is not the residence of the kings of the country; this is about 3 miles northeast of here near the shores of Lake Windmere.

5th and 6th August Jephson went over to see the king with a company of Zanzibaris.[...]
  Guides to Urigi were arranged and the king promised to send down quantities of food. These "quantities" turned out to be three jars of pombe, a few packets of beans, and some bananas–just enough to feed thirty to forty men, whereas we are 100 strong.[...] Since Rumanika's time things have gone down.[...][11]
  From 2 July to 4 August the pasha has lost 141 of his people by desertion, death, stolen by natives, and sold to natives for food. This is a great loss in numbers, but in reality a great gain to the strength of the column.

7th August Made a march of 7 miles to Rozaka on Speke and Grant's old track. Here the men got plenty of food. Stanley is sick again. It is strange how hard he tries to hide his illnesses from us. I fancy he likes to crow over us officers who cannot hide our feelings. He is terribly jealous of anyone being carried, though he himself has been carried every day since leaving Mazamboni. Jephson [has] fever again. So far we have found Karagwe much better watered than Ankori and the water nicer to the taste.

8th August Reached Uthenga. The morning was bitterly cold with a driving rain and strong wind. Many were knocked over (of the slaves and children) and it was only on the sun coming out that they recovered and came on. The men raided quantities of ground-nuts and beans. We are to stay here two days because Stanley wants a rest.
  Wanyankori and people of Karagwe have the finest and most useful looking spears I have yet seen. They are used for stabbing not throwing. Both tribes are very much afraid

of our guns, they have never seen many before and marvel at the rate of fire of the Watson and Remington. With four hundred rifles one could go clean through Karagwe, Ankori, Unyoro, or Uganda and take whatever one likes. The fighting powers of all these peoples have been exaggerated greatly by former travellers.[...]

9th August Halted at Uthenga. Held an inquiry into the conduct of W[illia]m Hoffmann, Stanley's former servant.

10th August Reached the Lake of Urigi.[...] Speke and Grant passed up the west side of this lake, but we go to the east to avoid the land of shark king of Usui and stride quickly for Victoria Nyanza.[...]

There are quantities of game her about: giraffe, zebra, rhinoceros, hippo, elephant, eland, hartebeest, native buck, springbok, and many others. The prettiest sight of all is to see the zebras running about just like ponies in a grass paddock at home.

I was in rearguard.

11th August Again camped on lake shore. [Travelled] 8 miles.

12th August Camped on lake shore. [Travelled] 7 miles.

On 13 August the column reached the county of Ihangiro where it halted the next day to obtain guides. After a long march on 14 and 15 August, it stopped again for two days in order to buy some food.

18th August Marched SSW, 8 miles. Shortly after leaving camp we came out on some bluffs right over the Victoria Nyanza and got one of the finest sights of anything we have yet seen. Far away to the east, to the horizons, stretched the lake glittering like gold in the morning sun, and here and there studded with islands of all sizes. Ahead of us is a big bay which we shall have to march round. It is unlike either the Albert or Albert Edward Lakes having bold shores and looking much like one of Canada's lakes.

19th August From this onwards to Mackay which we reached on twenty-eighth.[12] The country was covered with high bush. We all felt the hot trying marches very much and one can hardly express one's feelings of delight on putting up at the mission station [and] seeing two Englishmen—Mr. Deakes and Mr. Mackay. They were also very much pleased at seeing us and thus feeling certain we were not dead.

A mail for us had arrived from the coast. There were two letters for me—one from my mother and another from Jack.[13] Both told me the saddest and [most] heart-breaking news [I] could have read. Our dear old father had died in Cannes on the 21st March 1887.[14] This is a terrible blow to me. I am burning to know all about it and can find nothing except bare facts. How they all must have felt it at home. One hardly takes everything in now, there is so much in the way of news.

Poor Jameson died at Bangala on his way down [the] Congo.[...] The new German emperor is also dead and now it is Kaiser Wilhelm again:[15] My sister was burnt out in Burmah [sic] and appears to have had a terrible time of it.[16] What will become of our old home now? Will the place be sold? What a blow; our old home at the Arm broken up. It is too much. Shall I never again roam about the old place and potter [sic] about among the boats down at the shore? Shall we never have any more pleasant evenings together near the bathing house?

The brightest thing I always had to look back to when far away from home and the place I always delighted to return to was Fairfield. Shall I never go back there again among the brown birches and spruce trees, back by the side of the dear old Arm, back to the old places of our younger days? How many times have I started away from the old place with a well-loaded basket, off to the woods, off to the woods, trout fishing with Jack and Walter and Carlie.[17][...]

In what state my father's affairs were when he died I cannot tell. If we are left well or badly off I do not know nor can I guess. That he should have been buried in France is very sad I think! But what a blow to us all this is; however, I saw it coming, though those at home never did.

Mackay and Deakes made us very comfortable—good food, books, chairs, papers, and English tobacco. How we did revel in these things. Such stories have got about in England concerning us: how Stanley was wounded, how the "white pasha" was marching on Khartoum, etc., and the excitement caused in England over the expedition. Poor Barttelot's death caused a great deal of indignation against the Manyuemas, but in reality we know it to have been his own fault. Ward and Troup have been making statements apparently, though perhaps not actually publishing them over their names.

Here at Mackay's now we enjoy ourselves: first, there is the coffee in the morning and chat, then a little work and breakfast: biscuits, coffee, sugar, pepper, good stews, etc. Why, one hardly knows how to use all these things after such a long sojourn in the wilds. Mr. Deakes, though staying here, really belongs at Nyanza station, some four days off on the east side of the lake, and Mackay's real place is in Uganda.

Mwanga, the deposed king of Uganda, is now on Sesse Island with his forces gradually gathering strength to attempt an attack on Kalema, the present king, and get back his country. Mwanga, though a great scoundrel, has the sympathy of the missionaries, both French and English, and will in the end most probably succeed.[18]

We had a visit from the French missionary of Bukumbi, some five days off. We hear of the British East African Company being floated and its expedition under one Jackson had reached Usoga on the north side of Lake Victoria on its way to Wadelai!! Heavens, what a hole they will get into up there; they will certainly fall either into the Mahdists' hands or into those of the pasha's ex-soldiers—both equally fatal positions. We have no possible means of communicating with Jackson and stopping them.[19]

Mackay is the very ideal of a good chap for African colonization; he is wasted as a missionary in the position he is in. His treatment of us we shall never forget; a more kind-hearted and generous man I never met. We were able to obtain some European provisions here which will be a perfect godsend to us on the road. Mr. Deakes also has been very kind to us in a hundred different ways. Both of these missionaries are of the opinion that the Uganda mission will be a success.[...]

Between 28 August and 16 September the expedition stayed at the Usambiro mission station. As the caravan resumed its march to the coast, Stairs's entries in the diary lost their former continuity and covered only five days in September and eleven days in October. On 16 September the column resumed the 1,900 mile march to the coast. During the four days between 19 and 22 October, there were skirmishes with the unfriendly Wasukuma tribe. Further on, water became very scarce and people suffered considerably.

23rd October In Mgunda Mkhali all day long through low scrub. A great many Wanyamwezi are following us on their way to different places in Ugogo to settle and others to sell tobacco of which the Ugogo appear to plant little or none.

In this hot weather marching along a dusty track till one's throat is dried up and one's lips parched, how grateful one is for a drink of water no matter how muddy or salty, and think, then, how all these women must suffer when they, *have not got this cup full*. Nevertheless this is what actually does happen, for, poor creatures, they drain their gourds as a rule early in the day and so suffer all the rest of the march. But to me how good a cup or two of tea is when one is red hot on the march. Nothing that I know of quenches the thirst so thoroughly as hot tea. Cold tea or coffee are not thirst quenchers, but quinine, if taken in the morning, will stave off thirst for some time.[...]

Here at Migomera (camp) the old native wells are 36 [feet] to 40 feet deep, cut out of solid rock. No village exists here now, though, as there [has] been some tribal fighting going on with the result that this place has been wrecked.

The Wanyamwezi and Wasukuma carry their loads on poles resting on the shoulders and very rarely carry on the head as the coast people do.[...]

26th October Reached Muhalala in Ugogo. It is astonishing to us how people had apparently lost their heads in England about this expedition. Now, most probably, they have received Stanley's letters from Yambuya fourteen months ago and have stopped all this trash about cannibalism, slaving, etc. But the cuttings we have read from English and American papers show an ignorance about Africa and things African that is appalling.

A Mr. Wilmot Brookes (?) writes to his father a letter which is published in (I think) *The Standard*. This letter is either written in a vindictive and utterly spiteful tone or else is the result of a writer utterly ignorant of the true state of affairs at Yambuya. He had heard of arms and legs sticking out of cooking pots! Has he? Now, my experience of the very worst cannibal natives is that they know it is *wrong* to eat human flesh, and that they not only hide away any human meat from white man but also from other natives. They will never allow themselves to be caught with human flesh. Even Manyuemas who eat dogs are ashamed of it and hide the flesh away if one comes into their camp. Natives are always ashamed of themselves and try to put off any questions as to their cannibalistic propensities.

Here the diary ends. The march to the coast continued for another forty-one days and some of the events relating to this period were recorded by Stairs in an article written by him and published in 1891 in The Nineteenth Century, *and in a series of essays in* The Novascotian. *These two sources of information provide his reminiscences from the last lap of this long journey which, not surprisingly, ends on a highly emotional note.*

On the 19th November, about 10:30 a.m., we caught sight of the German flag waving over Fort Mpwapwa, and soon after halted under the two guns of the fort and made camp. Here we were welcomed by some German officers, who informed us that this was their farthest point west. Fort Mpwapwa was well able to withstand the attacks of any number of Arabs, provided its water-supply would hold out. It is very striking to see our Zanzibaris beside the Zulu and Soudanese soldiers of the Germans. Our men never salute us, and know no drill that could be of use to them, while, on the other hand, the Germans have their men drilled to almost perfection. While it is of the greatest importance to have men well trained in the use of their arms, i.e., to be good shots, I doubt if all this fancy drilling does much good; it is apt to break down in such a country as this.

Six days after leaving Mpwapwa we received as a gift from Major von Wissmann[20] some hams, champagne, and cigars. Needless to say, we soon made these disappear. Later on we received still further presents, this time from Mr. J. G. Bennett, of the *New York Herald*. These certainly showed we were approaching civilization, for among them were toothbrushes, Florida water, and soap.

On the evening of the 4th December we found ourselves encamped near the Wami River, and only 8 miles from Bagamoyo and the Indian Ocean.[21] The men were in great spirits, singing the whole day long, as the thought arose that home and friends were near.[22]

About eight o'clock in the evening, while the men were leaning over the camp-fires cooking their evening meal, all of a sudden came the long low "boom" of the sultan of Zanzibar's evening gun from the island far across the sea. It was the gun that summons all true Mahommedans to prayer in the evening. Like some long lost and forgotten chord being again heard it reminded the Zanzibaris that their homes were near. With a roar of cheering that I still can hear, the men bounded through the camp. Again and again the volley of cheers rang out in the still night air. The men left their fires and surrounded the tents of the officers.

"*Tumefika pwani.*" ("We have reached the coast.")

"*Tumefika Mwisho.*" ("We have come to an end.")

Reader, could you have seen how those men cheered Stanley, you would have felt that with such men as these he could go anywhere.

Next day, 5th December 1889, we marched into Bagamoyo.[23] The sea again boys; our work is done! With bursting hearts and quickened pulses we met Englishmen and Americans again. The feelings that came over us, when once again we saw the old flag flying from the peaks of the British men-of-war in the bay, are never likely to be forgotten by any of us.

Goodbye boys! Each and every one of you have passed through the fire and proved himself [sic] true as steel. Through the forests and across the plains of Africa, you have stuck to us like the men you are. Over 5,000 miles have some of you marched step by step with poor food. Backwards and forwards through that forest which seemed unending, through fevers, starvation, and scenes of death have you marched like Trojans. We white man [sic] who have served with you for three long years, who have fought and starved, have marched and camped with you, now go to our homes far across the sea.

But deep down in our hearts has sunk the remembrance of your deeds, and in the home of the white men [sic] who knows you, will your names be kept bright.

In afterlife we may meet with more brilliant examples of daring, more carefully wrought out schemes of progress than you were capable of achieving. But never are we likely to see again such splendid fortitude during dark and trying days as had been shown by you, the Zanzibaris of the Emin Pasha Relief Expedition!

"*Mekwisha Tumepata.*" (It is finished; we have won.)[24]

PART THREE

THE KATANGA
EXPEDITION DIARY

Slave caravan

CHAPTER 9

LONDON TO ZANZIBAR

18 MAY—3 JULY 1891

Stairs leaves London 18 May. He boards a ship at Naples for Port Said. The voyage continues via Aden and Mombasa. Zanzibar is reached on 14 June. After the recruitment of porters and the preparation of loads Stairs leaves for Bagamoyo on 1 July, his twenty-eighth birthday.

18th May Left London by the 10:00 a.m. train, departing from Charing Cross for Folkestone and Naples, and from there to take the steamer Madura to Zanzibar.

I have just spent fifteen months in England and during this time I have learnt a good deal and had a very good time. Goodbye, old England. I hope to be back in two and a half years, safe, sound, and successful. I would like to remain unknown until the day of my return and get back quickly to Europe.

20th May Left Paris by sleeping-car for Rome, where I arrived on the twentieth. In the afternoon I got off at Naples. There I found letters, among them a note for Alex. Delcommune who is at present in Central Africa, somewhere near the sources of the Congo.[1]

21st May Left Naples for Port Said. On board is Saleh, Stanley's boy, who was with him on the Emin expedition.[...] Among the passengers, I also notice the Reverend Ashe, formerly a missionary with Mr. Mackay in Uganda. He seems very well up in everything concerning East Africa and is, up to a certain point, an admirer of Stanley. Mr. Ashe has written a little book that is very learned and very useful, entitled *Two Kings of Uganda*.[...]

The names of the members of the expedition are: W. G. Stairs (English); Captain Bodson (Belgian); Marquis de Bonchamps (French); D. J. A. Moloney (English); [and] Thomas Robinson (English).[2]

25th May Arrived at Port Said. Landed, bought cigarettes and had dinner. It seems strange to see again these yellow Egyptians; a whole world of memories comes to mind, evoking those difficult days spent bringing the Emin clerks back to the coast.

During the year that I spent in England—1890-91—I must have made, in London alone, the acquaintance of at least three hundred people. But how few friends! How rare they are, those whom one can call by that name![...]

The ideas of the English on Africa are strange and of a sort that sometimes provokes irritation. But it must be admitted that for absolute ignorance as to African questions, the continental nations beat England hollow.

Shall I ever see again all the people with whom supped last year and the hundreds of young ladies with whom I waltzed in London and whom I have now practically forgotten? In general I don't much admire the London girls. They are absolutely empty beings and follow one another in ideas and dress like a flock of sheep. The young country girl, who comes to town only occasionally and makes the country her home, is far more interesting and also better educated.

30th May I've had long talks with the Reverend Ashe, the missionary from Uganda; he seems to me to have ideas on African questions. The more I read the reports on work done by missionaries and the more I talk with them, the more convinced I become of this truth: that before one can produce a real, lasting effect on the minds of African races by means of preaching, the laity must set up—if necessary, by force—a just, stable government.

Have we the right to take possession of this vast country, to take it out of the hands of its local chiefs and to make it serve the realization of our own goals?... To this question, I shall reply positively, yes.

What value would it have in the hands of blacks, who, in their natural state, are far more cruel to one another than the worst Arabs or the wickedest whites? And can one even suppose for a single moment that the Arab would ever leave the country to lie fallow? Certainly not. He will seize hold of the government of all these Central Africans and will introduce among them his semi-barbaric institutions unless white men intervene. And who would dare compare, for example, the rules of English government with those of the Arabs?

I repeat that, before the arrival of the missionary, stable government must be established. We've taken the wrong road in this respect and begun the task at the wrong end by first sending in advance some missionaries without the support of an armed force, so showing the blacks our weakness, and then [sending] traders without respect for either law or religion, so giving them an example of our perfidy and our lack of justice.

The experiment that Great Britain is attempting in Central Africa should be closely followed by all true friends of the natives. May real success crown England's efforts!

What a solid bond is the one that will always exist between Parke, Jephson, Nelson, and myself.[3] I have never read anywhere of the achievement of four Englishmen who bore together so many adversities and who remained such fast friends. I consider Parke, among others, as the bravest, noblest character I have ever encountered.

I have called one of my boats the *Dorothy* in honour of Mrs. Stanley, who christened her at the launching. The other has received the name of *Bluenose,* after the nickname given me by my compatriots.[4]

1st June Arrived at Aden. It was daylight. There I spent two very good, pleasant days waiting for the *Arcadia* of the P. and O. with the English mail.[5][...]

3rd June Left for Zanzibar in the evening. Received letters from Sir John Kirk telling me that the sultan has given up opposing recruitment.[6]

I've learnt that Cardinal Lavigerie's missionaries are seeking to recruit four hundred carriers in Zanzibar.[7] In all probability, there will be terrible starvation on the route. It will be one more difficulty to add to all those that we shall have to face.

11th June Arrived at Mombasa. I stayed Kilindini with Mr. Pigott who acts as administrator. There I noted considerable progress. The transport service under Ainsworth's orders is really very well organized.[8]

12th June Visited the tomb of my old friend, Captain H. B. MacKay, RE [Royal Engineers], in the cemetery of Free Town. Poor comrade! The news of his death is for me a terrible blow. To be young, strong, and active and to be thus cut down in one's flower is really frightening!

I've received a telegram from Nicol informing me that, to date, he has managed to enlist only about sixty men because he wasn't able to start signing-up operations until last Monday.[9] It's a disappointment, for in Aden I was wired that all was going well and that, on the day of my arrival at Zanzibar, I would find both my men and my cloth ready. With the help of Mr. Pigott I was able to procure about fifty-six carriers (in Mombasa), and I hope to obtain fifty more next week. Recently there has arrived here a great number of people taken on in Baluchistan.[10] As far as I could judge they form a pretty collection of absolutely useless creatures.

I've recruited a headman, fifty-six carriers, one cook, four askaris;[11] in all, sixty-two men, one of whom was missing on the day of embarkation.

13th June Embarked my men and had all the contracts signed for two years for the wage of £183 7s. From Zanzibar there is news of a great dearth of men as a consequence of the great number of caravans which are gong to the interior. Left Mombasa at 1:30. Learnt that Miss Sheldon, the American lady traveller, has reached the coast near Pangani on German territory.

14th June Arrived at Zanzibar. Got in touch with Nicol of Smith, MacKenzie and Company. I managed to hire a dhow to take the men I recruited in Mombasa as far as Dar-es-Salaam, for I fear they will desert if I let them get off here. I have wired Baron von Soden, the German governor, in order to obtain permission to land men and arms on German territory.

15th June Sent a dhow to Dar-es-Salaam with Captain Bodson carrying letters to Baron von Soden and to a Hindu merchant. Unloaded most of the merchandise for the expedition and stored the merchandise until my departure.

Saw at noon C. S. Smith, the English consul. I spoke for an hour with him. He is not at all hostile to me, but all my men must be free men; the contracts must be submitted to him and signed in front of him. I've obtained Johnston's contract and taken it as a model.[12][...]

The consul for Belgium, on his part, has put in a request so as to obtain permission for Captain Jacques to recruit his men here.[13] The latter, who is also going to Karema on behalf of the Belgian Anti-slavery Society, needs five hundred men.[...]

16th June Saw Bonstead and came to an agreement that he will send sixty loads of rice and two of biscuit to the Mamboia mission station on the Bagamoyo route.[14] I am also at this moment making arrangements with him for the dispatch of three postal couriers each month to Karema, if that is possible.

I was able to recruit about twelve carriers today. Met a large number of ex-members of our personnel on the Emin [Pasha] Relief Expedition. Unfortunately, they have already signed a contract to go with Johnston to Nyasaland.

17th June Sent letters of introduction to the sultan, to Toffa, Tharia-Thopan, Salim bin Azam and others. The sultan has promised me a personal audience for Saturday. Hired about a dozen carriers. Dined at the Shamba with Henderson, captain of the *Conquest,* one of Her Majesty's ships, Consul C. S. Smith, Sclates, RE [Royal Engineers], and Charlesworth, the English doctor here. Abedi, my old boy, will leave with me.

18th June Received a telegram from Bodson: in Dar-es-Salaam everything is going well and he was very well received by Governor von Soden. Wired Bodson to try and hire thirty Zanzibari carriers from among the Germans.

I hear that Ahse's caravan has broken up, and I hope to be able to get some of his carries. Had an interview with Jaffa Bhoy Topan who promised me letters for an Arab in Tabora. I'm getting worried as to means of obtaining carriers. I have only one hope: that the sultan will begin to look favourably upon me after the interview. Someone here has obviously prejudiced him against me.[...]

I have been presented to His Highness Segyid Ali [sic], or Seyd Ali bin Said-Segyid [sic], the sultan of Zanzibar, by C. S. Smith, the consul, at the same time as Bonchamps and Moloney.[15]

20th June Recruiting is going well, but the men enroled are principally those whom Ashe refused to accept and who might eventually come to an agreement with him. So it would be no surprise if I still happened to lose them.[...]

At 4:00 p.m. I went with Nicol to the sultan's for a private audience. I explained the goal of my journey to His Highness. I then asked him for help in recruiting men and to give me letters charging the people of Karema, Rua, Itawa, and Katanga to assist me. I also asked him to write to the consul instructing him to assist me in recruitment for my caravan. The sultan promised me the letters I requested.

22nd June Some of Ashe's men did not show up this morning. Total of recruits to date: about 220, of whom perhaps 150 will accompany me.

23rd June Received five autograph letters from the sultan for the Arabs of Tabora, Karema, Mpala, Rua, Itawa, and Katanga.

Today I registered the names of sixteen or eighteen old companions who crossed the continent with the expedition in search of Emin Pasha.

24th June I hope to send off 150 men on Saturday. I obtained from the consul the authorization to embark the men from the wharf of Smith, MacKenzie and Co[mpany]. I now have three hundred registered in my books and estimate that two hundred of them really mean to work.

I hear that Bonstead, Ridley and Co[mpany] are having difficulties sending my rice to Mpwapwa. As always, it's a question of carriers.

26th June Loaded all my merchandise onto two dhows and took every measure for embarking my men first thing tomorrow.

27th June At 7:15 a.m. I proceeded to register the men. By 11:00 I had assembled about 175 at the palace in front of the sultan's people. Next I had them line up in Smith, MacKenzie's courtyard and there I gave them their advance pay for four months. Then I saw them embarked on the dhows. Doctor Moloney took command of one of the boats, Bonchamps of the other. Bedoe, the headman of my caravan, has charge of a third.

At 2:30 p.m. the flotilla will set sail for Bagamoyo.[...]

Wired Bodson and the commanding officer in Bagamoyo. I'm expecting to have customs difficulties with this town.

Men recruited in Zanzibar up to the 27th June, 205; [those] recruited in Mombasa: first detachment, 56, second detachment, 61. General total to date, 322 men.

29th June I have started to register some more men, for I want another fifty.

Consul Smith asked me to come and see him. I went and he advised me of a telegram from the Foreign Office asking him if the sultan's refusal to allow me to engage slaves had been an obstacle to my departure. I told him to reply that now it was no longer an obstacle, but that this prohibition had been the causes of much trouble and a great waste of time. It had cost me £300 and held up my departure for twelve full days. I hope to leave here on Wednesday, 1st July.[...]

How many improvements are still necessary in Zanzibar! The customs, the police, and the army should be reformed, the coastal boats should be provided with licences and order maintained everywhere. When Portal arrives, he will perhaps make these changes.[16][...]

30th June I've been able to obtain a few more men. What a tedious task recruitment is !

1st July Today is my twenty-eighth birthday. I'm beginning to get old. I hope, over the two years to come, to be able to do good work for myself and for others.

Left Zanzibar about 2:00 p.m.[...] Arrived at Bagamoyo at 9:00 p.m. I stayed, with my assistants, at the house of Kajie Haussa, the Indian who serves as my agent in this place.

2nd July At this time caravans are leaving by the dozen for the interior. Numerous close columns of Wanyamwezi arrive almost every day. The Germans have bad news for me from Karema. It seems that the Arabs have driven away the French Fathers. If that is true, what a hard blow for me; the cloth which I sent on to Karema and which I'm supposed to collect there will be missing!

3rd July Finished putting together the loads for our caravan. I expect to begin our march forward tomorrow.

CHAPTER 10

BAGAMOYO TO MPWAPWA

4 JULY—3 AUGUST 1891

On July 4 Stairs's caravan leaves Bagamoyo. Problems of discipline and difficulties in obtaining foodstuffs arise. An encounter occurs with the ivory caravans heading for the coast. Health problems develop. Stairs curbs looting by his porters. Frequent desertions pose problems. There is evidence of a disastrous cattle epidemic and severe drought.

4th July I started the column off at nine o'clock and set off myself at 12:15 p.m. [sic]. Tippu Tib arrived this morning.[...]

My personnel consists of about 304 carriers, 30 askaris, 16 boys, and 9 headmen. As always when a safari gets under way, there's a certain confusion at the beginning.[...]

5th July This morning it took me not less than two and a quarter hours to get my caravan in marching order. One needs a great store of patience not to lose one's head or spirits. Everyone is still new and not up to his task.

There'll be desertions, I very much fear. Between here and Mpwapwa, I expect at least fifty men will decamp. These people tire easily at the beginning and get blisters on their feet. Besides, there's nothing easier for them than to slip away and return to Bagamoyo, just abandoning their tasks. A great number of carriers have no other trade except to sign up in order to get their advance pay, then pull their feet out and go and hide in the swarming hovels of Bagamoyo. I apply myself patiently to showing the new men what to do and feed all my people as well as possible.

The real route to Katanga is not this one, but, as I have always said, the one along the Zambezi or the Congo.

We crossed the Lufu by ferry. The crossing took us two hours and forty minutes. Then we set up our camp at about two-thirds of a mile to the west, having left behind us every vestige of coconut palms and coastal agriculture. If we were to take into account just the look of the landscape, we might well think ourselves in the centre of Africa, for the curtain of coastal vegetation extends only a few miles into the interior.

Today a letter from H. H. Johnston overtook me with a long explantation as to why he could not recommend the Nyasa way to me. There is famine everywhere there, and he could not let us have sufficient means of transportation.

Here is the list of my old companions on the expedition across Africa who are again with me this time: Massudi, Sudi M'Khamis, Songoro M'Kassim, Khamis Baruti, Mirabo

Mgumba, Kibaia, Khamis bin Chaudi, Almas Mshamgama, Khamis M'Kheri, [and] Idi M'Sulimini.

6th July Left at 7:10, marched for two hours and camped near the marshes where Stanley bivouacked for the last time before entering Bagamoyo.

Caught a man in the act of deserting. He was put on a chain. This threat of desertion hangs day and night over my head. It's almost impossible to prevent this misfortune. What is going to happen in this regard between here and Mpwapwa?

At every moment quarrels break out between the men. They lack order and it will still take some time before everything is licked into shape. The Zanzibaris are excessively quarrelsome and they all shout and talk at the same time. Imagine the cacophony! When they've been submitted to the white man's discipline for a certain length of time, they change completely, but during the first days following departure from the coast, they are totally undisciplined. In addition to that, our caravan comprises—besides the Zanzibaris—people from Dar-es-Salaam, Bagamoyo, and Mombasa, and all those fellows fight like cat and dog.

7th July Left camp at 4:50 a.m. I'm in command of the vanguard. After a march of two hours [and] forty minutes we set up camp. At 10:30 Dr. Moloney arrived to tell me that eight loads remain behind at the camp with Bonchamps who is in command of the rear-guard. It's the old story of men who've been badly grouped and Europeans who overload them with their personal baggage.

During the night a man from Dar-es-Salaam deserted again. I expect to lose them all one after another.

It's a curious spectacle to observe how aggressive a Zanzibari generally is to an inoffensive, peaceable native. He plays the bully and is often only a big coward.

If only the Jacques expedition doesn't catch us up and overtake us![1] From Bagamoyo to here the country is absolutely empty of inhabitants. These, for fear of being maltreated, have abandoned the roadsides, and it has become almost impossible to obtain provisions. The policy of the Germans should consist of encouraging the natives to erect villages along the routes and guarantee them their powerful protection. In this way there would be an abundance of food supplies in a very short time.

Bedoe, the headman of my caravan, is an old companion of Joseph Thomson's whom he accompanied on several of his expeditions to the Tangamilla, to the Kavirondo, and other places, too.[2] He was in charge of Bishop Hannington's caravan when the latter was killed, and told me that the poor bishop was stubborn to the point of madness.[3] He invariably pitched his tent away from his men in order to get away from camp noises.

Another of my section leaders is Khamis Ngoze who accompanied Stanley on his journey across the mysterious continent. He's a very active man and will be very useful, I think. Masudi, one of his colleagues in No. 1 Company, was a carrier on our last expedition. I think he is faithful and he has his men well in hand.

God be praised that I have in my column only twenty-one men from Dar-es-Salaam! They are absolutely no good.

So here I am again in the midst of a caravan, camping amongst grass and trees, far from the world and its bustle. How good that seems to me! In spite of all the worries, the difficulties, the bad food and the certainty of contracting fevers, I find this life, for various reasons, vastly superior to that which one leads between the four walls of a barrack!

Three months ago I was at Aldershot in the company of the best comrades in the world with pleasant society, delicious food, and the town in the neighbourhood. But I wasn't happy in the real sense of the word. I felt my life passing without my doing anything worthwhile. Now I am freely making my way over the coastal plain with more than three hundred men under my orders. My least word is law and I am truly the master.

A two years' stay in this country—with the mind continually on the alert, and interminable, arduous marches to accomplish—is quite enough, for the human system cannot bear longer physical and mental tension without cracking up. I do not think it possible to avoid fever in these regions. All who work, as we do, every day in the full heat of the sun are almost sure to succumb, sooner or later, to this disease.

8th July After a two hours' march we set up camp at Mbuyuni. By 10:50 all the personnel had assembled the camp. That's great progress.

We have about twelve sick and crippled men. That's an average of 5 percent which, in a few days, will reach 8 or 9 percent. This is always so with men freshly arrived from Zanzibar, not yet used to marching and not broken into carrying. Cases of sickness among the caravaneers are ordinarily caused by the weakening of their constitution, brought about by abuses of every kind, and their craze for smoking hemp. It is only after a month of assiduous work and substantial food that this poison is expelled from their system. Besides, the least scraping of the skin causes old, imperfectly healed ulcers to reappear.

Considerable quantities of very fine ivory tusks are now on their way towards the coast, coming from Unyamwezi, sixty-four days away from here. Not later than this morning, we saw almost fifteen hundred ivories file past which will net the Germans 14,200 dollars [M.] thanks to export duty.[4]

I have given my men their *posho:*[5] one *upandi*[6] for five days per man. As always in such cases I've been assailed by a considerable number of protest. Even if one were to give a *jora*[7] to every man, there would still be a veritable avalanche of complaints as to scanty distribution.

I've been obliged to send men back to Bagamoyo with orders to bring me twenty more bales of cloth. In five days I've had to hand out four and a half bales to buy supplies for the expedition.

9th July [...]The rearguard arrived at the camp about two hours after the head of the column. This delay is due to the slowness with which Companies No. 2 and [No.] 3 have been loaded. That's understandable; the commanders of these companies have difficulties with their men whose language and customs they do not yet know. Besides, I have to speak French with my officers, and I don't know the langauge. I hope to know it sufficiently well in three months' time.

10th July We marched today for barely two hours [and] twenty minutes and are camping two and a quarter hours away from Msua.

Bedoe woke me this morning with the cheerful news that seven of my men hired in Dar-es-Salaam deserted during the night. That already gives me a loss of eleven of these men out of a total of twenty-one—in all, sixteen desertions.

The most dangerous moment for a caravan is this: still unused to their loads, the men become stiff, their morale is affected, and they desert. It takes not less than a fortnight's march for the carriers' muscles to become supple while remaining firm. But it's a thankless task to draw this agility out of them. I exhaust every means in my power trying to coax things along. I've strictly forbidden that the men should be beaten, harsh words are prohibited, our stages are short, and I'm generous in the distribution of cloth. I hope, in this way, to advance slowly for ten more stages. We can then make a day's journey, averaging 8 miles, and pitch camp before noon. Unfortunately, there is still some hesitation and much complaining every morning in Companies [No.] 2 and [No.] 3.

My caravan is organized in the following order: Company No. 1 [includes] Captain Stairs, commander of the expedition, total, 121. Company No. 2: Captain Bodson, total 119. Company No. 3: the Marquis de Bonchamps, total, 114. [Plus] Doctor Moloney [and] Thomas Robinson. General total, 356 men.[8]

11th July On the road since 6:30 a.m. We camped about nine o'clock at one end of the village of Msua towards the west.[...] As soon as we arrived at the camp I sent on ahead Khamis Ngoze, one of my headmen. He has orders to go to Ngerengere, two days from here, in order to try and engage fifteen to twenty natives and bring them to me at Kisemo. Yesterday, seven loads did not have carriers in Bodson's company. It was only at the cost of the greatest trouble that we were able to get all our people under way. Today it's better.

Here is a [total] of our sick: [...] twenty-one.

12th July Three hours' march. We set up our camp at Kisemo. I obtained nine natives from Msua to carry our loads for two days. The average number of sick is rising steeply. Supplies in abundance. Heavy showers all morning.

I've just had a long conversation with one of the chiefs of Kisemo. It was very instructive. When I asked him why he had not sown onions, orange trees, or coconut palms instead of restricting himself to the cultivation of *mtama* and maize, he answered: "God forbid that I should plant anything here other than *mtama* and *corii* [sic]. If I tried another crop, we would all die."

Isn't that absolutely amazing? For two hundred years now this spot has been a much frequented place of passage, and yet, at a distance of six hours from the coast, only the toughest grains are grown—those that, even in Zanzibar, are given only to donkeys.

From the Lofu to Kisemo one doesn't see a coconut palm or an orange tree or a lemon tree. The Germans haven't succeeded yet in planting anything other than flags in the trees along the road. Certainly there's food here, but it's the same that was found a hundred years ago. No progress has been made either as to quality or quantity.

Would you like a little glimpse into the native character? Mungo, a native, made a bargain with me at Msua to carry a bale as far as Kisemo for the wage of *one* rupee. The contract was made very fairly; and he brought his load into the camp where I gave him his rupee. After a moment's hesitation, he accepted it but demanded, in addition, a bonus of four ells of cloth.[9] I refused and went to the trouble of explaining to him what a contract is. He listened to me, then ... asked for a little tobacco![...]

Endless arbitration takes up most of the time spent in camp.

13th July We stopped today at Kisemo. I sent ahead twenty inhabitants of the village with as many bales of cloth, under the orders of Khamis Ngoze, accompanied by three askaris. I hired them for twenty stages at the price of 7½ rupees a head. They will stop at Rudiwa where they will wait for us. In this way I hope to relieve my sick men and give them a chance of recovering. Three or four of them are seriously ill and will probably not recover. I'm thinking of sending them back to the coast, and this vexes me, for they each cost me an advance of twenty dollars [M.].

Today I set the *posho* at a half *doti* [10] for six days. That will take us to just beyond Simbamweni.

When we leave this place, we shall begin to make average stages, for I hope that by now the men have acquired the suppleness necessary for managing the regular march of a caravan. Up till now, desertions aren't as numerous as I anticipated. This happy result is due to the incessant vigilance that we never stop exercising.

The altitude of Kisemo is 330 feet.

14th July Our caravaneers are making great progress. They set out earlier and dawdle less on the way. We marched today from 6:20 a.m. to 10:20 a.m. and camped at Ngerengere on the banks of the river of that name. On the way we made a halt of twenty minutes. The distance covered was 8 miles.[...]

Near our camp are superb alluvial plains where one could grow almost anything one could wish. I am sure that mango trees and coconut palms would do wonderfully well. There is even a mango tree very near my tent, and the place near this was once the site of a village. At the present moment, there are only three little villages in Ngerengere. I am told that formerly there were at least ten or twelve. This is the result of the war two years ago between the Germans and the Arabs of Bushiri.

15th July Marched for three hours and forty minutes and camped at Mkoa in the tall grass. Mkoa was once a populous village, but the inhabitants, frightened by the continual pillaging by passing caravans, deserted the place and went off to build a village 2 miles further north. They are absolutely terrified of the Soudanese soldiers in the service of the Germans and their faces betray unspeakable terror when they speak of the extortions and raids conducted by these amiable creatures. That doesn't surprise me, for I doubt whether anywhere in the world there are brutes quite like these Soudanese.[...]

16th July Stage of three hours [and] thirty minutes. Bivouacked to the west of Makessi.

Because of the guides' stupidity we went beyond the wells and pitched a camp a good half-hour away from the water. All morning we scaled steep slopes and passed a number of fields of *mtama* which reached a height of 11 to 12 feet. The march was very tiring.

17th July In two hours [and] fifty minutes we reached a village to the west of Simbamweni and climbed a height of about 306 feet. Height of camp: 1,562 feet. The route was much better than it has been the last few days, so we reached the need of the stage sooner and the rearguard caught up with the vanguard in twenty minutes.

How little people in Europe understand of exploration in Africa! We speak of a road, whereas in reality there isn't the least trace of one in the countryside. What, in other countries, would be a road is here just a path which leads form one place to another in twists and turns which are far from constituting the shortest route. Along these paths we have to march in single file that often our personnel of 350 men stretches over a space of more than 2 miles. It is impossible for the white, who is at the head or behind, to ascertain how the men in the centre are behaving, whether they are sitting down, scattering about or moving ahead, for the long grass and the trees generally prevent one from seeing further than 80 or 100 yards.

Every morning I get up at 5:10 and breakfast as well as I can off the leftovers of last evening's meal with a cup of tea as well. I'm not a devotee of café noir, that is, coffee with a biscuit. As I see it, it's important to fill the stomach in the morning, more than at any other time of the day. One is out for hours in broad sunlight, so it is only rational that the stomach should be sufficiently full.[...]

On this question of the march made by an African caravan, sheer nonsense has been written in learned tomes that I could quote. One must, of course, first take into account the condition of the men one commands. If the stage is long, do it all in one go, not stopping for more than forty-five minutes. That should be a general rule. Take, for example, a stage of 20 miles. If one listens to orthodox authors, one should first do 12 miles, then rest during the heat of the day, and complete the rest of the way in the cool of the afternoon and evening. That's making a serious mistake. Indeed, if one does this, one must halt everything and set about finding a shady spot without delay. Result of this fine system: over these two or three hours of rest, the whole caravan, from the men to the boys, will become as stiff as logs. And what happens if one doesn't get into the shade? The white man can have his tent pitched and take his ease there, but his poor blacks have to remain exposed to the heat of the sun until it is pleased to curb its rays.

If everything is in good order, the best method to follow is this: start out at 6:00 a.m. Cover the first 12 miles with a twenty minutes halt at the tenth. At the twelfth, one stops long enough to allow the whites to eat, then one goes another 5 or 6 miles with another twenty minute halt. Then one completes the remainder of the stage resting only at the campsite. Experience has shown me that 16 miles a day for a caravan marching six days a week in a long column is the longest stretch it can make. After this exercise a daily rest of half a day is necessary.

In Africa the consumption of poor food badly cooked causes more diseases than too much eating and drinking [as] in Europe. Quite ridiculously, certain whites bring only tiny quantities of things which, for them, are an absolute necessity. In my opinion, all Europeans should supply themselves with, at least, salt, tea, coffee, and certain hard biscuits. They should, besides, have a provision of some sweet things in case of fever or dysentery. I've brought with me fifty-one boxes of European provisions, far more than what Stanley had for his ten white companions. I hope, besides, to be able to renew our stock of tea and salt at Unyanyembe[11] and to be able to buy coffee in Katanga.

Each of the whites in my caravan has his own tent, his own cook—who receives seven dollars [M.] a month or two more than a carrier—his own donkey, and three boys to look after his tent and his donkey. We are well provided with medicaments, chosen from among the best and packed with special care. Besides, each of my assistants has at least six personal carriers and may not have less than five without my authorization. I doubt whether ever officers of a caravan journeying into the African interior have travelled in better conditions than mine.

18th July Three hours' march. Camped at Mrogoro, or village of Kingo.

Our route was very interesting. On our left, mountains rose to a height of about 3,340 feet, their peaks disappearing into the clouds. Below us, to our right, stretched plains covered here and there with scrubby brush and dotted with villages. The French mission of Mrogoro is situated SSE of the village, over 2 miles away on the spur of a hill which overlooks the valley from a height of 405 feet. Jephson and I visited it when we passed this way with Emin and Stanley and both of us were charmed by the pleasant shades of the fresh, clear-water streams we saw there.

Let's be fair: all the French missionaries whom I have met have invariably chosen highly favourable spots for building their mission stations, while that is not the case with the posts set up by our English missionaries. French priests, in my opinion, do much more for the natives than ours. Indeed, they teach the blacks the trades of carpenter, mason, cultivator, and cook, while very often Protestant missionaries don't go beyond teaching the pagans to sing hymns horribly.[...]

Bonchamps seems to me to have been rather weary over the past few days. Oh, how I'd like to be able to speak French decently! It's especially in trying to speak of technical matters that I fail miserably.[...]

19th July Halt at Mrogoro.

I distributed a ration of cloth for five days: 4 cubits a man.[12] Given the slowness of our march, I begin to fear that we will not have enough cloth to take us as far as Mamboya. Our stages, so far, are still only three hours long. Water can be found only at these distances and my men are not yet sufficiently broken into marching for me to dare to make them do six hours on the road.[...] How irritating it is to have to halt as I have to do here so as to let the men buy food, then not be able to advance more than three hours a day!

Bonchamps continues to be in bad health. He is showing all the symptoms of dysentery.

I received yesterday as a present from Kingo, headman of this village, a sheep, *boyzas* (spinach), six eggs, and a bowl of curdled milk.

It is a pity that in all Central Africa the natives allow their milk to curdle before drinking it. In this state it is, it's true, more easily digested than when fresh. I suppose that it's because of their love of filth and their laziness that most of the time they refrain from washing their milk pots. The result is that, hardly has this liquid been poured, than it turns sour almost immediately.

The French Fathers sent me cabbages, onions, and vegetables. Father Horne is the superior of the Mrogoro mission. His assistant is ill. These Catholic missionaries are generally intelligent men with sound common sense.

Captain Jacques, I fear, is going to catch me up [sic]. At all costs, on this part of the route I must outstrip him, otherwise his five hundred men will eat everything still to be found in the villages.

A huge caravan overburdened with ivory passed through our camp at noon. From here to Gagamoyo a good courier would take only three and a half days.

It's hardly two months since I left England and it already seems to me like six. What an enormous amount of work I have accomplished in this short space of time! In the service, one would not do as much in a year. True, two years' work is more than enough in this country where physical and moral fatigue exercise such a harmful effect on the individual.

My tent is comfortable enough. There's a bed in it, a table, a chair, candles, and books to read in the night. What a difference from my former journey with Stanley! Then we had none of these articles of luxury, and during those three years I always slept on the ground. At that time I ate sitting on a packing case using another packing case as a table.

What a strange existence mine has been when I compare it with that of my army friends! I left my country when I was still only a youngster of twelve to go to school in a foreign country. Next I spent four years in Kingston. Then I found myself in the virgin forest of New Zealand where, for two years [and] nine months, I led an open-air life in the wilds working hard all through the rainy days of a New Zealand winter and eating coarse, tough food. And then, suddenly, I found myself transported to Chatham and London, leading a diametrically opposed life, eating my fill, sleeping as long as I liked, with no special precautions to take for my safety, and not having to work and think very hard.

Then another change of view: I exchanged this peaceful, monotonous life for a more rigorous one. I went to Africa with Stanley, fasting for three years, sleeping on the ground—never mind whether it is wet or dry—putting in hard daily labour of eleven hours a day on an average, and finally reaching the east coast with the feeling that I had performed deeds of which I had the right to be proud.

After that, once again I returned to London and Aldershot with any amount of time and money at my disposal, dining, dancing, making long stays in country houses, till I was heartily sick of it all. Then, everything changed again, and I find myself, this very day, on the way to the black centre.

Admit, that, in any case, I haven't let the grass grow under my feet. At the age of twenty-eight, I am the commander of a rather large expedition, charged with a confidential mission with the prospect of all sorts of difficulties to overcome.

There are three special goals in my mission that I would like to see accomplished: above all, obtain complete success with Msiri and a satisfactory outcome to my work in Katanga; [discover] mines in Katanga with the assurance that they can be profitably exploited; [and make] useful geographical discoveries when I cross the lands west of the Tanganyika. In short, I wish myself success all along the line and a speedy return voyage in order to reach home in good health.

Smith, MacKenzie and Co[mpany] should already have sent on to me the mail from England which was to arrive at Zanzibar on the 13th July. I like to get news of the external world for as long as possible. When I know that it is absolutely impossible, then it hardly matters.

My observations of altitude, longitude, and latitude are made with scrupulous care.

I've been forced to leave three of my men, incapable of marching any further, at the French mission station—a clear loss of seventy-five dollars [M.], for they each received twenty-five dollars [M.] paid in advance. Isn't this system iniquitous?[...]

On 20 July Stairs complained about the slow progress of the column which was due to the relative "flabbiness" of the porters. On the twenty-first, at Makata, the column had to cross a river which caused further delay.

22nd July We did a long stretch across the plains of the Makata as far as Ngomberenga, a little village where the water is foul. Our march—about 9 miles—took us nearly five hours.

From Kingo we have covered 28½ miles in a three days' march. I expect to arrive in Rudiwa tomorrow where my men will be able to find plenty of food and good water.

We are in Usagara, inhabited by the Wasagari. They are wretched travellers and speak of a three day excursion into the interior as a memorable event, standing for something in a man's life.

Last night I read part of Cameron's book *Across Africa*.[13] He had a hard time crossing exactly the same plains that we crossed in five hours. It was flood time; he had water and mud up to his knees, and it took him two days to pull out.

Ngomberenga is a very ugly, miserable spot for the site of a village. I can't understand how they could have settled in such a place when there are so many splendid rich sites near at hand. Only rarely do the natives think of improving their lot—that's the great weakness among the Africans. Their fathers' ways are theirs and their own customs will be those of their sons and grandsons.

This village has had the misfortune of seeing its name made a real hash of [sic] by white travellers. Some call it Mgombenga, others Ngarombenga, others still, Nbenga. As far as I can be certain the correct spelling is Ngomberenga.

Our stage today was the seventeenth since Bagamoyo and it's now nineteen days since we left the coast. If all goes well, we shall be at Mpwapwa on the 4th August.[...]

23rd July In two hours' time we arrive at Rudiwa, a rich well-populated village supplied with excellent water.

We left the main caravan route on our left and are now on the Mamboia road. To make good time, we ought to be at that place in five days.

The chief of Rudiwa is a feeble old man by the name of Waziri. He sent me, by his son, a goat and some flour.[...]

24th July Without stopping to take [a] break, made four hours' march and set up our camp at Mumi. The sun was beating down on us and the road was obstructed with high grass.

Bodson has had an attack of bilious fever and I myself don't feel up to scratch.

The natives of Mumi ran away as we approached. Why? I'm at my wits' end trying to guess. Every time something like this happens, it puts me beside myself. There is not, in fact, the least shadow of a motive for such behaviour. Besides, since yesterday these people have been told that we are a perfectly peaceful caravan.

I distributed rations of cloth at the rate of four ells for five days per carrier, six ells for every askari and one *doti* for company leaders. This method of provisioning the men is cumbersome and out of date. The Germans should force the natives to accept money payments.[...]

25th July Camped at Msomero (called Msamero by some) after two hours [and] thirty-five minutes on the road.[...]

Sudi, one of the men of No. 1 Company has deserted to Rudiwa. I sent off squads 30 miles all around and along the main route, and offered fifty dollars [M.] plus five bales of cloth for his capture. He has stolen a gun from me. If I catch him, I'll make a salutary example of him and that will prevent the others from entertaining the slightest desire to run off in their turn. My people are well fed, the stages are short, and strict justice is done on every demand. I am of the decided opinion that in such a case the white man should morally have the right to execute such deserters should they be taken. I could—as is only fair—act in this way, but in a country supposed, like this one, to have a good administration, it could be that I haven't the right over life and death.

One gains nothing and loses much in handing over to the authorities a man who has committed a reprehensible act. Indeed, his comrades are not present at his punishment, one loses a carrier and with him four months' advance pay.

The chief of Msomero, an old man, came to see me. He amused me greatly with his chatter and paid me the homage of a goat.

One does not notice among the natives the diversity that exists among Europeans. All these blacks lead the same kind of life, absorb exactly the same food and exercise their thoughts on the same sparse subjects. The result is that, little by little, they now have only one identical brain.

We whites, on the other hand, learn to know so many diverse countries inhabited by different peoples and to examine so many varied things that our ideas become thus as different as our characters[...]

26th July Arrived in Kideti after four hours' march on the direct road to Saadani towards Mpwapwa and beyond.

Encountered the caravan of [the] Reverend Ashe going towards Uganda. He has been twenty-one days on the road. Mr. Ashe told me that Mr. Greaves, one of his missionaries, fell ill with fever and dysentery two days away from the sea and has to be taken back, dying, to the coast. A great number of Mr. Ashe's servants have deserted and he has had to leave behind twenty loads, after sending one of his squadron leaders to the coast to see to new enrolments. Three other missionaries are with him, all making for Usukuma and Uganda. Something to note about Mr. Ashe is that, up till now he has done the whole journey perched on his bicycle. When the road becomes bad, he gets off his machine and gives it to a black who has always to be behind him. He gets onto his bicycle again as soon as the road becomes practicable. His black runs after him. In this way, he can arrive at the campsite two hours earlier than his caravan.

I'm writing these lines on the twenty-seventh, for on the twenty-sixth I had a bout of fever which kept me in bed all day. It's my first attack. The warnings of the sickness bring back the past to me. They are identical to the symptoms I had before: loss of taste and pains that I know so well for having felt them (so often).

Robinson is a shadow of his former self. I'm afraid that he can't take the climate.

27th July About 4 miles NW to Kifi. Altitude of the camp 1,198 feet. We are bivouacking in a deep gorge surrounded by mountains of which one is 3,475 feet high. We are two days away from Mamboya. Thank God my fever has abated.

On the route, corpses of abandoned carriers.[...]

On 28 July Stairs noted that Ashe's caravan overtook them the previous day. In the mountains, nights were very cold and the carriers, who slept in their light cotton clothes, tended to catch cold accompanied by fever and disagreeable complications. On the twenty-ninth the column reached Mamboia, where a mission station was located. It was the place to which Stairs previously had sent a consignment of rice for his men that it arrived safely. Stairs's column had been followed by a caravan of seventy-five Wanyamwezi, who felt more secure by the proximity of Stairs's column, feeling safety in numbers.

29th July If the temperature today was [sic] average, Mamboya must be a very cold place. For the whites it's bearable, but for the poor blacks it's hard and painful.

Two new desertions last night. I've taken all measures imaginable to put an end to this practice, but it is well nigh impossible to catch delinquents in countryside furrowed with paths like this one. The result is that it is difficult to impress sufficiently on the minds of those who remain how severe the punishment would be of those nabbed.

30th July A very full day. I've just, at 5:00 p.m., finished my work. To begin with, early in the morning we had an assembly of all the companies. We had roll-call, counted the guns, the billhooks, the axes, the hoes, and proceeded to a general clean-up. I found out that a great number of hoes had been sold. That's usual with the Zanzibaris.

In addition, two guns are also missing. One, I know, was taken by Sadi who deserted to Rudiwa.[...]

The population seems to me extremely mild for a place situated on a main caravan route and which is used every day as a point of passage by a number of troops. I had to spend hours explaining to these natives the difference in the value of cloth depending on whether one buys it here or at the coast.

The *dotis* sent by Sewa Hadju are worth 814 dollars [M.]. That will be enough for thirty-eight days at the end of which I expect to be in Unyanyembe.[...]

We are camped at an altitude of about 3,040 feet. The weather is clear and mild. The view one enjoys from the mission station is one of the finest I have every beheld. What joy one feels in one's soul, casting one's gaze far over mountains and valleys under the horizon endlessly poised about frail human beings. All poetry disappears, however, when one has to scale these same heights—so fascinating today from afar—with 350 carriers behind one, sweating, panting, heaving their loads along the abrupt slopes. The whites on the expedition seem, in general, to face up well to the dangers of the climate.

31st July The saffari [sic] set out at 6:15. Unfortunately, I had to remain behind because of the shortage of native carriers. I was only able to start at nine o'clock, leaving behind two loads of valuable cloth. Mwana Manuka, the Wanyamwezi chief, remains in Mamboya.[...]

The four carriers promised by Caidi, the mountain chief I hired yesterday for five days, haven't arrived. The robbers! I had already paid them their *posho* for five days! These Wasagara are scrimshankers to their very souls; a Wanyamwezi would never behave like that.

Bodson, who was in command of the caravan, pitched camp at 10:30. The rearguard caught up at 12:30. Distance: 10 miles. The agglomeration of villages we are in the midst of is called Kitangi.

Met Mr. Gordon, the missionary from Uganda, to whom I gave letters for the coast. He's marching as fast as he can in order to arrive in time to embark on the English steamer that is leaving mid-August. There are now 400 of us and we are followed step by step by two caravans of Wanyamwezi, 100 men in each, who have received my authorization to do so.

At the moment we were setting up camp, we were joined by another caravan of three hundred people, whose headmen asked me if they could put themselves under my protection, which would bring our total number to nine hundred. I gave a favourable answer to this request, on condition that my orders should be obeyed and that there should be no looting of the villagers' fowls and grain.

In Uganda, Smith, Williams, and Lugard joined battle with the Wanyoro, but Mr. Gordon told me they had to retreat because of the inundations which covered the whole country in an endless sheet of water.[14]

Three men deserted last night. Three! One of them was a certain askari, a deserter by profession, known as such. I've been watching him closely since our departure from the coast. If I'd got him this morning when I learnt that he'd slipped between my fingers, I think I'd have broken his head in.

1st August Three hours' march. Camped amongst the Rubehu mountains, at an altitude of 4,111 feet. The various chiefs of the surrounding area came to see me and gave me the customary presents. The carriers of the two boats, who up till now, have done their task to perfection, received a special ration of flour and a goat.

Another desertion, last night, in Saef bin Ali's group from Company No.1, and that in spite of sentinels posted all along the roads. It's enough to drive one mad.

The three Wanyamwezi caravans following us arrived an hour after my column. They came down along the mountains in a long undulating coil, a most curious sight.

These people travel very peacefully and comfortably. All the elders have their tents, their wives, and their cooks. The reason why the Wanyamwezi travel so well lies in the fact that their wives and daughters follow them, carrying their provisions, their tents and their dishes. When they reach the camping site, the carrier, exhausted, stretches out his stiff limbs, lights his pipe and has a chat, while the women do the cooking, cut the wood and help them in every way. Some of these caravans, made up of several hundreds of individuals, have not even ten guns for their protection.

We climbed today, not less than 1,213 feet up into the mountains, and I felt terribly sorry for my poor carriers as I saw them clamber up, bent under their heavy loads.

A great number of the inhabitants of the country are Wahumba or Wandorobo and speak Masai fluently. They twist their hair into long greasy braids and don't seem to be very bright creatures compared with other blacks whom I have met on my travels.

The cattle here and in all the countryside beyond Tabora have perished as a result of a pulmonary epizootic disease. The unfortunate inhabitants complain bitterly about the lack of milk. Nowhere in Central Africa, except amongst the Masai, do the natives eat their cattle. When a cow dies of disease, they might happen to eat it, but it is particularly the milk they want.

I had seven lashes given to each of the five men caught red-handed stealing fowls and eggs from the natives. These fellows showed themselves to be arrant liars. I've never met any more brazen, even amongst the Zanzibaris.

Each Wanyamwezi caravan sports the German flag and over each headman's tent floats the black, white, and red standard which adds a picturesque note to the spectacle of this swarming human anthill. At night the cold in these mountains is intense. Even today at noon the thermometer read 68°F. At night it goes down to 46°F and 50°F. The men suffer a good deal from the cold.

We are riding our donkeys now.

Tomorrow will be a rough march: we'll be going down to Mabala, 10 miles from here.

Great progress: the men are marching well and don't brawl any more. To get to this point, I've had to show infinite patience and go to the trouble of seeing to the settlement of all quarrels myself.

There's an abundance of guinea-fowls. I shot several. They are by far the best winged game that I have eaten in Africa.

2nd August From Rubehu to Mlali, where we are bivouacking: 10 miles crossed in two and a half hours. Road excellent nearly all the way. Met some German soldiers returning to the coast. They left Mpwapwa yesterday.

Saw some antelope. They were out of gun range. Delightful shade around our camp. The coolness is wonderful. It won't, I hope be a cold tonight as the two previous nights. From here we can see the site of yesterday's camp, on the other side of the plain. With a telescope I can make out the German flag floating above Rubehu's hut 11 miles from here.

Some natives have brought me baskets of *mtama* pounded into flour. They seem very poor to me.

Here there are Wagogos, Wasagaras, and Waseguhas. These natives have split ears and hang little iron chains from their hearing apparatus. They seem to have a great liking for bracelets on their legs and arms which they make out of very fine copper wire.

Khamis Ngoze, the second headman of Company No. 1, to whom I entrusted the command of the forty-two natives hired in Mamboia, carries out his duties wonderfully well and manages his men perfectly. He is something of an Uledi and is, in my opinion, one of the best headmen I have:[15]

The cold nights have brought on two or three cases of pneumonia, one of which will be fatal.

In England they must be getting ready now for the 12th August shoot,[16] and the subaltern officer of Aldershot will at last be able to glimpse the possibility of indulging in the sport far from the blare of the bugle and the claws of the general of the division. I don't think that I could ever again tie myself down to a regular soldier's life within the four walls of the barrack. It would be for me a slow death by inches. The work doesn't scare me. On the contrary, I like it, but it's mess life which gives me the shivers. Always the same faces in front of one and incessantly the same stupid, hackneyed jokes. I loathe the term "medal-hunter" applied by anteroom soldiers to military men who don't fancy an idle life.[...]

Look at my present existence! I have under my orders four hundred men and more power, more freedom of action that any English general in command of an army corps. On the other hand, I have great anxieties, exhausting labours, often intense moral qualms, but also how many opportunities I am given to distinguish myself! I have a sense of my responsibilities, but I feel I can breathe, and with the existence I lead here, life really seems worthwhile.[...]

3rd August Rough march of one and a half hours, 10 miles. Arrived at Tubugwe. The caravan marched badly, water is very far from the camp, and altogether a black mark must be put against the day, amongst those one curses.[...]

CHAPTER 11
MPWAPWA TO TABORA

4 AUGUST—6 SEPTEMBER 1891

The column arrives at Mpwapwa. There is scarcity of food. Hiring of porters becomes increasingly difficult. The expedition crosses the desert known as Pori of Shunio. Stairs observes and praises the Wanyamwezi's ability to organize caravans. He meets Arab caravans consisting of male and female slaves. Caravans seeking protection join Stairs's column. The expedition arrives at Tabora on 6 September.

4th August Arrived at Mpwapwa after a march of four and a half hours and immediately handed over my letter of introduction to Lieutenant von Elpon. I advised Mr. Price, a missionary of the CMS,[1] that I had arrived. I distributed rations of four hands of cloth to the men. That must last them six days.

I very much fear that starvation is rife in the countryside that lies before us; in this place there is nothing for my personnel to eat. The camping site is the same as the one where we stayed before. It is dirty and nauseating. It was scorching hot and we were covered with dust. Everyone seemed pleased and happy to be able to bathe their feet in the stream nearby.

We took a month coming from Bagamoyo to here, or twenty-seven stages in all. With luck we shall reach Unyamyembe in the same amount of time, for our men are in better condition now than the day they left Bagamoyo.[...]

As I was on my way to the fort, I met Lieutenant von Elpon and took him to my tent. We had a long discussion on African affairs. He has been here nearly two years and has almost never suffered from fever.

I sent letters to Europe and made arrangements to take advantage of the direct German postal service on Lake Victoria Nyanza, which takes forty-three days to make the trip via Tabora and the Usui. The couriers say that water is scarce in Ugogo and, according to what I hear, this will cause us much worry. Many heads of cattle (forty-five hundred) have died in the Mpwapwa region because of a pulmonary epizootic disease and the poor natives are powerless to do anything about the situation. The animals collapse in groups, suddenly, and there is now hardly a single herd in Ugogo.

Food supplies are extremely scarce here. Four cubits of cloth can't buy grain for more than three days. Famine and thirst are the two cries that echo to us from western Ugogo.

The garrison of the fort is made up of fifty-four soldiers, all that is needed to defend the fort of Mpwapwa against any attack.[...]

5th August We made a halt today at Mpwapwa and I allowed the men to get themselves some food.

I visited Mr. Price at his mission station, three-quarters of a mile east of the fort. He told me that, in three weeks' time, famine will be rife in his district. The crops have not been successful because of a lack of water. They were harvested and taken in towards the end of May and are now completely used up.

The people of Mpwapwa (Wagogos for the most part) go to buy their food some way away on the other side of the mountains; all their cattle have died of epizootic disease. Mr. Price examined some of the animal carcasses. The lungs were sound, but the livers and kidneys of [them] all were affected. According to him, epizootic disease does not affect the lungs, as has been believed, but the kidneys.[2] Mr. Price informs me that the ponds or little lakes SW of Mpwapwa are rapidly drying up. Seven years ago he used to buy fish in great quantities from the natives. Today it's a food that can't be found here. He adds that the Ugogo terrain is becoming barer and barer. In certain places where, three years ago, there was water in abundance, it has now disappeared, which has caused the natives to migrate.

In this valley I counted not less than fifty *tembes,* showing the traces of once quite dense population.[...]

Altitude of Mpwapwa (camp): 3,083 feet. I am without news of the two askaris whom I sent nearly a week ago from Mumi's in pursuit of a deserter. Can they have deserted, too, with their guns? I counted on seeing them return three days ago at the latest and at the present moment, they haven't, as yet, given a sign of life.

The men whom I had sent to look for food returned calling out that they weren't able to get any and that the country stretching out before us for another fifteen days has only very little. I expect new desertions, for the caravaneers are more afraid of hunger and thirst than of the mountains.

I visited Herr von Elpon, the German officer commanding the fort. He's a very pleasant man. He very kindly gave me a very plump sheep which we'll find very welcome.

I'm having a good deal of difficulty getting six carriers to go with me from here to Mabalala. Once arrived at that place, I hope to be able to recruit some men to go as far as Unyanyembe.[...]

6th August After a short march of two hours [and] forty-five minutes, we reached Kisokive, where we are camping. I wasn't keen to go any further for, at Kambi, 6 miles further on, is the nearest water after Kisokive. This village is 12 miles from the Gunda Kali where we shall have to make a forced march of 16 miles.

Tomorrow we are entering this desert and it will take us not less than twelve good hours to cross it. It's one of the worst obstacles on this difficult road into the centre of Africa. At this time of the year there is, in this region, an area of 19 miles where it is impossible to get the least drop of water. Kisokwe is one of the Church Missionary Society's stations, but as the mission is 2 miles away from the road, I'm afraid of venturing out under the broiling sun to visit Mr. Beverley, the missionary who, I am told, has recently been very ill. I've hired two men—a certain Almas from the Mpwapwa mission station and another, a native of Dar-es-Salaam, called Abdallah. They are engaged for two years.

The crossing is terribly monotonous: mountains, valleys, and plains are all covered in a single universal shade of a blackish grey. The eye tires of this gloomy sight and one sighs for green grass and trees. Great masses of rocks lie about the mountains and take on the same colour as the rest. For me, it's an impossible riddle as to how partridges and guinea-fowl can survive in these parts where they are miles from any water at all.[...]

7th August Left Kisokwe at 6:00 a.m. and marched until 7:30 to reach Kombi. We halted there until noon. Every man received the order to fill his gourd and prepare his food, then at noon we took up the march again to cross the waterless plain known as Pori of Shunio or Shunio Heath. We marched for five hours and arrived at Buguni, a place where caravans often spend the night. At 8:00 p.m. there was no water in the camp except for what the Europeans had. Everyone fell asleep with dry throats and the Zanzibaris' gaiety vanished completely.

8th August Left at 5:30 a.m., and after one of the most back-breaking marches I have made in Africa, we arrived at 10:00 at Unyangaru, where we set up camp. The heat was scorching and when we got to the water, it first had a salty taste. A great number of men swallowed whole barrels of this water and became ill. At the camp there was fresh water. My people were exhausted from the two days' march they've had to make without drinking.[...]

9th August Made a contermarch of 5 miles to Sanga where, thank God, we found fresh water not far from the camp.

En route we met a large Arab caravan of eight hundred people transporting a varied assortment of parrots, ivory, calabashes, etc. They are led by four or five Arabs from Unyanyembe and are going to Bagamoyo, having set off thirty-eight days ago from Tabora. Some of our men, who gorged themselves yesterday on salt water from the marshes we passed, are suffering today from stomachache.

The day before yesterday I learnt in the Pori of Shunio that Captain Jacques had arrived in Mpwapwa with his anti-slavery expedition.

10th August Set off at 6:20 a.m. and arrived at Ipala in the Marenga Kali at 10:00 a.m. Distance: 7½ miles. I went out last night at 9:00 p.m. with two askaris, and sitting in a shelter about two-thirds of a mile behind the camp, I kept watch until 5:50 this morning— that is eight hours of continuous surveillance—in the hope of nabbing a deserter. The result of my watch was that during the march this morning, I had to make a great effort not to fall asleep, even marching.

This Marenga Kali is an accursed place, imprinted in the memory of all Europeans who have travelled along this route. I had to bury a man who died of fatigue and thirst crossing it, but I consider myself lucky, for many caravans have been absolutely destroyed passing through this desert, and have lost scores of men and loads at a time. I doubt whether one can find a gloomier, more desolate spot than the Marenga Kali or "bitter waters" this month, seeing that for the last forty-two days no rain has fallen and that, curiously enough, even dew does not settle overnight.

These Wanyamwezi are really marvellous people. There are more than eight hundred of them around my caravan obeying my orders and accepting the discipline I impose on them. In exchange I guarantee them my protection against thieves. I'm always going through their camp and so observe their way of life on a caravan. It is hard to imagine anything more admirable than the skill with which they manage to meet all difficulties. One of the essential secrets of their success is that they bring with them so many women that there

Slave Caravan

are enough of these to carry the pottery, dishes, bedding, and tents. So the men just have to carry the loads of cloth, metal wire, and beads which are the currency of the country.

As soon as a caravan of Wanyamwezi arrives at the camp, some go in search of food, others go to draw water, while the shrewdest of all collect large bundles of firewood and come to my camp to sell them in exchange for food and cloth. These fellows are astonishing for the spirit with which they work and do their six hours' march without flinching, carrying on their heads a bale of the weight of 71 pounds—and this without shirking—in a manly fashion. They don't walk as fast as we do, but when we arrive at camp, they are never far behind us and we see them arrive in a long, uninterrupted file. I like them very much; they are so cheerful and such hard workers.[...]

The Arab caravans that passed by yesterday counted eleven hundred men and two hundred girls. They were, for the most part, slaves not intended for sale, for they will return to Tabora.

The Arabs have a healthy fear of the Germans now. They would not dare to sell a slave in Bagamoyo; they run too many risks in this dangerous game. At certain times, I am well aware that, after all, a large number of these slaves are in the custody of an Arab who feeds and looks after them, and that they are thus much better off than when they were in their own country, given over to fetishism and incessantly fighting one another. That slaves are well fed and well treated is true for 90 percent of the two thousand slaves I have encountered since I left the coast. They were plump and glossy and had a little tent in which to sleep at night and take shelter from the sun during the day.

It's the hunt for slaves which is a work of the devil. Once taken, their lot is much more enviable than that of thousands of slaves living in Christian England. I have never seen in Africa, for example, such deplorable misfortunes and such hideous sights as those which struck me in Whitechapel or Liverpool. It is true that here one can witness crueller acts and punishments by whipping that are not often encountered at home. I have only one thing to reproach the Wanyamwezi carriers with: they have filthy habits. Just listen: in Ugogo one gets well-water by making holes 13 [feet] to 17 feet deep in the sand. At this time of the year a great number of these cisterns are dry. Naturally, the camping sites occur near these water holes. Now the Wanyamwezi invariably use these cisterns—dry for the moment—for needs of an excremental nature. When the rains fall, these wells fill up with water, which they use again, without first cleaning out the cesspools!...

In the evening, up came the two askaris whom I had sent last 23rd July to Rudiwa in search of Sadi, the deserter from Company No. 1. They had been all along the main route to Bagamoyo, then had gone west of Farahani, had turned east up to Rogoro just 90 miles from the sea, all without result. In Rogoro they had met a courier sent by Smith, MacKenzie and Co[mpany]. He was sick and gave them his letters which they passed on to me.

People generally imagine that in Africa one finds delicious things like lemons, oranges, pineapples. If only that were true! Alas, in all East Africa, once you are twenty miles from the coast, the only food is what was there five hundred years ago, that is, tough grains and *batatas*.[3] The whites have introduced, here and there in the mission stations, fruits of various sorts, but not on any great scale.

11th August Arrived at Jassa, of which Mgulambua is the chief, in two and one-half hours. His investiture is signed by Emin Pasha, head of the Imperial German expedition. We passed by heaped-up carcases of oxen and cows killed by the epizootic disease. The water doesn't smell very pleasant, but it is sweet to taste.

12th August Five hours' march to get to Matangiri, of which the chief is Ulenca.

There's not much here in the way of food, but there is plenty of water and that's the main thing. This place is a little off the direct route.

I had to make a speech to my men this morning in order to get them to march straight on, for, during the first two hours, they were dawdling along in a deplorable way. The result of my speech was that for the next two hours they stepped out smartly. Water and mountains are two questions which preoccupy the Zanzibaris.[...]

We are in the heart of Ugogo. Some details about this people might be useful. As is known, the Wagogo have a bad reputation as caravan thieves. They don't behave like the Wahehe, who take ambush, stab loitering carriers them make off with their loads, but during the night they prowl in twos and threes waiting for a good opportunity, then slip into the encampment, lay their hands on what they can—guns preferably—then make themselves scarce.

Only two chiefs in Ugogo still ask for a *hongo;* the others don't dare imitate them, since they're not strong enough. At present, Europeans, if they have some fifty guns with them, only rarely pay a *hongo* any more. Just a few years ago, this had to be done at almost every village on the route. Many of their thieving inclinations have been cured by the whites, who let them have lead when they demanded *hongo,* and this fact, together with the loss of all their cattle, will perhaps induce the Wagogo to leave off their lazy ways.

They are not clever traders like the Wanyamwezi, and they do not want, on any account, to carry loads; they consider this work beneath them. One sees them flopping for whole days in front of their *tembes,* doing absolutely nothing.

In obtaining game they are not less awkward and clumsy, and are quite ignorant of the various skilful methods used by the inhabitants further up to trap game. As I see it, there's only one thing they excel at: the making of slender iron chains to adorn their necks and ears. They also make strong, pretty bracelets of yellow or red copper, but their spears are not at all well wrought.

Salt must be common in Ugogo, for the natives are plentifully supplied with it. Perhaps they obtain it from the salt ponds, of which there a number to the south of the district.

The altitude of our encampment is 3,587 feet, so that from Mpwapwa we have not stopped gradually climbing. That will no doubt continue until we reach 4,183 feet, which is the height near the longitude of Dabuwa. From this latter point the waters flow towards the Nile or the Congo and one begins to descend.

The average number of our sick stays at twenty men incapable of carrying loads. I have thirty-four extra Wanyamwezi carriers. At Mabalala, I'll have to try and get some more.

Latitude is 6° 3' S.[...]

13th August After four and a half hours, we arrived at Irindi with our caravan, quite worn out. All along the route we had to pass through nasty scrub, and nothing exhausts the men so much as having to continually bend down. The countryside is as unpleasant as can be; one sees nothing but scraggy trees and yellow, twisted grass. In addition, water is scarce and bad. Everyone suffered from the sun and, do what you like, encampments are always, more or less, exposed to its rays.[...]

The chief of Irindi has sent me six goats, as has the chief of Ugomvia. I've filled the heart of the latter with joy by giving him a letter asking passing whites to treat him properly and not to steal his fowls and his goats. I presented him with two elegant waistcoats and a little American cotton. I think that Ugogo is the least productive part of the German possessions, and its population is the most useless there is.

The number of sick increases, and every day I burn with impatience to be far from this accursed country in a healthy region where I could, as before on the Congo, enjoy shooting hippo and seeing them harpooned by the natives, as I saw done near the Aruwimi.

14th August Once again a four and a half hours' march through thick bush which is terribly exhausting for the Zanzibaris who carry their loads on their heads. At every step they have to bend to avoid the lower branches. In this respect, the Wanyamwezi method of carrying is far preferable, for they place their bales on their shoulders and not their heads.

On arriving at the camp, the Wanyamwezi began to loot the village. They stopped only when I came up with my people, who chased them with sticks. I've threatened their chiefs with refusing authorization to continue to travel under my safeguard. I warned them that I would ask Makenge, the chief of the village two days' journey further up, to levy tribute on them. Some time afterwards, they came to find me in a body and begged my forgiveness, which I accorded them after an hour of pleading. There are more than nine hundred Wanyamwezi who travel with my caravan. I have thus, under my orders, 1,350 men—quite a little army and the largest number of men that I've ever had to command.

The altitude of the camp is 2,937 feet, or a descent of 607 feet from Sanga. The latitude is 5° 56' [sic].

15th August After two hours and twenty minutes we stopped at Bubu or Rububu, and set up our camp near the river of this name, in the middle of the plain. The bed of the river is as dry as an old bone, but here and there are muddy puddles from where caravans draw their water. I shot a superb scaly duck when we arrived.

We had nearly fifty sick this morning, twenty incapable of carrying. We've managed to move our loads only by getting some askaris to carry cases of ammunition. The main cause of illness is the absorption of great quantities of alkaline water and grains of millet or maweli which irritate unaccustomed stomachs [sic] to this and cause diarrhoea and bodily weakness. This large number of sick causes me much anxiety. If we had at least mtama instead of this cursed maweli, everything would be all right and the men would soon be well again.

Among our people there are perfect savages. They come mainly from Mombasa and one would truly say that they had never seen whites before. At the beginning, their head-men, Mza and Sadick, were absolutely useless. The former has made considerable progress, but I've had to reduce the second to the condition of carrier, even though he can't carry more than 10 pounds, for he is a little, yellow, frail looking man. It's quite monstrous the way they swindle and cheat the white man who organizes a caravan in this country. All those Arabs in Zanzibar cling to one like vampires, squeezing everything they can out of one, and they even, once the caravan has set off, often persuade the men to desert.

16th August Arrived in three and three-quarter hours at the village of Makengi, where I expect to find the natives claiming *hongo* from me, as is their custom.

Most of my men have been exhausted by the continuous march of eleven stages from Mpwapwa across the dry, bare desert with bad water and insufficient food. From Mpwapwa here it is 85 miles. We have marched well, for one must consider that we are ill-fed, ill-watered, and encumbered with sick. Here the natives grow *mtama*. Heaven be praised, for one can, without inconvenience, eat great quantities of it and it doesn't swell after being taken into the stomach, like *maweli* or millet, which gives the men terrible stomachache[s]. Altitude of the camp, 2,600 feet.

17th August Here we took a well-deserved rest for a day. By bedtime yesterday evening, neither the chiefs nor the inhabitants of the village had yet come to see me. I had it conveyed to them that I was very displeased with this lack of courtesy and that it made me think that they were plotting some ill trick. One of their chiefs had an answer brought to me that they feared the white man had come to avenge the massacre of three hundred Wanyamwezi killed last year, and that was why they were holding back. They promised to come in the evening. Naturally, I put no faith in what they said.

The caravan of the Baluchi which we left behind near Sanga, 50 miles back, has just arrived this morning, after leaving this village the same day as I did.

The march in the full heat of the sun yesterday on a scorching day gave me an awful headache. I have a temperature (102°) today and sharp pains between my shoulders. There are still fifteen stages from here to Tabora.

The boys on the expedition are a constant source of disappointment to me. I had engaged two as stewards or *"stewedi,"* as they say in Zanzibar. They were supposed to be the leaders of the boys and receive seven dollars [M.] a month. Now, a *"stewedi"* is supposed to know what a white man requires as service. That doesn't prevent mine from not even knowing the purpose of the buckle on a strap. At present, when they wait at table, they hold the plate tilted so that everything on it slips to the ground. I've reduced them to five dollars [M.]–the wages of my other boys. Fortunately, I have a good cook.

18th August Arrived in Tiwi in three and a half hours, and camped near the river of that name, which now looks like a succession of puddles, of which the water is, fortunately, good. It's the best we've drunk since Mpwapwa.[...]

None of the chiefs of Makengi came to see me yesterday. They must have been in a mad panic seeing a white man arrive. They had indeed stolen four bales from the Baluchi, who has now put himself under my protection, and they could believe that I was coming to punish them for this deed.

This morning I counted the number of people arriving at the encampment and marching past me. There were 1,950, who are all under my protection and depend on my will. At Mualala 850 of them will leave me to go north towards the Victoria Nyanza. The rest are making for Unyanyembe, Ujiji, and Manyema. The Baluchis' caravan counts about 850 members, most of whom are going to Nyangwe and to Tippu Tib's station in Manyuema.

The intense heat has, for some time, caused suffering amongst the whites as well as the blacks. During the day the body is overheated; the night cold brings on shivering, and fever ensues.[...]

19th August Marched as far as Kilimantindi in three and one-quarter hours and scaled a hill of 557 feet. Altitude: 3,167 feet. The rivers flow west, then turn to the south, then eventually back to the east, where they empty into the Rufigi.

Kilimantindi now looks sad and dilapidated. One would say that its best days are over. It's not a place where one would want to end one's days near the natives. Sand and heat are the outstanding characteristics of all or nearly all Ugogo villages.

Our sick are increasing, and I think that two of them are going to die.

20th August Arrived in three hours at Mualala and camped west of the chief's hut. A caravan commanded by some Baluchi left this place for Tabora about three days ago. It was held up here for some time arguing over the amount of *hongo* to pay the natives. Several of my men, especially the sick and those who haven't any guns, were beaten by some Wagogo villagers. I don't consider myself justified in answering these procedures with reprisals, for it is probable that my people had rifled the huts for the fowls and flour they contained.[...]

It is often said that if 2,500 Wanyamwezi, heavily laden, set out en route from Bagomoyo to the interior, they would run a grave risk of dying of hunger on the way. I was also convinced of this, but I've changed my mind now that I'm acquainted with this people's habits. If, for example, 2,500 Wanyamwezi left the coast for Uzambiro, they would have a following of at least 250 women and 150 boys. At the coast, each man would get grain for thirty days and would take on his load as well. The first month over, if one gave cloth to only five hundred men a day, all would go well and there would be no famine to fear.

Most carriers are astonishing rummagers in filth and can live on very little. By giving them cloth each in turn and not all at the same time, and stopping only one day in nine, I myself would be willing to undertake to lead twenty-five hundred to three thousand Wanyamwezi into the interior. Our caravan counts at present about two thousand souls and I have become very familiar with the habits and customs of these people. Altitude: nearly 3,200 feet.[...]

There are moments when I almost feel my brain breaking down for want of someone to talk to, [someone] who has ideas to discuss and to whom I could present the opposite point of view. My ordinary companions are the Zanzibari and Baluchi headmen. They put me in touch with news of the country, but they don't say anything original or amusing. It's only at night that I can relax and read. I couldn't sit down during the day and take up a book. In fact, during the day I have so many things to plan, so much to think about, that every moment my mind is elsewhere and far from the book that I have before me. I spend my days in isolation.

This way of living, I know, makes one selfish and narrow, but it is also a necessity imposed by the care to behave capably and sensibly. If, for example, I took my meals with the other Europeans, quarrels would surely break out over mere trifles and the dignity of all of us would suffer.

21st August We are staying at Mabalala in order to give our sick some rest and to get about twenty-five Wanyamwezi to come and help them cross the Gunda Kali, a desert plain covered with thick bush. This begins just west of this village and goes on to Kwamba. The Gunda Kali is far from being such a terrifying region as it was ten years ago.[...]

Towards the end of the afternoon, Chief Mgogo arrived after I'd sent for him twice. I spoke to him very severely and addressed his subjects in the same manner. I told him that he was a thief and a coward when he set about robbing weak Arab or Wanyamwezi caravans and extorting from them two hundred or three hundred *dotis* as *hongo*. I showed him that he and Makengi would kill the route that passes through their territory, since caravans would eventually take a more southern route to escape being pillaged by them. I added that shortly the Germans would send about a hundred soldiers who "would eat Makengi's country and kill him and all thieves of his sort." "When one of my men," I told him, "steals a *single* fowl, your women scream and your men wave their arms about for a whole half-hour. Then, the next day when the fowl is returned to you, with cloth as well, you go off and rob a poor Wanyamwezi caravan. You Wagogo aren't men, you're just bags of meat. Just try to steal my bales, and I'll shoot at you like rats."

This reprimand seemed to make a deep impression on him. But I have no illusions: in a few days he'll fall back into his erring ways.[...]

The life of a native is limited to his tribe; he often doesn't speak any other language except his own and rarely, if ever, goes to a region other than his own. (Naturally, I'm not talking of the negroes who travel, like the Wanyamwezi, the Wasukuma, the Manyuema, and the Wangoni.) The result is that he gets his ideas from seeing and hearing those people who live cheek and jowl with him in the region his fathers have always inhabited. The thoughts of one are the thoughts of the other, the ideas of one chief are, more or less, those of another, and to channel and keep things going in the same way, there is nothing worse than their food and their customs.

The food they eat has been the same for centuries; the customs they observe date back to antiquity and have never changed, maintaining them always in the same fixed routine. A nation which, for example, has just one single type of solid food, whose huts are all of the same model, whose arms all seem to come from the same mould, whose men marry at the same age and pay the same price for their women, that nation will not very likely produce many original, independent thinkers. All real progress is rendered nil, for everything proceeds just as it did in their ancestors' time.[...]

Take even a Wanyamwezi carrier, who has travelled and who is, for a Central African, an enlightened man. If an event takes place in the camp which produces a reaction in his mind, you can be certain that this man thinks exactly in the same way as his three or four hundred carrier companions. Nine-tenths of the caravaneers who have seen an incident will make the same exclamation.

We speak of African natives too quickly, too superficially, and too generally. It's important to carefully study a race or tribe before judging it, and in order to arrive at a solid basis for what one says about blacks, they should be first analyzed in depth.[...]

A number of other caravans, seeking protection, joined Stairs's column which by 22 August had swelled to some 2,250 people. There were some problems with retaining the services of carriers, who asked for extra pay. This convinced Stairs that an average African did not understand the nature of a contract and that the whites who wish to live in Africa should take this into account. The column was experiencing problems with drinking water which was either salty or in short supply. On 25 August Stairs was glad to arrive at a place where he found enough water for eight hundred people.

25th August After three hours [and] forty minutes we arrived at Itawa, a dependency of Kwamba. We are now in a new district, that of the Wasanga. They are the remains of a tribe who used to occupy the region south of here. They were, in their time, famous *Rugga Rugga*, or highway thieves, but by now, in exchange for cloth, they have sold their powder and guns to passing Arabs and have subsequently been forced to take up the more peaceable occupations of tilling the soil and acting as carriers. So there you have, taken from life, the history of a little African tribe.

In 1877, the same men who today brought me food supplies were the terror of caravans crossing the Gunda Kali. Even now, more than one Arab passing through the area feels smarting memories revive when he remembers the loss of more than one fine bale of cloth. And now, at least half the adults of the district have been to Bagamoyo and have brought back loads for themselves or for the Wanyamwezi. There's not a pound of powder today in the village.

The chief of Itawa is called Charula. He is indeed a man of large views. He recommends the construction of several more villages in the Gunda Kali so as to break up the long stretches of terrain with its exhausting brushwood and help caravans by providing water and food. But before undertaking this work, Charula wants the Germans to guarantee that the villages would not be attacked by Muini Mtwana's men. With three villages more, one at Lali, the other 7 miles west, and a third to the east of Salalo, all the dangers of crossing the Gunda Kali during the dry season would disappear. Charuba lives very justifiably in fear of Muini Mtwana, who lives in the south. In order to avoid being surprised, he has made an alliance with Kwamba and the people of Mualala (Wagogo).

Yesterday, on arriving at the camp, out of curiosity I sat down near the cisterns, while eleven hundred individuals came to draw water. What an interesting study of African ways I was able to make there! It was just dusk when about three hundred Wanyamwezi arrived and threw themselves in to the puddles of water that were going to slake our thirst. The result of this fine exploit was to disturb the water, bring the mud to the surface and change the water-holes into a mass of mud. Hardly thirty or forty more people were still able to get what they needed to slake their thirst.

In that I recognize the African. There is, for example, enough water for five hundred men in a well. The first ten men who arrive will fill their gourds, then paddle in the water, mixing mud with the liquid. This, then, is no longer drinkable and because of their thoughtlessness, their thirsty comrades coming up with the rearguard, won't find anything to drink unless they eat mud. I've often noticed that if the blacks sometimes toil very hard in looking after their own needs, it's only very rarely that they will work with the same spirit for others, unless they find some personal profit in it. In fact, there exists among them no central power which obliges them to do certain works for the general good of the community. All will put their hands to the task if it's a question, for example, of building a *boma* for common defence or of planting crops; but if a cistern needs to be cleaned out, who bothers?[...] They dig a new one.[...]

26th August Arrived at Kwawamba after a march of one and three-quarter hours. At a distance, on a little hill I saw among the palmyra palms[4] growing in the savannah some giraffes raising their long necks to watch us pass about two-thirds of a mile from where they lay.

At noon the chief, who demanded *hongo* from all passing Arabs, came to see me, and was very mild. He gave me a goat, saying that he was very poor, which is untrue, for *tembe* is full of excellent cloth stolen from the Arabs and the Baluchi. For an hour I spoke to him and frightened him with the threat of the impending arrival of German soldiers.

This robbing of harmless caravans is quite monstrous, especially when the water comes from springs and can be obtained without difficulty and without having to dig wells. I told him that his land would die, that the white man would take his goats and grain, and that then he'd be really poor. Why should one let this man rob poor merchants of three hundred measure of cloth at one go? Water, firewood, and grain should not be taxed when nature provides them without any trouble to man, but if the native has dug wells, then it is only fair to pay for the use of them.

No *hongo* is exacted from me, or course, for people like Kwawamba are scared of me. I would refuse to pay, even if I had to fight, for this tax is pure theft on the part of a chief, who is, moreover, very weak.

27th August Halt at Kwawamba to give the sick some rest. I've hired twenty-five carriers, for those recruited at Mualala don't want to go any further. I had another meeting with Chief Wamba and spent an interesting hour talking to him of Europe and his own region. He is at the mercy of two or three chiefs above him, obeys their *shauri* and suffers for it. I've bought cattle to make a present of them to my men, but the price is almost prohibitive: six dollars [M.] for a cow in poor condition; it's exorbitant. But now that almost all the cattle have died, five dollars [M.] would be more than enough.

Our nights are made unbearable by the braying of countless donkeys, those of my troop and those of the adjoining caravans. My donkey, a fine, strong fellow, is the noisiest by far. He's the one who usually gives the signal, and immediately all the donkeys of the caravans answer him. Every half-hour the concert begins again, all the more irritating because the donkeys are tied right up against the tents and bray, so to speak, in our ears.

I have long conversations with a Baluchi [named] Sadoria. He's a Mohammedan, very attached to the Arabs, but he declares that his friendship for the English is stronger than any other feeling. He's an able merchant who can keep cool and collected in difficult moments, and who is well up on what East Africa needs. I count on his helping me at Tabora, and perhaps further on with the Manyema, and on his giving his people a good account of me, for I have been kind and courteous to him.

I am a great admirer of certain of these Arabs and Baluchis of the interior, but I think that they, on the other hand, hate the white man, although they respect his power and his intelligence. Our religions are almost diametrically opposed.[...] Although that doesn't matter very much to us, it is otherwise with the Arab, who never manages to get it out of his head that we are infidel dogs. Besides, there are very few Arabs who, when they can and when they're stronger than the white man, resist the temptation of stripping him of his least particle of wealth. Although he often doesn't show it, the Arab feels his fingers itch at the sight of the white man's *bitha* (merchandise), and often lets himself be led astray by his inferiors into a system of low extortion, the idea of which a man with the least sense of honour would indignantly reject.

They have much more contempt for the natives than for us and give all the savages a common name, that of *abeed* (slave), an expression which has a great number of meanings. Don't certain whites also give blacks the generic name of "nigger" attaching to it a contemptuous, offensive meaning? Fortunately, those people are either those who understand nothing of the question, or else people who have lost all illusions about the blacks.

I have tried, in my spare time, to write poetry. I certainly don't expect to do anything remarkable but if I manage to grasp and analyze faithfully the lights and shades of the daily life of an African expedition, I will fulfil a long dreamed of desire. How is it that African life has never been related in a poem? Yet it's far from being a monotonous, boring subject.

Between 28 and 31 August Stairs's caravan suffered badly from the shortage of drinking water. Moreover, an Arab whose caravan preceded them was spreading the falsehood that Stairs's people rob the villagers. The result was that at the approach of his caravan, the villagers were fleeing and there was great difficulty in buying food.

1st September In one hour we arrive at the Luali where we are camping. Because of the drought, the river has become a sort of rosary, in the beads of which, thank Heaven, we find more water than we need to drink our fill, cook our food and, at last, wash our bodies and clothes. Since our departure from Bagamoyo, this is the first time we have drunk water which empties into the Congo and from there flows into the Atlantic Ocean! In the rainy season, the river winds north, then suddenly turns west, flows into the Mlagarazi and gets to the Tanganyika a little below Ujiji.

No rain has fallen now for sixty-five days, and water, they say, is scarce in Tabora. We left Bagamoyo fifty-nine days ago and have marched for fifty-two days in stages averaging a little over 9 miles. It's an excellent average. The Arabs who are with us now have been on the road for eighty-five days.

2nd September Made a seven hour march. We have camped near sweet, fresh water. The Arab, Selim, arrived an hour after us. I forced him to halt for a while at Mtoni so as to prevent him from outstripping me and getting the natives to flee because of the lies he tells about me. The result of this measure was illuminating. We had hardly set up our camp when the natives came in crowds to offer us provisions, which allowed my people to cook their food without further ado, whereas on other days they had to scour the countryside for miles around to find some sparse fare.

I was able to nab a man who had deserted with a tool-box. Heavens, how pleased I was! This box contained bolt wrenches for my boats, a certain number of bolts, and all my tools. I couldn't sleep, haunted by the idea that my boats were perhaps going to be useless. Having learnt from this experience, I've just put my eggs into several baskets. I have a feeling that, when we are two or three days from Tabora, a certain number of my carriers will desert and go and sell my bales in Tabora. In any event, I am watching everything and everyone like a hawk and have organized a regular service of detectives who will be continually on the job.

Unyanyembe and Tabora are synonymous. All the natives call this town by the name of Unyanyembe, but twenty-five years ago the Arabs baptized it Tabora.[5][...]

3rd September Halt at Rubuga. I've received a letter from Captain Jacques to tell me that he's had a good deal of trouble en route and that he's had to engage in several fights.
There are here a crowd of carriers from Tabora on the lookout for some trick to play. A great number of them are professional deserters. They ask to be hired, then when they have been accepted, they make off into the *pori* with their loads, open the bale and so find themselves rich without doing any work. This theft means they can live for a month like fighting cocks, then they start their jolly tricks again.

I count on staying ten days in Tabora in order to rest my men and fill the vacancies that will be made in our ranks by the desertions that I foresee. I've put two deserters caught red-handed on a chain. I'm making an effort to keep an eye on the suspects. If they budge, they'll have the same fate.

Rubuga is a den of thieves and bad hats. The Germans should make a clean sweep of the broom through here.

4th September Arrived at Kigwa in four and a half hours. We crossed a curious native bridge made of an overturned tree with a liana stretched across the river as [a] parapet. Met a little caravan going to the coast.

From Kigwa to Kami there is a *pori* that takes six hours to cross before one reaches the outskirts of Tabora. This *pori* or jungle is, it seems, infested with robbers on the watch for passing caravans. It seems impossible to chase this riff-raff from their lairs, for they wreak their havoc over too large an area and the covers to which they retreat are too dense.

This morning I met Morjan Marjaliwa who is going to the coast. He is very intelligent and speaks pleasantly, one of the best types of Zanzibari I have ever met. For ten months he lived side by side with me on the Aruwimi and at Fort Bodo, and did me immense service. He told me that Emin Pasha is now in Ruanda [sic], south of Lake Albert Nyanza. He crossed Pororo, visited the district of Mfumbiro and Lake Alexandra. Marjaliwa went to Karagwe to buy ivory there, and is going to sell it in Bagamoyo.

Emin's geographical discoveries should be intensely interesting for there are not, in Africa, regions which have so many hidden, unknown marvels as those between Lakes Tanganika, Victoria, and Albert.[...]

5th September In three and a half hours we covered 7 miles and reached Toni (near the river) SSE of Kami. I wanted to go as far as Kami, but Sadoria's people were tired and he was frightened of the *Rugga Rugga* who were in the *pori*. I had to wait, and he arrived at 10:50 a.m. I hope that the kindness I'm showing to him as well as to Selim the Arab will find their reward in Tabora and that they will prove useful to me in that town. Every evening they spend an hour in my tent and we chat about one thing or another, especially the day's events.

Selim knows nothing of these parts to which he has come for the first time. When Arabs have not visited a place themselves, they know nothing of it. Sadoria, the Baluchi, knows the whole route from the coast to Nyangwe and is a pleasant conversationalist, full of information. Yet, he lacks initiative and has no authority over his people. From the point of view of discipline, the difference between a white man's caravan and an Arab's is very marked.[...]

6th September In four hours we reached the Unyanyembe clearing and camped 5 miles from Tabora.

My couriers returned with a letter for me from the German officer commanding the station, informing me that he has hired a *tembe* and that everything will be ready for the day of my arrival.

I think I've succeeded in giving the Arabs a good opinion of me. Will it be of any use?

Chapter 12
Tabora to Karema

7 September—8 October 1891

The expedition meets at Tabora with the local Wali, Baron von Siegl the German commander, and Captain Jacques of the Belgian Anti-slavery Society. Some observations are made on caravan routes. After a week's rest the expedition resumes its journey. There is high incidence of fever. Rumours circulate of Rumaliza raiding the northwest coast of Lake Tanganyika. Stairs observes desolation and depopulation of the areas close to Karema. Food and water are scarce.

7th September We arrived at Tabora at 9:50 a.m. and settled into the *tembe* near the Luali's. Shortly afterwards, the latter, called Saef bin Said—a man with a shrewd, intelligent look—came to visit me, along with some others. I've been to see Baron von Sigl [sic], the German officer who commands the place.[1] He is alone here, and has had a hard time with the Arabs.

Captain Jacques caught up with me yesterday. He's a magnificent man, who seems to me to be strong and healthy.

8th-10th September On the morning of the eighth, I received the visit of several Arab notabilities and had long, pleasant conversations in my *baraza*. It's very interesting being present at these talks between Arabs about passing travellers. A great number of the Arabs in Tabora are pure bred, and come from Muscat or other Arab places. They can all read and write and they talk intelligently. They are perfectly versed in the ivory trade.

On the 9th September I drew on the walls of my *baraza* a large map of Africa and explained the different ways to the interior by way of the Congo, the Nile, the Zambezi, and overland routes. Immediately they grasped the superiority of the Zambezi route for taking merchandise to Ujiji. It is better than going through Unyanyembe and Ugogo—regions strewn with deserts which take three months to cross. Next I showed how a load, for which transportation from Zanzibar to Ujiji costs 15 dollars [M.] per man's back, could be taken by convoy from Zanzibar to Quelimane, then by road from the Shiré to the Tanganyika for about 5.50 dollars [M.] to 7.50 dollars [M.].

Shortly, Tabora will be in jeopardy, when the stocks of ivory from West Tanganyika take the Congo route, those [stocks] of Unyoro and Uganda [take] the Mombasa way, and when those [stocks] of Karagwe, Mporo, and Ruanda [sic] are exhausted in three years' time. Just look at the difference: Bagamoyo to Tabora, twenty-five days; Tabora to Ujiji, fourteen days, or including three halts, forty-two days. Quelimane to Abercorn, thirty days; Abercorn to Ujiji, four days, [a] total [of] thirty-four days.

All the Arabs understood the truth of my remarks and agreed with me that the Tabora route will fall away one day, and that then they will emigrate to the coast or Nyangwe.

Tabora wheat is small and sometimes mixed with sand, but the flour is very good. My cook made delicious bread from it, thanks to some powered yeast that I have. The native chiefs don't plant wheat but persist in keeping body and soul together on *mtama* and sweet potatoes. There are many reasons for this. First, the transformation of wheat into flour would mean a certain amount of work; then this flour cannot be reduced to *ugari* or soup, and if it is swallowed in this form, it sticks to the intestines and obstructs the inner system. The result is that in this region the Arabs almost have the monopoly of the wheat crop.

A visit paid on the 10th September to Tabora market gave me the following prices for the things on sale. A *keti* of little beads—blue, red, black, yellow, and green—is the monetary standard: it's called *pesa mosa* (a piece). All articles are reduced to a size so as to cost only one *pesa* and I estimate that one *keti* is worth two *pice* (Indian coin).[2] We're here at a bad time of the year and prices are high now. There were perhaps three hundred buyers and sellers at the market when I went there. Here is a summary of the notes I took:

Article	Quantity	Price
Firewood	5 small pieces	1 *keti* of beads
Native salt	2 spoonfuls	1 *keti* of beads
Native hoes	1 hoe	1 *upandi* of cloth
Butter (rare)	1 thimbleful	1 *keti*
Beans	1 cupful	1 *keti*
Mtama flour	50 pounds	1 *doti* of cloth
Onions	1 onion	1 *keti*
Eggs	one dozen	1 *upandi*
Tobacco	cakes of one square inch	1 *keti*
Peanut oil	1 spoonful	1 *keti*
Native soap	1 small cake	1 *keti*
Rice	1 *pishi*[3]	1 *upandi*

When a seller has collected a certain number of *ketis* of beads, he exchanges them for cloth. The noise at the market is deafening, but Luali's police keep reasonably good order. It's a most interesting sight; there are natives of all tribes and all origins buying and selling.

11th September I am ready to leave. I notice that my men are beginning to become demoralized drinking *pombe*. Several of my boat carriers haven't had any solid food since they've been here. They've just imbibed *pombe,* which is both a drink and solid food.

Siegl [sic] and the Luali [4] get on well. Sigl [sic] has a very difficult mission to fulfil here, but he is equal to his task. He's very easy to get on with and completely in touch with African life.

Nyasso, the woman chief of Itura—a village to the south of Tabora—is Tippu Tib's mother, or rather his father's wife, whom she married without bearing him a child.

An Arab from here, Suleiman bin Zeber, was fined by the English consul of Zanzibar for going on a slave-hunt. All the Arabs are trying to discover the aim of my journey and I think that a large caravan is going to be organized to follow me closely and go and pillage the territory west of the Tanganyika. They know, in fact, that I'll clear the way for them and involuntarily prepare the natives by treating them well and so easing their minds as to the intentions of those who will follow me.

One *frasilah*[5] of ivory costs here, at the moment, 145 dollars [M.] but brings in only 115 dollars [M.] at the coast. That clearly indicates the present state of trade. News travels so slowly that one is rarely informed on time as to the fluctuations of prices on the coast. During the war with Bushiri, gunpowder sold at 100 dollars [M.] for a 10 pound barrel. It has now come down to the price of 23 dollars [M.] and will still descend steeply.

Sigl [sic] has managed to maintain admirable order here. Before his arrival, there was an average of forty murders a month, and now there are only two or three. If he were to leave, everything would fall into disorder.[...]

Tomorrow we set off.

13th September This morning at 6:43 a.m., I saw my column off. I stayed behind in Tabora until 10:00 a.m. in an attempt to round up four deserters. We arrived at Uruma—the village of Fundi Mabruki—where we camped. Since one of Jacques's assistants was ill, I ordered the doctor to stay with him and to come and join me tomorrow with twelve guns.

A curious fact [and a] result of the recent epizootic disease: all the hyenas have died from eating this tainted meat, and at night one no longer hears the howlings of this hideous beast. Everywhere one encounters hyena carcasses. This terrible epidemic has had at least this advantage and it has delivered the villages from this pest. They aren't needed here to eat the human cadavers that are thrown into the bush. The ants and insects see to that task. The hyenas steal goats and sheep and scare the natives.

14th September Marched for two hours [and] forty-five minutes and camped at Toni (river dried up at the moment) in order to await the arrival of Dr. Moloney and his men coming from Tabora. Our encampment is delightful—under large trees scattered over a grassy plain. How happy one feels here in the shade far from Tabora and its furnace, far from the lazy slaves which that town is full of!

I am happy to note signs that herald a lowering in the price of food. I can buy four good fowls for a *shuka* of cloth (2 yards). A large basket of fine peanuts costs a hand of cloth; the same price for two large portions of potatoes or *mahongo*. A man's *posho* will get him eight good portions of potatoes or else six fine portions of the same with two fowls.

The natives are very fond of cloth, for it's only a little more than fifteen months ago since this road was opened to ordinary caravans. Business is in a state of stagnation. An Arab caravan doesn't spread much cloth about a region since it usually transports grain which is distributed as rations. Consequently it stirs up little trading activity as it passes. Our camp, on the other hand, is today a veritable market-place where all is noise and animation while the bargaining goes on.

Since the Arabs are, according to what I have observed, poorer than the white man, they are closer-fisted, argue more over prices with the natives, pay less and keep themselves aloof from them. The result is that the latter, in the interior, prefer whites to Arabs. The blacks of the coast and the Islamised negroes, on the other hand, prefer the Arabs, although they know that the white man has better *dotis,* better guns, tents, etc. In general, the Arabs, especially those of the interior, think of us as silly fools. I think that twenty-five years hence they will have changed their opinion. The best respected people in all East

Africa are the Germans; that's because they showed the Arabs and the negroes of the coast that they were their superiors in the profession of arms and because they were able to inspire in them that fear which is the beginning of wisdom. Saw a group of elegant birds, Widowbirds, I think.[6]

15th September Marched for two hours [and] thirty minutes and camped at Pangalli to let the doctor catch up with us. Kapalata is the chief of this district, but actually it's Sike [sic] who's in command.[7] Every *tembe* has a name of its own, and if one asks a native the name of a village, he will answer by giving the name of the chief of this village preceded by the prefix *bwana* (son of).[8]

The natives are very inflamed, and although they bring us food, I'm well aware that, without the presence of the Germans in Tabora, we would have been attacked a long time ago. I've rarely seen more nervous mobile faces than those of the blacks I see every day in front of my tent. They are cowards, but for the sake of one or two bales of cloth, they'd have to go [sic]. We're going to have to cross a bad *pori,* a bush, and I expect to be attacked by some of the most ferocious of these people out to get cloth.

Moloney arrived at 11:20 a.m.

16th September Arrived at Guha in one hour [and] forty minutes. Mayoli, one of Cameron's camps, is a short distance WNW of this village. Guha has no chief, but there are daily *shauris* at Sike's [sic] as to who will win the prize.

17th September We made a good march this morning—four and a half hours—to Matamuna's. I chose the best place for our camp. It is nonetheless horrible, and under our tents we have dust two fingers thick and a temperature of 93°F. Matamuna, the chief, is a relative of Sike's [sic]; he left his village and went to settle at Karema, near the French Fathers. One should consider the feat of thus persuading a chief to leave his hearth and his people as representing a considerable feat on the part of the French Fathers. Perhaps Sike's [sic] influence also had something to do with it.

In front of us are the Waganda, a little tribe that occupies a territory six to seven days wide marching from east to west, and also, I think, from north to south.

18th September Arrived at Igonda in one hour and forty minutes. The chief is a woman by the name of Disa. She has one of the most beautiful *tembes* I have ever seen. It is very big, and in the courtyard are excellent wells of water.

Uganda goes from here to Kisindi in the west, where another district begins. This is very long and about [a] three days' march wide. The inhabitants are now, as to ways and customs, similar to the Wanyamwezi, but in earlier days they used to form a race apart and had their own language.

Some years ago, Igonda was the scene of battles between Mirambo and the Arabs. The natives remember Stanley very well and also Kaiser, both of whom passed this way.[9][...]

In Africa the only cause of war is often fear. If I hadn't taken the precaution of sending messengers to the natives telling them I did not intend to attack them, they would all have fled into the bush at my approach, then, some time afterwards, they would have prowled round the camp, and seeing my men return laden with food, one or other of them would have attacked, perhaps killing two or three. Naturally my people would have riposted and war would have begun. If the natives stay at home, there is no danger of my men stealing anything from them. I've trained them and they are fearful of being punished if they act otherwise.

19th September Left at 5:40 a.m. meaning to go as far as Zimbili, 12 miles away, and arrived at Wana-Myaga at 10:00, my rearguard marching very badly. Certain of my headmen are the worst old women I've ever seen. I mean to demote some of them, and put in their place really alive, virile men.

Robinson, my servant, has fever, seventeen of my men also, and as I write these lines I feel a pain in my knees. It's a warning; I'm going to catch it too. The men know now that we're going to Msiri's. I expect desertions at Mpala.

21st September Arrived at Kakoma after a two hour march. A great number of men down with fever. The cause: the terrible heat of the sun. Consequently we have camped in a *tembe,* so that everyone can have some shade. From 8:00 a.m. to 5:30 p.m. the sun is raging. Its heat becomes absolutely intolerable, and its rays pierce the sides of the tent as if they were made of calico.

22nd September The fever is better. Thirty-seven cases are being treated. From 7:30 a.m. to 5:50 p.m. the sun is blinding and at night its reverberations are stifling. Unless protected by a *tembe* the poor caravaneers can't get any rest; they lie on the ground and breathe in the air like fish out of water. They consume enormous quantities of water and since this is bad, they contract violent fevers. Most of the men looking very ill: the liver is attacked, the body reaches a temperature of 104°, and in two days' time the man is reduced to a wreck. Fortunately, the average length of an attack is only forty-eight hours.

Arrived at Kisindi, 6 miles' march. Camped in the chief's *tembe,* so that everyone is in the shade.

Arrived at Wana Ruika's in two hours [and] forty minutes. I led the caravan in a hammock.

Our camp is picturesquely settled in the village, and my men, although a bit spread out, are well sheltered. The sun is still terrible.

Wana Ruika lives in a village now, just a short distance from this one. He has handed his power over this [village] to his sons. The village is extremely well fortified surrounded by a clay-covered palisade. Around the *boma* runs the usual euphorbia bush. Inside, the *tembes* and huts are set in squares, each square being separated from its neighbour by a palisade of very solid wood. All that, I suppose, was once done out of fear of Mirambo's men.

The natives have very little cloth, and are very keen to get some. But what can they give in exchange except work? Nothing, absolutely nothing. They don't possess the least thing that they can sell in Tabora for an appreciable profit. There is only one means they have of getting cloth: going to the coast, getting themselves hired as carriers and having their salaries paid in cloth. There is no ivory. The Wanyamwezi are beginning to learn to travel, little by little, along the eastern shore of Lake Tanganyika, from Gongwe, then right into Upifa. It would be a good thing if one could persuade them to go still further south, right to Nyasaland, where they could serve as carriers for the government of English Central Africa. I doubt whether there are, in all Africa, better carriers than these of Unyamwezi.

27th September Reached Ukalala in five hours and set up our tents 1 mile west of the village, near the ponds. I travelled only 1 mile in the hammock, then, feeling myself stronger, mounted my donkey and only got off him at the camp. God be praised! I'm rid of the fever at least for twenty-four hours.

Chalala is, at the moment, full of foreigners who seem to me to earn their living by killing game and selling it to the villagers. It's the filthiest village we've been through for some time. In spite of my desire to find my personnel shelter from the sun, I was obliged to refuse to stay in such a pestilential place, and I had to come and settle here.

It is really wonderful to see how much certain villages differ as to cleanliness. In one, everything is in good order: the grain is piled up in orderly heaps, little hen-roosts have been set up, the paths are carefully swept and all rubbish thrown far away. In another village, the space between the huts is literally invaded by potato peel, banana skins, waste from grain, *mtama*. One never sees a broom. The stench is intolerable, yet the inhabitants live and are happy in their rotten nest! I'm always afraid lest my men contract smallpox in a village. That wouldn't seem absolutely impossible here.

A little river runs WNW to Ukalala, and it's near one of the pools formed by this waterway that we are camping. At 4:30 p.m. *tarishi* arrived from Karema. They are the men whom I had sent from Tabora on the 9th September to the lake. They gave me a letter from Father Camille Randabel, dated the 22nd September (five days ago), telling me that he has received my letters of the 19th September and that he will do all he can for me. He promises me three boats, advises me to go to Joubert's, south of Mpala, says that Rumaliza has laid waste all the northwest part of Lake Tanganyika and is now getting ready to do the same in the south. He was about to attack Captain Joubert when he heard of our approach and of Captain Jacques's, which kept him in the north.[10] The Father says that we have arrived at the psychological moment [sic].[...]

28th September After five hours of marching we bivouacked at Kilimani on the banks of a stream flowing just two-thirds of a mile from the mountain crest. Situated on the mountain, Kilimani is 253 feet above the level of the plain. The crest of the mountain stretches far NNW and SSE. Looking back, one can see 50 miles of forest without the least clearing. From Tabora to the lake there is continuous woodland. We are camping near springs which form a river 2 miles from here. I'm told that water is found there in every season.

29th September Camped near the village of Kalambega after a three hour march. The chief came to see me with about half a dozen of his subjects. They are Wagallas. Few Wanyamwezi are seen in the villages. The chief's tattoos were really artistic. All the inhabitants were likewise adorned on the chest, neck, stomach, and shoulders. The two top front teeth are not filed as amongst the Wanyamwezi. Wagalla country stretches from the Ugalla River in the east to Umkayala in the west, a place abut a day's journey from here. The chief of the tribe lives in Umkaiala where we shall camp tomorrow.

There's a semi-famine here; food is horribly expensive, whereas one day away from here, it's extremely cheap. Our camp is well situated and we all have shade.

I have, in all, six headmen or *Nyamparas* who render some service; the rest aren't up to much. As soon as the white man no longer has his eye on them, they dawdle or hide among their men. In this country it's not as it is in India. There, they have a whole number of non-commissioned officers (natives) who do the hard work, while the European sleeps in his tent or bungalow. Here, the white man must do the work himself and see to it that it's done if he wants everything to go well and speedily.

30th September Arrived at Umkayala in four hours [and] thirty-five minutes. We found plenty of food and water. That's all the more fortunate since I'm told that, further on, food is scarce and we shall have to sleep for two days in the jungle, away from any village.

A great number of my men got drunk this afternoon on beer bought from the natives. They get tipsy on a ridiculously small amount of drink. I could drink this *pombe* until I burst, and I still wouldn't feel any effect. Banana beer is also a very refreshing drink; when cold, it is delicious on a hot day. *Mtama pombe* is horribly bad.

1st October After four hours [and] fifty minutes, we arrived at Simbo (Toni). There was enough water for all our needs, although it was bad. We bivouacked in the bush, for there is no village.

We shall get to Gongwe tomorrow morning about nine o'clock, but war and pillage have left nothing of this village which was once so flourishing. The two Arabs have left for Karema. Some of the Gongwe natives came to see me at Simbo. I suppose they are frightened that I have come to punish them for chasing away the Arabs. The natives' wars are like children's squabbles: they end quickly and no real damage is caused, except perhaps a famine which lasts for a season.

2nd October We reached Gongwe in three hours [and] fifty minutes. As always, we crossed the *pori*. Just before reaching the place, one descends 200 feet. We set up our tents in the village, once populous and active, but now poor and depopulated because of the consequences of the war against Kasogera of Fimbwi.

About thirty-five days ago Kasogera, the chief of Fimbwi, who lives a day away from Gongwe, sent heralds to summon Sirundi, the chief of Gongwe, to come and pay him tribute in ivory, and recognize Kasogera as chief. Sirimbi responded by refusing to go to Fimbwi, adding that he was blood-brother to the whites of Karema, who would come to protect him in case of danger.

Meanwhile, Kasogera declared war and surprised the village three times during the night, made a breach in the protecting palisade, killed more than 100 men, carried off 100 women and 70 head of cattle. Gongwe, now, is unarmed and its people are in constant fear of another attack. Kasogera wants to close this route and open another through his village, in order to be able to exact *hongo*.

If Gongwe were completely wiped out, it would be a great pity, for then one would have a five days' march across the *pori* without being able to get food, and caravans would suffer terribly. So I wrote a letter to the Germans in Tabora, explaining matters and asking the German officer if he couldn't come to the chief's aid by giving him a flag or something.

Kasogera took most of the captured women to Umkaila to sell them there. From there, they must have been sent on to Tabora to be sold to the Arabs. That is the real reason for the war: Kasogera needs slaves and so will thus be able to obtain cloth.

Gongwe is in a pitiful state. The huts with their thatched roofs have been burnt down, and the chief is, in effect, camping in his own village.

Between the 3 and 7 October the column marched on without any significant events taking place.

8th October March of five hours [and] thirty minutes. We are camping about three-quarters of a mile west of the little village of Kifume, on the banks of the river which is dry except for puddles here and there in the river-bed.

This march has been one of the hardest since Bagamoyo. The road was marked out in sand that we sank into when marching. There was no wind, so no coolness.

From my tent I can make out the blue mountains which border the Tanganyika 35 miles from here. I am curious to see what longitude I shall give Karema, a point which has caused much discussion among geographers.

As we get nearer the lake, the landscape is beginning to change. At present, instead of the *pori* with short grass and tall trees we are crossing mountains dotted with little trees and valleys, tall mimosas, giant acacias, and long, dry grass. The countryside is intersected by streams on all sides and rocky ravines, which, in the rainy season, are transformed into torrents that empty into the Kifume and, from there, into the lake. The natives are few and poor. They seem lazier than those of Gongwe and Igonda. Game is scarcer than two or three days ago and the water somewhat briny.

Today the sun shed on our poor heads a barrage of incandescent rays, the burning heat increased by solar reverberation, for we were walking in the sand of the bed of the Kifume, which enveloped us in sweltering gusts that no breeze came to alleviate.

Since Mpwapwa we haven't encountered any running water. It will be so good to see again, at last, rivers with clear, streaming water and not have to dig holes to get a muddy, sickening liquid.

CHAPTER 13

ACROSS LAKE TANGANYIKA

9 OCTOBER—27 OCTOBER 1891

The caravan arrives at Karema on 9 October and the crossing of Lake Tanganyika begins. Stairs is entertained by the local missionaries. He learns from them that the level of this lake varies periodically over the years. Stairs is advised to avoid meeting with Captain Joubert to avoid antagonizing the Arab chief Ruamliza. Captain Jacques's caravan arrives. Stairs leaves Karema on 26 October and continues his march to Mrumbi.

9th October We left camp at 5:45 p.m. and sighted the Karema mission station, where I was given a kind welcome by the Fathers. After a short interview, I got the men to go down to the banks of the lake where I had the camp set up.

I immediately drank a long draught of lake water, which seemed like nectar after the muddy filth we'd been kept on for so long. The view of this vast sheet of blue water was heartening, and the view stretched southwest as far as Fimbwi camp. I immediately made my arrangements for crossing the lake, and [between] 10:00 [and] 11:00 at night, I sent off 110 men and 60 loads divided into 3 boats, their destination Mount Rumbi,[1] Captain Joubert's station, a little to the north on the other side, 24 to 30 miles away. At 3:00 in the morning one of the boats returned with a nasty leak, and could only get off again at 8:00 a.m. on the 10th October. One of the boats took sixty-nine loads, thirty-three men and fourteen sailors, which shows they have a large capacity. If I was able to have the priests' boats, it was because I had sent couriers ahead from Tabora, which means that I was thus able to send the caravan on ahead without losing a minute. Captain Joubert has two boats on the western shore. One of the priests went to Mount Rumbi to get them and bring them back. That will bring to five the number of boats to transport my men and Jacques's. I expect his arrival in three days' time.

At this time of the year, the return voyage takes five days. The best moment to leave this coast is midnight. You row until daybreak and once it is light, a SSW wind blows you on to Rumbi or Mpala, where you arrive at nightfall. Generally the men who steer the boat spend a night and a day on land, and are back here on the night of the fifth day. Mpala is 45 miles from here and not 20 miles as the maps show. The width of the lake opposite Karema is 23 miles.

The missionaries have given us a standing invitation to have our meals with them every day. How happy we were to taste vegetables and European bread! Our camp is well situated on a sandy grassy beach. About half a mile from here is firewood. I paid the crew one *doti* a head as passage fare.

10th October At 8:00 this morning, I was able to send off the boat that had sprung a leak. As the wind was good, they were out of sight in three hours.[...]

I've received from Sudi, Dosa bin Suleiman's agent, 500 *joras* of *satini*, 80 *joras* of *Bombay*, 90 of *amerikani* and 300 of *lesso*.[2] I got them all ready to be packed.

The trees that go to the making of the boats come from the western shore. They are ordinary boats hollowed out from a tree, with the sides raised by means of rough planks nailed together. They have a kind of poop. The oars used by the sailors are poor contrivances. They consist simply of a rod with, at the end, a little round plank shaped like a spade, tied and nailed to the end of the stick.

I've sent a load of my own oars with the Marquis de Bonchamps and his company, so he can see if they wouldn't be more useful to the men than these wretched spoons. The mast is a sort of ruin [sic] and the sails are rigged as for a dhow. One of these big boats can hold seventy-five men and about ten loads and move after a fashion.

I don't think that boat-building material is found on this coast; all the tall trees come from the western side.

Captain Joubert is the only white man living on Mount Rumbi, but there are four Fathers at Mpala and as many at Kibanga, seven days north of Mpala on the west side, north of the road which goes from Ujiji to Nyangwe. It is 20 miles from Rumbi to Mpala and, by going directly to the first of these stations, I save a long stage and I'll be able to climb up to the plateau much more easily than by setting out from Mpala, where high mountains present a great obstacle.

SSE about 28 miles from here is the Ras Pimbwe and, even further south, another cape.

The height of the mission station is 45 feet above the lake at this moment. The waters, according to the old inhabitants of the region, withdraw slowly and rise every twelve or fourteen years, depending on whether the Rufuga is open or dammed. My letter to Swan, [sic][3] who is at the southernmost part of the lake, should have reached him three days ago. I asked him for the use of his steamer. With this, I could send my men over in six days, whereas now I'm going to have to stay here twelve full days. I don't think it would be wise to launch my two boats on the lake, for it seems to me to have very strong waves and the steel they're made of is very thin. They were built only for crossing rivers or traversing waterways or little lakes, but they couldn't take a "sea" like the Tanganyika.

The water of the Tanganyika is fresh, clear, sweet, better, in my opinion, than that of Lake Victoria and immensely superior to the brackish water of Lakes Albert and Edward.

Today I engaged a guide to take me to Msiri's.[4] He tells me that he knows the route, the natives, and the countryside. I'll take him on trial for a few weeks. I estimate the distance from the lake to Bunkeia at about thirty-five stages.

11th October Bodson and the doctor went to church. I remained in camp and covered twenty-five bales of cloth with an old tent canvas that the Fathers gave me yesterday. Nothing could exceed the generous kindness of these men to us. They go out of their way to help us. They've given us a standing invitation to all their meals. I usually go to the mission station which is about half a mile from here every day at noon. I have lunch and stay there generally until three o'clock, the time of day when the temperature gets cooler.

Nevertheless, I'm desperately anxious to be off to the other side of the lake, for the men become incredibly demoralized staying in camp without doing anything. On the other hand, it's so pleasant to be able to chat with foreigners, and through them to know all about the lake and its inhabitants!

Father Randabel gave me today a curious specimen of a fibre that looks like flax, [...] and which would, without any doubt, serve to make excellent cloth. He has sown a certain quantity of seeds, and hopes when it is harvested, to make cloth. He made me a present of seeds which I shall take to Europe. The native name of this plant or shrub is *boluba*.[5] The spot where it is mostly found is Kibanga, the mission station northwest of the lake. The natives use it only for making string to be used for catching fish and other purposes.

The Wa-Marungu call the lake Bwembwa or Bwemba, but they all know the name Tanganyika.

By having wells dug lower than the mission station, Father Randabel found, 7 feet deep, a quantity of fragments of pots like those used by the natives. That shows definitely, in my opinion, that the lake was once at least 47 feet lower than now, and that what is at present solid ground was then on a lower level. Villages were built on this site. Then the lake raised its level and brought the sand and silt which now cover the plain that the mission station overlooks. The villages had to withdraw onto the heights. After a certain time, the waters dropped again and left this plain dry. According to what I hear from the Fathers, there is no doubt that the lake rises and falls every fifteen years. At this moment, it is about at its average level, and over the next ten years it will rise again until it reaches the old marks that can be made out under the mission station. This is now nearly half a mile from the shore.

The Lukaga is rapidly becoming dammed up at the moment with papyrus, plant debris, and sand which form a solid dike against the outflow of water from the lake. This, naturally—because of its tributaries which keep it supplied—sees its level rise and, to my mind, goes on rising until its volume of water is large enough to force a passage through the Lukuga dike. It thus makes an outlet which is effective until its surface is low enough for just a small amount of water to trickle through. Then the dike closes again.[...]

As our camp is pitched near a sandy beach, there are neither ducks nor geese, but there are quantities, and hour from here, in lagoons where these birds find plenty to feed on.[...]

The word Tanganyika comes from Tanga, the Kifipi word which means lake, and Nyika, which in Kifipi, Kinyamwezi, and Kiswahili means desert or solitude.[...]

The men have had a great ball, leaping about for seven to ten hours. I like to see them dance, and encourage them to do so every time I can, for that prevents them from thinking of other things. Especially in a stationary camp, the devil finds mischief for idle hands to do. Cabals are formed amongst the men who speak—and perhaps try to work—against the white man's influence. Those who are sick do not seem to be improving after five to six day's rest.[...]

12th October I had the boat, the *Dorothy*, assembled this morning and ventured out on the lake to try her.

We have had another nineteen bales of *satini* made up and covered by an old piece of canvas supplied by the mission station.

By midnight, no news of the return of the boats from Rumbi.

A huge forest fire broke out on the other side of the lake, to the west, just opposite Karema. It must be an enormous fire, for 24 miles away we can see the flames rise and fall.

13th October At 9:00 a.m. I was given a letter from Mr. A. J. Swann in reply to the one I wrote him from Tabora. It is dated from Kinyamkolo, mission station, Southern Point of Lake Tanganyika, 4th October 1891.

The couriers left twenty days ago: nine days to get there, nine days to return and two at the mission station. In answer to my request to lend me his steamer to transport my men across the lake, Mr. Swann tells me that he regrets not being able to bring it to me, as there is no one to look after his station in his absence. If I wished to send a white man to look after it, he promises me that he will come with his steamer and take my men across the lake, on condition that I do not interfere in Captain Joubert's quarrels with Rumaliza, Tippu Tib's man, who is making raids on the western side of the lake.

Mr. Swann, obviously, has a different opinion on Rumaliza than the French missionaries here. He advises me to go to meet the Arab chief and tell him frankly what my intentions are. He thinks that it would be safer and better for me not to pass by Captain Joubert's settlement, for the Arabs and Msiri will confuse my expedition with the antislavery expeditions of Jacques and Joubert. For a long time now I've been looking for a way of avoiding Joubert's station, but then all that remained open to me was the southern route, and I did not want to take that, because of the numerous complications which would ensue.

Some say that Rumaliza is at Ujiji, others that he is at Kirando. However that may be, wherever he is, he's watching my expedition and confuses it with Joubert's. If he is at Ujiji, all is well, but if he is at Kirando, my position is dangerous, for he could attack us whenever he wishes.

Swann has, as [an] assistant, another white man—the lay secretary of the London Missionary Society—who lives 31 miles away from him. I was pleased and thankful at 2:00 p.m. to see one of the boats arrive back from Rumbi. Received a letter from Bonchamps saying that everything is going well, but that the boats were too heavily laden and had taken on a good deal of water. At 10:00 p.m. the new sailors were ready; I embarked fifty loads and thirty men of Company No. 2, and had the steel ship, the *Dorothy* taken in tow by the boat, with orders to row her in calm weather, but tow her if it was windy. The departure took place in excellent conditions, no wind, the men happily rowing and singing. For crew, the *Dorothy* has four rowers and one helmsman. I count on sending the *Bluenose* off tomorrow in the same way, and, with this in mind, I assembled the sections today.

The donkeys will, I fear, give us much anxiety, for we can only embark, at most, one or two in each boat. To date we have already sent across 140 men and 120 loads. I hope that the two boats from Mpala will arrive tomorrow before Jacques and his expedition enter Karema. It is the Fathers here who choose the boat crews: they usually take a good fifteen hours to get to Mount Rumbi.

14th October God be praised! A boat arrived at 8:30. The north wind, which was blowing yesterday, had pushed her 19 miles too far south. Her crew says that the other boat must have been blown to Cape Pimbwi, 31 miles south. If that is true, the second boat will not be here before two days. These people, who are supposed to row, just let the wind take them, I imagine, in every possible direction.

If a white man were in the boat, they would possibly make good speed, but left to themselves, they idle along.

The name of the superior of Karema is Father Randabel. He's an extremely pleasant man, very gentle and hospitable, thoroughly acquainted with all questions concerning Central Africa.

It is very hot here during the day from 9:00 a.m. until 4:30 p.m. In spite of the breeze, under canvas one is very uncomfortable in the heat even if one is in shirt sleeves, but still there is an enormous difference between the shores of the lake and the camps in the *poris* to which we became accustomed over nine weeks. One is very happy to let one's eyes wander over the good lake water. The shore opposite disappears for eight hours of the day behind a hot, smoky wind. Pimbwi is usually visible only in the morning until noon and in the evening.

There is little or no animal life in the immediate surroundings of our camp, as the beach is too sandy and barren, but to the north and south are an abundance of hippos, crocodiles, antelopes, geese, ducks, plovers, curlews, and wild boars. There are also some magnificent sorts of kingfishers with long red beaks and sky-blue wings fringed with white and black feathers. I have noted two sorts of curlews and three sorts of ducks, but there is little time to go into these things.

Our guide and I have calculated the stages from Joubert's place to Msiri's capital. He estimates twenty-five days, or a month and would like to pass through the northern point of Lake Mweru. I, on the other hand, would like to keep north, further away from the influence of the Arabs, until the Mweru, at least, has been passed.[...]

After infinite difficulty, at 7:30 p.m., I was able to send off the boat which arrived this morning. Thirty-five men and a donkey were on board. There are only two dhows on the lake; both are at Ujiji and are very busy taking people over to that place. They are asking one *jora* a head as fare.

Half an hour after midnight the third boat arrives, and in forty minutes, I was able to send it off with another thirty-five carriers. I quite simply took the management of the whole business into my own hands and so saved at least two hours. Each boat that arrives needs a new crew, for the sailors on board are tired. It takes, to navigate it, an average of thirteen sailors, who cost me one *doti* of six hands per head.

To date, we've sent over to the other side of the lake 200 men and nearly 120 loads, as well as a donkey and a steel boat. No sign of the arrival of the boats from Mpala. They must have been blown by the wind beyond Cape Pimbwi.[...]

Between the 15 and 19 October the crossing of the lake was continued. Stairs, while sailing on the Bluenose, *caught a considerable number of large fish. On the eighteenth he was visited by Jacques's white personnel and two missionaries who were highly critical of Arab behaviour, resulting in enormous harm to the success of the missionaries' work.*

19th October The three Karema boats have returned. Two of them need repairs which will take all day tomorrow at least. I was able to send off the third at 9:30 p.m. with thirty men, fourteen loads, and one donkey.

I caught three very big fish this morning. Two were of the species called *pamlia* and weighed about 40 pounds each. The third was smaller, weighing 9 to 10 pounds, and is called *wangwa* by the inhabitants. This last is most curious. It is spotted yellow and green, has a bullet-shaped head, and teeth that are always visible, jutting out over the gums. It is great fun to fish as it runs and leaps like salmon. Its flesh is good to eat. The natives are very fond of it, but don't have the means to catch it.

In places, the beach is literally covered with shell-fish thrown up by the waves and which resemble our cockles or ordinary whelks.

20th October This evening, after much tinkering and idling, I managed to dispatch the two Mpala boats with seventy men, fifty-five loads, and one donkey bought at the mission station. To thank the Fathers for all their kindness to me I made them a present of twenty dollars [M].

The *Bluenose* takes to the water like a duck, and I'd give a good deal to take her back with me to England. One of Captain Jacques's officers came aboard this little boat. Captain Jacques is a very intelligent man and, I think, very clear-sighted. Unfortunately, he is imbued with the same idea as the French missionaries, that is to say, that all the Arabs should be massacred, which, in their opinion would bring peace to the land. Nonsense!

The country could not be pacified by the massacre of all the Arabs; first the natives must be subdued. More than one tribe would greet the white man as its saviour against the Arabs, but later would begin to hate him and try to get rid of him.[...]

21st October I got a boat again and went off fishing this morning since I had a few spare moments. I managed to catch a fish of at least 20 pounds. Then I got ready our mail for the coast, comprised of thirty-one letters, sewn into an envelope of very thick waterproof material.

The natives of Fipa make coarse but very durable cloth from the cotton which grows in quantities in their region. I've seen samples of it at the mission, where it is used to cover long armchairs. These materials are perfectly suited to this use, also for making clothes.

It's interesting to calculate what it costs to send my letters to England or elsewhere. For each letter, I've arrived at the sum of 4.35 dollars [M.] or about 14 shillings.

22nd October [...]I left camp last night at midnight in a boat belonging to the mission. I was making for the mouth of the Lifume, 3 miles to the north, to go duck-hunting.[...] I encountered four of five species of duck, two species of goose, one [was] the common Egyptian duck with ringed eyes, three sorts of plover, large curlews, red-footed waders, storks, cranes, herons, [and] dotterels. I saw several snipe and went towards them but without managing to shoot at them. I particularly admired the superb plumage of the big curlews. By 10:00 a.m., we had returned to camp.

The mission station was formerly an international Belgian station set up by the king. Captain Cambier was the founder. Storms succeeded him, then came the missionaries. While he was at the head of the station, Captain Storms quarrelled with Chief Kasagara, but compelled him to keep the peace. It's a mistake to have any post other than a mission at Karema, for this place is not on a much frequented route and news always reaches it late. For a mission it's a very advantageous site, for one is not under Mohammedan influence, which, in this country, runs counter to Christian preaching. I've noticed that the Arabs have seized possession of all the main centres in this part of Africa and that they have taken over the best routes. Kirando, for example, where the lake is narrow, would be an excellent post for the Germans. It would largely prevent the abominable pillage that is practised in the Free State.

I am anxiously wondering how I shall cross the Lake [Tanganyika]. No boat has arrived since Monday, and yet two should have been here a couple of days ago.

23rd October I've spent a day doing nothing, waiting for the boats which have not yet returned.

The Karema station is in a good situation, set on a gentle slope at the foot of some mountains which rise to an altitude of 150 to 250 feet above the lake. The buildings are 155 feet above the lake, although formerly the very base of the ramp on which they are was once washed by the water. This has now retreated half a mile so it has become difficult to obtain.

Here is a general picture of the station: large *tembe,* built in Wanyamwezi fashion, surrounds a raised, spacious central building in which the whites live. The children and servants of the mission live in the *tembe,* which is hexagonal in form. Outside, in huts of grass and hay, are the men and women in whom the priests are interested and who do the heavy work in the mission station. The church is outside the *tembe.* It is, without any doubt, the best built and most finished building I have seen up till now in the African interior. It is 70 yards long, proportionally wide and high. The roof is supported by arches made of stone and clay, an innovation that aroused the natives' admiration. It is formed of quite superior tiles of baked clay, solid and lasting.

About 300 feet away to the south is another *tembe* used as a dwelling by the natives who have been converted to the missionaries' religion. Below the rise on which the mission station stands, the plain stretches out SW and NW, formerly covered by the waters of the lake and now transformed into fields and gardens whose produce goes to feed the mission station.

Mtama, manioc, and maize are the staple foods of the blacks. The Fathers have at their disposal fields of rice and wheat of excellent quality for their own use. They also have a first class vegetable garden.

In spite of the dry season, we were served beans, onions, cabbages, and other vegetables during our stay. The Fathers planted pawpaw trees, banana trees, etc., which are overladen with fruit. I have noticed that wherever a French mission has been set up, one finds oil, bread, and vegetables, whereas few English mission stations possess these three useful additions to the African diet. Among other things, the Fathers make excellent tapioca with manioc, and vinegar from bananas. They have thirty head of cattle which have been here for years, neither increasing or diminishing in number, for the terrible *sotoka* or epizootic disease has not yet made its appearance.

Below and in front of the principal building is the cemetery where rest—in simple but decent looking graves—three Fathers who have given their lives trying to rescue the poor African from barbarism. There is one inscription in the cemetery, touching in its simplicity: that of Father Josset, the Superior, who died the very day we left Bagamoyo, and whose death the people on the coast must just be hearing about now.[...]

The mission is constantly in touch, by means of boats, with Rumbi, Mpala, and Kibanga. The Fathers frequently go from one place to another. These three points are now rid of the depressing influence of the Waswahili, who imitate the Moslems, and the Fathers conduct their mission with the assurance of having a certain influence over the natives. They don't teach them to read or write, and they don't insist on getting them to do things which can be of no use to them in the future, but they make *fundis* of them, that is to say, artisans, carpenters, blacksmiths, etc. They take them young and so easily initiate them into the practice of these trades.

I was deeply impressed by these Fathers, seeing their calm and all-quiet fervour with which they undertake and accomplish their task. It's something quite new, to which one is not accustomed in Africa, especially in caravans where noise and feverish haste are, alas, only too prevalent.

I am not as much in agreement with the Fathers concerning the political game they lend themselves to in the lake regions. Their aim and the motive of their acts seems to me, as a foreigner, the complete disappearance of any Arab or Mohammedan influence on regions where they hope to spread their teachings. That is perfect from their point of view, for the Mohammedan wields great power over the natives and is directly hostile to Christian doctrine. But something else must be taken into consideration: these Arabs are powerful, they know the country better than we whites do; they can work together when danger menaces them; they have arms and many men to use them. They [Arabs] hate from the bottom of their souls these "usurpers," these intruders, these dogs of Nazarenes.

If, in these circumstances, the Arabs were brought to fight, no one could predict what the end would be. Isolated mission stations, situated far off in the heart of the country, would be surprised and their inhabitants massacred. Life and property would run all sorts of risks. Have priests, whoever they are, out of their mistaken sincerity and ill-considered zeal for their branch of religion, the right to make such dangers possible? Certainly not. It is up to governments who have force at their disposal and who, by force, can get their principles of administration respected. It is up to governments, I say, to struggle openly with Arabs and bring them—if necessary by coercion—to behave in an orderly way, not because they are *Moslems,* but because they are slave-hunters. That brings me to insist again on what I have said before, which is that, in order to obtain real success, missionaries must come after the establishment of stable government, not before. They will thus have security and the native *will respect them*—the first necessary step to get him to believe in the teachings they are trying to instil in him.

24th October   It is useless to say that missionaries should not interfere in politics in the country where they find themselves. They almost invariably do. They are forced into it by the chief of the region under whose protection they really are. The latter begins by asking for advice, then he comes to tell the missionary about the trouble he is in, and finally he asks how he should behave towards another chief with whom he has been at war. In order to safeguard their interests and their property, the missionaries are obliged to take the side of one chief against another. That is somehow fatal; and yet it's a government's role, not a missionary's.

Three Fathers have died in Karema since the foundation of the mission; two died at Mpala and four at Kibanga. In addition, Carter was killed by Mirambo's people at Kasagera. I should add that Captain Cambier constructed the Karema enclosure, and Captain Storms the buildings inside.

Here is a copy of the letter Father Randabel wrote me:[6]

Karema/22nd September 1891.

Dear Captain Stairs,

Your men arrived at Karema on the 17th September. We were agreeably surprised to hear that you are coming to Karema. Your arrival is very opportune. Rumaliza, Tippu-Tib's [sic] famous companion, after seizing all the territory north of the lake, wants to make himself master of all the south. At this very moment, one of his men is with our neighbours, busy hiring *Rugga Ruggas* to go to fight Captain Joubert on the other side. The news of your arrival and Monsieur Jacques's reached the chiefs of the regions around us like a bolt from the blue. They have already spread it around that they won't send their men to Marungu.

Thanks to you, Rumaliza's expedition has, I think, failed. May you arrive soon and in good health. We shall do our very best to help you cross the lake. We can put three boats at your disposal. I shall, besides, send a courier to Mpala today to advise the missionaries at the station and also Captain Joubert to have theirs ready. Their boats are, I think, big enough. Perhaps you don't know that Captain Joubert has built a station a good day's march away from Mpala, further south, very near Rumbi, a point that is marked on the maps. I think it is more advantageous for you to prepare your expedition at Captain Joubert's since, from there, you are much nearer the goal of your journey. Besides, you will see him yourself.

Hoping to see you soon, my colleagues and I send our best wishes to you, Captain Bodson, the Marquis de Bonchamps, and to Monsieur the doctor. Yours sincerely, (signed) Camille Randabel.

This letter shows how anxious the Fathers were to help us.

25th October I drilled my askaris and gave each—man and boy—a *doti* of cloth so as to have shirts made for the rainy season. The Zanzibari has the habit of selling all the cloth he is given to get food. This time, I distributed this *doti* as part of the expedition, just like the guns and ammunition. I shall mark down each *doti* under the men's registration numbers. Tomorrow is Sunday, and all the men of the mission have to attend morning Mass, so if the boats return today, I shan't be able to leave before tomorrow evening.[...]

26th October Two boats returned in the course of the afternoon and I leave at nightfall. At last! The Fathers have been so good to us, and only their kindness has made the anguish of waiting bearable.

27th October Leaving yesterday at four o'clock with a slight breeze behind us, we were blown westwards to about 10 miles off the west coast, then the wind dropped. For two hours, the sailors set about rowing, then the breeze started up again and blew us to the coast, to the mouth of the F'ungwe, 20 miles south of Rumbi. There we camped for the night. At 5:00 a.m. we set off again and rowed steadily, then the wind rose again only to drop suddenly. All day long our paddlers toiled, and these astonishing mariners needed twenty hours to cover the remaining 10 miles. We arrived at Rumbi at 1:00 a.m. The whole population, black and white, were on the bank to welcome us.

I think it would be difficult to imagine lazier creatures than these Tanganyika paddlers! The oars they use are rods [about 7 feet] long, tipped with little round planks not even as wide as an oar blade. They dip these sticks into the water and flick them backwards; that's the only kind of stroke they make. They don't use any back muscles to speak of, and the sum total of the work of eighteen fine, fit chaps consisted in moving their little boat along at the rate of one mile an hour in calm weather!

CHAPTER 14

LAKE TANGANYIKA
TO BUNKEIA

30 OCTOBER—13 DECEMBER 1891

Stairs's caravan enters the Congo Free State territory. A meeting takes place with Captain Joubert at his station. The devastation of villages by Arab slave-raiders creates difficulties in the procurement of food. Stairs is involved in a dispute between the local African chiefs and the Arabs. He expresses his views on the behaviour of the Arabs. As Bunkeia is approached, famine becomes rife. Stairs sends presents to Msiri and receives a letter welcoming him to his capital.

30th October Here we are now in the Congo State! Captain Joubert told me that all the important chiefs of Uarungu have come to bring him presents, ask him for soldiers, guns, and his protection against Rumaliza, Uabatuba, and other Wangwana. In his hunt for slaves, Rumaliza has been ravaging villages within only three leagues of Rumbi. He considers all the country along the west of the [L]ake [Tanganyika] as part of his domain. For him, whites are intruders whom he cannot tolerate on his territory and who must be chased away by force.

Captain Joubert is a thin, sinewy little man with a very dark complexion, and he seems in poor health. For nearly twelve years now, he has been living near the lake and has given up all thought of returning to Europe. He's a character apart, a real "squatter priest." He looks energetic and lives rough; he's like the farmers who clear the bush in New Zealand. He has adopted the native way of eating and makes do with what they eat. A former Papal Zouave, he was sent here to set up an obstacle to the slave-trade. He built a chapel and has devoted himself body and soul to the cause of the salvation of the negroes quite as much as any missionary Father. His station is very well built. It is set on one of the hills at the foot of the mountains bordering the lake, one and a quarter mile away from the Tanganyika and at an altitude of 117 feet above its level.

He's a real hero. For a very long time, he was all alone here, faithful to his post, toiling hard and exposed to innumerable enemies. This man, so interesting to observe, is a first-class gardener. His plantations are superb. He is adored but not much feared by the natives who surround him. Calm, patient, paying little attention to his appearance, always working, wholly given over to his hard daily labour—such is Captain Joubert.

The Wamarungu are small and thin, and don't seem very capable of serving as carriers. They have more than one thing in common with the Wanyika of Mombasa. Speaking to them, one immediately grasps the profound difference there is between the people east of and those west of the lake. The hair of the inhabitants here is curled and frizzy like that of the natives of the Congo forests. Their voices rise and fall when they talk, as among the natives of the Aruwimi, but not in so pronounced a way. Their teeth are filed, their foreheads narrow and their general appearance is that of a race a little inferior to the one that peoples the country between the lakes and Mpwapwa. Set next to an Unyamwezi carrier, these people look like mere sticks.

From time to time one sees here cowries set in a head-dress or used as adornment.

The Tanganyika is a glorious lake with its fine, clear blue water resting in the midst of high-peaked mountains. What a lovely holiday spot and what delightful resorts could be built here once the direct line has been established by way of the Nyasa and the Shiré!

31st October Here we are, at last, en route again after a halt of twenty-two days on the banks of the lake. We camped at Monda, a little village two hours WSW of Rumbi. Smallpox is raging in the countryside. If we were infected, it would be a disaster for the expedition, for the news would spread and access to Msiri's country would be denied us on leaving Rumbi. We climbed to an undulating plateau 1,667 feet above the lake; it is furrowed by rivers with flowing water. We greeted them like old friends we hadn't seen for nearly three months. The trees are a fine, vigorous green and the soil is of red clay, a deeper colour than that on the Karema side.

One encounters less arid sand and the humus is deeper than on the eastern side of the lake. *Mahogo* is planted here, not in rows but in little hillocks a foot above the soil. Maize is the natives' staple food but it has not yet been planted, as the rains only really start to fall after the 15th November.

A large number of Wamurungu wear their hair long and twisted, like the Wagogo. They lengthen it by tying a long slender thread to each hair. That doesn't add very much to their beauty from our point of view, but they consider themselves very fine fellows decked out like that. Amongst themselves they speak five or six dialects, but near the lake, a great number of individuals speak a mixture of Kiswahili and Bantu. One also meets here people from Itawa and Unyamwezi.

1st November March to Gawe (east) which took us four [and] three-quarters hours. We were held up for one [and] one-half hours at the Mlagizi River; it took us this time to get the men across. It's a swift current of water and strewn with rocks at the place we crossed. To [the] right and left from the point where we viewed it, there are stretches of calm, deep water.

We are camping on the banks of the Kala, which gives its name to the little district Kala, whose chief, named Chula, lives in Gawe (west). Chief Gawe, subject to Chula, is like the latter, a Manyamwezi.

Chula once used to live in Msiri's country, as did Kassongomono, chief of Kassanza. Along with the others, they were chased out of the country and built a village at Kassanza. Later Kassongomono put Chula at the head of the Kala district.

Leaving this, one arrives at Kalola, whose chief is Kabongo, a Marungu. After Kabongo, one arrives in the country of Makatubu, the slave of Mohammed bin Suleiman bin Shaash of Zanzibar. After crossing the Rudifwa River, one gets into the country of Kakwale where Katumba is in command. This region is famous for the salt which is found there and which sells cheap.

The Lufuko is the Marungu frontier. Northwest of this river is Urua; SW, the Rufira or Lufira. The Arab, Kafindo, built his Mussumba on the Luapula where it joins the Lukenni, about [a] three days' walk to the south of Mpueto-Uturutu. The Baluchi, whose real name is Khamis bin Salem, now lives in Urua. He was beaten by Msiri and wants, I think, to keep a safe distance between him and the latter. Kafindo, as far as I can tell, is a friend of Msiri's.

Of the six splendid donkeys we had, now only two remain to us. Our nights are no longer troubled by their piercing brays, for the four strongest and bravest have bitten the dust. My fine little donkey was stricken with paralysis at Karema. I had to leave him behind and at the mission, buy a young donkey from Unyamwezi. The donkeys were placed on board, one at a time, under the care of the donkey-boys. Of the ten donkeys embarked, four died at Rumbi as a result of this voyage and of the barbarous cruelty of the donkey-boys who, to keep them quiet on the boat, tied their legs so tightly that the skin and muscles were destroyed. My animal was bound so tightly that three of the poor beast's hooves fell off.[..]

I forgot to say that my two boats, the *Dorothy* and the *Bluenose,* crossed the Tanganyika in very good conditions, towed by the boats or sailing in front. The *Dorothy* arrived four hours before the other.

Altitude [of camp]: 5,333 feet.

2nd November Marched for an hour to Gawe (west) where we camped so the men could get food for the three days we're going to have to cross uninhabited country. This region has been ravaged and depopulated by Makatubu. There is not a single village remaining along a 35 mile route.

Altitude of camp: 4,233 feet.

3rd November Arrived at Kaomba, a cluster of huts, in six hours [and] fifty minutes, covering a distance of 10½ miles.

This morning we went through our first heavy downpour. For an hour we were soundly drenched and the men seriously inconvenienced. At the camp, we were at last able to light a fire. The chief of this cluster of huts is Nanza, the country is called Kalalo, the village, or rather the huts, bear the name Kaomba, and the chain of mountains nearly 3 miles to the south is called Kalalo. Nanza was absent when we arrived; he has gone with his men to do battle against Kaiavalla, an enemy of Joubert's, who lives [a] two days' march from here.

Along the route, one sees many deserted villages and plantations, which proves that Makatubu has been completely successful in his attempt to devastate the land.

The natives fled at our approach, but I sent men to tell them that I wished them no harm, that I urged them to come back, and that very evening a great number returned.

The altitude of this camp is 5,777 feet—the greatest height the expedition has attained up till now. The country is mountainous and covered with bush. The trees stand apart, that is they don't grow in groups but separately; they are twisted, the trunks crooked. Here and there long grass shows through between the trees, but as a general rule, the grass is short and grows in little green sprouts. On all sides streams run towards the Lufuko, which makes a great change after the march across dry lands like those east of the Tanganyika. The mountain air is fresh and pleasant and every night the thermometer reads 65°F.

I have not yet encountered woods, properly speaking, but to the west of Lufuko there are, it appears, trees of 6 feet in diameter. The natives make boats out of them.

4th November Five hours [and] ten minutes' march almost as far as Makatubu's old camp, now abandoned. We met some men and women returning from Mpueto's district, near Lake Mweru, where the [River] Luapula flows out. They were forced to flee before the man of Kafindo, the Baluchi, who lives three days lower down than their village. The promoters of this devilish destruction are Kafindo and Uturutu, two Baluchis who live on the river, and Makatubu, a man from the coast who is in Zanzibar at this time. The country has been absolutely reduced to the state of ruin by these individuals; the unfortunate natives were forced to flee into the mountains to save their lives and they are dying for want of grain to eat.

There is much work in Marungu for Joubert. If he gave flags to the strongest chiefs and got them to form a confederation against these brigands, he could sit peacefully at home with the certainty that the Arabs would shortly retire west of the Luapula and that his region at least would be rid of a crowd of Moslem half-castes, the torturers of unfortunate natives too weak and cowardly at the moment to resist troops armed with guns. But if I am lucky with Msiri, and if I can pacify just a small part of his kingdom, how happy I would be to pounce on these villains! But that doesn't stop me from blaming the natives. In fact, even when they have powder and guns at their disposal, they flee, abandoning their wives. They never set up a watch at night or in the early hours of the morning. And yet, it's invariably at those moments that raiders attack the villages.

These raiders, in the service of Arabs and half-castes from the coast, give themselves grand airs, styling themselves Wangwana—free men—whereas it would be very difficult to find amongst them a single man from the coast who is not a slave or even the slave of a slave. Add to these individuals, who are Washwahili, some Wamerima and some Wanyamwezi, add also *Rugga Ruggas,* and you have thieves of all races and all tribes—from the east of Lake Tanganyika, from Ujiji, Tabora, Karema, Gongwe, Igonda, and other places—who have signed up for the sheer delight of wrecking and pillaging, and are moved by the hope of amassing wealth by selling slaves. Very often too, they take up this terrible trade in order to carry a gun and call themselves Wangwana. There are, in their number, many Manyuema belonging to Tippu Tib and other Arabs and who are, consequently, slaves.

A few heavy showers fell this afternoon and I think that the rainy season has definitely begun.

The Lufuko is a mile from the camp SWS [sic].

5th November We marched for four hours [and] ten minutes and camped three-quarters of a mile west of the Lufuko. We crossed the Ruvugwa and the Lufuko in a single stage. The Rufuko or Lufuko is, at this place, a waterway 8 to 10 yards wide, very rapid with pure, fresh water. At the height of the rainy season it floods a large area and discharges a considerable volume of water. The altitude of the point where we crossed is nearly 1,500 feet above the lake. To make such a descent, [the waterway] must be very rapid and precipitous; in fact, it runs from here to Mpala, where it joins the lake.

We passed by the former village of Makatubu, once a fortified, well-built place, but now in ruins. I estimate at eight hundred the number of people who must have lived in the *boma*. The countryside we crossed looked delightfully fresh and green. Oh, if I could only have 50,000 acres of similar land in a temperate climate, in New Zealand for example! I would then be absolutely independent. One could raise at least three sheep to the acre the whole year round. The sale of the trees would cover the construction costs of a house and a storeroom for the wool and would be enough, besides, to enclose the whole property. The soil would be suitable for every type of crop.

Makatubu must be a cunning man, as capable of using his head as his gun. He presented himself at first in the Lufuko Valley as a simple ivory-trader and must have asked the short-sighted chiefs of the country for permission to build his station. This permission was granted him, and, little by little, he attracted more and more soldiers around him and fortified his *boma*. One fine day, he threw off his mask and defied all the chiefs of the region. It was too late to protest against such an iniquity. As quick as lightening Makatubu's slaves fell upon the villages, shooting, stabbing and capturing every man, woman, and child.

The natives were reduced to camping in the mountains and sleeping out of doors. It took Makatubu three, or rather two, years of pillag[ing] to depopulate this valley completely. Then he crossed the Tanganyika at Kirando to sell all his human booty and ill-gotten ivory. Today he is in Zanzibar, rich and yet still the humble slave of Abdallah Shaash, the Arab you meet in the streets of that town and who says *"Yambo"* to you.[1]

Here I shall ask a question that must occur to everyone who has crossed this valley and seen the ravages caused by this man. Would it not be a thousand times less expensive for anti-slavery societies to seize and lock up for life men like Makatubu while they are at the coast, instead of sending expeditions here charged with putting an end to the slave trade and which do absolutely no good and cost a good deal of money? If Makabutu and Abdallah Shaash were imprisoned in Zanzibar, many other populous, fertile lands, would be saved and would be spared the fate of the unhappy regions we are now crossing. It certainly wouldn't cost the anti-slavery societies much. As things stand at the moment, Abdallah Shaash is a man who, in Zanzibar, is as good as any European, and who tells himself that the whites are downright fools. I have heard that Makatubu is organizing a large caravan of gunpowder, cloth, etc. That is being done openly at this moment in Zanzibar, where it is known that he is getting ready to come and conduct new raids in the Free State using Kirando as his base of operations!.[...]

The chiefs, without the least mistrust, authorize an Arab to enter their territory with a fixed number of guns in order to trade, that is, exchange ivory for gunpowder, cloth, hoes, etc. The Arab arrives with his soldiers, chooses a healthy spot that he first examines from the point of view of facility for his future attacks, and very shortly, is comfortably installed. He is a past master at intrigue, has great presence of mind, a good deal of composure and is gifted with astonishing lucidity compared with the poor, *pombe*-filled brains of the native chiefs.

Here is how he proceeds: he begins by stirring up chief A against chief B. Then he allies himself with A to fight B and, when the latter is rendered powerless, he turns against A and routs him in turn. Then the pillage and sacking of the countryside begins. Right, left, everywhere, the Arab attacks the natives [who are] too limited and too attached to their village to think of allying themselves with neighbours to organize common defence. When the region is soaked in blood, when the population has completely disappeared, the

Arab retires. That is the history of poor African tribes. Although one is moved by pity for the natives, one cannot, however, prevent oneself from despising them because of their narrow selfishness, which blinds them to the point of taking from them every sense of danger.

I never stop telling the district chiefs that their own drunkenness and their craze for chattering are the surest allies of the Arabs and the half-caste[s] from the coast. In the very course of a war, the villagers neglect to set up a watch, when they know very well that it is always at nightfall that the hunters of human flesh make their raids upon them. The palisades which enclose the villages are built according to half a dozen different plans, and the enemy is in the centre of the place before the occupants have had time to realize what is going on and seize their guns.

The chiefs have such a good opinion of themselves that they consider themselves superior to their colleagues on the other side of the mountain, and none of them wants to stoop to unite with another in order to join forces and fight the enemy. And yet, generally, these little chiefs govern (very badly) territory of the size of a good Canadian farm. It makes me boil to think that the pride of these small tribes make them such easy prey to the Arabs and Baluchis who come here just to ruin and depopulate the country, and not to set up flourishing establishments like the honest, right-thinking white man. We Europeans also have our sellers of alcohol and our stealers of men but, certainly, our administration can be examined, checked and made the instrument of serious government for these unfortunate blacks who, very often, are incapable of managing their own affairs. Should authority over the negroes be exercised by the Arabs, the half-castes, or the whites?[...] I have no doubt about the answer—authority should be exercised by the whites to the exclusion of all others, and the sooner the better.

The country we went through yesterday was Kavugwa. Msaka is the chief; he has taken refuge in the mountain. Today, after crossing the Lufuko, we are in Ruanda [sic], an Urua district of which Mambwe is the chief. Marungu and Urua are divided into little chieftainships which do not depend on a central chief. Hence, the weakness of these two large regions. They could be turned to good account by the cultivation of sugar cane and rice and the pasturing of thousands of head of cattle. But, alas, the country is depopulated and ravaged to such an extent that we outsiders have been marching for four days without being able to buy even a pound of any sort of food.

Once cotton cloth used to be fabricated in these regions and is still made in certain parts of Marungu, Urua, and Fipa. It is solid, long-lasting material to judge by the samples I was able to see at Karema and elsewhere. The principal element in the clothing of the Wamarungu is, however, a sort of waistcoat-jacket made from the bark of a tree called *Mirumba,* which grows nearly everywhere. Rope, too, is made out of it. Certain other fibrous trees are also used, and in various villages one notices the tree, a sort of ficus [plant], from which cloth is made in Karagwe and Uganda.

6th November March of six hours [and] ten minutes from the Lufuko to the Ludifwa. The latter is a very swift little river which goes NW from here. Six miles further up, it suddenly turns SW and on into the Lufunzo, [a] tributary of the Luapula.

The country we have been through can be considered as some of the best in Africa for cultivation and the raising of cattle and goats. In my opinion, it resembles Mambwe in

Nyasaland. We did over 14 miles this morning, which is very good, given the great number of muddy creeks we had to cross.

Yesterday evening at five o'clock Dr. Moloney came to inform me that he had found another case of smallpox. What a catastrophe if this disease were to spread in my caravan! For two years now this plague has been rife in Marungu. It has now passed into Urua and spread, south and west, to Msiri's territory. Yet, it seems that few natives die of it.[2]

The rain is having its usual effect on my people: we have a great number of stomach-aches. I make everyone put up dry huts, but the men's clothing is so light that they are very subject to feverish shivers.

7th November We marched for four hours [and] forty minutes in the same undulating countryside as yesterday. Then we set up our tents just as a torrential downpour started, which thoroughly drenched the men who were not yet provided with shelter, but did no damage to the bales already covered with oilcloth.[...]

We saw bamboos, cardamom plants, and other vegetation with a liking for humid air. The cardamom brought back to me memories of former difficult days in the forests of Aruwimi, when we were with Stanley, and these plants were almost the only food our men had.

8th November We marched for five hours [and] fifteen minutes and re-crossed the Ludifwa, which is now 17 yards wide and very deep. It's now four long days since the men have been able to get food. They are hungry, and long marches make them weak. We have covered 60 miles in six stages, going up and down mountains, and have found very little food. Oh, how happy I would be to have my men eat their fill! These famines, caused by devastation, put me in a furious rage against the Arabs.[...]

I've heard of a caravan from the Nyasa which has arrived in Mpueto, north of Lake Mweru. The Wasumbwa say they are English. If that is so, it must be Crawshay's expedition which is going to found a station of Lake Mweru [sic].[3] I've also heard of another caravan travelling south through Urua. Could it be Thomson or else Delcommune?[4] One can't get any trustworthy information, and I'm not keen on sending off any more men now in search of news. The truth is that my caravan is so heavily laden that it is difficult to do anything other than drag it from stage to stage.

The chief, Mlamira, came to bring me presents. He's pure Kinyamwezi and leapt with pleasure when I suggested that he come with me to see Kassongomona to arrange matters. This is the situation: there is a whole crowd of villages here that are under the domination of three chiefs: Kassongomona, Mpueto, and Gwena. Two of these are Wanyamwezi. Up till now, the two Baluchis who are on the Laupula–Uturutu and Kafindo–have remained at peace with them. The Baluchis, strong in their *Rugga Ruggas* and their Wangwana [supporters], want all the ivory from elephants killed in their territory to be their property. The three chiefs are opposed to this, for they are great elephant-hunters. This difference has caused a rift between the Baluchis and the Wanyamwezi, which is getting wider every day. The latter have asked me to settle matters by giving them the flag and forcing the Wangwana to remain west of the Luapula.

It would be a perfectly simple affair if, on my side, I did not want to attract the good will of these same Arabs and Baluchis, who are powerful in this territory. If I don't get on with them, I shall encounter great difficulties on my path. And yet, I would like to do the

Wanyamwezi a favour and take some of them with me to see Msiri, for he is of the same race as they are, and that would be an immense step forward in the path of negotiations with this powerful prince. I have letters for Kafindo and Uturutu, and shall write some myself that I shall send from the Luapula. The former is at war with Msiri, which further increases my difficulties in Katanga, for if I were Kafindo's friend, that would not please Msiri.

The Arabs of Itawa have forbidden Mpueto, the chief of the northern part of Lake Mweru, to build a *boma* around his village. To that this chief replied that he was not the slave of any Arab and that he had been to Joubert on the Tanganyika to ask him for his help and a flag.

Kassongomona arrived in Katanga before Msiri, but he soon had to withdraw before the latter's power. In this part of Africa there is an extraordinary mixing of Arabs, Baluchis, whites, Wasumbwa and natives, all criss-crossing, some to obtain ivory, others to seize possessions of pieces of the country. It's a truly sad spectacle to see these splendid valleys formed of alluvial soil and rich in humus, which [are] fallow, except here, where they cultivate maize. Tobacco, rice, vegetables of every kind, sugar cane could be grown in abundance, and all one sees is maize and millet! The blacks of the interior are very fond of mangoes, guavas, and pawpaws, but the very simple idea of planting these fruits has never occurred to them. I noted this in Tabora and Karema, where not a single fruit-tree has been planted by the natives.[...]

When one asks a native why he does not cultivate these vegetables when it is so easy for him to get seed, he invariably replies: *"Mungu Makatara"* (God forbid). What is the origin of this fatalistic expression? Mystery! The natives have never even tried planting rice or special grains! In any case, the native is always careful to cultivate the produce that requires the least attention for the largest yield. It is rare to note, from one period to another, any improvement whatsoever in their way of life. There are explorers who, on their return to Europe, have so praised the African that they've come to consider their opinion the truth. Why act like that? As for me, I prefer to depict him as he is, with his good and bad points, and leave it to those who have not seen him at home to form their own judgement. The optimists who find everything perfect really do more harm to Africa and Africans than the most passionate pessimists.

I have a foreboding of calamity, but can't tell where it will happen.

9th November We arrived in Kassongomona['s] in four hours [and] fifteen minutes, after a march of seven days in the rain, covering a distance of 78 miles. The men have done quite well; not one has had ulcers. Mlamira has been with me since yesterday when we left the encampment, and tomorrow we are having a great *shauri* with all the Wasumbwa chiefs of the region about the doings of the Arabs and the Baluchis. The Wasumbwa claim that they have the right to the ivory they get from hunting, the Baluchis say the opposite, so war is imminent. It is absolutely necessary for me to remain on good terms with both for I want to take the Wanyamwezi chiefs to Msiri's territory. So I must take their side and that will constitute an offence to the Arabs and the Wangwana. The Lufira [River] is over half a mile away from here.

The place where we are is Kassongomona's *kwikuru*, that is, the headquarters or principal village of the chief who governs this region. It's as gross an error to call this village *"kwikuru"* and to mark it thus on the map as designate London by the name of "capital."

Between two downpours we are exposed to the torrid rays of the sun, and constantly being in this state of warm humidity is like being in a sweating-room. Every day we come across superb flowers, many of them totally unknown to us. In particular, I've noticed a little shrub bearing a red flower with a white centre, which gives off an odour of almonds. This plant is very common here.[...]

Kassongomona has five villages under his domination. He has just been to see me. He is a young man of about twenty-two or twenty-three, quite small but well built. He looks quite unintelligent and his eyes are vague, probably the result of dissolute living and too much *pombe*. He has succeeded old Kassongomona, who died some time ago, so ridding Msiri of a powerful rival for the possession of Katanga. He talked to me for an hour and a half about the affairs of the country, with which, moreover, he is thoroughly acquainted. But, he draws no advantage from this knowledge as far as his authority is concerned, for he is completely dependent on two or three intelligent advisers who tell him what to do.

He would like to attack Msiri, his father's old enemy, and would be quite ready to follow me to fight him. I made a point of getting him to understand that, as he is, in fact, an enemy of Kafindo's, if he went off with his men to fight against Msiri, leaving his village to the women's care, this would mean abandoning them and their children as prey to this Baluchi Arab. He had never thought of that and my observations made him change his mind completely *for the moment*.

War, as it is conducted here, involves not only a struggle between two parties, but also tribes outside the dispute. Each hastens to seize the opportunity to avenge personal injuries. If Kassongomona made war on Msiri, he would thus aid his mortal enemy, Kafindo, who is also in conflict with the chief of Katanga.

These personal observations have allowed me to see that there are few African chiefs here who have any originality of their own except perhaps for a special method of brewing *pombe*. Each one obeys the inspirations of the elders and only rarely makes a decision of his own accord. They are all distinguished, besides, by their eternal chatter, praising their own strength and mocking [that of] others. To prepare a war for a long time and weigh the chances of success are things no one thinks of.[...]

The story of Uleki, the chief who is following me with twenty men, is very strange. He had a quarrel in Katanga because of one of Msiri's favourite wives. This woman became pregnant. Msiri noticed this and soon discovered that Uleki had meddled in his affairs. He sent warriors to seize him, but [Uleki] managed to reach the Lualuba. Chased from there, he took refuge on the Tanganyika. The poor woman and his child died. Every child of a wife of Msiri's bears the name of Mwanangwa, this is, "son of the chief." There are several hundreds [sic], it seems, of these children.

10th November Lombi, another chief, has been to see me and [to] bring me presents and food. Although I gave Kassongomona three *vitambi,* he gave me nothing.[5] After much discussion, Lombi has promised to follow me.

At 10:00 a.m. the village elders arrived. We had a *shauri* lasting two hours. They promised me to keep quiet and to intervene as peacemakers between their men and the Arabs or Wangwana. I handed over the state flag to Kassongomona.

His father was still called Bundala. His father, the grandfather of the present chief, bore the name of Kafassia and was a contemporary of Kalassa, Msiri's father, one of the first Wanyamwezi to visit Katanga.[...]

When one has managed to get the men to understand that it is pleasanter to camp in the woods, far from a village, one has much more peace and quiet. Near a village, one has the annoyance of having at one's tent door a crowd of curious people talking loudly and roaring with laughter. Usually I chase them away but today I can't, for I have to make a bid for the friendship of these people.

Near Kalola I picked up an iron ore which is either *specular oligist* [sic] or else magnetic iron. It is dark "iron grey," striped with black streaks, and from that I've concluded that it must be magnetic iron. *Specular oligist* [sic] has streaks of dark cherry red. If the same mineral is specular (red haematite), it is very valuable, and there are immense deposits of it on Mount Senga.[6]

12 November Walked for four hours [and] thirty minutes to Gwena, on the Luapula. At ten o'clock, we arrived at the Lufunzo. It took us two and a quarter hours to get the column over to the other bank. The river is over 50 yards wide and, at this moment, waist-high. It empties into the Lualubu about 5 miles below Gwena. What a magnificent spectacle to behold, at such a distance from the sea, this Luapula so large, so imposing, so powerful. I am reminded here of the Aruwimi. Before us rises a high steep mountain which plunges its base in the river.

I expect to have to stay here for five days but, from tomorrow, I shall begin sending my men across. I'm waiting here for Kafindo and also Mpueto, the chief of the large village on the Mweru, who wants to fly the state flag. He has been to Joubert to ask for it. Tippu Tib is powerful here, and his authority makes itself felt as far as Itawa. Rumaliza, his lieutenant, is an active, far-sighted man.

Chief Gwena is a Msumba and is subordinate to Kassongomona. He lives on an island in the middle of the [Lufunzo] River, but he has plantations on this bank. I think he favours the whites but, until now, it has been difficult to guess just what these Wasumbwa want. *I* think that they would like to chase away the Arabs with the help of the whites, then chase the latter in turn and so keep for themselves the land and the ivory.[...]

13 November My day has been very taken up in parleys with Gwena and the other chiefs. I've sent a deputation to Mpueto to ask him to send me some of his elders to listen to what I have to tell them. I've chosen a good point for crossing the river, down-stream from the island where Gwena is built. We shall transport our men as far as an island which is at that spot and, from there, they will wade across. From this island to another, there are 2 feet of water, and then one lands on the firm soil of the left bank. The bed for the river is rocky, but the current isn't strong. Even with a small boat, one must proceed with extreme caution, for fear of seeing sharp rocks stave in the hull. One couldn't launch a steamer on this mill-pond. It is possible that in January, however, when the river is in spate, the flow changes in this spot.

Crocodiles abound and fish also, though the natives don't seem to catch many. Unless they are starving, the Wasumbwa, like many other members of the Wanyamwezi tribe, never touch a fish. They consider it as food unfit for eating.

They are afraid of water and yesterday, crossing the Lufunzo, the Wanyamwezi carriers were the only ones to drop their loads. On the plains they are excellent carriers, but in woods, in mountains, crossing water, they don't have half the assurance and skill of the Zanzibaris.[...]

It was Kafassia who was the first Msambwa to penetrate Katanga. Kalassa followed him and made war with him. Kalassa was Msiri's father. After his father's death, Msiri chased Kafassia from the country and so became the only chief in the whole region. One sees that Msiri is not ashamed to make war, even on his compatriots who came with him from Ushirambo to Unyamwezi.

Food is expensive and scarce. Before us lies a five day *pori,* that is, five days of forests without provisions.

Oh, if only I knew where Delcommune is!

14th November Gwena village, Lualaba River, latitude 8° 09' 10" S, longitude 29° 09' E.

It is six months now since I left England, and I am approaching Msiri's kingdom. We have done some good hard work during that time, and it is to be hoped that this will be fertile in happy, lasting results. I am waiting here for the return of our couriers from Kafindo and Mpueto.

This morning I sent my *tarishi* or couriers to Msiri. Their escort is under the orders of Massundi, one of my most intelligent headmen, and is composed of five Zanzibaris, a chief (Mlezi), three of Gwena's men and a crowd of women and children who are return-ing to their homes near Bunkeia. I'm sending Msiri, [...] in all, £140 worth of goods.

I am extremely impatient to know Msiri's reply. If there are whites at present in Katanga, it is impossible to say whether it will be favourable or not to our expedition.

Taking a dozen men with me, I crossed the [Lualaba] River and prepared a site for our next encampment. I had all the brushwood removed from the points of crossing. We have had a very full day, given over to remaking our loads, etc.

I can't manage to obtain a satisfactory reply from Gwena on the subject of carriers; I need at least twenty.

Two men from Kipiripepi, the Mgwana of Kirando, arrived yesterday on their way from Mpueto's. They say that there are two white caravans in Mpueto's area. The first is building a station at Maputa, one day south of the Mweru; the second is coming to build on the Mweru. I think that the real goal of the latter is to visit Msiri.[7][...]

There are many Wama and Wamarungu, and also some Mafipa and Batawa in this place. The real native of the country files his teeth and, when speaking, his voice goes up and down with that intonation peculiar to the men of the Congo forests. The language of these bushmen talking amongst themselves is more like the barking of a dog than any-thing else, especially when, for example, they call to one another from one bank of the river to the other. I saw only two of them at Ngwena's. I also met two rather suspicious looking fellows, who seemed to me as though they might well be cannibals from lower down.

Chief Ngwena has built his village on a long, narrow island, about 20 yards from the bank where we have camped. Further on and a little higher up, is another little village. On both banks and on the islands are plantations of white *mtama,* maize, and manioc. One also sees some banana trees, but there is nothing remarkable about these and they don't look at all like the banana trees of the Congo and the Aruwimi. On the west bank of the river, about half a mile behind Ngwena['s], mountains rise to a height of 1,677 feet above the water, and these, with the river and the forest in the foreground, form a most imposing landscape.[...]

15th November There was an eclipse of the moon last night; I was thus able to obtain an exact observation of the longitude and determine our position as being 29° 6' 45" E of Greenwich. The altitude of the river is here 3,060 feet. At Nyangwe['s] the altitude of the Congo is 1,450 feet. So there is a fall of more than 1,613 feet between this point and Nyangwe for a distance which does not exceed 300 miles.[...] This is enough, I think, to show that the largest part of this Lualaba or Luvua is not navigable. Lualuba is the name given to the river by the Arabs, who at first confused it with the real waterway of that name nearly 188 miles west of this. The natives give it different names but Luvua is the most common.

All three words, "Luvua," "Loa," "Lua," mean river or water held in ponds. Nearly all the rivers of this part of Africa bear the prefix *lu;* thus, Lualaba, Lumami, Luwile, Lufuko, Lufunzo, Lufira, Luvua, Ludifua. The letter *v* is almost never used by natives west of the Tanganyika; it is replaced by the letter *l*.

When rubber becomes rarer on the coast, this will be a privileged spot for obtaining it and sending it on by way of the Nyasa. I have read Cameron's *Across Africa* for the third time and gleaned many interesting particulars.

The Kamalonda is a river into which the Lualaba and the Lufira flow. The junction is at Urua, [a] fifteen days' march from here. Papyrus grows in abundance along the banks, and one notices in the forests and on the banks many trees which are found on the banks of the Congo and the Aruwimi. Growing side by side, there are cardamoms, bamboos, etc.

Ngwena is a well-built man, but he is ugly and wears the long earrings of the Wasumbwa, which makes him even more ugly. He is very sad about the eye trouble his son suffers from, and has asked me to cure this during my stay with him. Kipirpiri's two men declare that they are absolutely certain that the caravan which is crossing Itama at his moment intends settling at Mpueto and building a post there.[...]

16th November I got all the men to do an hour's gun drill this morning. After that I went down the Lualaba on the *Bluenose* as far as the Lufunzo, then I went a mile up this waterway as far as the rapids. It is, on the average, 56 yards wide and, at its mouth, has a speed of nearly 2 miles an hour; in the middle it is from 7 to 8 feet deep, no rocks or snags. I caught a silvery fish with a tail like a salmon's. Along the banks of the Lufunzo, there is much rubber, growing in tree form as well as in lianas. The fruit of the rubber tree is delicious when it is very ripe, and is certainly the best fruit I have tasted in the African interior.

At five o'clock this evening, Kiboia, one of the men I had sent to Kafindo's, lower down on the river, arrived in camp. He had left the others at Kafindo's to wait for a reply from Uturutu, who lives even further down-stream, at a distance of about two days' march. Kafindo has let me know that he is coming to see me the day after tomorrow. Uturutu will perhaps accompany him. I shall wait for them here. Kafindo is [a] three days' march from this place along the river, and Uturutu [a] five days' march. Kibaia tells me that the river takes roughly a northern direction to just near Kafindo's place. It is strewn with rapids and whirlpools and isn't navigable, even by canoes. Kafindo had heard of my arrival. He wants to go to Msiri's either to trade or to fight.

About 7:00 p.m. Msena Feruzi, one of the men I had sent to Lake Mweru to arrange matters with Chief Mpueto, has returned to camp. Mpueto and the chiefs under his orders will arrive tomorrow morning. Msena [Feruzi] tells me that he met Mr. Crawshay's men, of the government of British Central Africa, now building a post in Rhodesia at Kapunto's. He brought me a letter from this gentleman. I answered him this very evening, and sent on to him letters for Europe, asking him to give our couriers a letter advising me of the costs, conditions, etc., for the letters I have just passed on to him for Europe. I shall not be able to leave before the sixteenth or the twentieth at the earliest.

17th November Cold, rainy morning.

I was wrong in saying that the river rises by 4 feet during the rainy season. That is not so; it only rises 2 feet above its level in the dry season. The natives cross it all the time to go to Ngwena's. Even in the rainy season, the water only comes up to their armpits.

If Kafindo comes here, I shall insist on obtaining a short, quiet route across country to the Tanganyika. He may or may not guarantee this state of things as he pleases. It is always a second string to my bow to remain in touch with Joubert. If I had known that Khamis Ngoze would be so long, I would have sent Bodson to Mpueto with the flag.

About 3:00 p.m. Chief Mpueto made his entrance into my camp, followed by eighty men armed with guns, bows, arrows, and spears. They looked imposing.

I invited them to sit down in front of my tent and began the *shauri* by wishing Mpueto long life and good health. After a conversation on usual matters, I started on our business. I told him: "I have asked you to come so I can settle the quarrel which has gone on for so long between your people and Ngwena, so that the country can be pacified, [so that] the inhabitants plant their fields and harvest their crops in peace, and so that the security of all be more assured than it is now. I know there are reasons for your bearing a grudge against Ngwena, but he too will produce grievances just now against you and your people. If you do not take care, the Arabs will seize hold of your land and ravage it. The best thing for you to do is to remain quiet and cultivate your lands in peace."

Mpueto replied with a long speech in which he went over his grievances against Ngwena, but he eventually said that peace was better. I promised to hand over to him the flag of the Congo Free State.

Then I got Ngwena to come, and brought the two enemies face to face. I delivered an address for half an hour to Ngwena and said the same things to him as to Mpueto. That done, I addressed myself publicly to the two chiefs in front of their vassals and principal subjects. They were reconciled, at least outwardly.

Tomorrow morning the two chiefs will receive the state flag. This has been by far the most interesting *shauri* I've seen for a long time. The two chiefs are intelligent men and very jealous of their interests. They have done a fair amount of travelling and are very well up in the etiquette of a *shauri*. Mpueto is a well-built man, 5 feet 10 inches tall, with a big chest, well-formed arms and neck, a round, firm head, a rather wide face, and determined chin. The general effect is pleasing. When he smiles, as he often does, one sees that his upper teeth have been filed, but the points are now blunted. He can line up many more men than Ngwena, but in the event of war, the latter would be aided by his Wasumbwa brothers.

In all *shauri* there is always someone who disturbs the order by interrupting or talking at the same time as one or other of the important personages. Today an old grey, toothless man from Urua kept on chiming in in spite of the silences of the young men. We finally had to take his bow and arrows from him for fear of a mishap.

Most of Mpueto's people are Wawembwa like himself, but a great number of Warua live amongst them and, by their intrigues, often sow discord in the country.

The bows that I saw were good, tipped with well-wrought iron heads and strung with the gut of large animals. The spears are rough. The guns represent the usual incongruous collection of arms of all sorts.

I have sent letters to Jacques and Joubert on the Tanganyika.

Food is scarce. I would very much like to cross the river and penetrate into the south-west, but I have to wait for Kafindo and the other Arabs.

18th November Mpueto signed this morning the act of submission to the Free State. I gave him the flag; some askaris are going to hoist it over his village. I have also raised the flag at Ngwena's.

Kansalo set off this morning for Tanganyika with my letters for Jacques and Joubert. It takes five days of *tarishi* from Mpueto to the south of Tanganyika, and eight days for merchandise. It takes twenty days to transport goods from Mpueto to Msiri's, which means that from Msiri's I could send to Abercorn for cloth and get it in two months. Direct *tarishi* would go to Kasongo, north of Lake Nyasa, in twelve days (from Bunkeia to Mpueto), plus seven days (from Mpueto to the Tanganyika), plus eleven days (from the Tanganyika to Kasongo), to equal thirty days. From Kasongo to the coast it takes sixteen days; which makes from Bunkeia to the coast by the Nyasa, forty-six days. From Bunkeia via Ngwena and Rumbi to the coast it takes [...] sixty-one days. By the Nyasa route the letters are in Zanzibar in [...] fifty-one days, via Tabora in [...] sixty-three days. Difference in favour of the Nyasa route, twelve days. The cost by way of the Nyasa is a quarter of the cost through Tabora.

19th November We set off very early so that by 8:30 a.m. men, boys, and loads, all had crossed to the other side of the Lualaba. The boats functioned splendidly. The *Bluenose* took twenty-two loads of all sorts, and the *Dorothy* about sixteen.[...] The men all crossed very rapidly in ten boats lent by Ngwena. I am having great difficulty in getting twenty extra carriers; but one way or another, I must absolutely leave tomorrow.

I am tired of waiting for those lazy Baluchis who imagine that a white man marches as slowly as they do. Here we are setting up our first camp in Msiri's territory. He claims that his rights stretch to the Lualaba.

At 2:00 p.m., I was informed of the arrival of Kafindo with a following of fifty people. I installed him in a tent and had coffee and food served him. I sent him a fat goat, four pigs, six butcher's knives, four pairs of scissors, one *jora* of red *vitambi*, one of brown *kangu*,[8] two tins of Scotch snuff, about three hundred pins and a thirty shilling watch. In exchange I received a goat, a load of rice, and a bunch of bananas, with six fowls as well.

Kafindo tells that some months ago three white men left a place west of Urua to go to Msiri's. They came from Nyangwe['s] and must by now have arrived at their destination. That must undoubtedly be Delcommune and his expedition. I would like to be at Msiri's before Bia, who is in command of another expedition coming from the north.[9] It would really be a pity to arrive last. If I manage to fix my itinerary, I shall march as quickly as possible to Msiri's capital.

Kafindo is a Baluchi, cousin to Shadoli, who travelled with me to Tabora. He talks in an open manner, but one can't trust too much to what these people say. He would like to follow me to Msiri's, but I insist on getting him to understand that he must wait another six or eight months. I am very anxious that the route should remain open behind me, at least Mpueto's.

Kafindo's rice crop was not successful last year, and he has nothing left for a new sowing. I gave him some onion seeds. For four years now this chief has not been out of the country. He tells me that his *tarishi* take hardly more than forty days to make the return journey from here to Tabora. That's very fast going.[...]

Between 20 and 24 November Stairs managed to recruit some badly needed carriers. He also discovered that the Arabs intended to take advantage of his entering Msiri's territory to rob him of his ivory and slaves.

24th November   At two o'clock Uturutu arrived.

Game abounds; we shot not less than twenty-two antelopes and a buffalo this morning. The plains here are large and fertile; unfortunately, they are not cultivated. Red antelope swarm there. The Luwule flows in the middle of the plain; its bottom is muddy, which would make crossing difficult in the rainy period. Between the Lufira and the Luapula there is, according to the Arabs, a high mountain whose base is covered with thick forests, but the summit is bare and rocky. It is isolated and, according to the same source, must be about 10,000 feet high. It is called *Kilimani,* a word which quite simply means "place of the mountain" (*Kilima* means "mountain").

At an advanced hour Madjid, the Arab from Kassenga, came in his turn to the camp, and until the middle of the night, he and Uturutu remained chatting with me in front of my tent. I did my best to show them how important it is for them to leave the route I am following open behind me. I added that if the Arabs want to remain friends with the whites, they must leave the natives alone so they can sow their crops in peace, that we Europeans were tired of these raids, pillagings, and destruction of villages, and that, sooner or later, we would put an end to it. I told them that if they wanted ivory, they could pay for it like honest people and not steal it from the weak, harmless natives, then oblige them to transport it to Tabora. They replied that they were ready to obey me in everything and to help the whites, and Uturutu asked me to give him the state flag. In all fairness, I told him that Jacques would no doubt let him have one and gave him a letter for that officer.

Madjid is only a tool of Kafindo's, placed here like a wedge allowing the latter to penetrate, should the occasion arise, into Msiri's kingdom. From the strategic point of view, Madjid's post is admirably situated for that objective. In my opinion, Uturutu is far from having Kafindo's tact, shrewdness, and quickness, but of these two men it is, obviously, Uturutu who better deserves to be trusted, although both are fickle, elusive creatures. As for Madjid, I would only trust him if there was no other way out.

Kafindo did not ask for the flag, but if he learns that Uturutu gets it, he will, perfect Arab that he is, ask for it in turn. These two men are, besides, in a state of war against one another at the moment. I have written to Jacques to cultivate Uturutu's friendship, to use it, if need be, against Kafindo, which would greatly strengthen the position of that valiant Belgian officer [Jacques].

Our men stuffed themselves tremendously with antelope meat. There was more than 40,000 pounds [sic] of it in the camp.

25th November We have reached Kassenga, the post of Madjid, who has accompanied me here. This situation has been admirably chosen. At this time everyone is busy sowing rice and maize.

The earth is astonishingly fertile and there is a marvellous abundance of big game. North of this place there is an impenetrable, impassable marsh six days long by two wide. It is formed by the Luwule. There is an abundance of clay, good for wattling.

The native chief of Kassenga and Iera, which is part of Urua and stretches from the Luapula to two days SW of Kimwambula, is a Mrua called Mwepo. Chona, who lives one day NNE, is subordinate to Mwepo, and the latter is subject of Kafindo, the Arab who claims all the Luapula [River] as far as Kamolondo, where Uturutu's territory begins.[...]

I told Uturutu that the whites are tired of these Arab "salaams" given with a corrupt heart in exchange for valuable presents, earnestly solicited. I showed him that I saw into his game, and that I knew the worth of the word of the Arab who says to you, "The country is yours, master, and no longer mine."

He answered me, "There is Arab and Arab. There are good ones and bad ones. I am amongst the first." I know what to think on that score!

The Warua call Msiri "Mshidi." It's a corruption of the word and the natural Warua way of pronouncing it, for they are incapable of articulating any word in which there is an *s* or *r*. The Wasumbwu, the compatriots of the great chief, say "Msiri."

27th November Arrived at Chaowela, the settlement of Kimwambula the Msumbwa, which consists of four or five agglomerations emerging from the papyrus on raised mounds. Rich country, but deplorably poor in food. Oh, this reluctance of the negro to sow even what he needs to subsist!

The chief came to see me accompanied by his wives, decked out in all their finery. They have bead necklaces artistically arranged and some of the wives are really pretty. At first, black women are shy and don't dare accost the white man. But, little by little, they get bolder and finally grow familiar with him. The husbands love their wives, but not love in the real sense of the term, for very often the latter are treated on a level with beasts of burden, like a thing that every man must have, on a par with a spear or a gun. I can vouch for it, lewdness and vice are unknown among these Warua people. Married women respect the conjugal bond, and it is extremely rare for a girl to be seduced by a fellow.

We have had good hunting. The best African game is, in my opinion, guinea-fowl, then quail. Giraffe or antelope meat is excellent, but antelopes have a dry flesh, rarely fatty like that of the zebra or giraffe.

28th November We left Chaowela this morning and are camping on the Luwule (2 feet and 6 inches deep). Kimwambula came to pester me with requests for presents, talismans "to kill elephant." I gave him a few trifles.

Negro chiefs capable of giving the white man something without asking for a much more valuable present in return are very rare. This chief is like all his fellows, he considers us as a walking depot, an inexhaustible gold-mine; it is impossible to get it into their heads that our goods have to last several years and that there are chiefs more powerful than themselves who have a right to presents.

The Warua are very brave: they accost lion, buffalo, and hippopotamus head on with poisoned arrows. This poison is very subtle but they know of a plant antidote, which works on an external wound. I imagine that for an internal wound this antidote works by injection.

30th November For two days now we have been going through absolutely devastated territory from which the Arabs have caused all the inhabitants to disappear. No food, and yet how fertile the earth is here. What better and more eloquent proof of the need for the white man's presence.

The Kiniamwezi [sic] names for the snakes from which the natives of the region take venom for poisoning their arrows are: *putira* (a water snake); *ngossia* (a long snake); *fwira* (the viper).

It's still raining cats and dogs![...]

On 1 December the column arrived at Gera, having covered a record distance of 42 miles in two days. One could buy palm oil from the villagers who were getting it in exchange for meat and beads. A good deal of copper was also available. The local craftsmen worked it into shafts for spears and axes which Stairs found well made. The caravan descended into the Lufira River Valley and arrived at Kafuntwe in the neighbourhood of which there were very impressive falls 167 feet high (about 51 metres). Famine was rife as the crops were not yet ripe. Fortunately Bodson shot fifteen antelopes.

8th December We began our stage by crossing the Lufira at 5:50 a.m. By 7:10 everyone had crossed the bridge which I had got the men to construct yesterday. After a two hour march, we camped in the plains near the river which here, is at an altitude of 3,000 feet.

At 3:00 p.m., my couriers, returning from Msiri's, arrived at the camp. They had crossed the Lufira by the eastern route and gone on to Kifuntwe where they were told I had taken the western way. They have brought me a letter from Msiri, written in English by Mr. D. Crawford, a missionary and a colleague of Mr. Arnot's, another, in Swahili, from Msiri himself, and a personal message from Mr. Crawford.[10]

Here approximately is the news contained in these missives: until my *tarishi* arrived no one had any inkling of my presence in the country. Msiri professes good intentions towards me and begs me to arrive as soon as possible. He expresses the hope we shall be friends and asks me for two head of cattle. Mr. Crawford tells me that famine is rife in the country. For nine months now there has been guerilla warfare between Msiri and the Wasanga. A great number of people are leaving the capital during the night and going to join the enemy. The Bihé route is closed by the Wasanga and Msiri's son has gone to the Luabula to help Mr. Arnot return to Bunkeia. Mr. Crawford's colleague is Mr. F. L. Lane. The missionaries have no provisions and are living in a very frugal manner. M. Le Marinel arrived in the country six months ago and had much difficulty in obtaining authorization to build a station. He left two whites in the region, who put up a post east of the Lufira, a place where the missionaries also have their settlement. Another expedition arrived from the north about three weeks ago and, after a short stay, went south, five days away from Msiri's capital. One of the members of this expedition, Carl Hakansson, was killed on Lake Likonia by natives, while he was in command of the rearguard marching south.[11]

Msiri is thinking of leaving the country and going to Kazembe on Lake Mweru. What is prompting him to make this decision is the famine which is rife in the vicinity, the drought, and the continual warfare he is engaged in against the Wasanga. Msiri eagerly desires my arrival for fear, I think, of his enemies.

Here is the official text of the letter Mr. Crawford has sent me in the name of the great chief of Katanga:

From Msidi [sic], Chief of Garenganze and Katanga,
To the Englishman, Captain Stairs.
Bunkeia, 24th November 1891
Your five men arrived yesterday bringing your letters and presents.

Here are the cloths I received: one piece of white cloth, one piece of ordinary white cotton, and a piece of the same cloth striped, one piece of fine cloth and striped silk ribbon. I am happy to receive you in my land and you should not delay coming straight to my capital. I notice that you are an Englishman. This is good, for I know that the English are sincere people. You say that the Wasumbwa and the other Wanyamwezi are your friends. This is also good; they are related to me. I too am a Wanyamwezi. I desire to transfer my capital to Kazembe on the Luapula. I would like you to bring me from Kavunda an ox and a cow. I desire to be on good terms with you and am happy to learn that that is also your intention.
Your friend,
(S.) Msidi [sic]

9th December This morning at about eleven o'clock we crossed the Lufira where it meets the Lufua. The crossing was made in four hours, including the dismantling and re-assembling of my two steel boats. Then we bivouacked in the plains on the western shore of the Lufira. This has a crossing point 76 yards wide and over 40 feet deep; its waters are gentle, calm and tranquil.[...]

The plains look magnificent. They stretch SSW as far as the eye can see and are bounded only 15 miles to the northwest. Red antelope are legion. One also encounters buffaloes and occasionally elephants. Pasture is excellent. The Lufira flows through the plains from north to southwest, carving out a deep bed in the rich, reddish soil. Fish are numerous, crocodiles frequent, and on the banks innumerable flocks of water-fowl paddle and wade. Seven and a half miles down-stream from the spot where we are camping, the Lujuruwe flows into the Lufira.[...]

We are 42 miles from Msiri to whom I am sending Chief Mlagarazi as ambassador. The countryside is peopled with Wasanga, always ready to fight Msiri or his friends.

10th December After five and a half hours' march, we camped on the Lukuruwe or Likulwe, about 5 miles up-stream from where it joins the Lufira. It is a fine waterway, not less than 50 to 55 yards wide, 20 feet deep, and rolls along waves, muddied now by the rains, at the rate of 1 mile an hour. The banks are 33 feet high.[...]

Two of our men who went off at night to loot were seized by crocodiles while swimming across the water. Crocodiles are much more dangerous at night than during the day. All through the day, they stretch out in the high grass that borders rivers and lakes, sheltered from the sun, and only emerge at night. Then they fall upon all that is flesh. When it is calm, they like to warm themselves in the sun, but when there are people, they take cover in the grass. I think that a crocodile can swim at a speed of 16 to 20 feet a second; I've never seen the water parted with such rapidity. It must be easy for them to catch fish as they swim.

In the dry season, these plains must be completely bare. Above the Lufira waterfall, we saw a cloud of vapour more than 100 feet high continuously rising above the falls. Going by that, I suppose that these must look very imposing.

Without the antelope which we shoot by the dozen, we would die of hunger.

11th December   After four hours, arrived at Mlagarazi's village on the Lukuruwe. This place is marked Kwamirando on the maps, after the name of the chief living in the vicinity. In certain places the banks of the Lukuruwe are 43 feet high, and the river glides along all of a piece like a wave of oil with hardly a ripple, here and there, on its surface. It is 7 feet higher than in dry weather and nearly everywhere a steamer, drawing 1 meter [sic]* of water, would pass easily.[...]

13th December   Camped on the plain after a five hour march. We are over 6 miles from Bunkeia.

A Belgian, M. Legat, who had received a letter last night, came to see me.[12] The news he brought me is hardly reassuring. The Wasanga have risen everywhere in rebellion against Msiri, and the old potentate is dogged by the fear of seeing the whites join them and chase him.

He shows himself to be touchy, demanding, and selfish in his relations with the whites. He tries to get as much out of them as he can without giving anything in exchange. Mr. Arnot has remained at Bihé and Mr. Thompson, another missionary, has just arrived. After a stay of seven days, Delcommune left Bunkeia, going towards Tenki in the south. Since then, there has been no definite news of him. Of the Bia expedition there is no news whatsoever. The two Belgians who have a post on the Lufira belong to the Paul Le Marinel expedition. They have been here for six months and have built a station on the Lufoi, a little tributary of the Lufira which comes from the east. Their post is about three days from the capital. Le Marinel, his assistants and Mr. Swan [sic], a Scottish missionary who followed them, have set out again for Luzambo on the Sankuru.

There are, at the moment, three missionaries with Msiri. It seems to me that Delcommune intends going westwards to the Lualaba, then to follow the course of that river. He does not know that he is no longer in the service of the *Compagnie du Congo pour le commerce et l'industrie* (Congo Company for Trade and Industry) and that he is now in the service of the *Compagnie du Katanga* (Company of Katanga).[13] The Wasanga declare that they do not want war, but that their only aim is to obtain the deposition of Msiri, who is behaving towards them like a savage beast.

M. Legat has been ten years in the Congo. He served under Stanley and has forty soldiers.

The missionaries are, it seems to me, in a difficult position. Msiri treats them very badly. Famine is rife in the country as a result of the wars against the Wasanga, who are the real owners of the land.

---

*The inconsistency between Imperial and SI measures can be explained by the fact that the *Katanga Expedition Diary* was written for a French/Belgian market. Belgians would have been using the SI measures at the time of the Katanga Expedition.

CHAPTER 15
AT BUNKEIA

14 DECEMBER 1891—2 JANUARY 1892

Stairs arrives at Bunkeia on 14 December. He finds ample evidence of Msiri's extreme cruelty to his people, and there is strong opposition to his rule. There is scarcity of food, good drinking water, and firewood. Stairs meets Msiri on 17 December and reproaches him for his crimes. Two days later, during the second meeting, Msiri refuses to accept the Belgian flag. He moves to a nearby village. Stairs sends Bodson and Bonchamps to persuade Msiri to return to Bunkeia or, if he refuses, to bring him back forcibly. During a skirmish Msiri is killed and Bodson is mortally wounded. Stairs appoints Msiri's successor and constructs a fort for the safety of his party. Many local chiefs make an act of submission to the Congo Free State.

14th December Purely out of greed and a desire for destruction, cruel Msiri has ruined for all time a magnificent region. We arrived at Bunkeia at 9:40 this morning and camped near the capital. Mr. Crawford, one of the English missionaries, came to meet me.

My first impression concerning the town is bad, but at the moment I am holding back from judging too hastily. I shall limit myself to a single remark: we first recognized Msiri's headquarters by the whitened skeletons fixed to stakes all round one section of the town and by a hideous pyramid of human heads and amputated hands placed on a sort of rustic pedestal table at the door of this chief's dwelling.

I had a long talk just now with Legat and Crawford. Msiri was furious when he learnt that the former had come to see me without his authorization, and got it into his head that this officer is intriguing to turn me against him.

The famine is such that, even if one were to offer a treasure, one could not buy food— there is none left. Firewood is wanting and the water is execrable. The missionaries are treated by the chief on a par with black slaves. They are terribly afraid of him.

If the king were deposed, the country would immediately return to order, the Wasanga would be our friends and one could achieve great things.

With the help of 150 Boers [Dutch settlers in South Africa], the Portuguese defeated and captured the black chief of Bihé who had sworn to kill all whites who fell into his hands, and who levied heavy *hongos* on travellers. Learning of this from the Portuguese merchant Coïmbra, Msiri exclaimed that a white would never dare tie him up!

I see that our first care must be to look out for a solid position, build a station there and live on meat until the next harvest.

Having arrived on the 15th May, Le Marinel set off again at the beginning of July. Delcommune arrived on the 6th September, spoke loudly and firmly to Msiri, then set off again on the 5th October for the south after a long stay at the Lufoi station, Legat's post.[1] He remained a week with Lukuku, then went towards Tenke via Katanga. Our couriers arrived here on the 23rd November. Msiri's sons are Mukanda Vantu (the man who fights); Chifamina-Chamundu (two bullets in the gun); Chidanika (the true son) who is ten; Mafingi, son of the wife Mahanga, who used to be called Chitambo and who lives in Mkurru.[...]

The three English missionaries in the country at the moment are D. Crawford, H. B. Thompson, [and] J. F. Lane. The first has been here for a year, the second several months, [and] the third two years. Mr. Arnot is at Bihé with Mr. Faulkner and others. Mr. Swan [sic] has returned to Europe. The missionaries have built a post on the Lufoi near the Free State station.[2]

15th December Yesterday evening, by making earnest entreaties to Crawford, I got him to induce Senhor Coïmbra, the Portuguese [sic],[3] to send two Bihenos in search of Delcommune to tell the explorer what is happening and get him to come back.

The famine is frightful, we are living only on meat and beans.

I have got ready the presents to make Msiri during our interview tomorrow. Here they are: two bales of cloth, one of fine assorted qualities and one of *kanikis* [4] and mixed *joras;* five rolls of copper wire; copper buttons; large quantities of needles and thread; six pairs of scissors; six razors; and assortment of jewels each worth between 200 and 250 francs; six sabre bayonets of the kind used by the navy; my own sabre; a box of beads; snuff; various trinkets; worth in all 6,000 francs. But I don't hide from myself that the chief will not be satisfied: what he wants is gunpowder. And often!

The three missionaries came to see me this morning. While we were busy talking, a messenger came up from Msiri to announce to Mr. Thompson that the missionaries may not go tomorrow to their Lufoi post, as they intend, unless they pay the chief a piece of cloth. I immediately advised the missionaries to go and take shelter behind the Lufoi before serious danger begins. Consequently, they propose to set out all the same tomorrow morning. The English missionaries are responsible for the contempt that Msiri shows the whites. They have been too weak and forbearing. Msiri has taken advantage of this and now imagines that all whites are the same.

Even now I can see already that the missionaries are going to put spokes in our wheels. That will not prevent me from doing all that is possibly human [sic] to do to help them. Another side to the question is the presence in Bunkeia of two or three of Msiri's advisers, Moslems and people from the coast.[...]

Mr. Thompson told me that Sharpe arrived here in November 1890 with thirty or forty soldiers. On entering the town, the latter fired a salvo of shots, which enraged the black chief. Seven days later Sharpe left. He had made every effort to get Msiri to sign a document declaring the country English, but he failed. It was Mr. Swan [sic], the missionary, who acted as interpreter during the interviews.

The missionaries solemnly promised me to leave tomorrow morning for their station. That is necessary, for their lives are in danger here. One of them said to me just now: "Oh, how I would like to give my life for Africa!" I remonstrated with him, getting him to understand that his death would be the signal for that of many others, and that it was very selfish of him to be so anxious to go to heaven by escaping the danger that lies in preaching the gospel in this country.

16th December I heard that the missionaries hadn't left. I anxiously had them sought out. Motive of their hesitation: the rain which fell during the night.

Senhor Coïmbra came to see me. He's an intelligent man who, although black, likes to be called a white man. He has already been six times on the Bihé-Katanga route and one could have no better testimony than his as to the extraordinary change which has recently come about in this country. He told me that, three years ago, one could count ten villages where one now sees only one; that the mountains to the southwest were covered, just a few years ago, with flourishing villages. Today, not a single one is left standing. Msiri's cruelty has caused the exodus of the greater part of the population. My interview with him is fixed for early tomorrow morning. We will exchange blood. Such is the desire of the great chief, who has sent me a message not to lend an ear to the gossip of the other whites, "all bad people."

Senhor Domingo came to see me this morning, imploring me to put an end to the butchering of men that is going on every day.

17th December The missionaries have at last set off for the Lufoi, in spite of all the threats of this miniature Nero.

At nine o'clock the interview with the chief took place. First I gave him his presents. I didn't mince matters with him. I told him how Uganda, Unyoro, Unyamwezi, and the country of the Masai had fallen into the power of the whites, and asked him if he knew that the king of Bihé was in chains. I reproached him with his brutal cruelty and asked him to explain the half-dry heads fixed to the stakes around his village. I added that the whole region was in a state of complete desolation thanks to his barbarous proceedings, that he is responsible for the famine and death hovering over this unfortunate land, that it is he who chased the terrified people from their houses and fields. "Who then would dare plant any more? That is what has become of this wealthy region which as been so much talked of. A powerful chief isn't even able to provide me with a handful of flour! I've met on my way a number of chiefs much more powerful than you! You are only a minor chief, very bad and hated by his subjects. You must change your way of behaviour if you want to become my friend."

He answered me: "I want you, rather than any other white, to be my friend. The other whites are bad and are trying to set you against me, lying about me, whereas I am good, while the Basanga are bad."

I walked towards him then, and looking him straight in the face, I said: "I don't need the testimony of any other white to know what to think of you. How many heads are there on the poles around your quarters, some of them five days old? What have you done to the Wanyamwezi, always so mild and peaceful? Where is the food with which this village should abound? Answer these questions, and then it will be proved [sic] that you are the author of all these calamities."

Then turning round, I addressed the assembled people: "Is it you who want your heads cut off? Do you or don't you want to be able to put down your houses in peace, raise your children and lead quiet lives. If yes, I am ready to help you!"

Msiri

(from a photograph by Ivens)

While I was speaking so boldly, Msiri was trembling with rage and threatening me with violence. I went on regardless and showed him that his fits of anger did not frighten me.

The interview ended with declarations made by the chief in a milder tone: "This country is yours; you are my *Munungu* [sic] (God).[5] Do what you think for the best and remain my friend!"

I answered that I was quite willing to consent to be his friend, but on condition that the human sacrifices cease immediately.

There were about 150 people present, and six or seven of the chief's wives. One of these was really very beautiful, with regular pretty features, and certainly the most beautiful woman I have yet seen west of the Tanganyika.

First, there is one palisade surrounding the town, then a second contained within the first. There are thus two quarters in the town. The interior palisade protects Msiri's residence and is in good condition. The exterior palisade is not very strong. The king's residence is made of *pisé* (puddled clay) and was built by Wangwana from *mrima* (coast) who came by the Kilwa route. The main square is clean but infested with weeds, and the number of adult men one meets in minimal. The huts are round with thatched roofs, just like the usual sort.

Msiri was wearing a woman's robe, made of red and white pieces of *kaniki,* flannel and cotton. He had a shell necklace—[a] mark of supreme sovereignty—had powdered his face with flour and put feathers in his hair.

As far as one can judge under the layer of flour with which he had masked his face, his features are full of sly craftiness. His laugh conjures up the memory of the human heads, fresh and grimacing which are strung along the stakes of the town. I counted a hundred of these hideous trophies. Some of these heads still preserve the expression they had at the moment of death, offering a weird, baleful testimony to the chief's cruelty and barbarity. When each man came up to greet him, one could feel the state of abject terror that gripped the unfortunate person admitted to this perilous honour.

18th December Legat tells me that Msiri spent the night in the village of Maria, making a great row and in a terrible temper, declaring that Legat had set me against him, and that the fire which had followed the explosion on Le Marinel's arrival—a fire which destroyed the present the king of the Belgians had meant for him—was a fire which had been lit on purpose.

The crafty old man is busy plotting something. I, for my part, don't lose an opportunity to repeat to his people that if they keep too close to the king, it won't be long before their heads are crowning the pillars of the *boma,* and I liberally hand out *bakshish* (tip) to make friends for myself.

If, after a second interview, I can arrange matters in a suitable way, I shall go towards the Lufira, where there is meat.

Bunkeia is halfway between two hills which overlook the *kwikuru* (capital) and does not have any defence works. The hills completely overlook the entire town. The Unkeia, a little river, flows alongside the town, but in the dry season, the inhabitants have to go far away to get drinking water. The result is that, washing so seldom, they are very dirty.[...]

19th December It rained last night. Msiri has let me know that he will receive me at 1:00 in the afternoon.

I received the visit of Mukanda Vantu and got him to sense what a ferocious, brutal creature this Msiri is. This fellow has unbounded ambition.

At 2:00 p.m. I visited Msiri. He told me a long, incoherent tale of the way in which he became master of the land; he chased the Wasanga and curses them as the cause of the war and ruin of the land. "You are," he added, "the only white man left me as friend." Delcommune, he said, fled from fear.

I replied that he, Msiri, is the only person responsible for the war which is rampant, and that he certainly didn't become master of the land to massacre its people. "You are bad and your people hate you. As for Delcommune, you are lying. He left because it suited him to do so."

Msiri started speaking again and went on for a whole hour. Once or twice he went into a rage, but each time he raised his voice, I lifted mine still higher.

After three hours' debate, I told him that since he is my friend and since I am shortly going to the Lufoi to shoot the game I need for my provisions, he should accept the flag and fly it in order to show the Wasanga that I am his friend. He answered me, "No, I refuse, for first I want to see if you really are my friend."

After another argument which lasted half an hour, he promised me to raise the flag tomorrow, when I had exchanged blood with his brother Kikako. I replied that that didn't suit me. Finally, with dusk approaching, he rose to retire to his dwelling. Then I said to him, "Good! If that's the way things are, I'll do without you and raise the flag myself."

Taking with me a picket of twenty men, I had the flag raised on a hill near the village. This act of authority has not provoked any disorder, and all night we are going to remain armed, ready for everything.

The king has left his residence and gone to a village an hour from here.

20th December Msiri fled during the night. The flag continues to fly on the hill where we placed it.

After vainly trying to get in touch with the chief, I started to march to the village of Maria. Next, I sent a troop of 100 men under the command of Bodson and Bonchamps with the mission of persuading Msiri to come and see me and, should he refuse, to lay hands on him.

Bodson and Bonchamps left at 11:50 for Maiembe where the chief was with 115 guns. They divided their forces. Bodson went with twenty men to the centre of the village to have an interview with Msiri, and Bonchamps waited outside with the rest of the troop, ready to rush up at the fist signal. Msiri, it is evident, had prepared everything to seize hold of the white man and was surrounded by sixty armed men, of whom several had their fingers on the trigger ready to shoot. The chief was carrying the sabre I had given him.

After talking for some time, Captain Bodson announced to Msiri that he was to accompany him to come and see me. If he would not do so of his own accord, he would by force.

The chief replied, "No, I don't want to come," and at the same time he drew his sabre, which was a sign agreed on by the conspirators. At that very moment, a man sitting near Msiri raised his gun and aimed at Bodson. It was the king's son, killed shortly afterwards.

Seeing that, the determined Belgian officer drew his revolver and fired two bullets into the king's chest, on which Hamadi, head of the squad from Company No. 2, fired a shot in turn. Msiri fell dead on the spot. But at the same moment Bodson received a bullet in the stomach. Poor fellow! The bullet lodged in his pelvis, perforated the bladder and worked awful havoc. He was transported by hammock to the camp, in terrible agony. That same evening he died.

Msiri is no longer, his body is in our camp, but that cost us poor Bodson's life!

A number of shots were fired and, back at the camp, I was very much afraid lest the fighting spread and our troop be divided in two if the camp were attacked. Fortunately, Msiri was so loathed by his subjects that almost no one ran to his assistance. [Instead, they were] crouching in their huts to see what turn events would take. Everyone understood that our intention was not to fight until the moment we seized Msiri.

Bodson is dead, but he has delivered Africa of her cruellest tyrant. That was one of his last words. His very last, as he breathed his last breath, was the cry of *"Vive le roi!"* ("Long live the king!")[6] He was a soldier from head to foot, full of initiative and energy, devoted to the interests of the expedition. He never, even for a second, argued about the least order I gave him; as soon as the order was given, it was executed. He was a practical fellow, knowing how to turn everything to advantage and always getting through. The expedition and the Belgian army have lost a valuable officer at a most critical moment.

Everything is in the most complete disarray. I can do only one thing at the moment: restrain my men and keep them in the camp.

21st December Everyone has fled except Chamundu, who came to see me. I told him that since Msiri was dead, I did not want to fight and that my sole desire was to see peace and prosperity return to the country. I have given him Msiri's body to have it buried and had Mulumanyama invited to come and see me.

Bodson was buried with all possible solemnity this morning at eleven o'clock. The body was wrapped in blankets and sheets. It was the doctor who dug the tomb at the foot of the hills which are about 200 yards behind the village of Maria. The body was borne by the headmen of Companies [No.] 1, [No.] 2 and [No.] 3. When we arrived at the place of burial, I had the askaris present arms, while earth was piled on the grave where our poor friend now reposes.

We erected a temporary cross at the place where his head lies. When we have a little more time, we mean to raise a cairn with a large cross at this place.

Legat left us this evening at ten o'clock. He is going to the Lufoi. For extra security he is taking ten of my men with him. He is hoping to reach his station tonight.

I have written to the missionaries telling them to go to the state station until the country is more secure, and I've had my column move back to a native village over half a mile from the village of Maria. I'm counting on building a temporary station while waiting for the harvest to ripen three months from now. From there I shall radiate out, making little expeditions in order to understand the lie of the land.

There is not a shadow of hostile blacks at the moment. What is most important is to construct solid defence works, so I can go off without fearing for the safety of those companions I would leave behind. I estimate that it will take me a month to construct my fort. We have quite an assortment of seeds, and Legat, I hope, will give me the ones I don't have.

22nd December We have begun the construction of Fort Bunkeia. Trenches have been dug and two-thirds of the *boma* has been formed of pieces taken from Msiri's former headquarters. The tyrant's dwelling is going to be destroyed and the debris will serve to build the house for the whites. There are fine poles, straight and solid. The fort will take the shape of an irregular hexagon with three towers, a trench, and a bullet-proof parapet made of palisades and earth.[...]

On 23 December Stairs decided that before nominating the new king he should consult with as many chiefs and other people as possible. Meanwhile, the construction of the fort progressed and a lot of building material from Msiri's old residence had been used. On Christmas Day the men had a holiday and Stairs invited Bonchamps and the doctor to a lavish banquet. A day later he came to the conclusion that Mukanda Vantu, Msiri's son, would be his best successor. Chiefs began to arrive in order to sign an act of submission.

28th December Bonchamps is seriously ill. Robinson too. The men are feeding only on *mbogas* or garden herbs. Even the whites can find no food to buy. The famine is frightful. The three principal herbs eaten are: the *machicha*, the *mboga maboga* or pumpkin leaf, and the *cassamvo* or tender manioc leaf.

29th December Today has been an important day. I nominated Mukanda Vantu chief of the Wagaranze. I had him sign an act of submission and got him to raise a flag above his village. There were a number of people present and I impressed upon them how dangerous it would be to try and pick a quarrel with the new chief. Chikako declares that he is coming to see me now that a new chief has been elected.

I gave Mukanda Vantu my sabre as a sign of the power with which he is now invested.

We have done good work on the fort which is now starting to take shape. The trench will be finished tomorrow, I hope. Two of the towers are more or less complete. The storehouse, in the shape of a *tembe,* is finished, as is my house. A cabin of [about 88 feet] for the personnel is being completed. A second dwelling, for the Europeans, is almost near completion, as also are other works.

The men need to be constantly spurred on. They are beginning to grow weak through living only on leaves, and one has to be constantly at their side under a pitiless, leaden sun.

Still without news of the Bia expedition. I've been told of the approach of an expedition led by whites, which is going to cross the Luapula. It must by an expedition from South Africa. I have informed Legat.

30th December I have sent a letter to Legat and given another to two of my men for Delcommune. They have orders to go as far as ten days south in search of this explorer.

31st December Mutwila [a chief] is asking me for the flag and asks to make an act of submission. The whole country is in disorder. The people are fleeing without rhyme or reason and shooting at each other with the sole aim of provoking pillage.

My men, crazed with hunger, have become absolutely unmanageable. They are robbing the natives. They are real demons, nothing can bring them to reason.

For six days now I've had nothing to eat except green leaves and meat.

1st January, 1892 The new year opens under very gloomy auspices. The famine is terrible, so it has become impossible to restrain the men.

Moloney and I are the only two able-bodied men. Everything falls on our shoulders, so we are worn out.

Oh, what bad omens 1892 has for me! May God grant that this year should pass happily and that our enterprise should be crowned with success!

What a country of famine! "I'm hungry." That is the cry that follows me everywhere and always. And I have nothing with which to appease the torments convulsing the empty stomachs of all these men who believe in me. Curses on that Msiri, author of all this misery!

A starving man is no longer a human being, he is a sack of meat. There are no coercive means of mastering him. He cheats and pillages the native, and that in the name of the white man, who thus acquires, through no fault of his own, a hateful reputation.

All is suffering, anguish, and famine!

2nd January The men are getting very low for want of enough food. There will be no harvest, alas, until six or seven weeks from now. Poor devils! I pity them from the bottom of my heart, and yet I have to show a face of stone and force them on to work, for the fort must be finished. Evening comes fast and once the dark falls, body and mind are equally exhausted....

CHAPTER 16
BUNKEIA TO CHINDE

1 APRIL—3 JUNE 1892

Stairs deals with the threat of a mutiny. Exhausted with fatigue and anguish he falls gravely ill on 2 January. Marquis de Bonchamps and Robinson are stricken with disease. Dr. Moloney is in charge of Fort Bunkeia. Famine decimates Stairs's party. New crops become available in the second half of January. The Bia expedition arrives at Bunkeia on 30 January. Dr. Moloney decides to return to the coast. The caravan departs on 4 February. By the middle of March Stairs takes over the command and on 1 April resumes writing his diary. The caravan follows the Stevenson's Road and sails along Lake Nyasa, and down the River Shiré to the mouth of the Zambezi. Stairs's last entry in his diary is dated 3 June.

1st April We have reached Makapula. Food is scarce, the *Rugga Rugga* Wanyamwezi have destroyed all the crops, all the villages have been absolutely wiped out and the wretched natives are wandering in the mountains.

2nd April We are in Kaputa, 8° 12' latitude N. All the natives go in terror of the Wanyamwezi. I've obtained from the chief a guide so I can go to Mwanangwa in the southeast where there'll be ructions, for I mean to say a few words to the Wanyamwezi and show them they must leave the people alone.

We are still in Marungu, so in the Congo State, but the natives are Wawembwa. The highest mountain we can see is 7,300 feet in altitude. The altitude we reached going through the passes was 6,000 feet.

8th April We had to cross the Choma by boat, which was very difficult as the river has a current of 5 to 6 miles an hour. Sharpe's salt lake is only one day SW of here. The Arabs of the district are Ramatha, two or three Zanzibaris, Abdullah bin Suleiman, and Khaliel. The Portuguese of the west coast come to sell their cloth, across Msiri's country, as far as the Wasumbwa or Chidobi, three days west of Tanganyika.

28th April We left Kituta this morning. Tsetse is rampant, and even without it the cattle couldn't survive, for the water is swarming with tadpoles which grow in the animals' stomachs and kill them. I've seen Mr. Swan [sic], who arrived from Ujiji on his steamer, the *Good News*. He has given me a leopard from Rumaliza for the queen of England. I am going to convey this feline to England.[1]

2nd May   Here we are in Cherezia, five camps away from Kituta, or 50 miles from that place. Yesterday we had to cross the Saizi. This part of Stephenson's [sic] route has never, it seems to me, been remade.[2] In spite of that, one marches quite easily, except in some places. But what is really missing are bridges.

Along this route the natives are well supplied as far as missionaries are concerned. There are missions at Iwando, Mambwe, and Kinymkalo.

3rd May   We are at Mambwe, the station of the French Fathers. We were received with touching cordiality by Father Van Oost, a Belgian and two other fathers.

We ate a delicious salad, lettuces, onions, radishes, tomatoes, sorrel, potatoes, cabbages, beetroot, etc., and have our bags literally stuffed with fresh vegetables.

I've noticed that wherever French Fathers have set up a mission in Africa one finds good water, very clear and fresh, and admirable vegetable gardens.

What a difference from the English missionaries who, all year long, eat only flour and preserved food! The Fathers have been here only five months and have, in this space of time, made astonishing progress, which covers [sic] me with amazement.

I've never seen anything like it in Africa. They have a superb fold for their sheep and goats, a cowshed with twenty-five head of cattle, and are busy building a large stone house for themselves. Patient, persevering, and energetic, they have dedicated their lives to the success of their enterprise.

4th May   We marched 13 miles and are camping on the banks of the Komba after having twice crossed the Kalisi. It is the birthday of our queen. God grant her many more. I am sure that foreigners must admire her. She is an honest, upright woman who always acts prudently and rationally.

The march is delightful with shady trees along the route. If a little breeze were blowing through these, one would think oneself in England. We are making forced marches so as to arrive on the fourteenth at the Nyasa. We still have 224 miles to cover to reach it. If we miss the steamer, that could hold us up for a month. I wonder how, once in England in a few months' time, I shall settle into the ways of my new regiment, the Welsh Regiment.

5th May   A long stage to the Nyramwanga. Our men are very tired. The guide has absolutely no idea of the route to follow. Fortunately, this is well-marked and very clear. So it is relatively easy to find the way.

On 6 May the column arrived at Mwengo where the African Lakes Company was located, halfway between the Lakes Tanganyika and Nyasa. From there Stairs hoped to reach Nyasa in eight days. During the march many men wanted to desert. They attempted this whenever they were approaching a place where they could get a thorough rest, which was indicative of their state of exhaustion. On May 10 the column entered the so-called Stevenson route which in reality was a mere track. Four days later Stairs received a letter from Karonga notifying him of the arrival of a steamer on 12 May.

14th May   We reached this place (Karongo) this morning at 10:45 and were received by Messrs. Whyte and Lagher of African Lakes Company.

Doctor Moloney arrived two hours ago, having done 110 miles in five days. My men are wild with joy. Two hundred thirty yards from our camp we can see the Domira which is going to take us to Matope, 400 miles from here. It has taken us 100 days to arrive here from Bunkeia.

15th May The whole day was taken up with embarking the men. Here are notes that I am copying on to my agenda: "Seven great Katanga chiefs have signed an act of submission."

1. 10th November 1891: Kassongomwana, living in his *kurkuru* in Kassansa. Latitude 7° 56' 55" S; longitude 29° 16' E of Greenwich. He is a stupid young man who gets drunk night and day and lets himself be dominated by his sub-chiefs. Is very frightened of the Arabs.

2. 17th November: Mpueto, of Mpueto, chief of Kabuire and Bukongolo. Intelligent fellow. Is afraid of the Arabs.

3. 18th November: Gueno, of Guena, on the Lualaba. Latitude 8° 4' 44" S; longitude 29° 06' 45" E of Greenwich. He is a Msumbwa chief, an old enemy of Mpueto's. Fears the Arabs. Peaceable, sensible man.

4. 19 November: Kimwambula, of Chaowela. Msumbwa chief. Lacks intelligence. Great enemy of the Arabs and Msiri.

5. 3rd December: Uturutu, residing on the Lualaba. He's a true Baluchi. His real name is Mohomed bin Selim bin Rashid.

6. 28th December: Mulumanyama. Residence: Myinga. Is a Msanga. Enemy of Msiri's. Lives two days west of Bunkeia.

7. 29th December: Mukanda Vantu, of Bunkeia, on the Unkeia. Latitude 10° 21' S. Nominated by me as Msiri's successor, 29th December 1891. Son of Msiri.

16th May We left at daybreak. We are camping at Ruaria (Ruawe) 98 miles distant from Karonga. We are sleeping in the woods. The scenery is very grand in places.

17th May We have arrived at Bandawa where we took on board Mr. and Mrs. MacCallum.[3]

18th May Left Bandawa travelling day and night.

20th May Arrived at Cape MacClear, mission station of the Livingstone mission.

21st May We have reached Fort Johnston, a fort built to the east of the village of Mponda on the Shiré, and which overlooks this river as well as the entrance to the lake. This fort is very solidly constructed.

22nd May We are resting today at Fort Johnston. One of my men was taken by a crocodile last night. I had long interviews with Mr. H. Johnston, the governor of the territories of British Central Africa.[4]

23rd May We are camping at Mpimbi which, later, thanks to its situation, will become an important place.

24th May Arrived at Matope where everyone left the steamer. Navigation stops here.[5]

25th May Left early and after a stage of 22½ miles, we are camping on the banks of the Lungu.

26th May Arrived at Mandala (Blantyre). We have enjoyed delightful hospitality in a real English house.

27th May A 22½ mile march to Katongo. There we shall go aboard the *Lady Nyasa*.

28th May We set out for the sea on the *Lady Nyasa,* towing five boats.

30th May Arrived at Chiromo, a station with a great future, at the junction of the Ruo and the Shire.

The Admiralty has established a little dock here. On the other side of the Ruo, the Portuguese have a very well-kept post.

I was able to wire Quelimane [a port in Mozambique] thanks to the Portuguese telegraph system which goes from here to the coast.

31st May We are continuing our descent. We crossed two English gunboats which are going up-river.

1st June Yesterday we camped at Port Harold, and now we have just crossed the Anglo-Portuguese frontier boundaries. We made our night quarters at Morambala at the foot of the mountain of the same name. It is a Portuguese post.

2nd June We arrived at Vicente Pass at the top of the Zambezi delta at 5:00 p.m. Vicente was once a very important place. Passengers and merchandise were then brought along the Kwakwa River and transshipped here. It is at Vicente that the ascent of the Zambezi used to begin.

3rd June We are stopping at Vicente to allow the up-going [sic] boats to pass.

Here Captain Stairs's diary ends. After the 15 May the entries became brief and staccato. One feels that the diarist was unable to pay the same attention, as before, to the details, and not even to such an important event as his meeting and a long conversation with Harry H. Johnston, who congratulated him upon the success of his expedition. Stairs also failed to report the mechanical breakdown of the SS Lady Nyassa, *and some navigational problems which had caused a serious delay.*

On 5 June the expedition arrived at Chinde, on the Indian Ocean. The steamer that was to transport it to Zanzibar was late. It arrived on the 8 June, but Stairs was not able to embark. Suffering a fatal attack of malaria, he passed away on the evening of the ninth. Thereupon the Marquis de Bonchamps took over the command. The expedition disembarked at Zanzibar on 20 June. One month later, the European survivors arrived at Marseilles.

Captain William G. Stairs's grave at Chinde

Appendix A

Chronological Table Of Events

1863 1 July William Grant Stairs born.

1878 Emin (Edward Schnitzer) appointed governor of the Equatorial Province.

1878-82 Stairs at Royal Military College, Kingston, Ontario.

1881 The beginning of Mahdi's uprising.

1882-85 Stairs in New Zealand as civil engineer.

1885 Stairs at Chatham, England. Attached to the School of Military Engineering.

1885 June Stairs gazetted lieutenant in the Royal Engineers.

1885 July Emin retires to Wadelai.

1886 Emin Pasha Relief Committee organized in England.

1886 December H. M. Stanley assumes the leadership of the Emin Pasha Relief Expedition.

1887 January Stairs accepted as member of the Emin Pasha Relief Expedition.

1887 20 January Stairs departs from London for Africa boarding SS *Navarino* at Gravesend.

1887 28 January Stanley meets Dr. Junker at Cairo and employs Dr. T. H. Parke as member of Emin Pasha Relief Expedition.

1887 12 February At Aden. Stairs boards SS *Oriental.*

1887 22 February At Zanzibar.

1887 25 February Boarding the SS *Madura* with Tippu Tib and his party on the way to the Cape of Good Hope.

1887 8 March At Cape Town.

1887 18 March At Banana Point.

1887 20 March At Matadi.

1887 24 March The march to Stanley Pool begins.

1887 28 March Herbert Ward volunteers as a member of the Emin Pasha Relief Expedition and is accepted by Stanley.

1887 21 April At Stanley Pool.

1887 1 May The expedition's flotilla steams up the Congo River.

1887 12 May At Bolobo.

1887 19 May At Lukolela.

1887 24 May Crossing the equator.

1887 30 May At the Bangala State station.

1887 2 June The boat *Henry Reed* takes Tippu Tib and his party to Stanley Falls. They are accompanied by Major Barttelot and a detachment of askaris.

1887 6 June At Upoto.

1887 12 June At the junction of the Congo and Aruwimi Rivers.

1887 15 June At Yambuya.

1887 28 June The departure of the advance column for Lake Albert, leaving behind the rear column at Yambuya under the command of Barttelot with Jameson as the first officer.

1887 13 August Stairs wounded with a poisoned arrow near Avisibba.

1887 17 September At Ugarrowwa's.

1887 6 October Nelson and a group of sick porters remain in the camp while the column marches toward Kilonga Longa's village.

1887 18 October At Kilonga Longa's (Ipoto).

1887 26 October Jephson returns to the temporary camp under Nelson's command at Kilonga Longa's.

1887 13 November At Ibwiri.

1887 16 November Jephson rejoins the column.

1887 30 November Sighting of the open country after 160 days in the forest.

1887 13 December At Lake Albert.

1887 15 December At the village of Kavalli. Unsuccessful attempt to find Emin Pasha.

1888 7 January Back at Ibwiri where Fort Bodo is to be constructed.

1888 19 January Stairs leaves for Ipoto (Kilogna Longa's) for the relief of Parke, Nelson, and their men.

1888 25 January Arrival at Kilonga Longa's.

1888 8 February Parke and Nelson arrive at Fort Bodo.

1888 12 February Return of Stairs, to Fort Bodo with the steel boat *Advance* which was left at Ipoto.

1888 16 February Stairs leaves for Ugarrowwa's.

1888 14 March At Ugarrowwa's.

1888 2 April Stanley, accompanied by Jephson and Parke, leaves Fort Bodo to establish a camp at Kavalli's and makes another attempt to find Emin Pasha.

1888 18 April Stanley receives a letter from Emin Pasha written at Tunguru and dated 25 March 1888.

1888 21 April Jephson departs on the *Advance* in search of Emin Pasha.

1888 22 April Jephson arrives at Mswa, Emin Pasha's station on the east coast of Lake Albert.

1888 26 April Stairs returns to Fort Bodo. Jephson meets Emin Pasha.

1888 29 April Emin Pasha arrives at Stanley's camp near Kavalli's.

1888 24 May Stanley departs from Lake Albert, leaving Jephson with Emin Pasha.

1888 8 June Stanley returns to Fort Bodo.

1888 11 June Barttelot marches to Banalya.

1888 16 June Stanley leaves Fort Bodo for Yambuya to bring the rear column. He takes with him Dr. Parke who is to recover the loads left at Kilonga Longa's. Stairs assumes command of Fort Bodo.

1888 6 July Parke returns to Fort Bodo.

1888 19 July Barttelot murdered.

1888 17 August Jameson dies of bilious fever at Lomami. Stanley arrives at Banalya and learns of the sad fate of the rear column.

1888 19 August Emin Pasha and Jephson imprisoned at Dufilé by the rebels.

1888 10 November Dr. Parke extracts the tip of the arrow from Stairs's chest.

1888 17 November Emin Pasha and Jephson, released by the soldiers, leave Dufilé for Wadelai.

1888 5 December Retreat from Wadelai to Tunguru in fear of the Mahdist invasion.

1888 20 December Stanley returns to Fort Bodo from Banalya with Bonny and the remnants of the rear column.

1888 23 December The expedition abandons Fort Bodo and marches to Lake Albert.

1888 30 December Stairs reaches Ituri River.

1889 9 January Stanley arrives. Decision is made to set up a camp at Kandekore where the sick, the weak, and part of the loads are left.

1889 11 January Stanley and Bonny depart for Lake Albert, leaving Stairs in command of Fort Kandekore.

1889 10 February Stairs receives news from Stanley and Jephson of the rebellion against Emin Pasha. Stanley instructs Stairs to abandon Fort Kandekore and to join him with the rest of the men.

1889 12 February Stairs leaves Kandekore and marches to Kavalli's.

1889 18 February Stairs arrives at Kavalli's and meets Emin Pasha.

1889 18 March Emin Pasha and Stanley decide to set off for the east coast on 10 April.

1889 25 March Letters received from Shukri Aga and Selim Bey in which they express their desire to leave Wadelai and to go with Emin Pasha to Egypt via Zanzibar.

1889 1 April Following Stanley's instructions, Stairs leaves Kavalli's for Mazamboni's village to set up a camp for the caravan which is to set off on its march to the east coast on 10 April.

1889 5 April Discovery of a plot organized by some of the pasha's men to seize arms and to refuse to return to Egypt. Stanley's prompt action saves the situation. An argument with Emin results in a cooler relationship between the two men. Stanley falls ill. (Stairs mentions the argument in his 12 April entry.)

1889 10 April The caravan, composed of 1,510 persons, marches to Mazamboni's and arrives there on the twelfth.

1889 2 May Rehan, a deserter and participant in the plot against Emin Pasha and Stanley, is tried and executed.

1889 8 May The march to the coast is resumed.

1889 6 June Stairs attempts to climb a peak in the Ruwenzori range.

1889 13 and 14 June Stairs discovers that the sources of the Nile extend to Lake Edward.

1889 20 June The crossing of the equator.

1889 3 July Decision is made to march via Ankole and Karagwe.

1889 18 August At Lake Victoria.

1889 28 August At Usambiro mission station.

1889 19 November At the German fort of Mpwapwa.

1889 3 December At Bagamoyo.

1889 4 December Emin Pasha's accident at a banquet in Bagamoyo.

1889 6 December At Zanzibar.

1890 21 January At Cairo.

1890 11 September Stairs presented with a sword of Nova Scotia steel and silver plate by the acting Mayor Mackintosh at a meeting of the City of Halifax Council.

1890 8 November Alfred Sharpe arrives at Bunkeia.

1891 25 March Stairs promoted to captain in the Welsh Regiment (the 41st). Moves to Aldershot.

1891 15 April Creation of the Company of Katanga.

1891 18 April Le Marinel expedition arrives at Bunkeia and stays there for approximately seven weeks.

1891 18 May Stairs leaves England for Africa to assume the leadership of a

Belgian expedition to Katanga sent by the Company of Katanga.

1891 14 June At Zanzibar.

1891 1 July At Bagamoyo. Stairs's twenty-eighth birthday.

1891 4 July Stairs's caravan leaves Bagamoyo.

1891 4 August At Mpwapwa.

1891 7 September At Tabora. Stairs meets Captain Jacques.

1891 6 October Delcommune expedition arrives at Bunkeia and stays there until 11 November.

1891 9 October At Karema mission station. Crossing of the Lake Tanganyika begins.

1891 17 October Arrival of Captain Jacques's caravan at Karema.

1891 27 October At Mrumbi.

1891 30 October Stairs's expedition enters the territory of the Congo Free State.

1891 14 December Stairs's caravan arrives in Bunkeia.

1891 17 December First meeting between Stairs and Msiri.

1891 19 December Second meeting between Stairs and Msiri at the conclusion of which Stairs raises the Belgian flag at Bunkeia against Msiri's will.

1891 20 December After Msiri's flight to Maiembe, Stairs sends Bodson and Bonchamps to bring him back to Bunkeia. In a skirmish which follows Msiri's refusal to return, Msiri is killed and Bodson mortally wounded.

1891 22 December Construction of Fort Bunkeia begins.

1891 29 December Stairs nominates Mukanda Vantu, Msiri's son, as his successor.

1892 2 January As of this date Stairs is down with malaria for nearly six weeks. Dr. Moloney takes over the command due to Bonchamps's illness.

1892 30 January Captain Bia's expedition arrives in Bunkeia.

1892 4 February Stairs's expedition begins its march back to the east coast.

1892 27 March At Abercorn (Kitutu), African Lakes Company station.

1892 3 June At Vicenti.

1892 5 June At Chinde.

1892 9 June Stairs's death. Marquis de Bonchamps takes over the command.

1892 11 June Embarkation for Zanzibar.

1892 20 June At Zanzibar.

1892 5 July Bonchamps, Moloney, and Robinson embark for Europe.

Appendix B

Glossary of Swahili Words*

baharia = sailor

bangi = hemp, hashish

baraza = reception room, entrance
    hall, meeting, assembly, council

barza *see* baraza

bhang *see* bangi

bitana = thin fabric

boma = palisade, enclosure, fort

bunda = bundle, package

chakula = food

chaouri *see* shauri

chungu = clay vessel, cooking pot

corii *see* kore

dodi = wire bracelet

doti *see* dodi

fimbo = stick, cane

fimto *see* fimbo

frasilah *see* frasila

frasila = unit of weight, about
    35 pounds (16 kilograms)

fundi = craftsman, skilled worker

gogo = a log

hongo = exaction, tribute, passage toll

jembe = hoe, spade

kanga = cotton cloth with designs
    in several colours

kangu *see* kanga

kaniki = dark blue cotton cloth

kipamba = tuft of cotton

kore = cultivated field, garden

korongo = heron, stork

mahindi = corn, maize

mahongo or mahogo *see* muhogo

masika = rainy season

mavele = millet

maveli *see* mavele

mayuba *see* mayungwa

mayungwa = leaves of taro

mboga = large pumpkin

mnyama *see* nyama

mohindi *see* mahindi

mrima = coast, coastal region

msiri = confidant, friend, secret agent

mtama = sorghum, millet

muhogo = cassava, manioc

Munugu = God

Munungu *see* Munugu

Muzungu *see* Mzungu

mwale = raffia palm

mwali *see* mwale

mzinga = cannon

*Other African or Arabic words used in the diaries are explained in the text or in the notes.

Mzungu = a European, white person

nyama = flesh, meat

pamba *see* kipamba

pishi = measure of capacity equal to ½ gallon (1.9 litres); measure of weight equal to 6 pounds (2.7 kilograms)

pombe = an alcoholic drink made from millet, bananas, and sugar cane

pori = uninhabited treeless plain, wilderness

ropoka = talk nonsense

ropoko *see* ropoka

rugaruga = irregular soldier, robber

Rugga Rugga *see* rugaruga

shamba = cultivated field, garden

shauri = advice, discussion, conversation

shuka = measure of cloth equal to 2 yards (1.8 metres)

sotoka = cattle plague, rinderpest

tarishi = courier, messenger

tembe = house with a flat roof, hut

ugali = porridge

ugari *see* ugali

Appendix C

Tippu Tib

Tippu Tib (Hamed bin Mohammed El Murjebi c. 1842-1905) was brought up in the Muslim faith. On his father's side he was a Mrima. His mother was a Zanzibari Arab of Muscat origin. As a teenager, he participated in his father's trading activities in East Africa. As an independent trader in ivory, he embarked on acquiring political power through a series of conquests west of Lake Tanganyika. He usurped the position of chief of the Watetera by falsely claiming close blood-relationship through his mother with the old ruler, who finally abdicated in his favour. Around 1870 Tippu Tib extended his domination over Manyuema tribes.

He established friendly relations with a number of European explorers including Livingstone, Cameron, and Stanley. He accompanied Stanley on his second African expedition opening the way for the Arabs into the Upper Congo region. In 1884 Tippu Tib gained control over Stanley Falls. In order to secure his cooperation during the Emin Pasha Relief Expedition, King Leopold II recognized his de facto control over Stanley Falls by offering him the governorship of that region.

There is considerable controversy regarding Tippu Tib's slaving activities. Some historians regard his behaviour as more humane than that of the other Arab traders; he did not engage openly in atrocities of slave-raiding. Others condemn him for collaborating with the notorious Arab slavers who were his business associates.

Above all, Tippu Tib was a skilled politician whose actions were guided by realistic assessment of the political situation. Realizing that the balance of power tilted in favour of the Europeans, he lessened his close ties with the sultan of Zanzibar, sensing that his control over the interior was rapidly dwindling. His presence at Stanley Falls came to an end when he departed for Zanzibar in March 1890. The move was prompted by news of Stanley's court action against him for losses sustained by the rear column as a result of his non-fulfilment of his obligations. Stanley, however, was forced to withdraw his case for lack of evidence. Tippu Tib never again returned to Stanley Falls, and did not witness the expulsion of the Arabs from the Congo by the Belgians in 1895.

During the course of his commercial activities, Tippu Tib acquired considerable wealth. As a young man, he owned a caravan of two thousand ivory porters and one thousand askaris. In the last years of his life, he owned landed property worth approximately £50,000. He died in Zanzibar of malaria, eleven months after Stanley's death.

For further particulars of Tippu Tib's life consult the following: Heinrich Brode, *Tippoo Tib* (London: Edward Arnold, 1907); Père P. Ceulemans, *La Question arabe et le Congo, 1883-1892* (Brussels: Académie Royale des Sciences d'Outre-Mer, Verhandelingen, 1960); Ruth Slade, *King Leopold's Congo* (London: Oxford UP, 1962).

Appendix D

Colonial Occupation: The Question of Priorities and Related Problems

In expressing his views on the priorities of the colonial occupation, Stairs failed to grasp the fact that so many of his contemporary missionary activities in Africa served as a necessary fist step to gain a foothold in a prospective colonial territory.

Missionaries spread the use of the English language and disseminated European culture. All this activity was achieved at no cost to the government, but with its tacit encouragement. Missions could exist, at first, in commercially unprofitable places and gradually pave the way for other Europeans once these stations became profitable. Consequently, it was not quite correct to say that the flag invariably followed trade. In some instances trade followed the cross carried by missionaries, as in Nyasaland, for example, where their activities prepared the way and provided an immediate pretext for British occupation. [See Roland Oliver, *The Missionary Factor in East Africa* (London: Longmans, 1965) 128.] This fact was admitted in a memorandum to the British South Africa Company by Harry H. Johnston, the then British commissioner in that country (Oliver, *The Missionary Factor,* 128 and 162).

In Katanga, too, the presence of missionaries was instrumental in attracting secular interest and eventually colonial domination. When Stairs arrived at Bunkeia he met the English Plymouth Brethren, who were the first Christian missionaries to have settled in Katanga. [See Ruth Slade, *English-Speaking Missions in the Congo Independent State, 1878-1908* (Brussels: Académie Royale des Sciences Coloniales, 1959) 109-110.] Subsequent events show that it was there that the missionary acted as the agent of European advance far more than in any other part of the Congo. According to Ruth Slade, the presence of Plymouth Brethren might have played a decisive role in the de facto incorporation of Katanga in the Congo State. R. F. Arnot, one of the Plymouth Brethren, was largely responsible for arousing interest in Katanga. His accounts of its natural wealth reached the ready ears of Cecil Rhodes, who became responsible for initiating the race for the spoils of Msiri's kingdom. During the course of this drama, the missionaries remained outwardly neutral, despite their tacit preference for the British occupation (Slade, *English-Speaking Missionaries,* 113-127).

So Stairs's contribution to the colonial occupation of Katanga cannot be divorced from the role played there by the missionaries. Yet, his own idea that missions should follow the flag proved mostly true in the rest of the Congolese territory, where they assumed significance only after the establishment of the colonial administration. Missionary activity there enjoyed the full support of King Leopold II, who insisted that missionaries be of Belgian nationality. Fearing that the work of Cardinal Lavigerie's White Fathers entering the country would serve French political interests, Leopold II succeeded in persuading the cardinal to recruit in Belgium his missionaries destined for the Congo.

In spite of the official policy to keep foreign missionaries out of the colony and give preference to the Belgian Catholics, Protestant missions were introduced, mainly on the initiative of English, American, and Scandinavian missionary societies. [See Slade, *King Leopold's Congo,* 141-148.]

APPENDIX E

MSIRI

Msiri was born c.1830 at Msene, northwest of Tabora.[1] His father, Mazwiri-Kalasa, a Nyamwenzi porter in the service of Arab caravans, eventually became a prominent trader. He developed commercial relations with Katanga, from where he imported ivory, copper, and slaves.

As a young man, Msiri often took part in his father's trading activities, and around 1858 permanently settled in Katanga with a small group of *Bayeke* (a name given by local Blacks to elephant hunters).[2] On his arrival, Msiri offered his services to the aging chief of the Wasanga, an old friend of his father's, who was then engaged in war with the Balubas. The enemy was defeated with the help of a few guns—then unknown in this part of Africa—which Msiri brought with him. Taking advantage of the chief's gratitude, Msiri promptly assumed the position of his successor, and upon the old man's death, became the ruler of the Wasanga.[3]

From his new base, Msiri launched a series of military campaigns, and by 1880 his rule covered an area of approximately 57,000 square miles (150,000 square kilometres). His territory extended to the Lualaba River in the west, the Luvua River in the north, to Lake Mweru in the east, and to the Congo-Zambezi watershed in the south.[4] In addition, he collected tribute from territories extending far beyond these limits.

In increasing the area under his domination, Msiri defied the powerful Kazembe, the ruler of a country situated in the east of Lake Mweru who treated the Katanga chiefs, including Sanga, as his vassals and collected tribute from them. Msiri refused to honour these obligations, provoking Kazembe to embark on a punitive expedition. Msiri won the battle, declared his independence,[5] and named his kingdom after one of the Wanyamwezi tribal designations—Ngaraganza—which eventually underwent a curious transformation to become Garengaze.[6] Bunkeia, the capital of the new state, became an important commercial centre attracting Nyamwezi and Arab traders from the east and the Portuguese from Angola. Copper, ivory, and slaves were exchanged for flint-lock guns, powder, cloth, beads, and various trinkets collected by Msiri himself. Salt, supplied by the thermic sources of Mwashya, was an important commodity of trade over which Msiri exercised a monopoly.[7]

Msiri introduced a centralized system of government in which he exercised absolute power, ruling the tributary political units through local chiefs nominated by him. The latter were permitted to enjoy their customary prerogatives, provided they obeyed his orders and paid tribute. Many of the chiefs were related to Msiri through marriage as young female relatives were offered to him, to cement friendships and alliances.[8] Some of the women became superintendents of various chiefdoms, administered by their own relatives.

It was the duty of all chiefs to provide warriors for Msiri's army which numbered between two thousand and three thousand men, led by the *batwale* (commanders). Warriors were not paid or fed, and they had to fend for themselves through pillage, the spoils of which were shared with the king and the chiefs. During the war they burned the enemy villages, enslaved women and children, and massacred the rest.

Msiri provided his country with legal framework when he reformed some of the old rules of customary law and created new regulations. In essence, he introduced absolute equality among all his subjects before law with himself as the supreme lawgiver. The absence of the institution of private property was the cornerstone of his system. Following the principle common in pre-colonial sub-Saharan Africa, his subjects were only the users of the tribal land. Msiri extended this principle to all other assets and goods in his kingdom, hence no one could own anything or was permitted to dispose of anything against his will. The king alone had the right of life and death over his subjects and judicial cases involving a death penalty had to be referred to him by the chiefs.

Powers exercised by the king had important economic connotations. Chiefs were required to hand over to him all ivory as tribute, which constituted the most important source of royal revenue. Copper was next in importance, and tax was imposed on all of its output. As Msiri conquered new territories, he forthwith confiscated all copper mines giving them to his faithful Bayeke and granting them sole rights of exploitation.

The sale of slaves constituted the third most important source of revenue. Msiri obtained his slaves from two sources: his military campaigns and through the judicial system which tended to condemn as many people to slavery as possible. As export of slaves by others was strictly forbidden, the law gave him practical monopoly over all the slave-trade in the land.[9]

At the time when Garengaze reached its maximum territorial expansion, Europeans began to call on its powerful ruler. Msiri wanted to establish contacts with the whites in the hope that they would provide him with gunpowder and weapons, so important for the control of his kingdom and for further expansion. He also saw an opportunity for lessening his dependence on the Arabs, who, until then, were the sole suppliers of these vital goods.

German explorers, Reichard and Böhm, were the first Europeans to enter Bunkeia. They led an expedition organized by the German committee of the African International Association. They arrived in Bunkeia on 20 January 1884. Although Böhm died two months later, Reichard continued his exploration of copper mines in the south of the country. Eventually the latter's activities aroused Msiri's suspicions as to his intentions, forcing him to flee the country. Before doing so, he managed to map, for the first time, the hydrographical system of Katanga and to ascertain the existence of copper in the area.[10]

In the autumn of 1884, a Portuguese expedition visited Katanga. Its two European participants were Capello and Ivens, whose aim was to investigate the possibility of a trade route between Angola and Moçambique with the view to justify Portuguese claims for a corridor between the two colonies.[11] At Msiri's invitation Ivens went to Bunkeia, reaching the capital on 22 November 1884, while Capello remained in the south of the country with the rest of the expedition. On his return journey to rejoin the expedition, Ivens came across some copper mines but failed to find any trace of gold, which seemed to interest him the most.[12]

In February 1886, Frederick Stanley Arnot, a lonely Protestant missionary of the Plymouth Brethren, made his appearance in Bunkeia. His interest in Central Africa was aroused by Livingstone. Msiri welcomed him as a prospective ally against the Arabs and granted him permission to settle in the country. Arnot founded Garengaze Evangelical mission and spent two years at Bunkeia. He was subsequently relieved by C. A. Swann and W. L. Faulknor, who, in 1890, were replaced by D. Crawford, F. Lane, and H. B. Thompson.[13]

The missionaries disappointed Msiri as they did not supply the African ruler with guns and powder. Although he continued to tolerate their presence, at the same time he mistreated them and closely watched their movements. Their plight was described by Dr. Moloney as follows:

> These worthy men had endured for several years the utmost contumely at the hand of Msiri. He used to call them 'his white slaves,' insult them before the public, and despoil them of their goods. The result of the royal displeasure was that, after six years' work, the mission had not secured a single convert.[14]

Meanwhile, Cecil Rhodes became keenly interested in Katanga, sending there an expedition headed by Alfred Sharpe. It arrived at Bunkeia on 8 November 1890, but it failed to realize its aim of subjugating the kingdom of Garengaze to the British South Africa Company. This attempt prompted King Leopold II to intensify his efforts towards "effective occupation" of Katanga by the Congo Free State. Consequently, three Belgian expeditions were sent out, reaching Bunkeia in 1891. The first expedition was headed by Le Marinel, the second by Delcommune, and the third by Stairs. A known sequence of events followed, culminating in the violent death of Msiri on 20 December 1891, and the realization of Leopold's aim of "effective occupation."[15]

Katanga attained its acme between 1870 and 1886. Thereafter, opposition of the subdued chiefs began to mount, so that in the last years of Msiri's life, the kingdom rapidly declined. There were various motives for the chief's dissatisfaction, but these were primarily of an economic nature. For instance, the Wasanga revolt was triggered by Msiri's monopoly of the exploitation of their copper mines and partly as a reaction against the brutality of the Bayeke overlords, and Msiri's own extreme cruelty towards his subjects.[16]

The Wasanga revolt began in February 1891, and serving as an example to the others, it spread like wildfire over the whole of the kingdom. Belgian expeditions saw prosperity disappear, and hunger became widespread while most of the population fled from the capital. Bunkeia, a town of about ten thousand inhabitants, soon became a village. With Msiri's death, his kingdom disintegrated into separate chiefdoms, including the little chiefdom of Bayeke with its centre at Bunkeia. Most of the chiefs declared their allegiance to the Congo Free State and the country came to be known again as Katanga. The name "Garengaze" fell into oblivion.

The short outline of Msiri's life reveals his strong and despotic nature. But what kind of man emerges from the few surviving intimate descriptions left by European travellers, who had brief encounters with this self-made ruler?

To Ivens, Msiri appeared to be a man of approximately sixty years of age, tall, strongly-built, rather unattractive, with a permanent forced smile on his face. His eyes were sly and his bearing was full of dignity, but his attire was grotesque. The photograph taken by Ivens depicts Msiri in a ceremonial uniform; his hair is covered with a handkerchief over which he wears a straw hat.[17]

Arnot found him an old looking man "with rather pleasant, smooth face, and a short beard, quite white. As I approached he rose from his chair and came forward to meet me, folding his arms round me in a most fatherly way; indeed his reception was quite affecting."[18]

In contrast, Dr. Moloney's impression is far more informative:

[H]is appearance was impressive, and his demeanour thoroughly regal. Though he had begun to stoop somewhat with age, he stood fully six [sic] feet high, and must have weighed, as I afterwards had occasion to know, some fourteen [sic] stone. He had good features, an aquiline nose, and a well-shaped head. His hair swept his shoulders, and he wore a short beard which had turned quite white. There was a sphinx-like impenetrability about his expression, yet his large gestures gave emphasis and variety to his conversation. In his prime, Msiri must have looked the ideal of a warrior-king; he was by no means contemptible in his decline. As for his attire, it consisted of a greasy handkerchief by way of head-dress, a silk cloak covered with gold lace, a pair of old trousers, and huge jackboots, in which he shuffled along, none too comfortably.[19]

Apart from his forceful and individualistic personality, Msiri must be seen also as a product of the environment within which he lived and which conditioned his behaviour and influenced his habits. Even if his deeds can hardly meet our contemporary standards, no one can deny that Msiri had created a legend, perhaps equal in its weight to those left by such other famous nineteenth-century African rulers like Chaka of Zululand or Mirambo of Unyamwezi. The latter was originally a petty thief who built up an entire empire to the west and northwest of Tabora.

Appendix F

Some Comments on Disease, Hygiene and Nutrition*

The purpose of this Appendix is to investigate the impact of tropical disease, hygiene, and nutrition on the lives and efficiency of the participants of the Emin Pasha Relief and the Katanga Expeditions. No claim is made to medical expertise, an approach which must be left to specialists in tropical medicine.

Diseases from which the participants suffered the most during the two expeditions were gastro-intestinal infections, malaria, and ulcers in the case of the Emin Pasha Relief Expedition. In view of the state of medical knowledge at that time, Dr. Parke and Dr. Moloney had no real understanding of the causes or the true nature of these diseases.

Ulcers were particularly common among the Africans. Early in August 1887, rapid spread of ulcerations became noticeable.[1] The two varieties of ulcers which are of relevance in the present context were those caused by the burrowing flea (*Tunga penetrans*), commonly known as the jigger, the chegoe, or the sand flea, and the so-called tropical ulcer, common in hot climates, including Africa.

Infection caused by a fertilized female jigger took place after it penetrated the skin, most commonly under the toenail, or other parts of the body. Eggs deposited there began to develop, causing inflammation and secondary infection. Gas gangrene could follow, leading eventually to the auto-amputation of the toes.[2]

During the march of the Emin Pasha Relief Expedition through the tropical forest, Dr. Parke was aware of the presence of jiggers. He observed that, once the flea penetrated the skin, its presence was indicated by a tender black spot. The affected Zanzibaris knew how to remove it with a pin or knife.[3] However, the most important part of the operation was to remove the *whole* flea with a sterile needle and to follow it with an application of antiseptic dressing. Unfortunately this was seldom, if ever, followed. Many victims suffered terribly as a consequence of these ulcerations and William G. Stairs tells us that, "some of their feet are simply rotting away, the toes being pulled out by the doctor with a pair of nippers; he says it is gangrene."[4]

It is uncertain whether Dr. Parke realized that there was a connection between the burrowing flea and the proliferation of ulcers among the bare-footed porters, as proper surgical removal of the parasites would have prevented this epidemic. We have no indication in his diary that this simple procedure was ever followed by him. Was it then neglect or ignorance that contributed to this disastrous state of health amongst the porters on the march through the African continent?[5]

According to Dr. Parke, jiggers disappeared after the expedition had passed Ugarrowwa's station.[6] This comment is of considerable interest as, in the opinion of some writers, the Emin Pasha Relief Expedition, in its eastward march, is credited with their introduction to

---

*An abridged version of Appendix F has been published as "The Emin Pasha Relief Expedition (1887-1889): Some Comments on Disease and Hygiene," *Canadian Journal of African Studies* 19 (1985): 615-625.

areas previously unaffected by them. One of these areas was Uganda, where, between 1893 and 1895, jigger infestation assumed alarming proportions. Gradually, they spread eastward, reaching the east coast by 1899.[7]

In a period of intense caravan movements in Central Africa, previously unknown diseases were introduced. Hence it is quite possible, that the Emin Pasha Relief Expedition was not alone in spreading the jigger in Uganda. On the other hand, one has to note that participants of the Katanga Expedition were relatively free form ulcers, which Stairs, its leader, was quick to observe in his diary on 9 November 1891, after four months on the march.[8]

The second type of ulcerations suffered by the participants of the Emin Pasha Relief Expedition can be attributed to the tropical ulcer, which is usually a superficial skin ulceration associated with the presence of *Bacillus fusiformis* and *Treponema vincenti*. It occurs most frequently in low-lying, hot, moist areas among open-air workers living in filthy conditions, who wear little clothing and are exposed to local injury, especially about the legs. Malnutrition, and particularly protein deficiency, predispose one to this type of affliction. The matter forming the ulcers is infectious and flies spread the disease to other victims. In the case of severe form of the tropical ulcer, there may be a deeper penetration to the underlying tissues, and bones may become necrotic or large blood vessels may be affected.[9] Ulcerations became noticeable during the sea voyage from Zanzibar to Banana Point. It is most likely that some of the men suffered form tropical ulcers, but Parke fails to provide description of the symptoms.[10]

During the march in the Congo, many men contracted new ulcers, which, according to Dr. Parke, were distinctly traceable to the bites of the flies that carried germs from one man to another.[11] As the caravan advanced into the interior, the incidence of ulcerations rapidly increased when starvation reduced men's resistance to infection.[12] In his Emin Pasha Relief Expedition Diary, Stairs provides a gruesome description of the desperate state of health of some of the Africans suffering form these ulcers: "tendons and muscles all round [their] ankle bones are just simply hanging out, the fleshy part has all rotten [sic] away."[13] The hopelessness of the situation is revealed when he admits that, "we have no medicine [...] except a little permanganate of potash; water and rest are the best medicines."[14]

Unfortunately even these elementary "first aids" were unavailable to the porters. Water was more often than not contaminated and prolonged rest was out of the question under the existing conditions of daily marches in the tropical forest.

As early as 27 August 1887, Stairs reports that out of eighty-three men in his company, thirty-five were suffering form bad feet. Two months later, he complains that, "many cannot carry their loads and are left behind to die or perhaps find shelter with the Arabs somewhere."[15] With improved nutrition on the return journey to the east coast, ulcers gradually healed up and ceased to plague the expedition.[16]

Gastro-intestinal afflictions, common to both Blacks and Whites, had a strong debilitating impact, resulting in numerous deaths. Dr. Parke's terminology is very vague, reflecting the state of European medical knowledge at the end of the nineteenth century. He used the term "dysentery" to describe various diseases such as diarrhoea, including the bacillary and amoebic dysentery, without being able to distinguish between them.[17] All he was able to do was to divide his patients into those suffering form "pure" dysentery and those showing symptoms of diarrhoea for some other reasons.

According to Dr. Parke, only one man had died during the sea voyage form Zanzibar to the Congo. Parke was convinced that he saw "comparatively little" of "pure" dysentery during the remaining time of the expedition.[18] In fact, he recorded only five deaths which he attributed to that disease. It is not known, however, how many African members of the expedition suffered form dysentery and managed to survive.

Parke also described abdominal disorders, to which he applied the term "gastro-intestinal catarrh." He referred to it as a very common ailment, which affected Whites in Africa and to which nearly all members of the expedition succumbed. Its symptoms were very similar to those of dysentery, except that the large intestine was not much affected and ulceration did not take place.[19] The afflicted person ran a moderate fever, had attacks of violent vomiting, cramps, straining, and diarrhoea. In modern medical terminology it is known as *Catarrhal diarrhoea*. Parke believed that it was mainly due to nocturnal chills,[20] and in his opinion, its incidence was "the most important physical obstacle to the prosperous progress of our expedition."[21]

The best documented history of gastro-intestinal ailment is that of Henry M. Stanley, as Parke paid much attention to the leader of the Emin Pasha Relief Expedition and described in considerable detail his illnesses. There seems to be little doubt that, in addition to gastro-intestinal problems, Stanley also suffered from malaria. Hence the possibility of dysenteric malaria must be seriously taken into account.[22] His gastro-intestinal disease dated back to the pre-Emin Pasha Relief Expedition times, when he contracted it on one of his previous African journeys.[23] As a consequence, he suffered from recurring attacks, even during his sojourns in England. One can only speculate that he must have acquired some form of chronic "sub-acute"[24] form of amoebic infection, which, without proper treatment, could drag on for years without causing much visible ill-health.

Members of the Katanga Expedition were not immune to the gastro-intestinal ailments. In his diary in July 1891, Stairs mentions that Marquis de Bonchamps was laid up with dysentery, although Dr. Moloney fails to mention the fact. In spite of scant information given by both diarists about this particular ailment, one can safely assume that many must have succumbed to it during the course of the expedition. Other ailments of the intestines were caused by tapeworms (*taeniasis*) and round-worm (*ascariasis*). During their stay at Fort Bodo, many Whites and Blacks had them. Dr. Parke attributed it to impure water.[25]

At times, Stairs complains bitterly of his sense of helplessness in controlling the spread of various diseases which afflicted so many of his companions.[26] Improper storage and handling of foodstuffs, improper refuse disposal, sewage problems, the inability to quarantine all those who suffered form infectious diseases, exposure to unhygienic conditions in camps and villages—all were hard to avoid and presented insurmountable problems to the white leaders of the two expeditions.

Parke provides an illustration of conditions at Ipoto (Kilonga Longa's) where: "the huts are crawling with body vermin. The rats are in corresponding abundance; they run over us at night in the most familiar and playful fashion. Vermin of all kinds, large and small, appear to multiply with the greatest rapidity here."[27] Stairs's experiences at Ituri River camp did not differ much form those at Ipoto:

This camp is getting too filthy to live in; the mass of filth in the bush on all sides of us is something astounding, as a matter of course this filth has attracted myriads of flies and midges which, alighting on the filth and then on the men's bodies, breed sickness.[28]

Malaria was the third common illness from which members of the two expeditions frequently suffered. Dr. Parke traced its source to the "clouds of malarious vapour" which hang about the swamps in tropical forests, to the "very miasmatic plain" around the shores of Lake Albert and to the "chilly breezes."[29] Dr. Moloney, on the other hand, blamed "the heat, bad water-supply, indifferent and indigestible food, and the altered conditions of living."[30] He did not differentiate clearly between malarial and gastro-intestinal diseases. Captain Stairs suspected "bad water, cold winds, and extremes of temperature between night and day for the onset of sickness."[31]

Malaria has been known from the earliest times and its connection with swampy areas is well established. Its name originates form the Italian word *mal'aria,* meaning "bad air."[32] The first known effective remedy was quinine, which made its appearance in Europe sometime during the seventeenth century, when it was brought form Peru.[33] The drug, used without any real understanding of the true nature of the disease, not only cured malaria but also prevented its onset when taken regularly in doses necessary to maintain its adequate level in the blood.

In 1880 Alphonse Laveran discovered minute parasites in the corpuscles of blood of malarious persons.[34] However, the discovery of the connection between malaria in humans and the *Anopheles* mosquito had to wait till 1894, when Patrick Manson identified this insect as the transmitter of the malarial parasite. Parke knew of Laveran's discovery, but sided with the latter's critics, who were more interested in the shortcomings of his findings rather than using it a basis for future promising research.[35]

As the Emin Pasha Relief Expedition took place between 1887 and 1889, Parke could not have been aware of the danger presented by the bites of the *Anopheles* mosquito, which the participants of the expedition viewed merely as a harmless nuisance. Consequently, they did not take any precautions, such as using mosquito nets at night, putting on adequate clothing after sunset, and avoiding campsites along stagnant waters. The only preventive measure taken by Dr. Parke was when he gave each officer four grains of quinine twice a day, ten days before their arrival at Banana Point. Between 18 March and 22 April 1887, quinine was taken sporadically. During that period there were only one or two recorded cases of malaria among the Whites. This convinced Parke that quinine was a preventive drug.[36]

Africans also suffered form malaria, in spite of their relative immunity to some malarial species, particulary the *Plasmodium vivax.* This can be explained by the fact that an individual who is immune to one particular strain of a species had no immunity to other strains of that species or to other species.[37] Emin Pasha told Parke on one occasion that many people in his province never suffered form fever, but that they had enlarged spleens. He saw a connection between these two facts. However, when they were removed to the Lake Albert area, they became susceptible to the sickness, as they had no immunity to the new local malarial species. It is not surprising then, to read in Dr. Parke's diary that in June 1889, when camping close to the stagnant waters of the lakes about one-third of the entire caravan came down with fever.[38]

Malarial fever of the *Falciparum* (malignant tertian) variety attacked all the white participants of the expedition. It could assume one of two forms, either uncomplicated or with serious complications. In the latter case, "bilious remittent fever" and "blackwater fever" were the most dangerous.[39] Both Stairs and Parke had them.

With monotonous frequency one reads of malarial fever attacks in Parke's, Moloney's, and Stairs's diaries. On the average, each victim suffered 150 attacks as they were constantly exposed to re-infection when the caravan moved form one malarious place to another.[40] Inadequate treatment contributed to the development of severe anaemia. Exertion, through long marches, and the existence of other diseases weakened those already afflicted, increasing the possibility of death.

During the Katanga Expedition, none of the Whites were spared the scourge of malaria, which also ravaged the ranks of the Africans. In the second half of September 1891, Dr. Moloney reported that thirty-five men suffered form "various kinds of fever" and cases of haematuria were quite common.[41] The situation deteriorated still further at the beginning of 1892 during the rainy season.

There was considerable confusion in distinguishing malaria form other diseases which had common symptoms. As knowledge of tropical medicine was still in its infancy, Dr. Parke tended to diagnose many ailments as "fevers," an umbrella term used by him frequently. He was incapable of carrying out differential diagnosis on dysentery from relapsing fever caused by a spirochaete (*Borrelia duttoni*). It was only described by Dutton and Todd, fifteen years later, in 1905. The common vector of this disease is the tampan tick (*Ornithodoros moubata*).[42] The possibility of infection with relapsing fever existed in many areas crossed by the Emin Pasha Relief Expedition.[43]

Evidence shows that many of its members were troubled by ticks including Dr. Parke himself,[44] who may have also suffered from relapsing fever. His partial blindness, which he ascribed to ophthalmia, points to this fact. Blindness in his right eye persisted until he reached the coast.[45] Impairment of his vision could have been caused by iritis—one of the frequent and severe complications of tick-borne relapsing fever[46]—or by vitamin A deficiency, which can lead to keratitis iritis (greatly reduced vision) and even complete destruction of the eye.[47]

Other diseases affecting the two expeditions were pneumonia and bronchitis. Exposure to chilly nights, often with hoar-frost lying on the ground, resulted in fevers from which every member of the caravan, of about one thousand men, suffered during the Emin Pasha Relief Expedition while on their march to the east coast.[48] Similar health problems dogged the Katanga Expedition at the end of July 1891, when it entered mountainous country, and some of the men developed pneumonia.

Smallpox presented a real threat. Already on board the *Oriental* at the beginning of the Emin Pasha Relief Expedition, one of the Nubian volunteers came down with what was regarded as the first symptoms of the disease. Immediate quarantine of the patient and prompt vaccination of other members of the expedition prevented its spread. Parke had every reason to be pleased with the long-term effects of his quick action. Stanley's caravan and the remnants of the rear column were exposed to the epidemic of smallpox at Banalya on their march to Fort Bodo in 1888. Only four men contracted the disease and all eventually recovered form it. Local Manyuemas, on the other hand, were dying of it in great numbers.[49]

During the Katanga Expedition, fear of smallpox caused Dr. Moloney some anxious moments. However, only two cases of smallpox were recorded during the course of the expedition, and in each case, these assumed a very mild form; the patients fully recovered.[50]

In his diaries, Dr. Parke reported a number of deaths from what he thought was tetanus. Most deaths occurred shortly after a man was wounded by a poisoned arrow. However, subsequent examination of the poison itself revealed that its chief active ingredients were erythrophoeine and strychnine, two substances which were responsible for the deaths of the wounded men. What misled Parke was the fact that when strychnine forms the principal ingredient of the poison, tetanic symptoms are present; however, they are more acute and less prolonged.[51] Symptoms of tetanus appear four or five days after contracting the disease. Parke's patients, wounded by poisoned arrows, developed similar symptoms and deaths occurred sooner than would have been the case with a tetanic infection.

Above all, progress of the two expeditions depended on adequate diet. Food intake affects both physical and mental performance of all human beings and the need for a balanced diet requires no explanation. Nonetheless, one must ask whether life and work in hot climates create any special dietary requirements. There is no evidence that tropical climates require any change in protein intake, while a low fat diet is indicated when conditions causing impaired liver function exist. Vitamin requirements of healthy persons are essentially the same as in temperate climates.[52]

Nutritional problems encountered during the Emin Pasha Relief Expedition and during the last stages of the Katanga Expedition were both of a quantitative and a qualitative nature. Form July 1887, when on the march form Yambuya to Ugarrowwa's camp, the caravan faced serious shortages of food, bordering on starvation. This situation lasted until the end of October 1887. Dietary imbalance also presented a serious problem. During the prolonged periods of hunger in the tropical forest, members of the caravan had to live, almost exclusively on plantains which consist primarily of carbohydrates (on the average 27 percent) and contain a minimal amount of protein (on the average 1.4 percent), the rest is mainly water.[53]

Even during the periods of relative food abundance, as for example at Fort Bodo, diet lacked in proteins particularly of animal origin. Food intake showed a high degree of imbalance relying on such staples as maize (average carbohydrate content 70 percent, protein 8.5 percent, water 13.5 percent, other 8 percent), and plantains with some other vegetables.[54] Similarly, cassava and rice, consumed by the members of the Emin Pasha Relief Expedition failed to provide a good source of protein.[55]

Shortage of salt led to serious mineral deficiency when its supply was soon exhausted by the expedition. The local foodstuffs contained far too little salt to satisfy the increasing requirement under conditions of tropical heat. Dr. Parke described the pathetic attempts at Fort Bodo to extract salt form a wild plant resembling leek, a procedure practised by the Africans who had no other source of it.[56]

Relatively little is known about vitamin deficiencies experienced during the expeditions, but a seriously unbalanced diet must have contributed to it. Dr. Parke's partial blindness could have been related to xerophthalmia caused by lack of vitamin A, which is not uncommon in the tropics. The loss of memory experienced by Stairs may have been also due to some form of mineral or vitamin deficiency.[57]

During the Katanga Expedition, drought and the mismanagement of local economy in Msiri's kingdom contributed to a serious shortage of food. In the summer of 1891, in the early stages of the expedition, 20 men a day out of 350, were incapable of carrying loads due to illness. By the beginning of 1892, starvation and disease assumed alarming proportions.[58]

The course of the Emin Pasha Relief Expedition (see chapter 1) indicates clearly that shortage of human resources had seriously undermined Stanley's plans and extended its duration beyond any reasonable expectation. When the expedition was to begin its return march form Lake Albert to Zanzibar, there were only about 230 men left of the original 700 who commenced the journey in February 1887.[59]

The Katanga Expedition, decimated by disease and hunger, had to cut short its stay at Garengaze and was forced to abandon its search for minerals in that area. During the month of January alone, the caravan had been reduced from 360 men to barely 200, of whom 73 died, "and the remainder were still wandering in the wilderness."[60]

Frequent references to health problems that beset the two expeditions show how little the planners understood the task they were undertaking, how limited was the science of tropical medicine at that time, and how ignorant many of the participants were of the elementary needs of nutrition and hygiene. Starvation and disease reached such proportions that the very fate of the two expeditions hung in the balance.

NOTES TO THE FOREWORD

1. Charles Ritchie, *Storm Signals: More Undiplomatic Diaries, 1962-1971* (Toronto: Macmillan of Canada, 1983) ix.

2. Charles Ritchie, *The Siren Years: A Canadian Diplomat Abroad, 1937-1945* (Toronto: Macmillan of Canada, 1974) 7.

3. Ritchie, *Storm Signals,* ix.

4. Henry B. Stairs, letter to Hilda Johnston nee Stairs, 7th May, 1908; Public Archives of Nova Scotia (PANS), M.G.1, No. 877.

5. H. B. Stairs, letter to Hilda Johnston nee Stairs, 7th May 1908; PANS, M.G.1, No. 877.

6. Hilda Johnston, letter to Henry Stairs, 21st May 1908; PANS, M.G.1, No. 877.

7. Of course, the stenographer received a fee. Fifty-four years later, according to my father, she sent a cheque for thirty dollars to Harry's widow, with a note indicating that she had just realized that she had over-charged Harry by that amount. The money was returned, it being recalled that Harry had been "well satisfied with the bill." A few days later there came the reply that the money had been given to charity, as the elderly stenographer's "conscience would not allow her to keep it." H. Gerald Stairs, "The Stairs of Halifax" (PANS, Cs.ST 1, 1962) 132-33. (Unpublished MSS). In the Victorian sense of commercial propriety, it seems, there were at least some qualities to be admired.

8. William G. Stairs, *Emin Pasha Relief Expedition Diaries.* PANS, M.G.1, Nos. 877 and 878.

NOTES TO THE PREFACE

1. Ruth Slade, *King Leopold's Congo* (London: Oxford UP, 1962) chapters 4 and 5 passim.

2. John Flint, "The Wider Background to Partition and Colonial Occupation," *History of East Africa,* eds. Roland Oliver and Gervase Mathew, vol. 1 (Oxford: 1963) passim.

3. Lord Rosebery's speech, *Proceedings, Royal Colonial Institute,* vol. 24 (1892-93): 227.

4. William G. Stairs, *Emin Pasha Relief Expedition Diaries,* PANS, M.G.1, Nos. 877 and 878. William G. Stairs, "De Zanzibar au Katanga," *Le Congo Illustré, Voyages et Travaux des Belges dans l'Etat Independant du Congo, 1893.* This journal was published in Brussels between 1891 and 1895 under the editorship of A. J. Wauters. Subsequently it merged with *Le Mouvement Géographique* which ceased to be published in 1922.

5. H. Gerald Stairs, "The Stairs of Halifax" (PANS, Cs.ST 1, 1962) 133.

6. W. G. Stairs, *Emin Pasha Relief Expedition Diary,* 18 May 1888.

7. W. G. Stairs, *Emin Pasha Relief Expedition Diary,* 18 May 1888.

8. W. G. Stairs, *Emin Pasha Relief Expedition Diary,* 1 June 1889.

9. Dorothy Middleton, ed., *The Diary of A. J. Mountenay Jephson. Emin Pasha Expedition 1887-1889* (Cambridge: published for the Hakluyt Society at the University Press, 1969) viii.

10. The published diaries and memoirs of the members of the Emin Pasha Relief Expedition are as follows: Henry Morton Stanley, *In Darkest Africa,* 2 vols. (New York: Charles Scribner's Sons, 1890); J. Rose Troup, *With Stanley's Rear Column* (London: Chapman and Hall Ltd., 1890); Herbert Ward, *My Life With Stanley's Rear Guard* (New York: Cassell and Company Ltd., 1891); Sir Walter George Barttelot, ed., *The Life of Edmund Musgrave Barttelot From His Letters and Diary* (London: R. Bentley and Son, 1890); James S. Jameson, *Story of the Rear Column of the Emin Pasha Relief Expedition,* ed. Mrs. J. S. Jameson (Toronto: Rose Publishing Company, 1891); A. J. Mounteney Jephson, *Emin Pasha and the Rebellion at the Equator* (New York: Charles Scribner's Sons, 1890); Thomas Heazle Parke, *My Personal Experiences in Equatorial Africa as Medical Officer of the Emin Pasha Relief Expedition* (New York: Negro UP, 1969); William Hoffmann, *With Stanley in Africa* (London: Cassell and Company Ltd., 1938); Middleton, ed., *The Diary of A. J. Mounteney Jephson.*

NOTES TO PART ONE

1. H. G. Stairs, "The Stairs," 1-7.

2. H. G. Stairs, "The Stairs," 14-16, 21-22, and 55.

3. H. G. Stairs, "The Stairs," 56-59 and 62. For his views on Confederation see his essay "Union of Maritime Provinces and Confederation," in *Family History Stairs, Morrow* (Halifax: McAlpine Publishing Company Ltd., 1906) 62-65.

4. H. G. Stairs, "The Stairs," 86.

5. H. G. Stairs, "The Stairs," 76-77 and 92-93.

6. H. G. Stairs, "The Stairs," 79. The Pilot Jack was the Union Jack defaced by a white border.

7. Thomas H. Raddall, *Halifax, Warden of the North* (Toronto: McClelland and Stewart Ltd., 1971) 206.

8. H. G. Stairs, "The Stairs," 79-82 and 84. Another indication of the relatively low level of wages and salaries and the large differentials in earnings was the rule imposed by the Halifax Bank, about 1800, that no employee could marry unless he earned a salary of at least $1,000 per annum.

9. H. G. Stairs, "The Stairs," 80.

10. H. G. Stairs, "The Stairs," 84.

11. H. G. Stairs, "The Stairs," 85.

12. H. G. Stairs, "The Stairs," 86.

13. H. G. Stairs, "The Stairs," 86.

14. H. G. Stairs, "The Stairs," 62.

15. William G. Stairs, *The Emin Pasha Relief Expedition Diary,* EPRE, 20 August 1888; PANS, M.G.1, Nos. 877 and 878.

16. H. G. Stairs, "The Stairs," 101.

17. H. G. Stairs, "The Stairs," 101; *Dictionary of National Biography,* ed. Sidney Lee, vol. 53, (London: Smith, Elder and Company, 1898); W. G. Stairs, letter to W. G. Jones, 3 and 7 July, 1883, Jones's Private Family Archives.

18. W. G. Stairs, "De Zanzibar au Katanga. Journal du Capitaine Stairs (1890-1891)," *Le Congo Illustré,* trans. Elizabeth Jones, 5 (26 February 1893). Translated from French and subsequently referred to as *The Katanga Expedition Diary.*

19. Joseph A. Moloney, *With Captain Stairs to Katanga* (London: Sampson Low, Marston and Company, 1893) 2.

20. Viscount Garnet Joseph Wolseley (1833-1913) was a British field marshal. Wolseley took part in several military campaigns, was in command of a number of expeditions to the various parts of the world and occupied administrative ports.

21. Henry M. Stanley, letter to General Lord Wolseley, Cairo, 30 January (no year given). A copy of this letter was sent to Stairs by Lord Wolseley. Stairs's scrapbook No. 63, PANS.

22. Stanley, *In Darkest Africa,* vol. 1, 43; Middleton, ed., *The Diary of A. J. Mounteney Jephson,* 3.

23. Interested readers are referred to note 4 in the Preface and to monographs written by Roger Jones, *The Rescue of Emin Pasha* (London: Allison and Busby, 1972), and Iain R. Smith, *The Emin Pasha Relief Expedition 1886-1890* (Oxford: Oxford UP, 1972).

24. Georg Schweitzer, *Emin Pasha, His Life and Work,* vol. 1 (1898; New York: Negro UP, 1969) 1-21.

25. Beshir Mohammed Said, *The Sudan, Crossroads of Africa* (London: The Bodley Head, 1965) 16.

26. Sir Samuel White Baker (1821-1893) was a traveller and a sportsman. After several years spent in Ceylon, he turned his attention to Africa, where he became engaged in extensive exploration during the 1860s. He became interested in the exploration of the sources of the Nile. In 1864, having discovered a lake that he named Albert Nyanza, he followed part of the course of the Victoria Nile.

In 1869 the Khedive Ismail secured Baker's services as governor-general of Equatoria, where he established his adminstration and fought slave-trade. In 1874 Baker was succeeded by George Charles Gordon (1833-1885), who distinguished himself in the Crimean War and in China. Gordon became governor-general of the Sudan in 1877 and held that position until 1880. He was called upon in 1883 to lead a mission to the Sudan, which was threatened by the Mahdi's uprising. He was killed in the fall of Khartoum.

27. I. R. Smith, *The Emin Pasha Relief Expedition*, 6-7.

28. He was promoted to the rank of pasha in November 1886 at the time when the Egyptian government instructed him to evacuate Equatoria. See also Stanley, *In Darkest Africa*, vol. 1, 391.

29. R. Jones, *The Rescue*, 59-61.

30. Wilhelm Junker (1840-1892) was a German explorer born in Moscow. Between 1875 and 1886 he resided in Equatorial Africa devoting his time to ethnographical studies and the exploration of the Nile-Congo watershed. The Mahdist uprising prevented his planned return to Europe via the Sudan but he managed to reach Zanzibar in December 1886.

31. R. Jones, *The Rescue*, 61-62.

32. Alexander M. Mackay (1849-1892) was a member of the Church Missionary Society.

33. Gaetano Casati, *Ten Years in Equatoria and the Return with Emin Pasha*, vol. 1 (1891; New York: Negro UP, 1969) 333-335.

34. R. Jones, *The Rescue*, 62.

35. Captain Gaetano Casati (1838-1892). After initial service in the Italian army in 1886, he became a member of the Topographic Department of the Leghorn Institute. In 1880 he accepted an offer from the Sudan to undertake cartographical work in the southern provinces where he worked over a number of years. In January 1885, at the invitation of Emin Pasha, he arrived at Lado. He remained in close contact with the latter through the difficult years.

36. Casati, *Ten Years in Equatoria*, vol. 1, 294 et seq., 334-335; R. Jones, *The Rescue*, 30.

37. Casati, *Ten Years in Equatoria*, vol. 2, 20-35; Roland Oliver and Gervase Mathew, eds., *History of East Africa*, vol. 1 (Oxford: Clarendon Press, 1963) 405.

38. R. Jones, *The Rescue*, 68-69; I. R. Smith, *The Emin Pasha Relief Expedition*, 37.

39. Sir William Mackinnon (1823-1893) was a first baronet. He was the founder and chairman of the British East Africa Company, which was incorporated on 18 April 1888. The territory of the company, which extended from the Tana River to the border of the German East Africa Protectorate, was taken over by the British government on 1 July 1895.

40. Mackinnon urged the Foreign Office to start immediate action in this matter, but the government was not prepared to commit itself in any way, or to undertake responsibility for the life of the British subjects taking part in the proposed expedition. See R. Jones, *The Rescue*, 71-72.

41. At the end of the expedition it was decided to give ten thousand rupees to the widows and orphans of the Zanzibaris who died on the journey. This sum of money equalled barely 12 percent of the excess of receipts over expenditure. See Stanley, *In Darkest Africa*, vol.1, 35 and vol. 2, 513-514.

42. R. Jones, *The Rescue*, 71.

43. Stanley, *In Darkest Africa*, vol. 1, 40-43.

44. Middleton, ed., *The Diary of A. J. Mounteney Jephson*, 3.

45. Stanley, *In Darkest Africa*, vol. 1, 43.

46. Stanley, *In Darkest Africa*, vol. 1, 49.

47. Stanley, *In Darkest Africa*, vol. 1, 83-84.

48. R. Jones, *The Rescue*, 73-74.

49. Stanley, *In Darkest Africa*, vol. 1, 37-39; R. Jones, *The Rescue*, 76.

50. Stanley, *In Darkest Africa*, vol. 1, 37-38.

51. Stanley, *In Darkest Africa*, vol. 1, 35.

52. Stanley, *In Darkest Africa*, vol. 1, 32-33; R. Jones, *The Rescue*, 77-78; I. R. Smith, *The Emin Pasha Relief Expedition*, 68-70. The first of these routes was suggested by Joseph Thompson, the second by the Emin Pasha Relief Expedition Committee, and the third route by Robert W. Felkin, a missionary.

53. Stanley, *In Darkest Africa*, vol. 1, 34-35.

54. R. Jones, *The Rescue*, 79; I. R. Smith, *The Emin Pasha Relief Expedition*, 69.

55. Stanley, *In Darkest Africa*, vol. 1, 36.

56. I. R. Smith, *The Emin Pasha Relief Expedition*, 54-56 and 61-62.

57. Stanley, *In Darkest Africa*, vol. 1, 31-32.

58. I. R. Smith, *The Emin Pasha Relief Expedition*, 62.

59. It is convenient, in this context, to paraphrase the expression used in the title of the book *Africa and the Victorians. The Official Mind of Imperialism* by Ronald Robinson and John Gallagher with Alice Denny (London: MacMillan, 1965).

60. A good introduction to this subject can be found in John Flint, "The wider background to partition and colonial occupation," *History of East Africa*, edited by Oliver and Mathew, vol. 1, 352-390.

61. Third Marquess of Salisbury (1830-1903) became prime minister and foreign secretary in June 1885.

62. I. R. Smith, *The Emin Pasha Relief Expedition*, 64; Robinson, et al., *Africa and the Victorians*, 199.

63. Stanley, *In Darkest Africa*, vol. 1, 43-44.

64. R. Jones, *The Rescue*, 79-82; Barbara Emerson, *Leopold II of the Belgians. King of Capitalism* (New York: St. Martin's Press, 1979) 157-161.

65. For further particulars on Tippu Tib see Appendix C.

66. G. N. Sanderson, *England, Europe and the Upper Nile 1882-1899* (Edinburgh: Edinburgh UP, 1965) 223.

67. Roger Anstey, *Britain and the Congo in the Nineteenth Century* (Oxford: Clarendon Press, 1962) 223.

68. Emerson, *Leopold II*, 160.

69. For details and exact dates see Appendix A, "Chronological Table of Events."

70. Stanley left written instructions to this effect, dated 24 June 1887, and addressed to Major Barttelot. See Stanley, *In Darkest Africa*, vol. 1, 116-119.

71. Barttelot, letter to W. Mackinnon, 4 June 1888, in *The Life of Edmund Musgrave Barttelot*, edited by W. G. Barttelot, 270-282.

72. For further details of Barttelot's death see Stanley, *In Darkest Africa*, vol. 1, 518.

73. H. Brode, *Tippoo Tib. The Story of His Career in Central Africa*, 208-210. A rather implausible explanation given for Jameson's trip was that he tried to reach the Congo Free State authorities in order to report Barttelot's death.

74. Parke, *My Personal Experiences*, 91.

75. Stanley, *In Darkest Africa*, vol. 1, 389-390.

76. Stanley, *In Darkest Africa*, vol. 1, 402.

77. Stanley, *In Darkest Africa*, vol. 1, 402-417.

78. Jephson, *Emin Pasha and the Rebellion*, 154-155.

79. I. R. Smith, *The Emin Pasha Relief Expedition*, chapter 9.

80. For details of these events see R. Jones, *The Rescue*, 218-225 and I. R. Smith, *The Emin Pasha Relief Expedition*, 252-261.

81. *The Morning Herald*, 13 January 1890, 1.

82. Most of the white participants of the Emin Pasha Relief Expedition died prematurely: Stairs in 1892, Nelson and Parke in 1893. Bonny is thought to have died some years before 1907. Stanley died of a stroke in 1904 and Jephson, who never recovered his health, in 1908. The fate of Hoffmann is unknown.

83. "Lieutenant Stairs' Account of his Ascent of Ruwenzori to a Height of 10,677 Feet Above Sea Level, June 8th 1889," *Proceedings of the Royal Geographical Society* 11.12 (December 1889): 726-730. Reprinted in Stanley's *In Darkest Africa*, vol 2, 276-280. See also Guy Yeoman, *Africa's Mountains of the Moon* (London: Universe, 1989) 51 and 170.

84. Stanley, "Geographical Results of the Emin Pasha Relief Expedition," *Proceedings of the Royal Geographical Society* 12.6 (June 1890): 313-331.

85. Parke, *My Personal Experiences*, 503-507.

After his accident Emin had been urged by Stanley to return to Europe. However, German doctors advised him against such a move as it could endanger his life. Eventually Emin entered German service and continued to explore East Africa until his death on 23 October 1892. He was murdered at Kinena station by Arab slave-traders, who were later-on captured by the Congo State forces, court-martialled and executed. The reason for Emin's murder has never been accurately determined. In all likelihood, it was prompted by the decision on the part of the Belgians to adopt more aggressive measures for the repression of the Arabs slavers. It is also possible that the murder was prompted by a conflict between Emin himself and the Arabs.

There is ample biographical material on Emin Pasha and interested readers are advised to consult Georg Schweitzer, *Emin Pasha, His Life and Work*.

86. W. G. Stairs, letter to the Editor of the *Morning Chronicle*, Cairo, 21 January 1890. PANS, M.G. 1, No. 877.

87. *Dictionary of National Biography*, vol. 53, 468.

88. *Dictionary of National Biography*, vol. 53, 468.

89. *Proceedings of the Royal Geographical Society*, 14.7 (July 1892): 476.

90. H. G. Stairs, "The Stairs," 119.

91. *Halifax Acadian Recorder*, 25 March 1890, 2.

92. *Proceedings of the Royal Geographical Society*, 14.7 (July 1892): 475. The name of Stairs's friend is not given.

93. *The Penny Illustrated Paper*, 19 July 1890, 38.

94. *The Morning Herald*, 12 September 1890, 3.

95. *The Morning Herald,* 12 September 1890, 3.

96. W. G. Stairs's scrapbook, No. 63, PANS.

97. Stella Margetson, in her study *Victorian High Society* (New York: Holmes and Meier Publishers, Inc., 1980), provides an excellent overview of the then fashionable cuisine. See page 78.

98. W. G. Stairs, *Katanga Expedition Diary,* 25 May 1891.

99. W. G. Stairs, *Katanga Expedition Diary,* 7 July 1891.

100. *The Novascotian,* 25 April 1891, 2.

101. *Dictionary of National Biography,* vol. 53, 468.

102. W. G. Stairs, *Katanga Expedition Diary,* 7 July 1891.

103. *The Morning Herald,* 20 February 1890, 2.

104. W. G. Stairs, *Katanga Expedition Diary,* 7 July 1891.

105. G. Cawston, letter to W. G. Stairs, 18 July 1890; British South Africa Company [BSAC] II, Misc., Rhodes House, Oxford.

106. W. G. Stairs, letter to G. Cawston, 20 July 1890; BSAC II.

107. W. G. Stairs, letter to G. Cawston, 26 July 1890; BSAC II.

108. René J. Cornet, *Katanga* (Brussels: L. Cuypers, 1944) 95.

109. G. Cawston, letter to C. Rhodes, 14 March 1890; BSAC II, Misc., Rhodes House, Oxford.

110. John S. Galbraith, *Crown and Charter* (Los Angeles: U of California P, 1974) 248-249.

111. Ruth Slade, *King Leopold's Congo,* 126-128. For further particulars see also Alfred Sharpe, "A Journey to Garengaze," *Proceedings of the Royal Geographical Society,* 14.1 (January 1892): 36-47.

112. Robert Cornevin, *Histoire du Congo* (Paris: Berger-Levrault, 1970) 122.

113. J. du Fief, "Les Expéditions Belges au Katanga," *Société Royale Belge de Géographie Bulletin* No. 2 (Mars-Avril 1892):110-122.

114. R. Cornet, *Katanga,* 92-93; Slade, *King Leopold's Congo* 130-131; Moloney, *With Captain Stairs,* 2-8.

115. Moloney, *With Captain Stairs,* 14.

116. H. G. Stairs, "The Stairs," 120.

117. See Daniel Crawford, *Thinking Black* (New York: George H. Doran, 1912) 303; "Haligonian saved Katanga for the Belgians," *The Mail Star,* 28 July 1960, 3; Fergus Macpherson, *Anatomy of a Conquest: The British Occupation of Zambia, 1884-1924* (Essex: Longman, 1981) 44-45.

118. Moloney, *With Captain Stairs,* 14-15.

119. With the exception of a few explanatory remarks, the material presented in this section is based primarily on Stairs's *Katanga Expedition Diary.* For details and exact dates see Appendix A, "Chronological Table of Events."

120. Slade, *King Leopold's Congo,* 119.

121. W. G. Stairs, *Katanga Expedition Diary,* 17 and 19 July 1891.

122. Armaments, scientific instruments and camping equipment: 31,829 francs. Victualling supplies, carriers (wages), and salaries, etc.: 154,702 francs. Total: 186,531 francs. [Compagnie du Katanga, "Rapport du conseil d'administration." *Le Mouvement Géographique* 9.5 (1892): 131.]

123. J. du Fief, "Les Expéditions Belges au Katanga," 114. Also, askaris are armed guardsmen who protected the caravans.

124. Crawford, *Thinking Black,* 303; Cornet, *Katanga,* 193.

125. W. G. Stairs, *Katanga Expedition Diary,* 14 December 1891.

126. According to Dr. Moloney, the name of the village was Muniema, and this is confirmed by Crawford, who spelled it "Munema."

127. Bia's expedition remained for about two months at Bunkeia but was forced to leave on account of acute famine affecting the whole region. While on the way towards Lake Mweru, Bia fell seriously ill and died on 30 August. Lieutenant Lucien Francqui took over the command of the expedition, which returned to Lusambo in January 1893. For further details, see J. du Fief, "Les Expéditions Belges au Katanga," 138-141; R. J. Cornet, *Katanga,* particularly part 2 which deals with the history of the Bia-Francqui expedition.

128. W. G. Stairs, letter to Walter G. Jones, 19 May 1892, Jones's Private Family Archives.

129. W. G. Stairs, *Katanga Expedition Diary,* 19 July 1891.

130. *Le Mouvement Géographique,* vol. 9 (1892): 40, 70, and 80. For further information on Stairs's expedition see also 17-18, 48, 62-65, and 131.

131. Stairs pointed out that the river was called Lualaba by the Africans and not Luapula as indicated on the contemporary maps.

132. *Le Mouvement Géographique,* vol. 9, 40.

133. *Le Mouvement Géographique,* vol. 9, 80.

134. *Le Mouvement Géographique,* vol. 9, 70 and 80.

135. In the present context, the problem as to whether and on what occasions Stairs considered himself either an Englishman or a Canadian is not directly related to his actual citizenship status. As a matter of fact, until 1 January 1947, persons born in Canada were British subjects. It is not surprising, therefore, that many of those whose families came originally from England referred to themselves as English, as Stairs did. For further information on Canadian citizenship see Donald Creighton, *The Forked Road: Canada 1939-1957* (Toronto: McClelland and Stewart, 1976) 129-130; Nicholas Mansergh, *Documents and Speeches on British Commonwealth Affairs,* vol. 2 (London: Oxford UP, 1953) 943; *Canada Year Book 1968* (Ottawa: Statistics Canada, 1968) 242-244.

136. For further details consult the following books: Sir Charles Petrie, *The Victorians* (London: Eyre and Spottiswoode, 1960); Gwyn Harries-Jenkins, *The Army in Victorian Society* (London: Routledge and Kegan Paul, 1977); Edward M. Spiers, *The Army and Society 1815-1914* (London: Longman, 1980).

137. Spiers, *The Army and Society,* 11.

138. H. Alan C. Cairns, *Prelude to Imperialism. British Reactions to Central African Society 1840-1890* (London: Routledge and Kegan Paul, 1965) 36.

139. Cairns, *Prelude to Imperialism,* 37-38.

140. Cairns, *Prelude to Imperialism,* 37.

141. See, for instance, comments on Stanley's behaviour made by Cairns, *Prelude to Imperialism,* 38.

142. Moloney, *With Captain Stairs,* 273.

143. Crawford, *Thinking Black,* 303.

144. W. G. Stairs, *Katanga Expedition Diary,* 15 June 1891.

145. W. G. Stairs, *Katanga Expedition Diary,* 25 May 1891.

146. W. G. Stairs, *Katanga Expedition Diary,* 17 December 1891.

147. W. G. Stairs, *Emin Pasha Relief Expedition Diary,* 6 April 1889.

148. W. G. Stairs, *Emin Pasha Relief Expedition Diary,* 28 May 1889.

149. W. G. Stairs, *Emin Pasha Relief Expedition Diary,* 5 December 1888.

150. W. G. Stairs, *Katanga Expedition Diary,* 2 August 1891.

151. W. G. Stairs, *Katanga Expedition Diary,* 2 August 1891.

Notes to Part Two, Chapter 1

1. They were Stairs's friends. G. Duff and P. G. Twining served as officers in the Royal Engineers.

2. Col. James Augustus Grant took part in Speke's expedition of 1860-1863 to the Upper Nile. He was a member of the Emin Pasha Relief Committee and a contributor to the relief fund.

3. East Indian sailors.

4. Mtese or Mutesa, king of Buganda, died in 1884 and was succeeded by Mwanga.

5. Dr. Wilhelm Junker, who previously accompanied Emin Pasha, arrived at Suez on 10 January 1887, and campaigned for his relief.

6. William Hoffmann was Stanley's white servant. Baruti was an African boy who accompanied Stanley to England and was now on his way back to Africa.

7. The correct name of the steamer was the *Oriental.*

8. Tippu Tib joined the expedition on his way to Stanley Falls. For particulars on him see Appendix C, "Tippu Tib."

9. The Sanford Exploring Expedition was organized in 1886 by Henry Shelton Sanford, an American diplomat, who served as United States minister to Belgium. He was a member of the executive committee of the African International Association and participated in the activities of the *Comité d'Etudes du Haut Congo,* later renamed *Association Internationale du Congo.* The Sanford Exploring Expedition's financial and organizational basis was a company created under the Belgian law with a capital of $60,000. Granted land tracts and various privileges, its trade was mainly in ivory and rubber. Sanford's company was the first commercial enterprise which pioneered trade on the Upper Congo and it opened the way for other companies that proved financially more successful. The Sanford expedition let its vessel the *Florida* to H. M. Stanley in 1887. For further details see James P. White, "The Sanford Exploring Expedition," *Journal of African History,* 8.2 (1967): 291-302.

10. The *Stanley* and the A. I. A. (Association Internationale Africaine) belonged to the Congo Free State.

11. Lt. Emory H. Taunt was hired by Sanford to act as the principal agent of the company and the leader of the expedition. His initial enthusiasm for "money-making" wore out within a year-and-a-half in the Congo and he left for Europe. The reason given for his discharge, in May 1887, was drunkenness. (White, "The Sanford Exploring Expedition," 294-298.)

12. Antone B. Swinbourne was Sanford's agent at the Kinshassa station (Léopoldville).

13. Mary Stairs (1857-1939) was one of W. G. Stair's sisters. She married George Deane Bourke, who was a British army surgeon.

Notes to Chapter Two

1. Mr. John Walker, a Scotsman, was an engineer who had joined the expedition at Cape Town and subsequently served on the *Henry Reed.*

2. Halifax lies on a peninsula surrounded by Bedford Basin on one side and the North West Arm on the other. Stairs was brought up in the home of his parents which overlooked what was commonly called the "Arm."

3. George Grenfell of the Baptist Missionary Society made seven exploratory trips between 1884 and 1886 and charted the main waterways of the Congo Basin. His map of the Congo was published in 1887 by the Royal Geographical Society.

4. Mr. E.J. Glove, an Englishman, acted as an agent of the Sanford Company. Captain Van Gele stayed at the station after his return from an unsuccessful attempt to explore the Mobangi River, further up than G. Grenfell had succeeded in doing a few months earlier.

5. Stairs refers to Edward Cornwallis's landing at Chebucto on 21 June 1749, the date of which Haligonians celebrate as the anniversary of the founding of Halifax.

Notes to Chapter Three

1. *Advance* was the name of the steel boat used by the expedition. It consisted of twelve sections, each of which was carried by two porters.

2. Jack was Stairs's younger brother and Walter was probably his cousin, Walter G. Jones.

3. Sambro Lakes are situated in Nova Scotia in a picturesque coastal area south of Halifax. Magdalen Islands—a small archipelago in the Gulf of St. Lawrence—had a particular significance in the history of W. G. Stairs's family. His father's firm had practical monopoly of the Magdalen Islands' trade. It provided the local fishermen with fishing gear and many other goods, which were paid for with salt fish that was subsequently exported to the West Indies and traded there for sugar, molasses, and rum.

4. The Manyuema, or Manyema, an African tribe that, from the 1870s, began to be penetrated by the Arabs who were attracted by a plentiful supply of ivory. Tippu Tib established himself as the ruler of the Manyuema.

5. Ugarrowwa was an Arab trader whose real name was Uledi Balyuz, although he was known to the local population as the former. He took part, as a tent boy, in the 1860-1863 expedition of Captains Speke and Grant. Ugarrowwa came from Zanzibar and settled in the Manyuema country.

Notes to Chapter Four

1. The Lenda River, a tributary of the Aruwimi.

2. Abed bin Salim was an Arab of considerable importance in the ivory trade.

3. Stairs misspelled the word "cummerbund" meaning a waist sash or loin band.

4. Nepoko River, a confluence of the Aruwimi to the west of Ugarrowwa's.

5. Stairs used this term to describe persons of Arab origin. However, the common Swahili term is *Mwarabu.*

6. According to Stanley the name was Mambungu (*In Darkest Africa,* vol. 1, 262).

7. Stairs's recording of African words was often inaccurate. Stanley noted that the greeting was *Bodo, Bodo, ulenda, ulenda* (*In Darkest Africa,* vol. 1, 269).

8. In all likelihood, Stairs had in mind the Ituri and Ihuru Rivers.

9. Romolo Gessi Pasha (1831-1881) served under Gordon, explored the Upper Nile and made the first circumnavigation of Lake Albert (1876). Eventually, Gessi became governor of the Province of Bahr el Ghazal.

10. Stairs makes a rather unclear reference to a hill from which Stanley first saw the "Promised Land." In Stanley's own words, "This [...] was the long promised view and the long expected exit out of gloom! Therefore I called the tall peak terminating the forest ridge [...] Pisgah—Mount Pisgah—because, after 156 days of twilight in the primeval forest, we had first viewed the desired pasturelands of Equatoria." (*In Darkest Africa,* vol. 1, 281). For a biblical reference to Moses and Mount Pisgah, see Deuteronomy 3.

Notes to Chapter Five

1. Ismaili was a Manyuema headman who was responsible to Kilonga Longa. He was reputed to hate Europeans.

2. Stairs refers here to Stanley.

Notes to Chapter Six

1. Sir Francis de Winton (1835-1901) was a soldier and an administrator. In the course of his long military and administrative career, he was administrator-general of the Congo (1885-1886), and in 1887 acted as secretary of the Emin Pasha Relief Committee. In 1890 he retired from the army with the honorary rank of major-general.

2. Abdullah was the headman in charge of the party sent to Yambuya to contact Major Barttelot.

3. A mountain which is an extension of the Ruwenzori Range.

4. Rev. Alexander M. Mackay (1849-1892) was a member of the Church Missionary Society.

5. Stanley managed to establish friendship with Mazamboni, the paramount chief of Undussuma, who had previously molested the expedition under the false impression that they had been sent by Kabba Rega to attack him. Later on, Stanley successfully fought off chief Musiri, Mazamboni's enemy, who planned to attack Stanley. For further particulars of these events see Stanley, *In Darkest Africa,* vol. 1, 433-435.

6. *Bula Matari* (Breaker of Rocks) was Stanley's African nickname, which had been given to him by the Africans when constructing a road in the Congo's cataract region—a feat they considered almost superhuman.

7. Stairs refers to an experiment with the poison used by the Africans for their arrows. Jokingly, he called Washenzi (or Monbuttu) woman a doctor; she stayed at Fort Bodo and knew how to prepare both the poison and its antidote. The experiment is mentioned subsequently in his diary. A more detailed description of the preparation of the poison can be found at the end of Stairs's journal written at Fort Bodo, covering the period 3 to 19 December 1888. This description has been omitted from the present volume and the reader is referred to pages 304-331 of Dr. T. H. Parke's *My Personal Experiences,* previously cited in full. Dr. Parke's report is more complete than that written by Stairs and includes a scientific statement on the identification of the plants used in the preparation of the poison.

8. A place on the way from Fort Bodo to Ipoto.

9. Georgina (1861-1916), Stairs's sister, married Edmund Twining, a well-to-do cotton broker of New York. Mary, Stairs's elder sister, married George Deane Bourke. (See note 13, chapter 1.)

10. Presumably, Stairs refers to Alfred Jones, who was married to his father's sister, Magaret Stairs.

Notes to Chapter Seven

1. Kavalli was the chief of the Wahuma people who were pastoralists and, according to tradition, had fled from Unyoro from the tyranny of its kings.

2. Mpinga was the chief of the Bavira, with an hereditary title of Gavira.

3. Stairs misspelled the name of Joseph Thomson.

4. Robert W. Felkin (1853-1926) was a missionary, a physician, and a traveller who became Emin Pasha's close friend. Upon his return to Europe, he was active in promoting the relief of Equatoria. See note 30, Part one for details about Wilhelm Junker.

5. Vita Hassan was a Tunisian apothecary who lived in Equatoria for about ten years when Stairs met him in March 1889. In his words, Hassan "at times has been very useful to the pasha."

6. Danagla or Donagla, inhabitants of Dongola, served as irregular soldiers. They revolted against the government. Stairs expects that Emin's followers will suffer punishment for their rebellion at the hands of the Mahdists.

7. Matera Selim Bey, a senior officer of Equatorial troops, took part in the revolt against Emin Pasha.

8. Shukri Agha was commandant of Mswa station, situated about 60 miles (100 kilometres) north-east of Kavalli's.

9. Hawash (or Hawashi) Effendi was an Egyptian administrator and for some time the commanding officer at Dufilé.

10. He is mentioned in other memoirs as Rehan. According to a version provided by Stanley, the party which caught Rehan was led by Stairs and this event is recorded under the date of 17 April. Dr. Parke's version, on the other hand, is consistent with Stairs's entry, and so is Jephson's.

NOTES TO CHAPTER EIGHT

1. In actual fact the highest peaks of the Ruwenzori Range are Mount Margherita 16,795 feet (5119 metres) and Mount Alexandra 16,750 feet (5105 metres).

2. Muta Nzige was Lake Edward, originally named Albert Edward. Stairs also called it Lake Usongora.

3. Stairs's report of his ascent of the Ruwenzori was first published in the *Proceedings of the Royal Geographical Society* 11.12 (December 1889): 726-730, and subsequently in Stanley's *In Darkest Africa*, vol. 2, 276-280. As a matter of interest, Sir Harry Johnston had pointed out that the name Stanley gave to this mountain range did not correspond with the local African name which was Runsororo. See H. Johnston, *The Nile Quest*, (New York, 1903) 261.

4. Stairs's exploration had solved part of the problem of the Albertine source of the Nile by extending it to Lake Edward to which he applied the local name "Muta Nzige." He ascertained that the two lakes were connected by the Semliki River.

5. Kakuri Island

6. Stanley ascribed the colouration of the water to matter in suspension, which was probably of an organic nature. For the results of chemical analysis of the water, see Stanley, *In Darkest Africa*, vol. 2, 340-341.

7. Wara Sura tribesmen were the subjects of Kabba Rega. They devastated the country periodically.

8. Stairs refers to Stanley's expedition of 1874-1877.

9. Antari was king of Ankori (Ankole).

10. Mpororo: a country situated to the southeast of Lake Edward.

11. Rumanika, the ruler of Karagwe between 1855 and 1878, was Stanley's friend. The young King Ndagara (or Unyagumbwa) who met the representatives of the expedition was Rumanika's grandson.

12. The mission station in which Mackay resided, at that time, was at Usambiro. According to Stairs it was located at Msalala, but it is most likely that he was mistaken.

13. Stairs's brother.

14. The correct date is 22 March 1888.

15. In 1888 Emperor William I died and was succeeded by his son Frederick III. The latter, however, died of cancer three months after his accession and was succeeded by his son William II.

16. Stairs's sister Mary.

17. Stairs refers to his brother Jack and possibly to his cousins Walter Jones and Guy Carleton Jones, Walter's brother.

18. Stairs's conjecture proved correct; early in 1890 Mwanga regained his throne.

19. Stairs refers to an expedition organized by Mackinnon under the auspices of the Imperial British East Africa Company in relief of Stanley, whose fate, at that time, gave rise to serious concern. It was headed by Frederick Jackson (1860-1929), a traveller and colonial administrator. Jackson reached Mount Elgon and then turned back, thus avoiding the dangers anticipated by Stairs.

20. Herman von Wissman (1853-1905) was a German soldier, an explorer, and an administrator. According to Stanley he was, at that time, the Imperial Commissary of German East Africa.

21. According to the records of Stanley, Jephson, and Parke, this had happened on 3 December.

22. W. G. Stairs, Lieutenant, RE, "From the Albert Nyanza to the Indian Ocean," *The Nineteenth Century* 172 (June 1891): 967.

23. The correct date appears to be 4 December.

24. Captain W. G. Stairs, "Capt. Stairs' Letters (Part IV)," *The Novascotian* (30 May 1891): 2.

NOTES TO PART THREE, CHAPTER NINE

1. Alexandre Delcommune headed an expedition equipped by the Commercial and Industrial Company of the Congo *(La Compagnie du Congo pour commerce et l'industrie)*, on 17 October 1890. Its objective was to investigate the future potential of Katanga, with particular attention to gold deposits. Delcommune was to reach Bunkeia, the capital of Garengaze, and to persuade its ruler Msiri to accept the Belgian flag, and then to proceed to the south, where the gold fields were reported to lie.

Delcommune reached Bunkeia on 6 October 1891. After Msiri had declined to accept the flag, he moved southward in search of gold. His whereabouts were unknown to Stairs, whose attempts to open communications with him proved unsuccessful. Delcommune's expedition returned to Bunkeia on 8 June 1892, and on 7 January 1893, it reached Luzambo, on the Sankuru River. Delcommune had ended his mission upon his return to Kinshasa on 5 February 1893. See also Alexandre Delcommune, "Relation du voyage de Mpala à Luzambo," *Mouvement Géographique* (1893): 39; Delcommune, "Voyage au Katanga," *Bulletin Societé de Géographie d'Anvers* (1893): 237; J. du Fief, "Les Expeditions Belges au Katanga," *Bulletin Societé Royale Belge de Géographie,* No. 2 (1893): 116-122.

2. For particulars of the European members of the expedition see chapter 1.

3. Parke, Jephson, and Nelson were members of the Emin Pasha Relief Expedition.

4. A nickname given to Nova Scotians from a potato grown by them and shaped like a human proboscis with a blue tip. Also, in the old days, the ships of Nova Scotia were known among the sailors as "Bluenoses," which may have had something to do with a Nova Scotia privateer in the War of 1812 called the "blue nose" from a cannon painted blue. Presumably, Stairs might have followed some of these traditions when christening one of his boats. The famous schooner the *Bluenose I* was built much later, in 1920.

5. Pacific and Orient Line.

6. Sir John Kirk (1832-1922) took part in David Livingstone's expeditions into Central Africa between 1858 and 1863. From 1866 he worked in Zanzibar as medical officer, and between 1868 and 1873 acted as British consul there. In 1873 Kirk was appointed consul-general and in 1898 was knighted. He retired six years later.

7. The French Cardinal Lavigerie was the founder of the White Fathers Mission *(Societé de Notre-Dame d'Afrique)* which was sanctioned by Pius IX in 1868. Originally the White Fathers worked among the Muslims of Algeria. As the order grew in strength, Lavigerie's missionaries moved into

East Africa and also became interested in the schemes of King Leopold's Belgian Committee of the International African Association in Central Africa.

8. Presumably, Stairs refers to John Ainsworth (1864-1946) who was active as an administrator in Kenya at that time. Ainsworth later became the Chief Native Commissioner.

9. At Zanzibar, Stairs had dealings with a Mr. Nicol of Smith, MacKenzie and Company in matters related to his expedition.

10. The Indo-Iranians of Baluchistan appeared in large numbers earlier in the century when they were employed as mercenaries by the sultans of Zanzibar. Stairs refers to them in his diaries as "Baluchis."

11. Askaris were European-trained African soldiers. In Stairs's caravan they carried only half a load.

12. Sir Harry Hamilton Johnston (1858-1927) was a noted British explorer, botanist, and colonial administrator. He joined consular service in 1885 and for three years administered a British protectorate in eastern Nigeria. Between 1891 and 1895 he served as the first commissioner in Nyasaland (now the Republic of Malawi). He was knighted in 1896. At the time when Johnston was organizing a caravan to Nyasaland, he drew up contracts which now served Stairs as a model for his own use.

13. Captain Jacques headed the second expedition sent by the Belgian Anti-slavery Society. The first one departed on 16 June 1890. Having followed a route similar to that of Stairs's caravan, Captain Jacques reached Karema on 17 October 1891.

14. Mr. Bonstead of Bonstead, Ridely and Company acted also as Mrs. Sheldon's agent, an American lady mentioned by Stairs in his entry of 13 June.

15. Stairs misspelled the names of both Sayyid Ali and Said Sayyid, the founder of the sultanate of Zanzibar.

16. After the declaration of the protectorate over Zanzibar by Britain in 1890, Gerald Portal assumed the office of consul-general and commissioner for the British sphere of influence. He created a new administration there and the reforms were well under way when by the end of 1892, he was transferred to Uganda. Thus, Stairs's expectations, related to the role which Portal was to play in the reorganization of the government of Zanzibar, proved correct.

NOTES TO CHAPTER TEN

1. It appears that the main reason for this fear was the difficulty of obtaining provisions.

2. Joseph Thomson (1858-1895), an explorer, was the author of *To the Central African Lakes and Back* (London, 1881) and *Through Masai Land* (London, 1885). In 1878 and again in 1882 he led expeditions in East Africa, which were sponsored by the Royal Geographical Society. In 1883-1884, he made the first journey by a European from Mombasa to Lake Victoria.

3. Bishop James Hannington was murdered in October 1885 in Busoga on Kabaka Mwanga's order.

4. Stairs used this designation—dollars M.—for the Maria Theresa dollar which was used in East Africa as a standard of value. Actual coins were already scarce, and the main currency in circulation was the Indian rupee. The dollar (or *talari*—Arabic form of *thaler*) originated in Austria during the reign of Maria Theresa and it bears the date of 1780. In Austria it went out of use in 1854 but over 2 million were minted for export between 1891 and 1896. This impressive coin weighs 28.06 grams (about 1 ounce) and contains 83.3 percent of silver. One dollar M. was equivalent to 3s. 23/4d.

5. The *posho* was the provision of cloth given to caravans for the purpose of buying food. The Zanzibaris preferred this system to that of direct intervention by the white man to obtain their provisions.

6. The *upandi* varied according to place from 6 feet (183 centimeteres) to 4 feet 5½ inches (136 centimetres).

7. The *jora* is a piece of calico about 88 feet (27 metres) long and about 16 inches (42 centimetres) wide.

8. The total number of 356 men excluded the three commanding officers.

9. An ell is a former English unit of length equal to 45 inches (114 centimetres) and used for measuring cloth.

10. The *doti* varied according to place. At Zanzibar and on the coast, as far as Mpwapwa, it was the equivalent of 4 yards (about 4 metres), at Tabora 3½ yards (about 3 metres), and at Ujiji 3 yards. The varying length of the *doti,* which was used for the purpose of the *posho,* reflected the cost of transport as one penetrated into the interior. Thus, cloth gained in value, whereas under normal conditions, food was becoming cheaper.

11. Stairs used this designation for Tabora, then an Arab trading post.

12. The cubit was measured from the elbow to the tip of the finger. It averaged about 18 inches (45 centimetres). On the coast, 8 cubits were the equivalent of 1 doti. At Tabora the *doti* was equivalent to 7 cubits, and at Ujiji it measured 6 cubits.

Stairs had related, in a footnote to his entry made on 19 July, that the *mikomo,* or *cubit,* when measured for the *posho* often gave rise to amusing scenes: " The caravaneers choose from amongst themselves the one with the longest arm, and when the cloth is measured, nothing is funnier to see than this new-style standard of measurement stretching out his fingers to gain a fraction of an inch."

13. Stairs refers to Verney Lovett Cameron, *Across Africa* (London: G. Philip, 1877), who explored Eastern and Central Africa. The regions, through which Stanley's caravan was progressing, were crossed by Cameron eighteen years earlier when the latter left Bagamoyo in March 1873 and reached Lake Tanganyika in February 1874.

14. Stairs refers to a military campaign initiated by Lugard, which resulted in the conquest of the Bunyoro empire. Frederick J. D. Lugard (1858-1945) was a soldier and colonial administrator who played a prominent role in Britain's imperial history and was raised to the peerage in 1928. The other two names, mentioned by Stairs, were probably those of Capt. W. H. Williams, a subordinate of Lugard, and Capt. Eric Smith. Both were active in East Africa at that time.

15. Uledi was a much appreciated member of Stanley's Emin Pasha Relief Expedition.

16. The twelfth of August was the beginning of the shooting season.

NOTES TO CHAPTER ELEVEN

1. The Church Missionary Society.

2. It was the epidemic of rinderpest which ravaged East Africa at that time.

3. *Batatas* means sweet potatoes.

4. Palmyra palm is a tall, fan-leaved African palm (*Borassus flabellifer*).

5. Many modern writers on East Africa make no clear distinction between Unyanyembe and Tabora, using them as synonymous terms. It is more correct to treat Unyanyembe as the name of a province, which was headed by a chief and Tabora as its capital.

NOTES TO CHAPTER TWELVE

1. Lieutenant Baron von Siegl was an Austrian aristocrat. Stairs misspelled his surname.

2. *Pice* is a fraction of the rupee, a currency used in India.

3. *Pishi* is a measure of capacity or weight: 1/2 gallon (1.89 litres) or 6 pounds (2.72 kilograms).

4. Luali: Stairs probably had in mind the term wali meaning a governor. The Germans had nominated Seef bin Saad for that post. This term was also used in the Moslem countries to indicate a saint. It originated from the Arabic root *walinga* meaning to govern, to rule, or to protect someone.

5. *Frasila* is a unit of weight equal to about 35 pounds (16 kilograms).

6. The Widowbird is also known under the name of Whydah. Its distinctive feature is a long black tail suggesting a funeral veil.

7. Siki (spelled by Stairs as "Sike") was Mirambo's successor who fought the Germans. On being attacked by them in 1893, he blew himself up in his fort.

8. Stairs was mistaken as the word *bwana* is a term of address equivalent to "sir," or "mister." It may also indicate a proprietor or owner.

9. E. Kaiser was a member of an expedition sent in 1881 by the German African Society to East Africa. He died at Karema in 1882.

10. Captain Joubert, a Frenchman, joined the Belgian Anti-slavery Society in 1880. He built the station of St. Louis Mrumbi on the western shore of Lake Tanganyika. At the time of the arrival of Stairs's caravan at Mrumbi, Joubert had been about a year on his mission. Rumaliza, the chief of Ujiji who allied himself with the notorious slaver Tippu Tib, was determined to destroy him, as well as Captain Jacques.

NOTES TO CHAPTER THIRTEEN

1. Stairs misspelled the name of this mountain. The correct spelling is "Murumbi."

2. *Satini* is a kind of glossy cloth; *bombay,* a rough blue cotton fabric; *amerikani,* a coarse, unbleached cotton cloth; *lesso* (the correct spelling is *leso,* a word of Portuguese origin) denotes a handkerchief or shawl.

3. Alfred J. Swann of the London Missionary Society, resided at the mission station situated at the southern point of Lake Tanganyika. Stairs occasionally misspelled his name as "Swan."

4. For particulars relating to Msiri, the ruler of Garengaze, see Appendix E entitled "Msiri."

5. Eventually, Stairs tentatively identified this plant as hemp.

6. This letter was originally written in French.

NOTES TO CHAPTER FOUTEEN

1. *Yambo:* a common form of greeting.

2. William H. McNeill, in his thorough study on the spread of infectious diseases and their effects on human history—*Plagues and Peoples* (New York: Anchor Press/Doubleday, 1976)—notes that after 1500, when African slaves came into contact with European diseases, their mortality rate was moderate. This indicates an earlier exposure, in their African habitat, to the standard European childhood diseases. In East Africa, this exposure was most likely due to the penetration of Moslems from the Middle East.

3. Richard Crawshay, of the British Central African Administration, was sent to open a station on the shores of Lake Mweru, the purpose of which was to protect the claims of the South Africa Company against incursions from the Congo Free State.

4. Stairs's suspicions regarding the movements of Thomson's caravan were aroused by rumours that Cecil Rhodes, a prominent empire-builder who made his millions on the South African diamonds and gold-mining, had become interested in Katanga and had sent an expedition, headed by Thomson, to annex that territory.

5. *Vitambi* is a kind of cotton cloth.

6. Stairs refers to hematite (ferric oxide) of which there are two varieties: red and black, and micaceous.

7. In all likelihood, Stairs refers to an expedition whose presumed purpose may have been the same as that mentioned in note 4 above.

8. *Kangu* (or *kanga*) means cotton cloth with designs in several colours, suitable for women's garments.

9. Captain Lucien Bia, of the Belgian Army, was placed in command (with Lieutenant Emile Francqui as his second) of an expedition to reinforce Captain Stairs and to take over the administration of Katanga. The expedition left Matadi on 8 August 1891, and on 30 January 1892, it arrived at Bunkeia, where it met what was left of Stairs's caravan.

10. D. Crawford was a member of the Wesleyan mission, situated close to the Congo Free State station near Bunkeia, which was founded by Frederick S. Arnot in 1890. Arnot was originally accompanied by William H. Faulkner (a Canadian) and Charles A. Swann (an Englishman). They were later replaced by D. Crawford, F. L. Lane, and H. B. Thompson, who resided at the mission when Stairs's caravan arrived.

11. Stairs refers to the Delcommune expedition which arrived at Bunkeia on 6 October 1891, that is, over two months earlier and not three weeks previously as stated by him. Carl Hakansson, a topographer and a lieutenant in the Swedish army, was a member of this expedition. The rear-guard, composed of twelve soldiers under his command, was massacred by the Baluba of Kikondja while marching along the Lualaba River.

12. Lieutenant Amede Legat was in command of the station on the Lufoi, set up by Le Marinel.

13. The Company of Katanga was established on 15 April 1891, after Alexandre Delcommune's expedition had left Kinshasa (17 October 1890). This new company was an offshoot of the Compagnie du Congo pour le commerce et l'industrie (Congo Company for Trade and Industry) which had originally organized Delcommune's expedition.

NOTES TO CHAPTER FIFTEEN

1. Stairs's dates are incorrect. Le Marinel arrived at Bunkeia on 18 April 1891, and left at the beginning of June. Delcommune reached Bunkeia on 6 October and subsequently spent about three weeks at the Lufoi station. He left for the south on 11 November.

2. For further information see note 11 in chapter 15.

3. Lourenço Souza Coïmbra was a son of a Portuguese man of Bihé and an African woman. He was nicknamed "Naha-Honjo" by the inhabitants of Garengaze. His niece Maria de Fonseca became one of Msiri's many wives. Earlier in his life, Coïmbra had served with the notorious slaver José Antonio Alvez. V. L. Cameron remembered him as a slave-raider who "reached the highest grade of ruffianism among them all." (Cameron, *Across Africa*, 324).

4. *Kaniki* is a cotton cloth, usually dark blue.

5. The proper spelling is "*munugu*."

6. Another version of Bodson's last words had been given by Dr. Joseph A. Moloney, according to whom he had whispered, "Doctor, I don't mind dying now that I have killed Msiri." To Captain Stairs, he delivered the following message: "Thank God, my death will not be in vain. I have delivered Africa from one of her most detestable tyrants" (Moloney, *With Captain Stairs*, 194-194).

NOTES TO CHAPTER SIXTEEN

1. Rumaliza, an Arab sheikh who controlled the region around Ujiji, sent a leopard cub as a present to Queen Victoria. The animal died during the voyage to England.

2. The correct spelling is "Stevenson." Stevenson Road led from the southern tip of Lake Tanganyika to the northern tip of Lake Nyasa. This track had been cleared in 1881-1882 when the London Missionary Society moved a steamer in sections to Lake Tanganyika.

3. Dr. Moloney's spelling of this name is McCalmont. (See Moloney, *With Captain Stairs,* 268.) Mr. McCalmont, of the Scotch Livingstonian mission, was going home on leave of absence.

4. For information on Sir Harry Johnston, see note 12 to chapter 9.

5. According to Dr. Moloney, the expedition reached Matope on 26 May, or two days later than the date given by Stairs. (See Moloney, *With Captain Stairs,* 271).

NOTES TO APPENDIX E

1. Msiri's original name was Ngwelengwa. The name he adopted subsequently signifies "confidant" or "friend" in Swahili. Auguste Verbeken speculates that Msiri's name could have been a corruption of an Arab title "*Sidi,*" meaning "lord" or "master." It is also possible that the young Ngwelengwa assumed the name of Mushidi—a seventeenth century emperor of the Lunda, of whose outstanding territorial conquests he might have heard. See August Verbeken, *Msiri Roi du Garengaze* (Brussels: Editions L. Cuypers, 1956) 34.

2. Robert Cornevin, *Historie du Congo* (Paris: Editions Berger-Levrault, 1970) 55-56.

3. Frederick Stanley Arnot, *Garengaze or Seven Years' Pioneer Mission Work in Central Africa* (London: Frank Cass and Company Ltd., 1969) 231-233. (Originally published in 1889.)

4. In contrast to Msiri's kingdom, the Province of Katanga, on the eve of independence in 1960, had about 193,000 square miles (500 000 square kilometres).

5. Arnot, *Garengaze,* 232-233.

6. For an explanation of the origins of this name, see Verbeken, *Msiri,* 70-72.

7. Verbeken, *Msiri,* 132.

8. According to Daniel Crawford, who was familiar with Msiri's court, the king's wives and concubines numbered over five hundred. See Crawford, *Thinking Black,* 229.

9. Verbeken, *Msiri,* 101-116, 123-127, and 130-133; Arnot, *Garengaze,* 234-235.

10. Cornet, *Katanga,* 38-41.

11. James Duffy, *Portuguese Africa* (Cambridge, Massachusetts: Harvard UP, 1959) 198-199.

12. Cornet, *Katanga,* 41-46.

13. Ruth M. Slade, *English-Speaking Missions in the Congo Independent State, 1878-1908* (Brussels: Academie royale des Sciences coloniales, 1959) 110-112; Verbeken, *Msiri,* 157-162.

14. Moloney, *With Captain Stairs,* 180.

15. For particulars, see the following sections in chapter 1: "Intermezzo" and "The course of the Katanga Expedition."

16. For details see Verbeken, *Msiri,* 116-122; Moloney, *With Captain Stairs,* 177.

17. Verbeken, *Msiri,* 152.

18. Ernest Baker, *The Life and Explorations of Frederick Stanley Arnot* (New York: E. P. Dutton and Company, 1920) 183.

19. Moloney, *With Captain Stairs,* 180-181.

NOTES TO APPENDIX F

1. Parke, *My Personal Experiences*, 88.

2. George W. Hunter, William W. Frye, and J. Clyde Swartzwalder, *A Manual of Tropical Medicine* (Philadelphia: W. B. Saunders Company, 1966) 734-737.

3. Parke, *My Personal Experiences*, 84.

4. W. G. Stairs, *Emin Pasha Relief Expedition Diary*, 30 September 1887.

5. Dr. Parke admitted that during the forest march men frequently got jiggers in their feet, which, according to him "gave them great annoyance." His ignorance of the connection between the parasite and the ulcers seems rather strange, as Frederick S. Arnot, a missionary who resided in Central Africa (Garengaze) for a number of years, wrote in 1888 of "the troublesome insects known as *chegoes* [...] [which] lay their eggs in the sole of the foot and cause abscesses." For further details see Parke, *My Personal Experiences*, 500; Arnot, *Garengaze*, 354-355.

6. Parke, *My Personal Experiences*, 500.

7. W. D. Foster, *The Early History of Scientific Medicine in Uganda* (Nairobi: East African Literature Bureau, 1970) 78.

8. W. G. Stairs, *Katanga Expedition Diary*.

9. Adams and Maegraith, *Clinical Tropical Diseases* (Oxford: Blackwell Scientific Publications, 1980) 443-447.

10. Parke, *My Personal Experiences*, 60, 88, and 100.

11. Dr. Parke's detailed descriptions corroborate the clinical characteristics of tropical ulcer that can be found in any modern manual of tropical medicine.

12. Parke, *My Personal Experiences*, 208, 256, and 352.

13. W. G. Stairs, *Emin Pasha Relief Expedition Diary*, 2 July 1888.

14. W. G. Stairs, *Emin Pasha Relief Expedition Diary*, 9 July 1888.

15. W. G. Stairs, *Emin Pasha Relief Expedition Diary*, 2 November 1887.

16. Parke, *My Personal Experiences*, 482.

17. The former is caused by bacteria of the genus *shigella*, discovered by Shiga in 1898, the latter by the protozoan *entamoeba histolytica* first described by Lösch in 1875. See Charles Singer and E. Ashworth Underwood, *A Short History of Medicine* (Oxford: Clarendon Press, 1962) 391; Adam and Maegraith, *Clinical Tropical Diseases*, 1-10 and 31-37.

18. Parke, *My Personal Experiences*, 489.

19. Parke, *My Personal Experiences*, 54.

20. Parke, *My Personal Experiences*, 54, 88, and 349.

21. Parke, *My Personal Experiences*, 355 et seq.

22. This form of malaria may be clinically indistinguishable from bacillary dysentery.

23. Parke, *My Personal Experiences*, 198.

24. "Sub-acute gastritis" was the term used by Parke to describe Stanley's illness.

25. Parke, *My Personal Experiences*, 224 and 271.

26. W. G. Stairs, *Emin Pasha Relief Expedition Diary*, 25 September 1888.

27. Parke, *My Personal Experiences*, 126.

28. W. G. Stairs, *Emin Pasha Relief Expedition Diary*, 3 January 1889.

29. Parke, *My Personal Experiences*, 76 and 225.

30. Moloney, *With Captain Stairs*, 38.

31. W. G. Stairs, *Emin Pasha Relief Expedition Diary*, 18, 19, and 20 July 1889.

32. Gordon Harrison, *Mosquitoes, Malaria and Man* (New York: E. P. Dutton, 1978) 25.

33. Paul F. Russell, *Man's Mastery of Malaria* (London: Geoffrey Cumberlege, Oxford UP, 1955) chapter 6.

34. Malaria is caused by sporozoa of the genus *plasmodium* (P). Its symptoms are periodic fever, anaemia, and splenic enlargement. Other organs viz., the brain, the liver, and the kidneys, may also be affected. Malarial species include the following four *plasmodia*: *P. falciparum* (malignant tertian); *P. vivax* (benign tertian); *P. malariae* (quartan); and *P. ovale* (ovale tertian).
　By 1890 the first three species were known and in 1922 the fourth was identified. The most common malarial infections are those caused by the first and second species. In West, Central, and parts of East Africa, *falciparum* is the dominant form of malaria. See Adams and Maegraith, *Clinical Tropical Diseases*, 240-242; Singer and Underwood, *A Short History of Medicine*, 459.

35. Parke, *My Personal Experiences*, 231.

36. Parke, *My Personal Experiences*, 480.

37. Hunter, et al., *Tropical Medicine*, 334-335.

38. Parke, *My Personal Experiences*, 391 and 445.

39. The bilious remittent fever is characterized by gastro-intestinal syndromes which arise from severe liver damage. The patient suffers from abdominal pain, remittent fever, vomiting, enlarged liver, and diarrhoea. The stool contains blood and bile. Blackwater fever involves haemoglobinuria associated with haemolysis, jaundice, fever, and vomiting. The spleen and liver are enlarged and tender. For further details see Adams and Maegraith, *Clinical Tropical Diseases*, chapter 15.

40. In those who leave the endemic area, the parasites of malaria usually cease to be active within one year.

41. Moloney, *With Captain Stairs*, 91.

42. Don R. Arthur, *Ticks and Disease* (Oxford: Pergamon Press, 1961) 110 and 293-294.

43. David Livingstone suggested its presence in northwest Angola in 1857. The tick-borne relapsing fever found its way to the Congo from eastern Africa and from Portuguese territories in the south, where it was endemic. Its carriers were Arab caravans from the east and European traders from Angola. Evidence published in 1905 indicates the presence of infected domestic ticks in the Congo. Infected insects were found in villages dominated by the Arabs and in rest houses along the caravan routes. See Charles M. Good, "Salt Trade and Disease: Aspects of Development in Africa's Northern Lakes Region," *The International Journal of African Historical Studies* 5.4 (1972): 582.

44. Parke, *My Personal Experiences*, 84, 126, 186, and 499.

45. Parke, *My Personal Experiences*, 459-461 and 482.

46. Adams and Maegraith, *Clinical Tropical Diseases*, 368.

47. See Michael G. Wohl and Robert S. Goodhart, *Modern Nutrition in Health and Disease* (Philadelphia: Lea and Febiger, 1960) 542-543.

48. Parke, *My Personal Experiences*, 447.

49. Parke, *My Personal Experiences*, 13-17, 23, and 490.

50. Moloney, *With Captain Stairs*, 131.

51. "The Arrow Poison of the Pigmies: by Surgeon Parke D. C. L., Army Medical Staff and E. M. Holmes F. L. S." in Parke, *My Personal Experiences*, 308-319.

52. Hunter, et al., *Tropical Medicine,* 592-593; Wohl and Goodhart, *Modern Nutrition,* 1028-1032.

53. H. Kraut and H. D. Cremer, eds., *Investigations into Health and Nutrition in East Africa* (Junchen: Weltforum Verlag, 1969) 64.

54. Kraut and Cremer, eds., *Investigations into Health and Nutrition,* 59.

55. One could argue that in many parts of Africa local populations survive almost exclusively on such staples as cassava, maize, or plantains, but the fact remains that they are malnourished.

56. Parke, *My Personal Experiences,* 326-368.

57. See *Emin Pasha Relief Expedition Diary,* 14 July 1888.

58. Moloney, *With Captain Stairs,* 214.

59. Stanley, *In Darkest Africa,* vol. 2, 210.

60. Moloney, *With Captain Stairs,* 234.

SELECTED BIBLIOGRAPHY

Adams and Maegraith. *Clinical Tropical Diseases*. Oxford: Blackwell Scientific Publications, 1980.

Alexandre Delcommune, "Relation du voyage de Mpala Luzambo," *Mouvement Géographique* (1893): 39.

Anstey, Roger. *Britain and the Congo in the Nineteenth Century*. Oxford: Clarendon Press, 1962.

Arnot, Frederick Stanley. *Garengaze or Seven Years' Pioneer Mission Work in Central Africa*. London: Frank Cass and Company Ltd., 1889, 1969.

Arthur, Don R. *Ticks and Disease*. Oxford: Pergamon Press, 1961.

Baker, Ernest. *The Life and Explorations of Frederick Stanley Arnot*. New York: E. P. Dutton and Company, 1920, 183.

Barttelot, Sir Walter George, ed. *The Life of Edmund Musgrave Barttelot From His Letters and Diary*. London: R. Bentley and Son, 1890.

Cairns, H. Alan C. *Prelude to Imperialism. British Reactions to Central African Society 1840-1890*. London: Routledge and Kegan Paul, 1965.

Cameron, Verney Lovett. *Across Africa*. London: G. Philip, 1877.

Canada Year Book 1968. Ottawa: Statistics Canada, 1968.

Casati, Gaetano. *Ten Years in Equatoria and the Return with Emin Pasha*. 1891. New York: Negro UP, 1969.

Cawston, G. Letter to W. G. Stairs, 18 July 1890. British South Africa Company II, Misc., Rhodes House, Oxford.

Compagnie du Katanga, "Rapport du conseil d'administration." *Le Mouvement Géographique* 9.5 (1892): 131.

Cornet, Ren J. *Katanga*. Brussels: L. Cuypers, 1944.

Cornevin, Robert. *Historie du Congo*. Paris: Editions Berger-Levrault, 1970.

Crawford, Daniel. *Thinking Black*. New York: George H. Doran, 1912.

Creighton, Donald. *The Forked Road: Canada 1939-1957*. Toronto: McClelland and Stewart, 1976.

Delcommune, Alexandre. "Voyage au Katanga," *Bulletin Societé de Géographie d' Anvers*. 1893.

———."Relation du voyage de Mpala à Luzambo," *Mouvement Géographique* (1893): 39.

Dictionary of National Biography, ed. Sidney Lee. London: Smith, Elder and Company, 1898.

du Fief, J. "Les Expéditions Belges au Katanga," *Bulletin Soceité Royale Belge de Géographie*, No. 2 (1893): 116-122.

Duffy, James. *Portuguese Africa*. Cambridge, Massachusetts: Harvard UP, 1959, 198-199.

Emerson, Barbara. *Leopold II of the Belgians. King of Capitalism*. New York: St. Martin's Press, 1979.

Foster, W. D. *The Early History of Scientific Medicine in Uganda*. Nairobi: East African Literature Bureau, 1970.

Galbraith, John S. *Crown and Charter*. Los Angeles: U of California P, 1974.

Good, Charles M. "Salt Trade and Disease: Aspects of Development in Africa's Northern Lakes Region," *The International Journal of African Historical Studies* 5.4 (1972): 582.

Halifax Acadian Recorder, 25 March 1890, 2.

Harries-Jenkins, Gwyn. *The Army in Victorian Society*. London: Routledge and Kegan Paul, 1977

Harrison, Gordon. *Mosquitoes, Malaria and Man*. New York: E. P. Dutton, 1978.

Hoffmann, William. *With Stanley in Africa*. London: Cassell and Company Ltd., 1938.

Hunter, George W., William W. Frye, and J. Clyde Swartzwalder, *A Manual of Tropical Medicine*. Philadelphia: W. B. Saunders Company, 1966.

Jameson, James S. *Story of the Rear Column of the Emin Pasha Relief Expedition*, ed. Mrs. J. S. Jameson. Toronto: Rose Publishing Company, 1891.

Jephson, A. J. Mounteney. *Emin Pasha and the Rebellion at the Equator*. New York: Charles Scribner's Sons, 1890.

Johnston, H. *The Nile Quest*. New York, 1903.

Johnston, Hilda. Letter to Henry Stairs, 21st May 1908. PANS, M.G.1, No. 877.

Jone's Private Family Archives.

Jones, Roger. *The Rescue of Emin Pasha*. London: Allison and Busby, 1972.

Kraut, H. and H. D. Cremer, eds. *Investigations into Health and Nutrition in East Africa*. Junchen: Weltforum Verlag, 1969.

The Mail Star, 28 July 1960.

Macpherson, Fergus. *Anatomy of a Conquest: The British Occupation of Zambia, 1884-1924*. Essex: Longman, 1981.

Mansergh, Nicholas. *Documents and Speeches on British Commonwealth Affairs*, vol. 2. London: Oxford UP, 1953.

Margetson, Stella. *Victorian High Society*. New York: Holmes and Meier Publishers, Inc., 1980.

McNeill, William H. *Plagues and Peoples*. New York: Anchor Press/Doubleday, 1976.

Middleton, Dorothy, ed. *The Diary of A. J. Mountenay Jephson. Emin Pasha Expedition 1887-1889*. Cambridge: published for the Hakluyt Society at the University Press, 1969.

Moloney, Joseph A. *With Captain Stairs to Katanga*. London: Sampson Low, Marston and Company, 1893.

Morning Chronicle, Cairo, 21 January 1890. PANS, M.G. 1, No. 877.

The Morning Herald, 13 January 1890, 1.

Oliver, Roland, and Gervase Mathew, eds., *History of East Africa*. Oxford: Clarendon Press, 1963.

Parke, Thomas Heazle. *My Personal Experiences in Equatorial Africa as Medical Officer of the Emin Pasha Relief Expedition*. New York: Negro UP, 1969.

Petrie, Sir Charles. *The Victorians*. London: Eyre and Spottiswoode, 1960.

The Penny Illustrated Paper, 19 July 1890, 38.

Raddall, Thomas H. *Halifax, Warden of the North*. Toronto: McClelland and Stewart Ltd., 1971.

Ritchie, Charles. *Storm Signals: More Undiplomatic Diaries, 1962-1971*. Toronto: Macmillan of Canada, 1983.

Ritchie, Charles. *The Siren Years: A Canadian Diplomat Abroad, 1937-1945*. Toronto: Macmillan of Canada, 1974.

Robinson, Ronald, John Gallagher, Alice Denny. *Africa and the Victorians. The Official Mind of Imperialism*. London: MacMillan, 1965.

Rosebery, Lord. Speech. *Proceedings, Royal Colonial Institute*, vol. 24 (1892-93): 227.

Russell, Paul F. *Man's Mastery of Malaria*. London: Geoffrey Cumberlege, Oxford UP, 1955.

Said, Beshir Mohammed. *The Sudan, Crossroads of Africa.* London: The Bodley Head, 1965.

Sanderson, G. N. *England, Europe and the Upper Nile 1882-1899.* Edinburgh: Edinburgh UP, 1965.

Schweitzer, Georg. *Emin Pasha, His Life and Work.* 1898; New York: Negro UP, 1969.

Sharpe, Alfred. "A Journey to Garengaze," *Proceedings of the Royal Geographical Society,* 14.1 (January 1892): 36-47.

Singer, Charles and E. Ashworth Underwood. *A Short History of Medicine.* Oxford: Clarendon Press, 1962.

Slade, Ruth M. *English-Speaking Missions in the Congo Independent State, 1878-1908.* Brussels: Académie royale des Sciences coloniales, 1959

———. *King Leopold's Congo.* London: Oxford UP., 1962.

Smith, Iain R. *The Emin Pasha Relief Expedition 1886-1890.* Oxford: Oxford UP, 1972.

Societé Royale Belge de Géographie Bulletin (Mars-Avril 1892):110-122.

Spiers, Edward M. *The Army and Society 1815-1914 .* London: Longman, 1980.

Stairs, Henry B. Letter to Hilda Johnston nee Stairs, 7th May, 1908. Public Archives of Nova Scotia, M.G.1, No. 877.

Stairs, H. Gerald. "The Stairs of Halifax." Public Archives of Nova Scotia, Cs.ST 1, 1962.

———. "Union of Maritime Provinces and Confederation," in *Family History Stairs, Morrow.* Halifax: McAlpine Publishing Company Ltd., 1906.

———. "De Zanzibar au Katanga," *Le Congo Illustré, Voyages et Travaux des Belges dans l'Etat Independant du Congo, 1893.*

W. G. Stairs's scrapbook, No. 63, PANS.

———. "De Zanzibar au Katanga. Journal du Capitaine Stairs (1890-1891)," *Le Congo Illustré,* trans. Elizabeth Jones, 5 (26 February 1893).

———. Letter to Walter G. Jones, 19 May 1892. Jones's Private Family Archives.

———. "From the Albert Nyanza to the Indian Ocean," *The Nineteenth Century* 172 (June 1891): 967.

———. *Emin Pasha Relief Expedition Diaries.* PANS, M.G.1, Nos. 877 and 878.

Stanley, Henry Morton. "Geographical Results of the Emin Pasha Relief Expedition," *Proceedings of the Royal Geographical Society* 12.6 (June 1890): 313-331.22.

———. *In Darkest Africa,* 2 vols. New York: Charles Scribner's Sons, 1890.

———. Letter to General Lord Wolseley, Cairo, 30 January. Stairs's scrapbook No. 63, PANS.

Thomson, Joseph. *To the Central African Lakes and Back.* London, 1881.

———. *Through Masai Land* (London, 1885).

Troup, J. Rose. *With Stanley's Rear Column.* London: Chapman and Hall Ltd., 1890.

Verbeken, August. *Msiri Roi du Garengaze.* Brussels: Editions L. Cuypers, 1956.

Ward, Herbert. *My Life With Stanley's Rear Guard.* New York: Cassell and Company Ltd., 1891.

White, James P. "The Sanford Exploring Expedition," *Journal of African History,* 8.2 (1967): 291-302.

Wohl , Michael G. and Robert S. Goodhart, *Modern Nutrition in Health and Disease.* Philadelphia: Lea and Febiger, 1960.

Yeoman, Guy. *Africa's Mountains of the Moon.* London: Universe, 1989.

INDEX